Sir Gawain & the Green Knight

A New Critical Edition

Theodore Silverstein

The University of Chicago Press
Chicago and London

THEODORE SILVERSTEIN is professor emeritus of English at the University of Chicago. His many studies of medieval English and continental literature include a translation of *Sir Gawain and the Green Knight* into modern English.

The University of Chicago Press, Chicago   60637
The University of Chicago Press, Ltd., London

© 1974, 1984 by The University of Chicago
All rights reserved. Published 1984
Printed in the United States of America

91 90 89 88 87 86 85 84   1 2 3 4 5

LIBRARY OF CONGRESS CATALOGING IN PUBLICATION DATA

Gawain and the Grene Knight.
  Sir Gawain and the Green Knight.

  Bibliography: p.
  1. Gawain—Romances.   I. Silverstein, Theodore.
II. Title.
PR2065.G3   1984   821'.1   83-9126
ISBN 0-226-75767-6
ISBN 0-226-75768-4 (pbk.)

For Mary
And wener þen Wenore, as þe wyʒe þoʒt

Contents

Preface

Sir Gawain and the Green Knight has been fortunate in its editors and to print it once again may require some justification. The manuscript in which the poem survives, though carefully written, is not without its faults and time besides with its offsets has multiplied the imperfections, whose study has helped to produce over the years what has come to be, with small discrepancy, the accepted text. The present edition, indebted as it is to its predecessors and to the Early English Text Society's facsimile, yet starts afresh from a reexamination of the manuscript that has tested old and yielded new corrections. Among the many new stands the disenchantment of that second rustic monster in the poem, conjured up by Madden long ago, Sir Doddinaual de Sauage, may his true name live forever!

The explanatory notes are full and preoccupied by matters previously unobserved. Many are lexical in nature, as in the case of words like *auinant*, *borȝ*, *couetyse*, *craþayn*, *kest*, *pentangel*, *querré*, and *recreaunt*, among others; and of course the two crucial terms, both connected here with the chivalric virtue justice, which have deeply concerned the critics, *trawþe* and *clannes*, the former meaning *fides*, i.e., the keeping of word and agreement, the latter meaning *innocentia* as defined by the twelfth-century treatise *Moralium dogma philosophorum* and naming a quality here discovered to be Sir Gawain's own and known as such in England in at least one other piece, *The Parlement of the Thre Ages*, around the mid fourteenth century, hence thirty or forty years before its appearance in our poem. Some have to do with ornaments, which are part of a poet's style and have hitherto on the whole been neglected: *traductio*, *double entendre*, *repetitio*, aphorism, epithet, the ancient military topos "heart and hand," the play on the name of Arthur's queen and the reflection of traditional literary similes, like the comparison of Sir Gawain's robing to that of spring, called Ver or Flora in the Latin texts. The relations with the poem's other sources, some of them familiar to scholarship, particularly the various versions of the *Perceval*, are noted in considerable detail, but also in new ways with those texts and with Laȝamon, Robert Mannyng, and the contemporary English lyric and romance. In addition, the notes consider the poet's probable Senecan knowledge and his use of a Ciceronian tradition, influential on knightly morality in general and on certain of the romances in particular from the twelfth century on, a tradition that seems to lie at the center of his argument and makes a considerable difference to the reading of the poem. Their conclusions, incidentally, tend to support, against Ernst Curtius's notorious attack, a view advanced long ago by Gustav Ehrismann. All together the notes seek to enrich with fresh particulars the picture, already outlined by modern commentary, of a poet intimately acquainted with the literature of his time and of a poem which appropriates that knowledge happily to its very own special use.

The introduction does not fail to cover the usual range of topics, though it is sometimes argumentative, as in the discussion of Gawain's "ambiguity" and in the contention that the piece is a comedy, not simply in some of its happier details but more formally in its plot; and the vocabulary, though perforce and gratefully it draws on other editions, especially Gollancz and Tolkien-Gordon-Davis, is newly studied and made.

Debts to predecessors are witnessed throughout the book, but the editor is especially happy to acknowledge here what he owes his colleagues, Professors R. P. McKeon, David Smigelskis, and Jay Schleussener of Chicago, and in very pleasant circumstances Professor John Burrow of Bristol University in England, with all of whom he canvassed some of his ideas about the poem.

And he also would wish to thank Dean Karl Weintraub and the Division of the Humanities in the University of Chicago for supporting with a financial grant the publication of this book.

T. S.

Chicago and Wotton Underwood, 1981−83

The text of MS. Cotton Nero A. x. is published by kind permission of the British Library.

Introduction

1. The Poem: Sources, Conventions, Form

Sir Gawain and the Green Knight is an Arthurian adventure, whose fable would appear to have its roots in Celtic story; whose social norms, touched by their settlement in England, are those of the courtly French romances; whose moral psychology follows the Roman rhetoricians, among them especially Cicero; and whose writing joins to local native convention the Latin schoolroom and the romance practices of its time. In form, molding all these elements into one, *Gawain* is a comedy of manners, whose plot contrives to trap its hero in a dilemma from which there is no possible escape, then happily lets him go—though in himself he is forever caught.

The story is about a Christmas "game," spanning two festive seasons. It tells how a gigantic green stranger comes to King Arthur's court and challenges anyone in it to a head-chopping contest. He will stand a blow on his neck on condition that a year and a day hence his opponent will take a similar blow from him. Sir Gawain assumes the challenge and chops off the head of the Green Knight, who picks it up and, after it reminds Sir Gawain of the condition he has promised to observe, rides away. The rest of the story tells Sir Gawain's adventures in search of his adversary, particularly the love temptation to which he is subjected by the wife of his host in the castle where he spends his second Christmas, and how in the end he survives the return blow.

The head-chopping and the lady's temptation, these were the chief concerns of a scholarly generation preoccupied by genetics and the transmission of inherited narrative motifs. The earliest surviving Western example of the head-chopping incident seems to be in a Middle Irish piece evidently older than the twelfth century, the *Fled Bricrand (Bricriu's Feast)*, where the hero is Cuchulainn. By the thirteenth century it was known in the Arthurian romances, chiefly in French: the Carados episode of *The First Continuation* of the *Perceval* of Chrétien de Troyes; the prose *Perlesvaus*, where it is connected with Lancelot; and *La mule sans frein, Hunbaut*, and the High German *Diu Crône*, in all of which Sir Gawain is the protagonist. As for the episode of the love temptation, it does not appear in any of these pieces and has been sought separately elsewhere, in such romances as *Yder*, the Vulgate *Lancelot del lac*, and Ulrich von Zatzikhoven's Swiss *Lanzelet* translated from a twelfth-century Anglo-Norman original, as well as in various "fairy mistress" tales, the contemporary *Châtelaine de Vergi*, and, further afield, the ancient traditions of Joseph and the wife of Potiphar. Indications like these have formed the foundation for the attempted reconstruction of what may be called the prehistory of *Gawain*'s story, one in which challenge and temptation appear in ordered shape together. The most precise and cogent of these attempts is that by G. L. Kittredge, who attributes to the ingenuity of an unknown French precursor the basic features of the fable as received and set down by the English poet. But reconstruction like this may appear to be schematic rather than fact, there being otherwise no evidence for the actuality of such a predecessor or his work. It assumes, moreover, that for the fable there had to be a well-contrived literal source. But our poet is among the most original of his time, one who seems to reshape the basic matter that he uses; and this is true of *Pearl* as well, and perhaps its most persuasive claim to be by him. Except in those details that are the verse conventions and decorative devices of his art, he seldom is simply translator or adaptor; in this respect he differs from Chaucer, who for other artful reasons frequently is, even in the *Canterbury Tales*.

Parallel to the studies of the material development of *Gawain*'s story are those which have examined what its traditional connections make it "mean," as folk belief, philosophy, or otherwise. They depend on finding the right ancestral theme and their method often enough involves peeling down an artistic object to its core. For literature in general that method is illustrated by Robert Graves, in *The White Goddess*, who seeks by its means to unearth the fundamental nature of poetry itself; and Fierz-Monnier, in her psychological study of the romances, who finds in recurring details that deep, embedded experience of the psyche which they supposedly symbolize: the extent to which they appear in any work (the color green, for example) will determine its importance as literature; if enough of them are present, even accidentally, that work is, willy-nilly, a masterpiece. For A. K. Coomaraswamy *Gawain* is significant for what he detects in it as an ancient Indian theme, the speaking head, connected by him with the god Indra and the primordial myth of the One and the Many. Since in the course of time, he tells us, poetry regressively forgets the *philosophia perennis* that once gave it meaning, to recover the proper myth in any poem is to recognize the original source of its power. Others have associated the Green Knight with the Green Man of English popular festival, with Death, with the folklore of the weather and the seasons.

Whatever the ultimate sources of its story, *Gawain* reflects the interests and reading of its time. In it there are various points of contact with the English Arthurian tradition of Geoffrey of Monmouth as found, among others, in the *Chronicle* of Robert Mannyng of Brunne and in Laʒamon's earlier alliterative *Brut*. Long ago Oakden catalogued the word tags and conventional phrases widely found in the contemporary English alliterative poetry, including those in *Gawain*. Among the poems are *The Quatrefoil of Love*; *Wynnere and Wastoure*; *The Avowynge of King Arther*; *The Awntyrs off Arthure at the Terne Wathelyne*; *Morte Arthure*; and especially *The Wars of Alexander*, a striking number of whose verses echo or are echoed by *Gawain*; and *The Parlement of the Thre Ages*, where the seasonal poetry, the hunting scene, and the figure of the elegant youthful horseman in green all bear a special relationship to our romance. Which way debt among them for their similarities goes, is difficult in some instances to determine since their dating is not yet secure; but *The Quatrefoil*, *Wynnere and Wastoure*, and *Parlement* seem to be roughly of the third quarter of the fourteenth century, some time before *Gawain* was composed. In any case they disclose together a current fashion which our poem likewise represents.

It also shows the influence of the French Arthurian romances, perhaps the Vulgate texts, but certainly the vastly popular *Perceval*, and of this some form of the Long version of *The First Continuation*, which the English poet recalled with minute intimacy. That version evidently contained, as Professor Benson has suggested, touches not found in the surviving poetic redactions but present in the prose text, the *Tresplaisante et recreative hystoire*, printed at Paris in 1530. In those romances he discovered the world of chivalry and manners which shapes the acts and outlook of his characters; he makes a point indeed of the self-conscious Frenchness of their behavior in that distant courtly outpost Hautdesert, where Sir Bertilak rules as country master. (That Camelot at the center knows its Gallic manners goes without saying.) The debt to France includes as well the conventions of its treatises on hunting, as exemplified in the Anglo-French adaptations of William Twiti and as translated with additions of its own, a decade or two later than *Gawain*, in *The Master of Game* by Edward Duke of York. The poem also discloses an acquaintance with the ancient Latin moral treatises, among them Cato's *Distichs*, Cicero's *De officiis*, and probably the *De beneficiis* of Seneca, the first accessible also in vernacular form and the second in such influential transformations of its doctrine as the *Moralium dogma phi-losophorum*, ascribed to the twelfth-century philosopher Guillaume de Conches, and Brunetto Latini's popular *Tresor*. From the second of those sources, Cicero and its adaptations, *Gawain* drew that secular scheme of virtues based on justice which, sitting beside his Christian sensibilities, de-termines Sir Gawain's character as a knight. The details of the scheme (*Trawþe* and its five compeers, *Fraunchyse, Felaȝschyp, Clannes, Cor-taysye, Pité*) are listed with particular attention by the poet when he tells us what the five-pointed figure on our hero's shield intends. The tradition which that scheme denotes had reached other romances of the period as well and touched Sir Gawain in them, especially with the distinctive virtue *innocentia*, i.e., *clannes*, which becomes peculiarly his in such texts as the French *Continuations* of the *Perceval* in prose and the English *Parlement of the Thre Ages*. He who possesses this virtue, the *Moralium dogma* tells us, cannot bear to bring any harm to anyone and will, moreover, deem to be great, as does our own Sir Gawain, the very tiniest of his faults. The poet may likewise have had access to the thirteenth-century dictionary of Hugutio of Pisa since it contains, among other relevant matters, the word *pentangulus -um*, previously unrecorded, which he anglicizes as *pentangel*, using it to name that same figure so crucially connected in what it represents to the progress and outcome of the story. (Many of these associations are wit-nessed in the editor's "Sir Gawain in a Dilemma," *Modern Philology* 79 (1977): 1–17, and, with important additions, in the explanatory notes be-low, especially 619ff., 623, 626, 651–53, 653, and 2508–14.)

The complex effect of such associations surfaces everywhere in the poem, but let us take example from the person of the Green Knight when first he appears at Camelot. He is both a giant and a man, with red-rimmed eyes and an oral thunder that stuns the whole Round Table and leaves it still as stone; but also preternatural, a green-faced elvish creature—is it magic or illu-sion?—who coolly lifts his chopped-off head and faery-like rides away to no one knows just where. The giant in this apparition has been analogized to the rustic creatures wielding club or axe who turn up in the Welsh *Mabinogion*, the French *Yvain* by Chrétien de Troyes, the *Continuations* of the *Perceval*, and as woodland wight, the Green Man, in older English lore. He is indeed a scion of such fabled stock, as on the way to the Green Chapel a year later Sir Gawain's guide describes him, meaning to scare our hero from his duty, and as he is in fact at the Chapel itself, grinding the fatal axe and, with it as a monstrous walking stick, striding across the brook to meet Sir Gawain.

But when he first appears at Camelot he is also a knight of fine physique, long-limbed, slim-waisted, and got up in high style. This is not the tradition of the clod, rather that of Carados in *The First Continuation* of the *Perceval*

where, among its various versions, a chevalier *molt grant* comes riding into
King Arthur's court at dinner time, singing a *chanson* and bringing with him
the head-chopping challenge. He is dressed in green satin furred with er-
mine, has a chaplet of flowers on his bonnet, and bears a sword with baldric
of beaten gold and pearls. Closer still in detail to the Green Knight, and rem-
iniscent of this chevalier as well, is the green-clad mounted youth of *The
Parlement of the Thre Ages*, different though his circumstances are from
theirs:

He was balghe in the brests and brode in the scholdirs
His axles and his armes were I-liche longe
And in the medill als a mayden menskfully schapen
Longe legges and large and lel for to schewe. . . .
He ne hade no hode ne no hatte bot his here one
A chaplet on his chef-lere chosen for the nones. . . .
He was gerede all in grene alle with golde by-weuede
Embroddiride alle with Besanttes and Beralles full riche.

[112–23]

Dressed here as he is for peaceful intercourse, he also possesses, though not
with him, arms and armor for use on more military occasions.

It has been suggested recently that the episode in *Gawain* reflects the
contemporary reality of mounted men and servants riding into feasts, espe-
cially the English custom at coronation dinners where the king's champion,
seated in his saddle, defends the royal right against all challengers. In such
instances, however, the challenger is accoutered as a warrior like the cham-
pion, though the combat may in fact be a tableau and the armor ceremonial,
whereas the Green Knight comes in peace and riding shoeless, without the
warlike gear he has left behind at home. Nevertheless, one point in these
challenges at dinner deserves the attention that thus far it has failed to at-
tract, that they normally occur in the interval between the first and second
courses, and this is so, not only in *Gawain* and the coronation feasts, but
also in the French *Perlesvaus* where one of the adventures brought to King
Arthur's court arrives exactly at that customary moment (see n. 134–36 in
the explanatory notes below).

The texts in which these analogues appear all perform more gently than
does *Gawain*. Even the action of the French Carados, with its well-developed
climax, vivid as it is and touched with magic, does not produce so awesome
a figure as the Green Knight nor the drama that the English poem contrives
by the mingling of its creature's lavish elegance with his daunting rude out-
landish look and manner.

Other examples of the complexity of *Gawain*'s sources and the poet's
rise above them as he shapes them to his purpose can be found in the nature
poetry that occurs throughout the narrative. Among them are the lines on

the bitter storm during the second New Year's night before Sir Gawain arises from his bed to be armed and go to meet the giant (1998–2005). Its formulaic phrases about the weather and the wind ("wylde wederez of þe worlde," "þe werbelande wynde wapped"), found elsewhere in the alliterative literature of the day, join art to actuality. The even more striking line, "þe snawe snitered ful snart, þat snayped þe wylde," appears in *The Awntyrs off Arthure*, which also reflects the reality of a northern English winter. Yet the whole description in *Gawain*, active, formed and strong, is matchless among the romances, where winter is seldom a season for adventure. Our poet, we may add, displays a seeing eye and talking tongue, beyond mere literary example, at other parts of Sir Gawain's uncomfortable wanderings. Thus he tells us (726–32), making things more trying for our hero:

For werre wrathed hym not so much þat wynter nas wors,
When þe colde cler water from þe cloudez schadde
And fres er hit falle my3t to þe fale erþe.
Ner slayn wyth þe slete he sleped in his yrnez
Mo ny3tez þen innoghe in naked rokkes
Þer as claterande from þe crest þe colde borne rennez
And henged he3e ouer his hede in hard iiseikkles.

Or to take a further instance, he notes that weary moment when the good steed Gringolet goes plodding with his master through a wintry wood "With mony bryddez vnblyþe vpon bare twyges, / Þat pitously þer piped for pyne of þe colde" (746–47). Later, on the way to the Green Chapel, he leads Sir Gawain and the guide across a raw, resounding landscape, as

Þay bo3en bi bonkkes þer bo3ez are bare,
Þay clomben bi clyffez þer clengez þe colde.
Þe heuen watz vphalt bot vgly þervnder;
Mist muged on þe mor, malt on þe mountez,
Vch hille hade a hatte, a myst-hakel huge.
Brokez byled and breke bi bonkkez aboute,
Schyre schaterande on schorez þer þay doun schowued.

[2077–83]

Perhaps the best example, however, in a piece of nature poetry of the intricate weaving of subject-matter, commonplace, literary device, and language, reflecting old tradition and immediate implication, is in the elaborate group of stanzas (500–531) on the passing of the seasons that intervene between the first Christmas at Camelot and the approach of the second nearly a year later when Sir Gawain must begin his "anious uyage." Its analogues include *The Parlement of the Thre Ages*, whose description of spring is often like Gawain's in observed minutiae and in language; La3amon, which offers a phrase for the rising hot dry wind of autumn; and *The Wars of Alexander*, whose words "aftir wele comys wa, for so þe werd askis" make explicit the darkening implication of *Gawain*'s seasons' ending: "And wynter wyndez aȝayn, as þe worlde askez." The *cursus annorum*, the endless cycle of the seasons, as these vivid verses give it to us, is analogized, in the tradition of Seneca and the Christian homilists, to the journey from human youth to age, from life to death. The related theme of each day's swift decline into a phantom yesterday is also both Senecan and Christian. Its tradition is reinforced in the High Middle Ages by Pope Innocent's influential *De contemptu mundi*, also known as *De miseria humanae conditionis*, which cites Psalm 89 ("For a thousand years *in thy sight* are but as yesterday") and perverts it: "*To the man about to die* a thousand years are but as yesterday"; and remembered in a current English lyric *Sum Tyme Thenk of Yusterday*. And so our poet sums up his group of moving stanzas: "þus ȝirnez þe ȝere in ȝisterdayez mony." The whole account, running seasons and troubling implication, is introduced by a set of monitory aphorisms on the shifting fortunes of the year translated from the Book of Proverbs and Cato's *Distichs*: "Bot þaȝ þe ende be heuy haf ȝe no wonder / . . . / A ȝere ȝernes ful ȝerne and ȝeldez neuer lyke, / Þe forme to þe fynisment foldez ful selden." (See explanatory notes 526 and 496–99 below.)

Nor have we yet done with these remarkable stanzas, for they possess, despite a rich wrought luxury that might have encumbered their progress, a speed arising, not only from their restless subject-matter, but also from their artful function that makes them more than just a *tour de force* for saying "a year goes by," that lends to them, in fact, the crucial role of stating indirectly, hence with added power, the mounting apprehension of Sir Gawain and the Round Table, indeed of the very reader himself, as only too quickly time comes flying headlong, bringing ever nearer the unavoidable journey that can only lead our hero, save for God, to death.

Gawain's meters, poetic words, and other ornaments are treated in section 4 of this introduction. Nevertheless, three of its devices which witness the poet's acquaintance with the various technical conventions of his age and at his hands lend particular color to their moments in the poem, have almost entirely escaped critical notice, and they may be considered briefly here. Two are what the medieval school manuals call *traductio* and *repetitio*, the other concerns his use of aphorisms.

The first of these, *traductio*, consists in the use of two or more words that sound alike but differ in meaning. In *Gawain* that use is sometimes serious, sometimes witty, at other times charmingly romantic. The explanatory notes below list many instances, but three may be especially mentioned here. Line 498, "A ȝere ȝernes ful ȝerne and ȝeldez neuer lyke," provides a sort of double *traductio*, in which verb and adverb, *ȝernes*, *ȝerne*, may descend from either OE *(ge-)eornan*, "run," or *geornan*, *georne*, "yearn," "yearningly, eagerly," hence the phrase can signify "runs runningly," as it were, "yearns yearningly," "runs yearningly"—an interplay in meaning and suggestion that contributes to the sense of life and speed. In line 1641, when Sir Gawain gives two kisses to his host in return for the boar's flesh won by the host that day at the hunt, he plays it oh so jolly, bearing down a bit to make the point: "Now ar we euen in this euentide," says he. But by far the most delightful word-play of this sort, improving on the Latin craft of the medieval *artes poetriae*, which notably illustrate the device, arises when first Sir Gawain sees his hostess of Hautdesert (941ff.). King Uther first beheld Igerne at a festival, Achilles first Polyxena among the ladies at a tomb, Troilus first saw Criseyde from the distance in a temple as the crowd parted to grant the fateful view. So Sir Gawain down the chapel aisle beholds the lady fair as, moving among her dames and demoiselles, she comes at last out of her private pew: and he, dazzled by her grace, plays elegant *traductio* with the name of Arthur's queen, the very model of courtly beauty in that world: and she was "wener þen Wenore as the wyȝe þoȝt." (See explanatory notes below, esp. 945.)

Of *repetitio* one notable example occurs (1007) in the description of Sir Bertilak's Christmas dinner: "Þer watz mete, þer watz myrþe, þer watz much ioye." The device may have been blessed by the manuals and their examples taken from the ancient tongue, but the closest words to *Gawain* are to be found in Laȝamon's "lewed" native English: "her wes mete her wes drænc. / men þer of dræmden / her wes unimete fare"; and in a rather different context: "Þer com Hengest þer com Hors. / þer com moni mon ful oht. / þer comen þa Saxisce men" (5104–5, Madden 10234–38; and 6991–93, Madden 14009–11). Other evidence suggests that our poet may have remembered the *Brut* as he wrote, and if so then the use of this device should perhaps be credited also to that memory.

Aphorisms, proverbs, and proverbial phrases are features of many of the French romances, and some occur as well in *Gawain*. Chrétien de Troyes often seasons sophisticated narrative with the salt of rustic wisdom, quoting what his age knew as *dits au vilain* and often placed beside other sayings based on ancient and subsequent monkish tradition. *Gawain*'s aphorisms and proverbial phrases are less rustic than Chrétien's. When at the end of the second day's exchange of gifts Sir Bertilak compliments Sir Gawain's keeping of the agreement between them, he reserves final judgment for the third day: "þrid tyme þrowe best," he says (1680), using a proverb no doubt of popular origin. But the source is unknown, whether popular or literary, of the phrase by which he later praises our hero's knightly excellence (2364): "As perle bi þe quite pese is of prys more, / So is Gawayn, in god fayth, bi oþer gay knyȝtez." All the rest are drawn from what are patently literary sources, in most instances directly from the texts. King Arthur's injunction to Sir Gawain (371), that "his hert and his honde schulde hardi be," derives from an ancient Latin word tag, *animo manuque*, that provides a topos to

medieval and renaissance literature and appears here early in English. Sir
Gawain's words of resignation (564–65), "Of destinés derf and dere / What
may mon do bot fonde?" have all the character of aphorism; they may derive
from two different phrases in Vergil that had already become *Sprichwörter*
in the Middle Ages. In lines 1499–1500 Sir Gawain puts aside the lady's
come-on that no woman could resist his masculine strength, with a notable
piece of courtly instruction against rape: "Bot þrete is vnþryuande in þede
þer I lende / And vche gift þat is geuen not with goud wylle." Its source is
the saying "force n'est droit," current in both Latin and French, applied to
love in the romances, but of more general application as well. Geoffrey of
Monmouth has King Arthur use it as a principle of international law to
counter the Roman imperial claim against Britain, and it is found similarly
used but in words very like *Gawain*'s in the chronicle of Robert Mannyng of
Brunne. One of the ways of beginning a literary piece, according to the *artes
poetriae*, is with an aphorism, and *Gawain* follows this principle, as we have
seen, in the long passage on the changing seasons, citing both the Book of
Proverbs and Cato's *Distichs*. Another phrase also resides among these two
that has all the look and feel of a proverb (497): "For þaʒ men ben mery in
mynde quen þay han mayn drynk." Familiar as it sounds, to find it elsewhere
frustrates inquiry; the only convincing analogue thus far recovered is a line
which registers uniquely the word *ebriolatus*: "Ebriolati mentem hilariam
accipiunt." It turns up, unexpectedly, in that bundle of ancient Latin lexical
scraps brought together to instruct his son by one Nonius Marcellus in the
fourth century A.D. (See below, explanatory notes 1680, 2364, 366, 564–65,
1499–500, 497.)

The fiction which this poetry embellishes continues to inspire a variety of
present "readings" explaining what *Gawain* is about, many of which fall
into the realm of rhetorical rather than poetic criticism. Some have stressed
the importance of the motif of the journey, a commonplace of epic and ro-
mance, seeing in it the theme of perfection found wanting, and drawing for
support on the evidence of the shield. In such a view the group of virtues
symbolized by the pentangle signifies that perfection in our hero. Chrétien
in *Charrette* uses the journey to test, in *Perceval* to educate his hero, and no
romance, short of sheer adventure, fails to teach somebody something.
There are many "themes" in *Gawain*, and one of them is suffering and en-
durance and the protagonist's embarrassment at his failure in the end, but to
read the poem therefore as essentially a journey of instruction or self-
discovery is to ignore other aspects of the plot hence to misread it, as will
appear further in the present essay. Nor is the poem about perfection,
though that topic lends some necessary substance to the story. To be sure,
Sir Gawain may be the pearl of chivalry, as the Green Knight describes him,
above all others of his kind, and possess in gold-fined purity the five virtues

symbolized by the device on his shield. But the poet, like his French masters in the *Perceval Continuations*, never makes him a mummy of perfection, nor does the pentangle signify that scarcely human state; it means, as the poet plainly tells us, *Trawþe*, that is, faithfulness to word or oath or other sworn agreement, which is a very different matter from perfection and plays a different role in *Gawain*'s plot. (See explanatory notes below, esp. 626, 651–53, and 653.)

Other readings of the poem turn to metaphor and allegory, as in the case of the three days of hunts and love temptation. In a recent book on the medieval chase Marcelle Thiébaux points out that some of the treatises draw lessons from the sport, attributing moral benefit to its practitioners. That Sir Gawain lying in luxury at the castle is open to temptation while his host is exercising virtue in the woods echoes the frequent warnings of the homilists against such idleness leading to license, and enriches the implication of these interwoven moments, but attempts to fathom in them something deeper have stirred up more problems than they have settled.

A further consequence of the current search for "poetic meaning" is the notion, widely held, that *Gawain* is ambiguous. That is not the same as observing that the story, like most stories, raises a number of unanswered questions: for example, what becomes of the three days' take that Sir Gawain wins by wager with his host, and about which there is so much talk? To analogize the fox's pelt to the embroidered girdle given him by his hostess and so preserve it in symbolic transformation to the climax of the tale, may exercise some smallish ingenuity in a modern reader, but to ask what happens to our hero's share of deer and boar and what that intimates, or whether in fact he carries the fox's pelt at his saddlebow as fate beckons him to the Green Chapel, is as futile (and no doubt irrelevant) as to seek out from the ancients what song the Sirens sang. Ambiguity proper, seen as a poetic virtue which lends "richness" to a piece, provides its own temptation. Going back to the French Symbolists, William Empson, and some of the American New Critics, this view tends to give the interpreter full rein. One may be enticed into fancying the Green Knight a sort of Janus figure, at once a good thing and a bad, though Sir Gawain, and the reader as well, know him for one unchanging figure throughout, the antagonist threatening our hero's life. That he is the same as Sir Bertilak is something vouchsafed us only at the denouement. Who he is and how we feel about him is thus a function of the plot. To be sure, in books as in life ambiguity is a common condition and there are some obvious occurrences in *Gawain*, besides the occasional *double entendre* and a straight-faced prologue that arguably masks a comic purpose. When at the beginning of the story the Green Knight appears at Camelot, fear among the guests arises out of the doubt which his outrageous figure portends (is it magic or illusion?). The play between Sir Gawain and his host at Hautdesert over the lady's kisses relies on an indefinition as to what her husband knows or guesses, to give the game its piquancy. In the French romances there can be a dangerous dark ground between dalliance and the rise of passion; and that is the case with our hero and the lady, who also has a hidden, perhaps sinister, purpose, as the poet intimates, without, however, telling us what it is. Sir Gawain spends an entire Christmas season with his hosts, presumably without learning who they are. Nor does the reader think of it until Sir Bertilak identifies himself at the Green Chapel (if he thinks of it even then) when obscurity in the matter no longer is important. These are instances of deliberate ambiguity, whose literal function is to build suspense and let the story work out as it must. But that *Gawain* is ambiguous, in fact or intent, about the major issues of its plot is contrary to all the evidence. The one literally stated allegory in the poem lies in the pentangle device on Sir Gawain's shield, which immediately on describing it, the poet interprets for us, even interrupting the narrative to do so because it tells us something about our hero's character that will define his role in the story. The central issue is, of course, the agreement that Sir Gawain makes about the head-chopping contest, whose terms are formally laid out, with the entire Round Table as witness, by the Green Knight, reiterated by him just before the first blow, repeated further by the severed head and referred to by the giant once again a year later at the Green Chapel. When afterwards Sir Gawain accuses himself of cowardice and covetousness he says it, not just once but twice, the second time in the full public presence of King Arthur's court, which witnessed the original transaction. Similarly guest and host at Hautdesert twice repeat their agreement to exchange each day's winnings indoors and out, an agreement out of which arises Sir Gawain's final dilemma. It is hard to see how in important points like these the poet could have been less ambiguous.

In the French romances conflicting moral views sit side by side and are never fully reconciled, and this is so as well in *Gawain*. Unresolved but accommodated conflict, however, is also not the same as ambiguity. The normal ways of knighthood, especially in the matter of sexual love, reflect moral customs at variance with those of the Christian culture into which the romances came to be naturalized. A text of *The First Continuation* of the *Perceval* (MS *R*) illustrates the conflict and the accommodation it produced. At the confession in which the good Mesire Gavains discloses that he has loved many women in his time, Bishop Salemon says that God will forgive those who are gentle, if not those who are ungentle in their love. *Gawain* faces our hero in the love temptation scenes with the conflicting demands of courtliness, of *loyauté* to host, and of Christian chastity, from which he escapes by surrender to another sort of temptation, the acceptance in secret of the supposedly magic girdle.

A third ingredient also enters into the combination, that of the secular moral psychology of the ancients, especially Seneca and Cicero, which had long persisted in the Christian moralists and was renewed in the twelfth century, affected the romances, and here plays a major part in *Gawain*, where it provides the secular virtues listed by the poet as what the pentangle means, virtues associated with the principle of justice, whose maintenance is peculiarly appropriate to a Christian knight, as John of Salisbury, Ramon Lull, and some of the French Arthurian texts aver. The basis of justice, Cicero tells us, is *fides*, or in our poet's word *trawþe*; *fides* is the keeping of agreements, and what prevents a man from keeping his word are *metus* and *avaritia*, *timor* and *cupiditas* as the twelfth century and after phrased it, *cowarddyse* and *couetyse* as Sir Gawain names them, accusing himself of failure. This is what the poem at its center is about. (See explanatory notes 623, 626, 632, 651–53, 2508–14.)

The intrusion into the narrative of this secular tradition produces the curious phenomenon of two separate confessions by Sir Gawain, the first to a priest at Hautdesert, who "asoyled hym surely and sette hym so clene / As domezday schulde haf ben diȝt on þe morn" (1883–84). Gollancz observes that our hero makes a sacrilegious confession here, for he conceals the fact that he has accepted the girdle with the intention of retaining it. Professor Davis points out, however, that because of his absolution a man of Sir Gawain's devotion would hardly have felt merrier than he ever had in his life, as the poet tells us he did, if the absolution were not valid; and we may add, though disagreement about the matter still remained in contemporary treatises, Thomas Aquinas himself, in his account of the sins opposed to justice, provided the principle (*Secunda secundae*, q. 66, art. 8) on which such validity might be based, namely, that grave necessity, in this case the imminent threat to Sir Gawain's life, would in Christian terms have justified his keeping the girdle. The second confession is a secular one, its penance made, as the giant sees it, at his hands and beneath the blade of his axe: "'Þou art confessed so clene, beknowen of þy mysses, / And hatz þe penaunce apert of the poynt of myn egge, / I halde þe polysed of þat plyȝt and pured as clene / As þou hadez neuer forfeted syþen þou watz fyrst borne.'" (2391–94). These two confessions represent two different aspects of the received moral world of the romances, differences that may raise a problem for the finicky modern critic but evidently gave our poet no qualms, who used them as his story required and timed to build suspense and, in keeping with his hero's moral sensibilities, to offer explanation and completion. (See, *inter alia*, explanatory note 2508–14.)

That story has been summarized already in terms of its two original inherited motifs, the head-chopping and the love temptation. Let us do it now another way. Two adversaries make an agreement, to fulfill which will evi-

dently lead one of them to death. In the effort to keep his word, the protago-
nist engages in a dangerous journey, at the end of which he undertakes two
further agreements whose conflicting conditions place him in an unresolva-
ble dilemma which could affect his keeping the original compact, but do
not, as it turns out, prevent his doing so. This sort of résumé adds motivation
beyond the inherited matter of the story and the use of devices like the
knightly quest or journey. It may be particuliarzed further by the observa-
tion that the poet sees the action as an exercise in justice, appropriate to
Christian chivalry, and clothed in the ideas of Cicero, as the High Middle
Ages perceived them. The protagonist, Sir Gawain, is a set-up, intended pre-
cisely for such an action. The book-made schema of his virtues, specified in
the pentangle of his shield, produces what may be called rhetorical, rather
than natural, character, a character that the trials of the story are deliber-
ately designed to play upon. If this, however, were all the poem is about,
Gawain would seem to be an essay on conduct, or rather an exemplary fic-
tion embellishing a treatise or a homily. But there are other features which
humanize Sir Gawain, his rising apprehension as the year too quickly passes
by, the welling up of fear at Hautdesert stimulated by an early morning
dream, his instinctive sudden anger after the giant has made, not one, but
three passes at him with the axe, his embarrassment at what he considers his
knightly failure and his masculine chagrin at having succumbed to feminine
deceit. More basic than all this is the perception that the entire plot is de-
signed to exploit its protagonist's noble being to entrap him and then hap-
pily grant him release, with laughter and approval by foe and friend alike. If
the story comes out happily, as it does (despite our hero's blushing discom-
posure), then the plot is a comic one, and if the issues turn on social princi-
ple and habits, then (despite the hard scar tissue on our hero's knightly con-
science) the poem is a comedy of manners. In short, if the poem touches its
characters with serious considerations integral to its plot, as do, for exam-
ple, eighteenth-century English sentimental comedies, Jane Austen's *Pride
and Prejudice*, Bernard Shaw, and, more recently, James Goldman's play
about Henry II and Eleanor of Aquitaine, *The Lion in Winter*, which en-
tangles them in a web of Christmas games; that does not transform it, as
some readers would wish to do, into a tragedy, almost.

There is a tradition in Middle English of Gawain comedies, *The Marriage
of Sir Gawaine*, *The Weddynge of Sir Gawen and Dame Ragnell*, the re-
lated story by the Wife of Bath, and Gower's funny Tale of Florent. Each
turns on its own and different point, but all are alike in catching the protago-
nist in a difficulty from which an unforeseen circumstance releases him. But
no difficulty is as difficult as our hero's in *Gawain*, for it adds to the physical
peril in which he finds himself a dilemma in the very strictest sense. Sir
Gawain gives his word that each day he will exchange his winnings in the

castle for his host's that day at the hunt. On the third day the lady gives him a girdle, requesting that he say nothing about it to her husband, and he agrees. The dilemma then is this: If he keeps the girdle he breaks his word to the host; if he tells his host he breaks his word to the lady. *Catch-22.* The only way to resolve this unresolvable dilemma is, as in that comic novel, to break the loop and run away from it. This Sir Gawain does by confessing to his host and the host in turn by admitting that the whole affair is a trick deliberately contrived to catch out his guest. One more trick remains unspoken and unnoticed, perhaps the crowning trick of the story. This is that the girdle is supposed to have the magic to protect its wearer from death or injury. But wherein lies the magic? The giant lifts his axe twice, twice withholds the stroke, and the third time gives Sir Gawain a blow that cuts the flesh. Had he wished he could, for all we know, have chopped our hero's head off and so put sorry *finis* to the story. But the plot would not let it end that way. The real magic lies in human will and social principle, and healing, especially of the heart, comes with time, and with love and laughter among one's fellows in the world of Camelot.

The prologue with which this all begins, at once conventional *prohemium* for a poem of noble content and *insinuatio* by reason of its devious comic intention, takes us through a history whose primal Trojan hero Aeneas was a traitor, its founding British father Brutus a parricide and outcast, and its outcome a chronicle of "blysse and blunder," of which the present instance, subtle in its shaping by a very great poet, is Sir Gawain's unhappy-happy case.

2. Manuscript, Date, Subsequent History

Gawain survives in a single manuscript, British Library Cotton Nero A. x, written on vellum toward the end of the fourteenth or early in the fifteenth century. In the seventeenth Sir Robert Cotton, to whom it belonged, had it bound up as article 3 with other unrelated works, from which in 1964 it was made separate again. It consists of ninety folios, 17.3×12.3 cm: at the beginning a single sheet of two leaves containing illustrations, followed by eight gatherings, seven of twelve leaves each and at the end another of four leaves, the last two of which also have illustrations. Two different modern hands have marked these eight gatherings, one H through P, the other 2 through 9, respectively. As a guide to the binder, the end of each gathering contains catchwords from the beginning of the next in the hand of the original scribe, and it may have been he who set down the marks in the margins which distinguish stanzas and other line divisions, just as he set the rhyming "bob" near the end of each stanza in *Gawain* to the right beside, or above the level of, the line to which it belongs. The folios were designated 37–126, and afterwards renumbered beginning with 41, both when the manuscript was part of Cotton's composite volume. Editors from Madden on have used the older of these numberings and it is retained for convenience in the present edition.

In the manuscript there are four poems, which seem to have been composed in the last two decades of the fourteenth century: *Pearl*, *Purity*, and *Patience* on folios 39–90ᵛ, and *Gawain* on folios 91–124ᵛ. Errors in writing and some small differences in language suggest that they are a collection based on slightly varying copy texts; and there is some slight evidence in *Gawain* that the writer had two versions of the piece in front of him. (See n. 552 in the explanatory notes below.)

All the poems are written by a single scribe in a distinctive, rather delicate angular hand. Notable among its characteristics is its use of yogh (ȝ) for the sounds /x/, /w/, /y/, and for final -s or -z. It also employs tȝ for s or z, evidently from Anglo-French convention, and the 2-form of r following o. Th occurs, as well as þ, the latter always in the OE *wen* form, that is, without the verticle ascender at the top. But most idiosyncratic is the regular fusion of d and e and of p and e, its ligature of sch, and the curious formation of its w. The same scribe has made corrections by erasure and rewriting, and a later hand has redone some letters, faded or blurred by discolorations of the vellum. Over the years the manuscript has continued to fade so that the EETS facsimile, made in 1923, is now in many places more legible to the naked eye than the original. Offsets from facing folios in some instances complicate, in others assist, the reading of the text. The colophon (fol. 124ᵛ), "AMEN/HONY SOYT QUI MAL PENCE" (lacking the telltale fusion of p and e), is perhaps by another hand. Two further hands have inscribed names on the margins: on folio 91ʳ "Hugo de," which has been hypothetically expanded as Hugo de Mascy in connection with the most recent attempts to identify *Gawain*'s author; and on folio 111ᵛ "Phares" in a somewhat later script, evidently by a moralizing reader who, when he came to the lady's second love temptation (1534ff.), "Whil my lorde is from hame . . . ," was reminded of *Purity*, folio 80ᵛ, that is, King Baltazar's wanton ladies and the mysterious hand that spelled out Babylon's doom: "MANE TECHAL PHARES." A third marginal note on folio 111ᵛ is discussed in the next section.

Throughout the manuscript, initials are rubricated in blue with flourishing in red pen-stroke designs, the letters and flourishes being larger and more elaborate for the opening of each piece and in *Gawain* also for the major parts of the narrative. In addition there are five smaller rubricated letters in *Gawain* at 619 (Sir Gawain's shield), 763 (approaching Bertilak's castle), 1421 (the boar hunt), 1893 (turning from Sir Gawain among the ladies to the last part of the fox hunt), and 2259 (the Green Knight getting set to give his blow)—why has been a subject of critical speculation, related to the question of the poem's stanzaic symmetry (see Michael Robertson, in

Speculum 57 [1982]: 779–85). None of the pieces in the manuscript have titles, all of which are modern inventions.

The manuscript is unusual for its time in having illustrations: four for *Pearl* (folios 37ʳᵛ and 38ʳᵛ), two each for *Purity* and *Patience* (folios 56ʳᵛ and 882ʳᵛ), and four for *Gawain* (folios 90ᵛ, 125ʳᵛ and 126ʳ). They are crudely drawn, colored in red, blue, green, and yellow, their manner reminiscent of rural wall paintings, and not always accurate representations of the text. The isolated pictures at the beginning and end, Gollancz observes, would suggest that the illustrations were later in date, except that several are found in the body of the manuscript. There is, moreover, other evidence, thus far unobserved, that they were contemporary with the writing. On folio 125ʳ, above the drawing of the wife's third visit to Sir Gawain's bedroom, are the lines: "Mi minde is mukul on one [on *added above the line erroneously after* one] þat wil me noȝt amende / Sum time was trewe as ston and fro schame couþe hir defende." The handwriting, somewhat larger and rounder than that of the text of the poem, Gollancz judges to be the illustrator's; yet it displays the three most notable traits of the texts themselves: the fusion of d and e, the peculiar w, and the ligature of sch.

Gawain and the other poems of this manuscript seem never to have been widely read in their own time, as were the works of Chaucer, Gower, Lydgate, Hoccleve, and others; in the subsequent centuries they were virtually unknown until their rediscovery in the later eighteenth and earlier nineteenth century. A popular fifteenth-century remaking called *The Greene Knight*, a version of which appears among the Percy manuscripts, has been shown by Kittredge to be dependent on it and may be the piece recorded in an inventory of the Paston library dated between 1475 and November 1479. The present manuscript itself was acquired by Henry Savile of Banke, Yorkshire, in the later sixteenth or early seventeenth century and went in turn soon afterwards with other Savile manuscripts to Sir Robert Cotton, thence to the British Museum. A catalogue of Savile's books (British Library MS Harley 1879) lists "an owld booke in English verse beginninge Perle plesant to princes pay in 4° limned [i.e., illustrated]." There is no evidence that Savile or his cataloguer read the manuscript further to distinguish the various pieces in it, and this is true also of the later cataloguers, Thomas Smith (1696) and J. Planta (1802), as well as Thomas Warton, in *The History of English Poetry* (3 [1781]: 107–8), who quotes *Pearl* but takes no notice of *Gawain*. With the ferment of interest in the older poetry and other popular antiquities characteristic of the Romantic movement of the early nineteenth century, *Gawain* was rediscovered by many English and Scottish scholars, Warton's editor Price, J. J. Conybeare, Joseph Stevenson, David Laing, Edwin Guest—it was even called to the attention of Sir Walter Scott—and the *editio princeps* by Sir Frederick Madden was published in 1839, in keeping with its supposed Northern or Scottish connection, by the Bannatyne Club.

But the full season of its reflorescence has been, for scholar and reader alike, the twentieth century.

3. Author and Provenience

Gawain is anonymous, like the other three poems in the manuscript, and the best efforts of nearly a century and a half of literary scholarship have failed to recover with certainty the name of its author. The claims of the Northern poet Huchowne of the Awle Ryale, advanced by Madden and others of his time, have retired before the increasing knowledge of Middle English dialects, which distinguishes the poem's language as a form of Northwest Midland. The character of the manuscript would seem to limit the provenience of this scribal copy even further, to an area in southeast Cheshire or just across the border in Staffordshire; and while we do not have the poet's language pure, the results of independent topographical investigation of the supposed local originals of the Green Chapel and the terrain of Sir Bertilak's Hautdesert imply that it was not very different from the scribe's.

The most recently proposed candidate for author is connected with the locale which these observations suggest. He is one John Massy of Cotton in east Cheshire, a life retainer in the Lancastrian service under John of Gaunt and King Henry IV until his death between 1409 and 1415. In a book sent to Henry's son John of Lancaster after 1411 but before 1414 the poet Thomas Hoccleve refers to a man skilled in the rhetorical arts whom he calls "maister Massy." The scribal language of another poem, *Saint Erkenwald*, which in many respects is like *Gawain*, has been associated with an area roughly ten miles in radius from Holmes Chapel in Cheshire, a center lying one mile east of Cotton. On the outer margin of folio 111ᵛ of the *Gawain* manuscript, slightly below the level of line 1544: "As I am oþer euer schale in erde þer I leue [Sir Gawain is speaking of King Arthur's court, where he lives]," are the letters *oton* in a hand not unlike that which wrote the o's, t's, *on*, and *ston* of the verses above the illustration on folio 125ʳ, hence may be by the original scribe himself or someone near to him in time and place. Unfortunately, the margin has been trimmed close at this point, with some apparent loss of writing, and it has been suggested that the full word was *Coton*, an older form of Cotton. An attempt has already been made, unconnected hence providing a convergence with this case, to relate the fictional setting of the Green Chapel to the valley of the River Dane, which runs just behind Cotton Hall.

These are in essence the chief material points in support of the claim for John Massy. They assume the common authorship of *Saint Erkenwald* and at least *Gawain*, if not all four poems of Cotton Nero A. x—a view on which there is as yet some disagreement. Together they produce, once again, rather less than certainty, though a fair presumption in Massy's favor and a start to further search for the evidence that could turn that favor into fact.

4. Meter, Diction, Ornamental Devices, Style

The alliterative revival of the fourteenth and fifteenth centuries, to which *Gawain* belongs, is a phenomenon chiefly of the Northwest Midlands and the North. Based on the older native poetry, it produced a number of historical and didactic pieces in long unrhymed alliterative lines with no stanzaic division, like *The Parlement of the Thre Ages* and *Wynnere and Wastoure*. But it was also affected by the rhymed and short-lined poems of the French, not simply the romances but the brief stanzaic pieces, and this no doubt influenced the verses of such poems as *The Quatrefoil of Love*, *The Awntyrs off Arthure*, and others, written in regular stanzas of thirteen lines that, with some small variation, mix nine long lines with four short at the end, all rhymed a b a b a b a b c d d d c.

Gawain displays a somewhat similar mixture. It is written in 101 stanzas of long, unrhymed alliterative lines, varying in number from twelve to thirty-seven, which are followed in each stanza by a "bob" and a "wheel" of five short lines rhymed a b a b a. The bob has two or three syllables with the stress on the last. The short lines of the wheel have three stresses and usually begin unstressed and end with a stressed syllable. There are some, however, that start with a stress and a few others that have a feminine ending, though the general loss in pronunciation of historical final -e indicates that most of the written instances are in fact silent.

The long alliterated lines are made up largely of four stressed syllables, with a varying number of others that are unstressed, but there are many lines (more than 500) that have five stresses. A caesura, usually between the antepenultimate and the penultimate stress, produces a pattern of half-lines that reflect, with appropriate differences arising from the shift in the language of length to stress, the half-line structure of Old English verse.

Alliteration is of consonants, single or in groups, or of vowels or breathers initially at the point of primary stress. There are usually three such alliterations in each line, though some lines have four or five and others only two. In the pattern that dominates throughout the poem (1236 lines) the alliteration occurs in the two primarily stressed syllables of the first half-line and the first stressed syllable of the second; a variant shifts to the second stress in the second half-line:

[2062]   Gordez to Gryngolet with his gilt helez
  [4]   Watz tried for his tricherie, þe trewest on erthe
  [27]   Forþi an aunter in erde I attle to schawe
[475]   For I haf sen a selly I may not forsake

In other four-stress lines the first or second stressed syllable of the first half-line alliterates with both stressed syllables of the second:

[1082] Dówelle and éllez dó quat ʒe démen
[2378] Ló! þer þe fálssyng, fóule mot hit fálle!

There are perhaps a third as many lines with five stresses as with four and they are arranged in nine alliterative patterns, among which one appears four times and three others only once each (1082, 1154, 1406, 1965, and 1701, 1682, 2417). All the rest have either three alliterations or, more heavily, four and a few (twenty-one instances) have five; these are illustrated by the following lines:

  [417] The gréne knýʒt vpon gróunde gráyþely hym drésses
  [549] To sech þe gome of þe gréne, as God wyl me wýsse
  [905] Þat is þe rýche rýal kýng of þe Róunde Táble
  [591] Þe lést láchet oþer lóupe lémed of gólde
 [1151] Dér dróf in þe dále, dóted for dréde

All such metrical patterns are verse conventions based on oral performance that are mounted on and limited by the natural rhythms and stresses of the language. This relationship is implied in Davis's analysis of *Gawain*'s verse and more fully worked out by Borroff, who takes into account those shifts and nuances of stress without which meters become stiff and merely formal. More recently, in a study of the larger body of Middle English alliterative poetry, Sapora offers an account of *Gawain*'s meters supported by a newly ordered theory of their interconnection with the language substrate, and illustrates the consequences of that account with a complete scansion of the poem.

Meter, diction, syntax, and ornamental devices are all elements of style, and many of *Gawain*'s practices in these respects it shares with other alliterative poems of its time. As to diction, there is abroad among these poems a common stock of word tags and phrases, whose presence in *Gawain* is noted frequently in the explanatory notes below: *in londe, in stedde, in toun, so foule and so felle, glam and gle, lufsum vnder lyne, word þat he warp*. Subtler than the use of such clichés is that of a vocabulary which adds to its not unusual mix of words of older English and romance origin a smaller but distinctive Scandinavian component that enriches the texture of the poetry. Technical terms occur, especially those, largely French, connected with the chase. But there are other points about the diction, as representative of a current poetic language, which our poem also shares with its contemporaries—shares and then surpasses them in its art. The quality of that art can be seen in the description of a spring day in *The Parlement of the Thre Ages*:

In the monethe of Maye when mirthes bene fele,
And the sesone of somere when softe bene the wedres . . .

Als I habade one a banke be a bryme syde,
There the gryse was grene, growen with floures—
The primrose, the pervynke, and piliole þe riche—
The dewe appon dayses donkede full faire,
Burgons & blossoms & braunches full swete,
And the mery mystes full myldely gane falle;
The cukkowe, the cowschote, kene were þay bothen,
And the throstills full throly threpen in the bankes,
And iche foule in that frythe faynere þan oþer
That the derke was done & the daye lightenede.

[1–2, 7–16]

Here language and observed detail remind us of, but do not reach, the effect
of *Gawain*'s early summer season:

Schyre schedez þe rayn in schowrez ful warme,
Fallez vpon fayre flat, flowrez þere schewen,
Boþe groundez and þe greuez grene ar her wedez,
Bryddez busken to bylde and bremlych syngen
For solace of þe softe somer þat sues þerafter
              bi bonk,
      And blossumez bolne to blowe
      Bi rawez rych and ronk;
      Þen notez noble innoȝe
      Ar herde in wod so wlonk.

After þe sesoun of somer wyth þe softe wyndez,
Quen Zeferus syflez hymself on sedez and erbez,
Wela wynne is þe wort þat waxes þeroute,
When þe donkande dewe dropez of þe leuez
To bide a blysful blusch of þe bryȝt sunne.

[506–20]

This, too, is part of a tradition, newly stated, whose more scholastic parallels
appear in the Latin *artes poetriae* and whose movement stems to some de-
gree from the dynamics of the verbs. No other instance, however, is as
charming as the one in *Gawain*, which adds to observation a sense of the
life of little things, nor has any other caught, in a verb-centered, antithetic,
simple line like this (505),

Colde clengez adoun, cloudez vplyften,

the hard frost and sweeping skies of late winter.

   Some of the ornamental devices used by our poet, drawn from his read-
ing, both English and Continental, have been described above in section 1 of
this introduction. They are *double entendre*, aphorism, and a figure called
repetitio. *Double entendre*, in particular, a form of witty decoration belong-
ing with what is called *traductio* in the *artes poetriae*, appears with a vari-

ety of effects appropriate to the different moments of the story, and there are many further occurrences than those already observed, e.g., *dubbed in a dublet* (571) and, to take another which adds antithesis to its witty play, *My hede flaȝ to my fote and ȝet flaȝ I neuer* (2276). The well-known Lenten joke in line 503, which turns in a single appearance of the word on the two meanings of *flesch*, suggests the first meaning, "body," with the verb *fraystez*, then suddenly shifts with *fysche* and *fode* to the second, "meat":

þe crabbed Lentoun,
Þat fraystez flesch wyth þe fysche and fode more symple.

Conventional epithets for many of the persons in the poem likewise constitute a portion of its stock; some instances, always found in the first half-line, alliterate properly with the pattern of the verse and represent a survival from the older historical poetry: *þat athel Arthure, Ennias þe athel, Gawayne þe gode*. The others, which occur in the second half-line, do not alliterate and probably mark the influence of the short-lined French romances, in which many similar epithets appear (see explanatory note 5 below).

In the end, devices are not style but help to form it. Style presumes a functional relation with what the author conceives to be the nature of his work, its internal economy; in a narrative its events, its persons and their interactions. The richly textured weaving of the Green Knight's fancy dress as he rides into King Arthur's hall at dinner, the noise and high excitement of the hunts at Hautdesert, the mock-pathetic chorus in prayer for Reynard's soul, the rough speech of the Green Knight at Camelot and King Arthur's *þou*'s in response to one not the equal of his peers, the gay and dangerous dialectic of the lady in her three days' temptation of our hero, the broken syntax of her speech imitating talk (1508ff.), her bright colloquialism as she throws open a window and rallies Sir Gawain from his dream-raddled sleep, Sir Bertilak's cursive history of Morgan la Faye crowded into his account, after Sir Gawain's ordeal at the Green Chapel, of the plot against Queen Gaynour and the Round Table; these are illustrations of the principle and, in a work providing varied opportunity, of the poet's singular mastery of that aspect of his art.

5. Language and Dialect

The language of *Gawain* has been variously localized in areas including southeast Lancashire, the Peak district of Derbyshire, southeast Cheshire and neighboring Staffordshire, and even more northerly in northeast Lancashire and parts of Cumbria. Current studies propose a narrower focus on the Cheshire-Staffordshire border near the valley of the River Dane (see section 3 of this introduction). In contents the manuscript has the character of a collected edition; but whatever small differences in language there may be among the individual pieces in it, no firm evidence emerges that the scribe's speech varied notably from the poet's.

From Knigge to Menner, Serjeantson and Davis, accounts of the language have raised questions about its sounds that are even yet not fully answerable. Many of the questions arise from the history of the language itself and from the varying spelling habits embodied in the practices of the scribe, which produce multiplicity in the representation of similar, and likeness in that of different, sounds. Those practices have been systematically studied by McLaughlin for MS Cotton Nero A.x as a whole.

Spelling and Sounds

Vowels Unstressed and with Secondary Stress

The text is full of nonhistorical final e's, many of them in discontinuous sequence with other vowels marking length in stressed syllables, and these are unpronounced (see next sections). There are, besides, occasional e's with short vowels, as in *þikke* (175), rhymed with *quik*, and *blysse, blys, mysse, Iwysse*, rhymed with *þis* (1888ff., 2526ff.); and in the presence of r *yourez* rhymes with *honours* (1812ff.). Such practices are, however, not uniform. The rhymes show some historical survivals of pronunciation, e.g., *for soþe, to þe* (413ff.) and *scaþe, waþe* (from ON i), *ta þe* (2353ff.). Four forms, not in the rhymes, end in ee and oe (*eldee* 844, *madee* 1565, *trwee* 1274, *trowoe* 813) but what that signifies is unclear. Other letters appear also in unstressed or secondary syllables. Thus the shift away from the stressed syllable in French loan-words ending /ayn/ produces /en/, with the notation unchanged, and it may be this in turn which by a reverse spelling gives *etayn* (140, 723), from OE *eoten*. *Resoun* (227, 392, 443, etc.) has a moveable stress without effect on the spelling of its second element, though no doubt with a changing allophonic quality when the stress falls forward; and this may explain the "French" spelling of *lentoun* (502), from OE *lencten*, and perhaps *moroun* (1208), which is affected by the presence of the r. Among proper nouns the king appears regularly as *Arthur(e)* and *Arth(þ)our*, but also *Arthor* (2275, at the end of a line) and *Arþer* (467, 536); *Gawayn(e)* alternates with the weakened *Gawan, Gawen* and their variants (109, 387, 463, 476, etc.) as the stress shifts forward (the form *Gawan* rhyming with *frayn*, 487, may be a scribal error), Yvain is named *Ywan, Aywan* (113, 551), and Morgain is written, unstressed, *Morgne* (2446, 2452). Others survive unchanged in the writing, as is the way of names: *Mador, Lucan, Gaynour* (*Gwenore, Wenore*).

Short Stressed Vowels

The letter a is written for /a/ coming from OE /æ/, /a/, and /ɑ/; examples: *last(e)* (1023, 1027, etc.), *harme* (2272, 2277, etc.), *rande* (1710). The significance of the West Midland variant spellings a/o for Anglican /α/ before nasals is uncertain. They may be simply haphazard or represent a survival of OE doublets in some words or an allophonic range between /a/ and /o/. Examples: *wrang* (1494), *þronge* (1021), *songez* (1654).

The letter e is written for /e/ coming from OE /e/, /ə/, /e:/, /ə:/; examples: *bent* (605, 827, etc.), *heuen* (323, 2057, etc.), *blessed* (1296), *frendez* (714, 987). The tendency of /e/ to rise to /i/ in the presence of dentals, r, g, 3, and l is evident in words like *geserne*, *giserne* (326, 288), *3ernes*, *3irnez* (498, 529), *quel*, *quyl(e)* (822, 814). The spelling e for the later fourteenth-century unrounded /ö/ coming from OE /ə/ occurs elsewhere in the manuscript but some uses of u and o indicate the preservation of the rounding, especially in the presence of palatals and w, and this is apparently the case in *Gawain* in words like *worth* (adj. 1269), *worþe* (vb. 1214, etc.), and *chorle* (2107). Some spellings of ar for er represent the later fourteenth- to fifteenth-century shift in pronunciation for this combination; examples: *start(e)* (431, 1567, etc.), and perhaps *charres* (1674), *marre* (2262), *3ar(r)ande* (1595, 1724). The form *ernd(e)*, which occurs throughout (257, 559, etc.), may simply be a traditional survival though the phoneme is in fact /a/, and an indication therefore of some allophonic range for /e/ and /a/. This possibility is supported by such other variants as in *kest*, *cast* (64, 2317, etc.), *waschen*, *wesche* (72, 887), which also survive in related modern dialects.

The letters i and y, and in some instances u, are written for /i/ coming from OE /i/, /y/, /i:/ and /y:/; examples: *in*, *inn* (645, 1096, etc.), *dyn* (47, 1159, etc.), *busyly*, *bysily* (68, 1824), *fust* (391). Before r, Late OE /i/, untensed from earlier /y/, is spelled with i, y, or e; examples: *miry*, *myry*, *mery*, *meré* (1691, 1086, 153, 497, etc.), *mirþe*, *myrþe*, *merþes* (45, 1007, 40, etc.). It is uncertain whether this represents two different pronunciations or a shift to /e/, as in modern dialects of the area, with the i, y spellings conservatively retained.

The letter o is written for /o/ from OE /o/ and /o:/; examples: *blossumez* (512), *ronk* (513).

The letters u, initial v, occasionally o, are written for /u/ coming from OE /u/; examples: *ful* (41, 44, 1820, etc.), *vp* (789, 820, 884, etc.), *dust* (523), *sun*, *son* (1064, 113), *somer* (510, 516), *wonder* rhyming with *blunder* (16ff.).

Lengthened Vowels

The letters a, e, o, singly or in discontinuous sequence with e, are written for the following sounds, respectively, in open syllables: /a:/ from OE /æ/ and /α/ and OE, ON, and OFr /a/; /e:/ from OE /e/; and /o:/ from OE /o/. Examples: *mane* (187), *race* (2076), *face* (445, etc.); *brek*, *breke* (1333, 1764), *mete* (45); *fole* (196, etc.). Words of AN origin in /a:/ before final n, nd, nt, ns, nc, ng, nch, or mp, mb are regularly written with au, which thus indicates a characteristic nasalization. Examples: *ble(e)aunt* (879, 1928, etc.), *chaunce* (1406, 2068, etc.), *laumpe* (2010). There are, however, instances in a (*graunt* adj., 838, as well as *grant*, 1037, 1392, 2126; *grant[e]* v., 273, 1110, 1861, and *graunte*, 921, 1841; *lance* v., 526, 1212, 1343, 1350, 1766, 2124, and *launce*, 1175, 1464, 1561, and *launce* n., 667, 2066, 2197; *pentangel* n., 620, 623, 636, and *pentaungel*, 664). The same distinction appears in two words of Germanic origin, neither apparently found in AN or OFr, *trantes* v. (1707) and *traunt* n. (1700), where nasalization in the second is witnessed in its au spelling by analogy. Wyld has argued that the distinction is not merely graphic but may reflect an upper-class French nasalization which was foreign to local speech hence ignored by it as in the two surviving modern pronunciations of such words; and *auinant* (806), rhyming with *plesaunt, erraunt* (808, 810), has been considered in the light of this circumstance. (See explanatory note 806 below.) The variant *stronge* for *straunge* (1028) is chiefly Southern but found sometimes elsewhere (Davis).

The letters o, oo, ou, once uo, and the discontinuous sequence of each of these with e, are written for /uː/ from OE /oː/, as in *god(e), good(e), goud(e), guod* (1029, 109, 129, 381, 702, 1625, 2430).

The manuscript represents variously /iː/ coming from /æː/, /eː/, /əː/ and /ə/ and OFr /e/ and /ie/; in *Gawain* are examples in e, eʒ, yʒ, ei, alone or in discontinuous sequence with e: *dreʒ, dryʒe* (1750, 335), *grene* (172, 211, etc.), *pecez* (1458). Whether *leude* (1124) rhyming with ʒede belongs with /iː/ or /uː/ remains doubtful.

The letters ay and eʒ, each sometimes in discontinuous sequence with e, are written for /ay/ coming from OE /æj/, /æːj/, /ej/, /eːj/ and AN /ey/; examples *day(e)* (61, 1075, etc.), *gray*(e) (82, 1024, 1714), *play* (1014, 1379, etc.), *saynt* (1644), *sweʒe* (1796), *way(e)* (689, 1077, etc.).

The letters ay, e, and the discontinuous sequence e-e are written for /ey/ coming from OE /æː/, /aː/, and AN /ey/ before liquids, dentals and /s/; examples: *mene* (233), *dede* (1047, etc.), *resoun, raysoun* (392, 227).

The letters y, ii, ie, i, y, yy, uy and the discontinuous sequence y-e are written for /iy/ coming from OE /iː/, /yː/, AN /i/ and /üy/; examples: *myn(e), myyn* (1942, 342, 1067), *hyde* (1332, 2312), *nye* (2141, from AN /anüy/ with rising stress). See *fut, fuyt* under /iw/ below.

The letters o, oo and a and their discontinuous sequence with e are written for /ow/ from OE /aː/; examples: *ston(e)* (789, 2230), *colde, coolde* (727, 2474, etc.), *hom(e), ham(e)* (2121, 408, 2451), *so* (frequently), *foo* (716, 2326).

The letters o, u, uu, ow and their discontinuous sequence with e, and in addition oʒ and uʒ, are written for /uw/ from OE /uː/, /uːx/, /oːx/, /əː/ and AN /u/; examples: *burn(e), buurn(e)* (20, 73, 825), *burnyst, bornyst* (212, 582), *flowre* (507), *roʒ(e), rogh, ruʒe, rugh* (2198, 745, 1432, 2166, 953). A form like *yorseluen* (1394) evidently represents a weak pronunciation unstressed.

The combinations au, aw, ow, sometimes in discontinuous sequence with e, are written for /aw/ from OE /ɑːw/, /oːw/, /uːw (eoːw)/, /ɑx/, /ɑːx/ and ON /aːg/; examples: *lawe* (790, 1643, from OE *lagu*) and also *lawe* (765, 2171, 2175, from OE *hlāw*), *lowe* (972, 2236, from ON *lágr*), *snaw(e)* (2088, 956, etc.), *auen, aune, awen, owen* (408, 836, 10, 293), *trawe, trowe(e), trawþe* (70, 373, 813, 626 etc.).

The letters ew, w, eau, u are written for /iw/ from OE /ɑːw/, /iːw/ and AN /üy/, /ü/, /ew/; examples: *nwe, newe* (118, 132), *duk* (552, 678), *endured* (1517), *pure* (262, 654, 808, etc.), *beau* (1222), *bewté* (1273). The variants *fut, fuyt* (1425, 1699) also perhaps belong here, from an AN development of OFr /üy/ with falling stress. See *nye* in /iy/ above.

The combination oy is written for /oy/ from OFr /ɔy/; examples: *noyce, noyse* (134, 118), *poynte* (1009). The variants *coynt, koynt* (1525, 877) and *quaynt* (999) reflect OFr /oy/ becoming /ey/ in the twelfth to the thirteenth century, AN *queinte*, giving ME /ay/. The forms *boyled, byled* (2174, 2082) possibly show the influence of OFr /ɔy/ and /uy/ as these differ in the 1st singular and plural of the verbs.

Consonants

Notable is the scribe's use of þ and th, ȝ and its variants gh and w, and z and especially its combination with t.

The letter þ is normally used initially and alternates with th in medial and final position. No certain instance of it occurs in majuscule form. Th, on the contrary, appears eighteen times in majuscule, including three where it is rubricated (491, 619, 2259), and as these are all at the beginning of stanzas the circumstance probably reflects the scribe's tendency to write th rather than þ where a capital was required or suggested. Only 1177 seems to start with a minuscule th and this in a short line near a stanza's end. By *Gawain*'s time words like *þat, þaȝ, þe, þis, þou*, and *þus* were most probably voiced. There is evidence elsewhere of the employment of þ and th to distinguish voice and voicelessness in the sounds which these symbols represent, but that their alternation here has that significance is unlikely.

The letter ȝ has a number of uses and is paralleled by alternative spellings which confirm the sound intended by this symbol: (1) It is written for the front fricative voiceless sound before OE /xt/ (*ht*); and for the back fricative voiceless after back vowels in words from OE ending in /xt/ (*ht*) or /x/ (*h*): *myȝt* (2446), *riȝt, ryȝt* (1790, 2346), *nyȝt* (2347); *aȝte* (767, 843), *oȝt* (300), *þaȝ* (350, 1391). Occasionally gh appears in such situations. Here also may be observed the use of ȝ possibly for /k/ in *Meȝelmas* (532; McLaughlin, pp. 132f.). (2) The scribe also writes ȝ for /y/ mainly initially, from OE /j/, as in *ȝe, ȝef, ȝonge, aȝayn*, but also from an initial stressed palatal combination: *ȝowre* (1065, from OE /ə:wer/, *ēower*), though the alternative spelling with y occurs more frequently. It is further written with y and gh, for OE /x/, when this was preceded by palatal vowels: *heȝe* (281), *neghe*

(697), *hyȝe*, *hyghe* (2087, 844). (3) The ȝ is also written for /w/ when preceded by /ɑ/, /o/, /u/, /l/, /r/: *draȝez* (1031), *innoȝe*, *loȝe* (1170). Such words also are spelled or rhymed with words in w: *drawen* (1233), *innowe* (1401, and *innoȝe* rhymed with *blowe*, 514), *lowe* (972). A form like *broȝes* (305, 961, plural of *browe*, from OE *brū*) shows a reverse spelling for an etymological w and confirms the pronunciation. A further spelling is gh: *innoghe* (730), *loghe* (1373), *oghe* (1526).

The letter z comes from Anglo-French convention and represents the sounds /s/ and /z/. In the scribe's hand it is in form exactly like ȝ; the present text prints it as z. Appearing as it does, with one exception, in final position, it alternates there with s, but their distribution makes uncertain when it intends the voiced or the voiceless consonant. Thus words like *cauelaciounz* (683), *domezday* (1884, compound from OE *domes dæg*), *gyrdez* (2160), *rennez* (731) are surely voiced, but others that are voiceless are also written with z: *lipernez* (1627; cf. *diamauntez*, 617). In addition, there are many words written both ways, and this suggests that perhaps the distinctions in sound are not everywhere strongly felt: *eftersones*, *eftsonez* (1640, 2417), *shankes*, *schonkez* (160, 431, 846), *ones*, *onez* (2218, 895, etc.), *renkes*, *renkkez* (432, 862, 1134). See also the rhymes *slokes*, *cnokez*, *strokes* (412ff.). The only initial use of z is in the loanword *Zeferus* (517), which, it should be observed, the poet alliterates with s, standing no doubt for /s/. Old French provides the combination tz, which, with z alone, represents the sound /ts/. That sound then developed into /s/ and the same letters could be written for it. In *Gawain* they represent /s/ or /z/ in a particular group of monosyllabic verbs: *hatz*, *dotz*, *gotz*, *watz*, the last three also written with s; but that in such instances tz is only used for /s/ as has been suggested (Gordon for *Pearl*) is not the case, nor is it limited to such monosyllables in stressed positions (see *hatz*, 17, 330, *watz*, 4, 5, 603, 652, etc.).

Among the other characteristics of *Gawain*'s writing is its use of consonantal u (regularly, but not exclusively, v when initial) for the sound/v/, the intervocalic voicing of /f/ in Old English. The voicings of /þ/ and /s/ to /ð/ and /z/ are written þ or th and s. With the loss of endings such intervocalic consonants become final: *rise*, *dryue*, *boþe* (from ON *báðir*), *eþe* (379, 2467). *Waþe* (2355, from ON *váði*) retains the sound of final -e as the rhyme *ta þe* testifies. The original Old English long consonants /ff, þþ, ss/, when quantity as a feature was lost, evidently maintained their unvoiced distinction in contrast to the voiced forms, and this distinction survives in *Gawain*, written doubled, but sometimes with the single letter: *offred* (593, from OE *offrian* or OFr *offrir*), *messe* (1690, from OE *messe*), *wrathed* (726, from OE *wræþþu*; cf. *wrathþe* in *Pearl*, 362), *siþen*, *syþen* (6, 43, etc., from OE *siþþan*). See also the rhymes *blysse*, *kysse*, *iwysse* (1553ff.) and *blys*, *Iwysse*, *þis* (1888ff.). That the distinction between at least one of these voiced and voiceless sounds was not always sharply felt is suggested by the rhymes *knyffe, bilyue, ryue* (2042ff.).

The significance of the alternative spellings with wh, qu and sometimes w, as in *whyle, quyle, wyle, quy, why, whene* for *quene, whyssynes* for *quyssynes, wheþen, queþen, wich* (918), *where* but also *were* (in *were-soeuer,* 1459), is not certain. Old English hw normally became wh or w, whereas cw appears as qu. That the use of qu for the former may be a Northern feature is disputed by the discovery that qu was regularly used for /w/ in south Lancashire (Whitehall), hence in fact characteristic of Northwest Midland. Another possibility is that the writer knew a dialect in which older /xw/, spelled wh here, had either remained /xw/ or become /kw/, and that, living as he did in a border area, he was at home with the Northern /kw/ (written qu) from Old English /xw/, and the Northwest Midland /w/ (written wh, w) from the same Old English sound. McLaughlin hypothesizes that the mixture is directly used for the stylistic purposes of the poem, and if so, this would imply that the idiosyncrasy detected in the spelling is the poet's, not the scribe's.

The variants d and t in words like *bronde, bront* (561, 588), *lorde, lortschyp* (849) exemplify in the unvoicing a characteristic of Northwest Midland; and some spellings with d evidently stand for /t/, as in *bry3t bronde* (1901; cf. *bry3t bront,* 1584) and perhaps in lines with internal rhyme, though these are not always certain: "Þe bor3 brittened and brent to brondez and askez" (2), "Syn 3e be lorde of þe 3onder londe þer I haf lent inne" (2440). The sound /d/ regularly becomes /t/ in the preterite and past participle of verb stems ending in /l/, /ld/, /rd/, /m/, /n/, /nd/, and with original t analogically in verb inflections: *blende, blent* (1361, 1610), *gyld, gilt* (569, 777, 2062). Further instances of unvoicing can also be found in the weakening of /g/ to /k/ following a nasal, and its disappearance sometimes in the spelling when followed in turn by þ: *rynk, rynkande* (1817, 1827, 2337), *þynk* (1526), *strenkþe* (1496), *lenkþe* (210) but more often *lenþe* (1627, 232, 2316). The /g/ evidently tended to survive in stressed positions in the poetic line, as with *syng(en)* in 472, 509 and 923 and *3ong(e)* in 492, 951, 1510 and in the rhyme in 1317; but the sound is /k/ when followed by þ in 1526: *3onke þynk*.

The letters sch, ssch, ch and sc are written for /š/ from OE /sč/: *flesche(e)* (943, 2313), *blusschande* (1819), *worchip* (1267, also *worschip,* 1032), *schaped* (1832). The unique form *scade* (425) may come from Northern convention (McLaughlin), though scribal error cannot be ruled out. The spellings *schere* (334, but also *cher[e],* from OFr *ch[i]ere*), *cheldez* (1611, also *schelde[z],* from OE *scéld*) indicate that the French and English sounds were not essentially distinguishable to the scribe.

The names Gaynour and Gawayn are written variously with g, gu, gw and w: *Gaynour, Gwenore, Guenore, Wenore, Gawayn, Gawan, Gawen,*

Wawan, Wawen, Woven, Wowayn. These variations arise from the differing treatments of Celtic /gw/ and /w/. In Welsh the initial /g/ tended to disappear before /w/, but in French the Celtic /w/ in that position was treated like Germanic /w/, becoming g. In some northern French dialects and sometimes in Anglo-Norman, however, this sound /gw/ became w. Though not every variation need be the author's own, rather than the scribe's, there is at least one piece of evidence that the poet had a hand in it, i.e., in line 945 (see explanatory note below).

Inflections

Nouns

Inflection in the nouns survives principally in the -es, -ez endings of the genitive singular and in -es, -ez for all forms of the plural. Some genitives occur uninflected in nouns ending in er or s, or before a word beginning with s: *kinges sister sunes* (111), *þe hors fete* (1904), *þe duches doȝter* (2465), *Renaude saule* (1916). Besides these there are a few others without ending: *fro fole houes* (459, OE gen. *folan*), *þe segge fotez* (574). With them may be listed the plural genitive *rach* (1907). Nouns used attributively, as in *heuen quene* (647) and *trweluf craftes* (1527) are no longer genitive but uninflected, and *iisseikkles* (732, OE *ises gicel*) has become in effect a single word.

To the normal plurals in -es, -ez can be added the variant in -us, *auenturus* (491), which may have simply a tachygraphic origin (cf. 95 and the gen. *Arthurus*, 2522, in the manuscript). Some French loanwords ending in r or n have -s or -z without the e: *arsounz* (171), *botounz* (220), *cowters* (583), *trystors* (1146). A few plurals without ending are found among older feminine nouns and neuters and nouns of measure following a number: *halue* (2070), perhaps *hond* (494), *der* (1151), *þynge* (652, 1080, but *þingez*, 645, etc.), *two dame* (1316), *fowre fote* (2225), *two myle* (770), *þre mote* (1141), *seuen wynter* (613). *Chylde* has as plural *chylder* (280), and *breþer* (39), *men(ne)* (28, 45, 466, etc.) and *fete* (428, 859, 1904, after prepositions) preserve the old vowel mutation. But *fotez* (574) also occurs, a plural re-formed by analogy. It is doubtful whether the instances of *fote* following prepositions (329, 2276, 2363, etc.) are plurals from OE *fotum*, with the possible exception of 2229. The weak plural survives in *yȝen* (82, 304, 684, 963, but *yȝe*, 228), and the plural genitive once in *nakryn* (118).

Definite Article, Demonstratives, Adjectives

The definite article is *þe*, singular and plural, but *þo* also occurs for the plural (39, 68, 466, etc.). *Þat* survives in *þat ilke, þat on, þat oþer* (173, 771, 110, etc.). The demonstratives, both adjective and pronoun, are *þat* (singular), *þo, þose(e)* (plural), and *þis, þys* (singular), *þis(e), þyse, þese* (plural).

The varied use by the scribe of final -e in discontinuous sequence with lengthened vowels, as well as elsewhere, makes it difficult to distinguish inflection in the plurals of adjectives. Such words as *stif* (322), *bolde* (2043), *quyte* (2088), in the traditionally weak position between article and noun, all seem better pronounced without the e. A discernible genitive plural occurs only in the forms *alder-*, *alþer-*, used in combinations like *aldertruest*, *alþergrattest* (1486, 1441, from OE *alra*). The comparatives and superlatives of adjectives in *-li(ch)* become *-lok(k)er*, *-lok(k)est*, from Late OE *-lucor*, *-lucost*.

A notable piece of the poet's syntax is his frequent substantive use of adjectives, singular and plural, and sometimes in the vocative, for persons and things: *þat gay* (970), **gracios* (1213), *þe hende* (827), *hende of hyȝe honours* (1813), *þe naked* (423), *þe schyre* (1331).

Pronouns

The first person singular nominative is *I*, accusative and dative *me*, genitive *my*, *myn* (before a vowel); plural nominative *we*, accusative-dative *us* (the scribe sometimes writes *v*, together with the -us abbreviation, meaning, no doubt, simply *us*). The second person singular nominative is *þou*, *þow*, accusative and dative *þe*, genitive *þy*, *þin* (before a vowel); plural nominative *ȝe*, accusative and dative *yow*, genitive *ȝour(e)*, *ȝowre*, *your(e)*, *yowre*, unstressed *yor* as in *yorseluen* (1394). (See also *yourez*, *ȝourez* [1106, 1037, 1387, etc.].) Notable is the discriminated use of *þou* and *ȝe* in the talk between King Arthur and the Green Knight, Sir Gawain, and the lady, and the guide and Sir Gawain to mark out nuances of relationship (see explanatory note 1068–78 below).

The third person singular masculine is for the nominative *he*, accusative and dative *him*, *hym*, genitive *his*, *hys*; feminine nominative *ho* but also *scho* (969, 1259, 1550, 1555, 1556), accusative and dative *hir*, *her*, genitive *hir*, *her*; neuter nominative, accusative, and dative *hit*, *hyt* (impersonal with plural verb *hit ar[n]*, 280, 1251). Reflexive or intensive forms of *he* are *hymself*, *hisselue(n)*. The plural nominative of the third person is always *þay*, but the genitive is *her*, *hor*, though *þayr* and *þayres* both appear exceptionally (1359, 1362, 1019), and accusative and dative are *hem*, *hom*, with some instances of *him*, *hym*, but never forms with þ-.

Verbs

The use of final -e with other vowels as a spelling device throughout the text and with verbs in the rhymes where it is seen to be mute (*strayne*, 176, rhyming *sertayn*, *gayn*; *synge*, 923, rhyming *bryng*, *talkyng*; *payne*, 1042, rhyming *Gawayn*), indicates that the infinitive is uninflected; and this is the case with the first person singular present. Deviations in the infinitive end in -en (*byden*, 374, *chepen*, 1271, *demen*, 1529, *lyþen*, 1719, sauen, 2040, seruen, 827) and now and then with monosyllables in -ne (*bene*, 141, *sene*,

712). The ending of the single form *fayly*, 1067, evidently comes from OFr *faillir*. The present participle regularly ends in -ande, but there are a few instances of -yng (gruchyng, 2126, sykyng, 753).

The second and third person singular end in -(e)s, -(e)z and -tz: *deles* (397), *fles* (2272), *cnokez* (414), *hatz* (392), *habbes* (327), *spekez* (2302); *answrez* (1044), *closes* (186), *gotz* (375), *hatz* (330), *rides* (160). *Ricchis* (8) is exceptional. The traditional *me þynkes* (111, 1241, 1793) is paralleled by *me þink* (348, 1268, 2428), where the meaning has evidently caused the shift in the verb to first person, and by the doubly irregular *hym þynk* (2109).

The plural of the present usually ends in -en, but there are a few Northern plurals in -es, -ez: *beres* (2523), *folȝes* (1164), *hyȝes* (1351), *traylez* (1700), *walkez* (1521), and possibly *dares* (315), *desyres* (1257) and *hatz* (17, 19), though these are doubtful because of the syntax. In addition, there are many instances without ending and some written with -e.

The past indicative of strong verbs is uninflected in the singular. A few are written with final -e: *sate* (339), *loȝe* (2389), but *come* (116, 502, 1004) also appears as *com* (807). The plural is -en, but again there are instances without ending or with -e. Forms like *brek* (1333), *com* (556), *drof* (1151), *fonde* (1329) are taken from the singular. The past participle ends regularly in -en, with rare instances having no ending but written -e: *biholde* (1842), *fonge* (1315), *funde* (396).

In the weak verbs the first and third person singular of the past end chiefly in -ed but -d and -t alone occur frequently, as also -de, -te: *bisied* (89), *meued* (90), *louied* (87); *layd* (419), *lut* (418, but also *lutte*, 2236, 2255), *myȝt* (201), *raȝt* (432); *bende* (305), *bledde* (441), *herde* (31), *grypte* (214), *sette* (422). The second person singular ends in -des, -de, -tes (-z), -te. *Myntest* (2274) and *fayled* (2356) are notable exceptions, both perhaps simply by scribal error. The plural ends in -ed, -den, -ten, with some forms in -t: *bult* (25), *hent* (1597), *kest* (1147), *went* (1143). The past participle has -(e)d(e) or -t: *sesed* (1), *layde* (156), *wont* (17).

The subjunctives *be* and *were* are found very frequently, but for other verbs this mood is not distinguishable in form from the indicative, except in the second and third person singular present, where there is no ending, though some instances occur written with -e: *lymp* (1109), *worth* (2374), *arȝe* (2301), *craue* (277), *telle* (380). The imperative singular is uninflected, but sometimes written with -e: *com* (456), *heng* (477), *let* (414), *ta* (413), *chose* (451), *loke* (448), *ryde* (2144). The plural ends in -(e)s, -ez, or without ending, written -e: *comaundez* (2411), *dos* (1533), *letez* (2387), *slokes* (412); *layne* (1786), *make* (2468).

Among the preterite-present verbs *schal(e)* is used for all persons of the singular and plural. *Schyn*, plural (OE *scylon*) appears once (2401) and *schulde* is normal for the past tense. *May(e)* is regular for the present, sin-

gular, and plural, with *mowe* for the plural once (1397). Past forms are
moȝt and *moȝten*. The Northern form *connez* is used once as the plural of
con (1267). The verb "to be" is, infinitive *be*, present singular *am*, *art*, *is*,
plural *ar(n)*, sometimes *be(n)* with future meaning (1646, 2111).

The strong verbs as a group have experienced a number of changes.
Among them is the tendency for one stem within a verb to dominate the
others, for one class to influence another, and for a shift from strong to weak
in individual forms. Notable are the cases where the past plural becomes the
type of the singular as well. In particular, in classes IV and V the leveling of
the past singular vowel to plural e produces such forms as *brek(en)* (cf.
1333 and 1564 with 2082), *spek(en)* (cf. 1288 with 1117). Other examples
are to be found in *bere* (class IV), *get(e)*, *gif* (class V) and *sitte* (class V).
Singulars like *gafe* (1861), *forȝate* (1472), *forgat* (2031), all of class V, are
exceptions which keep the original stem vowel. The shift of strong to weak
shows in such forms as *boȝed*, past of *boȝe* (481, 1189), *lutte*, past of *loute*
(2236, 2255) and *sleped*, *slepte*, past of *slepe* (729, 1190), and in verbs
which have both strong and weak forms, like *blowe* (1141, 1913), *falle*
(430, 2243), *fonge* (646, 919), *rys(e)* (1148, 1313), *speke(n)* (1288, 2461).

Fundamentum est iustitiae fides, id est dictorum conventorumque constantia et veritas.

The foundation of justice is *trawþe*, that is to say truth and fidelity in word and compact.

Cicero, *De officiis*, i.7, 23

Dilemma . . . is when the reason consisteth of repugnaunt members, so that whatsoeuer you graunt, you fall into the snare.

Thomas Wilson, *The Rule of Reason* (1551)

O dignitosa coscienza e netta,
Come t'è picciol fallo amaro morso!
O conscience clean and clear, precise and prim,
How bitter seems so small a sin to thee!

Dante, *Purgatorio*, 3:8–9

I would tell them, too, what I don't have to tell this particular congregation, that jokes can be noble. Laughs are exactly as honorable as tears.

Kurt Vonnegut, *Palm Sunday*

Sir Gawain and the Green Knight

I

f. 91ʳ

SIÞEN þe sege and þe assaut watz sesed at Troye,
Þe borȝ brittened and brent to brondez and askez,
Þe tulk þat þe trammes of tresoun þer wroȝt
Watz tried for his tricherie, þe trewest on erthe;
Hit watz Ennias þe athel and his highe kynde   5
Þat siþen depreced prouinces and patrounes bicome
Welneȝe of al þe wele in þe west iles,
Fro riche Romulus to Rome ricchis hym swyþe,
With gret bobbaunce þat burȝe he biges vpon fyrst
And neuenes hit his aune nome, as hit now hat;   10
Tuscius to Tuskan and teldes bigynnes,
Langaberde in Lumbardie lyftes vp homes,
And fer ouer þe French flod Felix Brutus
On mony bonkkes ful brode Bretayn he settez
        wyth wynne,   15
    Where werre and wrake and wonder

Title   *Modern editors'; none in MS*
I   *Division by roman numerals into parts is modern; MS indicates divisions by rubricated initial in the beginning stanza of each part*
11   Tuscius]   *Or Tirius; Ticius MS: see explanatory note 11 below*

Bi syþez hatz wont þerinne
And oft boþe blysse and blunder
Ful skete hatz skyfted synne.

Ande quen þis Bretayn watz bigged bi þis burn rych   20
Bolde bredden þerinne baret þat lofden,
In mony turned tyme tene þat wroȝten.
Mo ferlyes on þis folde han fallen here oft
Þen in any oþer þat I wot syn þat ilk tyme.
Bot of alle þat here bult of Bretaygne kynges   25
Ay watz Arthur þe hendest, as I haf herde telle.
Forþi an aunter in erde I attle to schawe   f. 91ᵛ
Þat a selly in siȝt summe men hit holden
And an outtrage awenture of Arthurez wonderez.
If ȝe wyl lysten þis laye bot on littel quile   30
I schal telle hit as tit as I in toun herde,
         with tonge,
     As hit is stad and stoken
     In stori stif and stronge,
     With lel letteres loken   35
     In londe so hatz ben longe.

Þis kyng lay at Camylot vpon Krystmasse
With mony luflych lorde, ledez of þe best,
Rekenly of þe Rounde Table alle þo rich breþer,
With rych reuel oryȝt and rechles merþes.   40
Þer tournayed tulkes by tymez ful mony,
Justed ful jolilé þise gentyle kniȝtes,
Syþen kayred to þe court caroles to make.
For þer þe fest watz ilyche ful fiften dayes
With alle þe mete and þe mirþe þat men couþe avyse;   45
Such glaum ande gle glorious to here,
Dere dyn vpon day, daunsyng on nyȝtes,
Al watz hap vpon heȝe in hallez and chambrez
With lordez and ladies, as leuest him þoȝt.

41   bi *Madden and Morris*
43   make]   ake *rewritten in another hand MS*
46   glaum ande]   *Emerson*; glaumande *MS*

With all þe wele of þe worlde þay woned þer samen,   50
Þe most kyd kny3tez vnder Krystes seluen
And þe louelokkest ladies þat euer lif haden
And he þe comlokest kyng þat þe court haldes.
For al watz þis fayre folk in her first age,
    on sille,   55
   Þe hapnest vnder heuen,
   Kyng hy3est mon of wylle:
   Hit were now gret nye to neuen
   So hardy a here on hille.

Wyle Nw 3er watz so 3ep þat hit watz nwe cummen,   60
Þat day doubble on þe dece watz þe douth serued.
Fro þe kyng watz cummen with kny3tes into þe halle,
Þe chauntré of þe chapel cheued to an ende,
Loude crye watz þer kest of clerkez and oþer,
Nowel nayted onewe, neuened ful ofte;   f. 92ʳ
And syþen riche forth runnen to reche hondeselle,   66
3e3ed 3eres 3iftes on hi3, 3elde hem bi hond,
Debated busyly aboute þo giftes;
Ladies la3ed ful loude þo3 þay lost haden
And he þat wan watz not wrothe, þat may 3e wel trawe.   70
Alle þis mirþe þay maden to þe mete tyme.
When þay had waschen worþyly þay wenten to sete,
Þe best burne ay abof as hit best semed,
Whene Guenore ful gay grayþed in þe myddes,
Dressed on þe dere des, dubbed al aboute,   75
Smal sendal bisides, a selure hir ouer
Of tryed tolouse, of tars tapites innoghe,
Þat were enbrawded and beten wyth þe best gemmes
Þat my3t be preued of prys wyth penyes to bye
    in daye.   80
   Þe comlokest to discrye
   Þer glent with y3en gray,

58 were] werere *MS*
81 discrye] discry *rewritten in another hand over stain as in 43, which is on opposite folio in MS*
82 glent] e *written over another letter MS* y3en] n *rewritten MS*

> A semloker þat euer he syȝe
> Soth moȝt no mon say.

Bot Arthure wolde not ete til al were serued,   85
He watz so joly of his joyfnes and sumquat childgered:
His lif liked hym lyȝt, he louied þe lasse
Auþer to longe lye or to longe sitte,
So bisied him his ȝonge blod and his brayn wylde.
And also an oþer maner meued him eke   90
Þat he þurȝ nobelay had nomen: he wolde neuer ete
Vpon such a dere day er hym deuised were
Of sum auenturus þyng an vncouþe tale,
Of sum mayn meruayle þat he myȝt trawe
Of alderes, of armes, of oþer auenturus,   95
Oþer sum segg hym bisoȝt of sum siker knyȝt
To joyne wyth hym in iustyng, in jopardé to lay,
Lede, lif for lyf, leue vchon oþer
As fortune wolde fulsun hom þe fayrer to haue.
Þis watz þe kynges countenaunce where he in court were   100
At vch farand fest among his fre meny
> > in halle.   f. 92ᵛ
> > Þerfore of face so fere
> > He stiȝtlez stif in stalle,
> > Ful ȝep in þat Nw ȝere   105
> > Much mirthe he mas withalle.

Thus þer stondes in stale þe stif kyng hisseluen,
Talkkande bifore þe hyȝe table of trifles ful hende.
There gode Gawan watz grayþed Gwenore bisyde
And Agrauayn a la Dure Mayn on þat oþer syde sittes,   110
Boþe þe kynges sistersunes and ful siker kniȝtes;
Bischop Bawdewyn abof biginez þe table,
And Ywan, Vryn son, ette with hymseluen.

---

88 longe *(1st)*]   lenge *MS*
95 Of *(1st)*]   Of of *MS*
100 þe *supplied Madden*
103–5 *Ink faded in letters at beginning of lines,* stiȝtles *only legible by ultraviolet though clear in facsimile*
113 with]   wit *MS*

Þise were diȝt on þe des and derworþly serued
And siþen mony siker segge at þe sidbordez.   115
Þen þe first cors come with crakkyng of trumpes,
Wyth mony baner ful bryȝt þat þerbi henged;
Nwe nakryn noyse with þe noble pipes,
Wylde werbles and wyȝt wakned lote,
Þat mony hert ful hiȝe hef at her towches.   120
Dayntés dryuen þerwyth of ful dere metes,
Foysoun of þe fresche, and on so fele disches
Þat pine to fynde þe place þe peple biforne
For to sette þe sylueren þat sere sewes halden
    on clothe.   125
  Iche lede as he loued hymselue
  Þer laght withouten loþe;
  Ay two had disches twelue,
  Good ber and bryȝt wyn boþe.

Now wyl I of hor seruise say yow no more,   130
For vch wyȝe may wel wit no wont þat þer were.
An oþer noyse ful newe neȝed biliue
Þat þe lude myȝt haf leue liflode to cach;
For vneþe watz þe noyce not a whyle sesed
And þe fyrst cource in þe court kyndely serued,   135
Þer hales in at þe halle dor an aghlich mayster,
On þe most on þe molde on mesure hyghe;
Fro þe swyre to þe swange so sware and so þik
And his lyndes and his lymes so longe and so grete,
Half etayn in erde I hope þat he were,   f. 93ʳ
Bot mon most I algate mynn hym to bene   141
And þat þe myriest in his muckel þat myȝt ride;
For of bak and of brest al were his bodi sturne,
Both his wombe and his wast were worthily smale
And alle his fetures folȝande in forme þat he hade   145
    ful clene.

115 siker] i *altered from* e *MS*
124 sylueren] syluen *with* ' *slightly misplaced over* n *MS*
137 on *(2nd)*] o *faded, but clear in some copies of facsimile*
144 Both] *Napier;* bot *MS*

For wonder of his hwe men hade,
Set in his semblaunt sene;
He ferde as freke were fade
And oueral enker grene.   150

Ande al grayþed in grene þis gome and his wedes:
A strayte cote ful streȝt þat stek on his sides,
A meré mantile abof mensked withinne
With pelure pured apert, þe pane ful clene
With blyþe blaunner ful bryȝt and his hod boþe,   155
Þat watz laȝt fro his lokkez and layde on his schulderes;
Heme wel-haled hose of þat same hewe,
Þat spenet on his sparlyr, and clene spures vnder
Of bryȝt golde vpon silk bordes barred ful ryche,
And scholes vnder schankes þere þe schalk rides.   160
And alle his vesture uerayly watz clene verdure,
Boþe þe barres of his belt and oþer blyþe stones,
Þat were richely rayled in his aray clene
Aboutte hymself and his sadel vpon silk werkez.
Þat were to tor for to telle of tryfles þe halue   165
Þat were enbrauded abof wyth bryddes and flyȝes,
With gay gaudi of grene, þe golde ay inmyddes.
Þe pendauntes of his payttrure, þe proude cropure,
His molaynes and alle þe metail anamayld was þenne,
Þe steropes þat he stod on stayned of þe same   170
And his arsounz al after and his aþel skurtes,
Þat euer glemered and glent al of grene stones.
Þe fole þat he ferkkes on fyn of þat ilke,
           sertayn,
       A grene hors gret and þikke,   175
       A stede ful stif to strayne,
       In brawden brydel quik—
       To þe gome he watz ful gayn.   f. 93ᵛ

157 hewe]   grene *MS; see explanatory note 157 below*
168 þe *(2nd)*]   pe *MS*
171 skurtes]   *Gollancz*; sturtes *MS*

Wel gay watz þis gome gered in grene
And þe here of his hed and of his hors swete.   180
Fayre fannand fax vmbefoldes his schulderes;
A much berd as a busk ouer his brest henges,
Þat wyth his hiȝlich here þat of his hed reches
Watz euesed al vmbetorne abof his elbowes,
Þat half his armes þervnder were halched in þe wyse   185
Of a kyngez capados þat closes his swyre;
Þe mane of þat mayn hors much to hit lyke,
Wel cresped and cemmed, wyth knottes ful mony
Folden in wyth fildore aboute þe fayre grene,
Ay a herle of þe here, an oþer of golde;   190
Þe tayl and his toppyng twynnen of a sute
And bounden boþe wyth a bande of a bryȝt grene
Dubbed wyth ful dere stonez as þe dok lasted,
Syþen þrawen wyth a þwong a þwarle knot alofte
Þer mony bellez ful bryȝt of brende golde rungen.   195
Such a fole vpon folde ne freke þat hym rydes
Watz neuer sene in þat sale wyth syȝt er þat tyme
        with yȝe.
    He loked as layt so lyȝt,
    So sayd al þat hym syȝe;   200
    Hit semed as no mon myȝt
    Vnder his dynttez dryȝe.

Wheþer hade he no helme ne hawbrgh nauþer
Ne no pysan ne no plate þat pented to armes
Ne no schafte ne no schelde to schwue ne to smyte,   205
Bot in his on honde he hade a holyn bobbe,
Þat is grattest in grene when greuez ar bare,
And an ax in his oþer, a hoge and vnmete,
A spetos sparþe to expoun in spelle, quoso myȝt.
Þe lenkþe of an elnȝerde þe large hede hade,   210

180   and] *supplied*
182   as] as as *MS*
210   lenkþe . . . hede] *Davis*; hede . . . lenkþe *MS*

Þe grayn al of grene stele and of golde hewen,
Þe bit burnyst bry3t, with a brod egge
As wel schapen to schere as scharp rasores.
Þe stele of a stif staf þe sturne hit bi grypte,
Þat watz wounden wyth yrn to þe wandez ende   f. 94ʳ
And al bigrauen with grene in gracios werkes;   216
A lace lapped aboute þat louked at þe hede
And so after þe halme halched ful ofte
Wyth tryed tasselez þerto tacched innoghe
On botounz of þe bry3t grene brayden ful ryche.   220
Þis haþel heldez hym in and þe halle entres,
Driuande to þe he3e dece, dut he no woþe,
Haylsed he neuer one, bot he3e he ouer loked.
Þe fyrst word þat he warp, "Wher is," he sayd,
"Þe gouernour of þis gyng? Gladly I wolde   225
Se þat segg in sy3t and with hymself speke
          raysoun."
          To kny3tez he kest his y3e
          And reled hym vp and doun;
          He stemmed and con studie   230
          Quo walt þer most renoun.

Ther watz lokyng on lenþe þe lude to beholde,
For vch mon had meruayle quat hit mene my3t
Þat a haþel and a horse my3t such a hwe lach
As growe grene as þe gres and grener hit semed,   235
Þen grene aumayl on golde glowande bry3ter.
Al studied þat þer stod and stalked hym nerre
Wyth al þe wonder of þe worlde what he worch schulde.
For fele sellyez had þay sen bot such neuer are;
Forþi for fantoum and fayry3e þe folk þere hit demed.   240
Þerfore to answare watz ar3e mony aþel freke
And al stouned at his steuen and stonstil seten
In a swoghe sylence þur3 þe sale riche;
As al were slypped vpon slepe so slaked hor lotez

216   gracōs MS
236   glowande]   Emerson; lowande MS

in hyȝe—   245
I deme hit not al for doute
Bot sum for cortaysye—
Bot let hym þat al schulde loute
Cast vnto þat wyȝe.

Þenn Arþour bifore þe hiȝ dece þat auenture byholdez   250
And rekenly hym reuerenced, for rad was he neuer,
And sayde, "Wyȝe, welcum iwys to þis place,
Þe hede of þis ostel Arthour I hat;   f. 94ᵛ
Liȝt luflych adoun and lenge, I þe praye,
And quatso þy wylle is we schal wyt after."   255
"Nay, as help me," quoþ þe haþel, "He þat on hyȝe syttes,
To wone any quyle in þis won hit watz not myn ernde;
Bot for þe los of þe, lede, is lyft vp so hyȝe
And þy burȝ and þy burnes best ar holden,
Stifest vnder stel gere on stedes to ryde,   260
Þe wyȝtest and þe worþyest of þe worldes kynde,
Preue for to play wyth in oþer pure laykez,
And here is kydde cortaysye, as I haf herd carp,
And þat hatz wayned me hider, iwyis, at þis tyme.
Ȝe may be seker bi þis braunch þat I bere here   265
Þat I passe as in pes and no plyȝt seche;
For had I founded in fere in feȝtyng wyse
I haue a hauberghe at home and a helme boþe,
A schelde and a scharp spere, schinande bryȝt,
Ande oþer weppenes to welde, I wene, wel als;   270
Bot for I wolde no were my wedez ar softer.
Bot if þou be so bold as alle burnez tellen
Þou wyl grant me godly þe gomen þat I ask
bi ryȝt."
Arthour con onsware   275
And sayd, "Sir cortays knyȝt,
If þou craue batayl bare
Here faylez þou not to fyȝt."

"Nay, frayst I no fyȝt, in fayth I þe telle;
Hit arn aboute on þis bench bot berdlez chylder.   280

If I were hasped in armes on a heȝe stede
Here is no mon me to mach for myȝtez so wayke.
Forþy I craue in þis court a Crystemas gomen,
For hit is Ȝol and Nwe Ȝer and here ar ȝep mony.
If any so hardy in þis hous holdez hymseluen,   285
Be so bolde in his blod, brayn in hys hede,
Þat dar stifly strike a strok for an oþer,
I schal gif hym of my gyft þys giserne ryche,
Þis ax þat is heué innogh, to hondele as hym lykes,
And I schal bide þe fyrst bur as bare as I sitte.   f. 95ʳ
If any freke be so felle to fonde þat I telle   291
Lepe lyȝtly me to and lach þis weppen,
I quitclayme hit for euer, kepe hit as his auen,
And I schal stonde hym a strok, stif on þis flet,
Ellez þou wyl diȝt me þe dom to dele hym anoþer,   295
            barlay,
        And ȝet gif hym respite
        A twelmonyth and a day.
        Now hyȝe and let se tite
        Dar any herinne oȝt say."   300

If he hem stowned vpon fyrst, stiller were þanne
Alle þe heredmen in halle, þe hyȝ and þe loȝe.
Þe renk on his rouncé hym ruched in his sadel
And runischly his rede yȝen he reled aboute,
Bende his bresed broȝez, blycande grene,   305
Wayued his berde for to wayte quoso wolde ryse.
When non wolde kepe hym with carp he coȝed ful hyȝe
Ande rimed hym ful richely and ryȝt hym to speke.
"What, is þis Arþures hous," quoþ þe haþel þenne,
"Þat al þe rous rennes of þurȝ ryalmes so mony?   310
Where is now your sourquydrye and your conquestes,
Your gryndellayk and your greme and your grete wordes?

282 so] fo *MS*
283 gomen] gome *with n-stroke slightly misplaced over third minim of* m *MS*
301 he] *altered from* ee *MS*
308 richely] *Davis*; richley *MS*
312 gryndellayk] gry dellayk *MS*

Now is þe reuel and þe renoun of þe Rounde Table
Ouerwalt wyth a worde of on wyȝes speche,
For al dares for drede withoute dynt schewed!"   315
Wyth þis he laȝes so loude þat þe lorde greued;
Þe blod schot for scham into his schyre face
   and lere;
  He wex as wroth as wynde,
  So did alle þat þer were.   320
  Þe kyng as kene bi kynde
  Þen stod þat stif mon nere

Ande sayde, "Haþel, by heuen, þyn askyng is nys
And as þou foly hatz frayst, fynde þe behoues.
I know no gome þat is gast of þy grete wordes;   325
Gif me now þy geserne, vpon Godez halue,
And I schal bayþen þy bone þat þou boden habbes."
Lyȝtly lepez he hym to and laȝt at his honde.   f. 95ᵛ
Þen feersly þat oþer freke vpon fote lyȝtis.
Now hatz Arthure his axe and þe halme grypez   330
And sturnely sturez hit aboute, þat stryke wyth hit þoȝt.
Þe stif mon hym bifore stod vpon hyȝt,
Herre þen ani in þe hous by þe hede and more.
Wyth sturne schere þer he stod he stroked his berde
And wyth a countenaunce dryȝe he droȝ doun his cote,   335
No more mate ne dismayd for hys mayn dinte
Þen any burne vpon bench hade broȝt hym to drynk
   of wyne.
  Gawan, þat sate bi þe quene,
  To þe kyng he can enclyne: 340
  "I beseche now with saȝez sene
  Þis melly mot be myne.

"Wolde ȝe, worþilych lorde," quoþ Wawan to þe kyng,
"Bid me boȝe fro þis benche and stonde by yow þere,
Þat I wythoute vylanye myȝt voyde þis table   345
And þat my legge lady lyked not ille,

336 hys] hȳs *MS* *dinte*] dintez *MS; see explanatory note 336 below*
343 Wawan] Gawan *MS*

I wolde com to your counseyl bifore your cort ryche.
For me þink hit not semly, as hit is soþ knawen,
Þer such an askyng is heuened so hy3e in your sale,
Þa3 3e 3ourself be talenttyf to take hit to yourseluen   350
Whil mony so bolde yow aboute vpon bench sytten
Þat vnder heuen I hope non ha3erer of wylle
Ne better bodyes on bent þer baret is rered.
I am þe wakkest, I wot, and of wyt feblest
And lest lur of my lyf, quo laytes þe soþe,   355
Bot for as much as 3e ar myn em I am only to prayse,
No bounté bot your blod I in my bodé knowe;
And syþen þis note is so nys þat no3t hit yow falles
And I haue frayned hit at yow fyrst, foldez hit to me.
And if I carp not comlyly let alle þis cort rych   360
          bout blame."
               Ryche togeder con roun
               And syþen þay redden alle same
               To ryd þe kyng wyth croun
               And gif Gawan þe game.   365

Þen comaunded þe kyng þe kny3t for to ryse;   f. 96ᵛ
And he ful radly vpros and ruchched hym fayre,
Kneled doun bifore þe kyng and cachez þat weppen.
And he luflyly hit hym laft and lyfte vp his honde
And gef hym Goddez blessyng and gladly hym biddes   370
Þat his hert and his honde schulde hardi be boþe.
"Kepe þe, cosyn," quoþ þe kyng, "þat þou on kyrf sette,
And if þou redez hym ry3t, redly I trowe
Þat þou schal byden þe bur þat he schal bede after."
Gawan gotz to þe gome with giserne in honde   375
And he baldly hym bydez he bayst neuer þe helder.
Þen carppez to Sir Gawan þe kny3t in þe grene,
"Refourme we oure forwardes er we fyrre passe.
Fyrst I eþe þe, haþel, how þat þou hattes,
Þat þou me telle truly as I tryst may."   380
"In god fayth," quoþ þe goode kny3t, "Gawan I hatte

365   Gawan]   w *rewritten MS*

Þat bede þe þis buffet, quatso bifallez after,
And at þis tyme twelmonyth take at þe anoþer
Wyth what weppen so þou wylt and wyth no wyȝ ellez
               on lyue."   385
      Þat oþer onswarez agayn,
      "Sir Gawan, so mot I þryue
      As I am ferly fayn
      Þis dint þat þou schal dryue.

"Bigog," quoþ þe grene knyȝt, "Sir Gawan, me lykes   390
Þat I schal fange at þy fust þat I haf frayst here.
And þou hatz redily rehersed, bi resoun ful trwe,
Clanly al þe couenaunt þat I þe kynge asked,
Saf þat þou schal siker me, segge, bi þi trawþe,
Þat þou schal seche me þiself whereso þou hopes   395
I may be funde vpon folde and foch þe such wages
As þou deles me to-day bifore þis douþe ryche."
"Where schulde I wale þe?" quoþ Gauan, "Where is þy place?
I wot neuer where þou wonyes, bi Hym þat me wroȝt,
Ne I know not þe, knyȝt, þy cort ne þi name.   400
Bot teche me truly þerto and telle me how þou hattes
And I schal ware alle my wyt to wynne me þeder,
And þat I swere þe for soþe and by my seker traweþ."   f. 96ᵛ
"Þat is innogh in Nwe ȝer, hit nedes no more,"
Quoþ þe gome in þe grene to Gawan þe hende.   405
"Ȝif I þe telle trwly quen I þe tape haue
And þou me smoþely hatz smyten, smartly I þe teche
Of my hous and my home and myn owen nome,
Þen may þou frayst my fare and forwardez holde;
And if I spende no speche þenne spedez þou þe better,   410
For þou may leng in þy londe and layt no fyrre—
          bot slokes!
      Ta now þy grymme tole to þe
      And let se how þou cnokez."
      "Gladly, sir, for soþe,"   415
      Quoþ Gawan; his ax he strokes.

384 so] fo *MS*

The grene knyȝt vpon grounde grayþely hym dresses,
A littel lut with þe hede þe lere he discouerez,
His longe louelych lokkez he layd ouer his croun,
Let the naked nec to þe note schewe.   420
Gauan gripped to his ax and gederes hit on hyȝt,
Þe kay fot on þe folde he before sette,
Let hit doun lyȝtly lyȝt on þe naked
Þat þe scharp of þe schalk schyndered þe bones
And schrank þurȝ þe schyire grece and scade hit in twynne   425
Þat þe bit of þe broun stel bot on þe grounde.
Þe fayre hede fro þe halce hit to þe erþe
Þat fele hit foyned wyth her fete þere hit forth roled;
Þe blod brayd fro þe body, þat blykked on þe grene.
And nawþer faltered ne fel þe freke neuer þe helder   430
Bot styþly he start forth vpon styf schonkes
And runyschly he raȝt out þereas renkkez stoden,
Laȝt to his lufly hed and lyft hit vp sone,
And syþen boȝez to his blonk, þe brydel he cachchez,
Steppez into stel bawe and strydez alofte   435
And his hede by þe here in his honde haldez;
And as sadly þe segge hym in his sadel sette
As non vnhap had hym ayled, þaȝ hedlez nowe
           in stedde.
       He brayde his bluk aboute,   440
       Þat vgly bodi þat bledde;   f. 97ʳ
       Moni on of hym had doute
       Bi þat his resounz were redde.

For þe hede in his honde he haldez vp euen,
Toward þe derrest on þe dece he dressez þe face   445
And hit lyfte vp þe yȝelyddez and loked ful brode
And meled þus much with his muthe, as ȝe may now here:
"Loke, Gawan, þou be grayþe to go as þou hettez
And layte as lelly til þou me, lude, fynde

432   runyschly]   ruyschly *MS*
438   nowe]   ho we *MS*; he were (?) *Madden*; he were (?) *or* nowe (?) *Morris*
440   bluk]   *MS*; bulk *Onions and others; see explanatory note 440 below*

As þou hatz hette in þis halle, herande þise kny3tes. 450
To þe Grene Chapel þou chose, I charge þe, to fotte
Such a dunt as þou hatz dalt—disserued þou habbez—
To be 3ederly 3olden on Nw 3eres morn.
Þe Kny3t of þe Grene Chapel men knowen me mony;
Forþi me for to fynde, if þou fraystez faylez þou neuer. 455
Þerfore com oþer recreaunt be calde þe behoues."
With a runisch rout þe raynez he tornez,
Halled out at þe hal dor, his hed in his hande,
Þat þe fyr of þe flynt fla3e fro fole houes.
To quat kyth he becom knwe non þere 460
Neuer more þen þay wyste from queþen he watz wonnen.
What þenne?
Þe kyng and Gawen þare
At þat grene þay la3e and grenne,
3et breued watz hit ful bare 465
A meruayl among þo menne.
Þa3 Arþer þer þe hende kyng at hert hade wonder
He let no semblaunt be sene bot sayde ful hy3e
To þe comlych quene wyth cortays speche,
"Dere dame, to-day demay yow neuer. 470
Wel bycommes such craft vpon Cristmasse—
Laykyng of enterludez, to la3e and to syng—
Among þise kynde caroles of kny3tez and ladyez.
Neuer þe lece to my mete I may me wel dres,
For I haf sen a selly I may not forsake." 475
He glent vpon Sir Gawen and gaynly he sayde,
"Now sir, heng vp þyn ax, þat hatz innogh hewen";
And hit watz don abof þe dece on doser to henge, f.97ᵛ
Þer alle men for meruayl my3t on hit loke
And bi trwe tytel þerof to telle þe wonder. 480
Þenne þay bo3ed to a borde, þise burnes togeder,
Þe kyng and þe gode kny3t, and kene men hem serued
Of alle dayntyez double, as derrest my3t falle.
Wyth alle maner of mete and mynstralcie boþe,

456 behoues] behoue + us-*abbreviation MS*

Wyth wele walt þay þat day til worþed an ende   485
    in londe.
    Now þenk wel, Sir Gawan,
    For woþe þat þou ne wonde
    Þis auenture for to frayn
    Þat þou hatz tan on honde.   490

II

THIS hanselle hatz Arthur of auenturus on fyrst
In ȝonge ȝer for he ȝerned ȝelpyng to here,
Thaȝ hym wordez were wane when þay to sete wenten.
Now ar þay stoken of sturne werk, stafful her hond.
Gawan watz glad to begynne þose gomnez in halle   495
Bot þaȝ þe ende be heuy haf ȝe no wonder;
For þaȝ men ben mery in mynde quen þay han mayn drynk,
A ȝere ȝernes ful ȝerne and ȝeldez neuer lyke,
Þe forme to þe fynisment foldez ful selden.
Forþi þis ȝol ouerȝede and þe ȝere after   500
And vche sesoun serlepes sued after oþer:
After Crystenmasse com þe crabbed Lentoun,
Þat fraystez flesch wyth þe fysche and fode more symple.
Bot þenne þe weder of þe worlde wyth wynter hit þrepez,
Colde clengez adoun, cloudez vplyften,   505
Schyre schedez þe rayn in schowrez ful warme,
Fallez vpon fayre flat, flowrez þere schewen,
Boþe groundez and þe greuez grene ar her wedez,
Bryddez busken to bylde and bremlych syngen
For solace of þe softe somer þat sues þerafter   510
    bi bonk,
    And blossumez bolne to blowe
    Bi rawez rych and ronk;
    Þen notez noble innoȝe
    Ar herde in wod so wlonk.   f. 98ʳ

II and 491   This]   *with large rubricated* T *MS; see note to I above*

After þe sesoun of somer wyth þe soft wyndez,   516
Quen Zeferus syflez hymself on sedez and erbez,
Wela wynne is þe wort þat waxes þeroute,
When þe donkande dewe dropez of þe leuez
To bide a blysful blusch of þe bryȝt sunne.   520
Bot þen hyȝes heruest and hardenes hym sone,
Warnez hym for þe wynter to wax ful rype;
He dryues wyth droȝt þe dust for to ryse,
Fro þe face of þe folde to flyȝe ful hyȝe;
Wroþe wynde of þe welkyn wrastelez with þe sunne,   525
Þe leuez lancen fro þe lynde and lyȝten on þe grounde,
And al grayes þe gres þat grene watz ere;
Þenne al rypez and rotez þat ros vpon fyrst.
And þus ȝirnez þe ȝere in ȝisterdayez mony
And wynter wyndez aȝayn as þe worlde askez,   530
          no fage,
     Til Meȝelmas mone
     Watz cumen wyth wynter wage.
     Þen þenkkez Gawan ful sone
     Of his anious uyage.   535

Ȝet quyl Al Hal Day with Arþer he lenges;
And he made a fare on þat fest for þe frekez sake
With much reuel and ryche of þe Rounde Table.
Knyȝtez ful cortays and comlych ladies
Al for luf of þat lede in longynge þay were   540
Bot neuer þe lece ne þe later þay neuened bot merþe:
Mony ioylez for þat ientyle iapez þer maden.
For aftter mete with mournyng he melez to his eme
And spekez of his passage and pertly he sayde,
"Now, lege lorde of my lyf, leue I yow ask;   545
Ȝe knowe þe cost of þis cace, kepe I no more
To telle yow tenez þerof neuer bot trifel;
Bot I am boun to þe bur barely to-morne
To sech þe gome of þe grene, as God wyl me wysse."

531   fage]   *Onions*; sage *MS*

Þenne þe best of þe burȝ boȝed togeder,   550
Aywan and Errik and oþer ful mony,
Sir Doddinal de Sauage, þe Duk of Clarence,   f. 98ᵛ
Launcelot and Lyonel and Lucan þe gode,
Sir Boos and Sir Byduer, big men boþe,
And mony oþer menskful, with Mador de la Port.   555
Alle þis compayny of court com þe kyng nerre
For to counseyl þe knyȝt, with care at her hert.
Þere watz much derue doel driuen in þe sale
Þat so worthé as Wawan schulde wende on þat ernde,
To dryȝe a delful dynt and dele no more   560
                    wyth bronde.
          Þe knyȝt mad ay god chere
          And sayde, "Quat schuld I wonde?
          Of destinés derf and dere
          What may mon do bot fonde?"   565

He dowellez þer al þat day and dressez on þe morn,
Askez erly hys armez and alle were þay broȝt.
Fyrst a tulé tapit tyȝt ouer þe flet
And miche watz þe gyld gere þat glent þeralofte.
Þe stif mon steppez þeron and þe stel hondelez,   570
Dubbed in a dublet of a dere tars
And syþen a crafty capados, closed aloft,
Þat wyth a bryȝt blaunner was bounden withinne.
Þenne set þay þe sabatounz vpon þe segge fotez,
His legez lapped in stel with luflych greuez,   575
With polaynez piched þerto policed ful clene,
Aboute his knez knaged wyth knotez of golde;
Queme quyssewes þen þat coyntlych closed
His thik þrawen þyȝez, with þwonges to tachched;
And syþen þe brawden bryné of bryȝt stel ryngez   580
Vmbeweued þat wyȝ vpon wlonk stuffe,
And wel bornyst brace vpon his boþe armes,

552 Doddinal] doddinanal *MS, second* n *written over what may be erased* s; *see explan-*
atory note 552 below

With gode cowters and gay and glouez of plate,
And alle þe godlych gere þat hym gayn schulde
     þat tyde;   585
   Wyth ryche cote-armure,
   His gold sporez spend with pryde,
   Gurde wyth a bront ful sure
   With silk sayn vmbe his syde.

When he watz hasped in armes his harnays watz ryche: f. 99ʳ
Þe lest lachet oþer loupe lemed of golde.   591
So harnayst as he watz he herknez his masse,
Offred and honoured at þe heȝe auter.
Syþen he comez to þe kyng and to his cort ferez,
Lachez lufly his leue at lordez and ladyez,   595
And þay hym kyst and conueyed, bikende hym to Kryst.
Bi þat watz Gryngolet grayth and gurde with a sadel
Þat glemed ful gayly with mony golde frenges,
Ayquere naylet ful nwe, for þat note ryched;
Þe brydel barred aboute, with bryȝt golde bounden; 600
Þe apparayl of þe payttrure and of þe proude skyrtez,
Þe cropore and þe couertor acorded wyth þe arsounez;
And al watz rayled on red ryche golde naylez,
Þat al glytered and glent as glem of þe sunne.
Þenne hentes he þe helme and hastily hit kysses,   605
Þat watz stapled stifly and stoffed wythinne.
Hit watz hyȝe on his hede, hasped bihynde,
Wyth a lyȝtly vrysoun ouer þe auentayle,
Enbrawden and bounden wyth þe best gemmez
On brode sylkyn borde, and bryddez on semez,   610
As papiayez paynted peruyng bitwene,
Tortors and trulofez entayled so þyk
As mony burde þeraboute had ben seuen wynter
     in toune.
   Þe cercle watz more o prys   615

590 *catchword* when he watz *MS*
591 oþer] *Morris*; ouer *MS*

Þat vmbeclypped hys croun,
Of diamauntez a deuys
Þat boþe were bry3t and broun.

THEN þay schewed hym þe schelde, þat was of schyr goulez
Wyth þe pentangel depaynt of pure golde hwez.   620
He braydez hit by þe bauderyk, aboute þe hals kestes,
Þat bisemed þe segge semlyly fayre.
And quy þe pentangel apendez to þat prynce noble
I am in tent yow to tell þof tary hyt me schulde:
Hit is a syngne þat Salamon set sumquyle   625
In bytoknyng of Trawþe, bi tytle þat hit habbez,
For hit is a figure þat haldez fyue poyntez   f. 99ᵛ
And vche lyne vmbelappez and loukez in oþer
And ayquere hit is endelez; and Englych hit callen
Oueral, as I here, þe endeles knot.   630
Forþy hit acordez to þis kny3t and to his cler armez,
For ay faythful in fyue and sere fyue syþez
Gawan watz for gode knawen and as golde pured,
Voyded of vche vylany, wyth vertuez ennourned
          in mote.   635
     Forþy þe pentangel nwe
     He ber in schelde and cote,
     As tulk of tale most trwe
     And gentylest kny3t of lote.

Fyrst he watz funden fautlez in his fyue wyttez,   640
And efte fayled neuer þe freke in his fyue fyngres,
And alle his afyaunce vpon folde watz in þe fyue woundez
Þat Cryst ka3t on þe croys, as þe Crede tellez;
And queresoeuer þys mon in melly watz stad
His þro þo3t watz in þat, þur3 alle oþer þyngez,   645
Þat alle his forsnes he fong at þe Fyue Joyez
Þat þe hende Heuen Quene had of hir chylde.
At þis cause þe kny3t comlyche hade

620 Wyth þe] th þe *rewritten MS*
629 endelez] emdelez *MS*
634 vertuez] v'ertuez *MS*

In þe inore half of his schelde hir ymage depaynted,
Þat quen he blusched þerto his belde neuer payred.   650
Þe fyft fyue þat I finde þat þe frek vsed
Watz Fraunchyse and Felaȝschyp forbe al þyng,
His Clannes and his Cortaysye þat croked were neuer,
And Pité þat passez alle poyntez—þyse pure fyue
Were harder happed on þat haþel þen on any oþer.   655
Now alle þese fyue syþez, for soþe, were fetled on þis knyȝt
And vchone halched in oþer, þat non ende hade,
And fyched vpon fyue poyntez þat fayld neuer
Ne samned neuer in no syde ne sundred nouþer,
Withouten ende at any noke I oquere fynde,   660
Whereeuer þe gomen bygan or glod to an ende.
Þerfore on his schene schelde schapen watz þe knot
Ryally wyth red golde vpon rede gowlez,
Þat is þe pure pentaungel wyth þe peple called   f. 100ʳ
          with lore.   665
        Now grayþed is Gawan gay
        And laȝt his launce ryȝt þore
        And gef hem alle goud day;
        He wende for euermore.

He sperred þe sted with þe spurez and sprong on his way,   670
So stif þat þe ston fyr stroke out þerafter.
Al þat seȝ þat semly syked in hert
And sayde soþly al same segges til oþer,
Carande for þat comly: "Bi Kryst, hit is scaþe
Þat þou, leude, schal be lost þat art of lyf noble!   675
To fynde hys fere vpon folde, in fayth, is not eþe.
Warloker to haf wroȝt had more wyt bene
And haf dyȝt ȝonder dere a duk to haue worþed;
A lowande leder of ledez in londe hym wel semez
And so had better haf ben þen britned to noȝt,   680
Hadet wyth an aluisch mon, for angardez pryde.

653   þat] *supplied*
658   fayld] f *and* d *rewritten MS*
659   nouþer] e *now lost in MS but legible in facsimile*
660   I oquere] (?) jquere *MS*

Who knew euer any kyng such counsel to take
As kny3tez in cauelaciounz on Crystmasse gomnez!"
Wel much watz þe warme water þat waltered of y3en
When þat semly syre so3t fro þo wonez   685
                    þad daye.
            He made non abode
            Bot wy3tly went hys way;
            Mony wylsum way he rode,
            Þe bok as I herde say.   690

Now ridez þis renk þur3 þe ryalme of Logres,
Sir Gauan, on Godez halue, þa3 hym no gomen þo3t.
Oft leudlez alone he lengez on ny3tez
Þer he fonde no3t hym byfore þe fare þat he lyked.
Hade he no fere bot his fole bi frythez and dounez   695
Ne no gome bot God bi gate wyth to karp
Til þat he ne3ed ful neghe into þe Norþe Walez.
Alle þe iles of Anglesay on lyft half he haldez
And farez ouer þe fordez by þe forlondez,
Ouer at þe Holy Hede, til he hade eft bonk   700
In þe wyldrenesse of Wyrale; wonde þer bot lyte
Þat auþer God oþer gome wyth goud hert louied.   f. 100ᵛ
And ay he frayned as he ferde at frekez þat he met
If þay hade herde any karp of a kny3t grene,
In any grounde þeraboute of þe Grene Chapel;   705
And al nykked hym wyth nay þat neuer in her lyue
Þay se3e neuer no segge þat watz of suche hwez
                    of grene.
            Þe kny3t tok gates straunge
            In mony a bonk vnbene,   710
            His cher ful oft con chaunge
            Þat chapel er he my3t sene.

Mony klyf he ouerclambe in contrayez straunge,
Fer floten fro his frendez fremedly he rydez.

683   cauelaciounz]   cauelounz MS
697   neghe]   noghe MS
705   Chapel]   clapel MS
707   hwez]   w written over another letter MS

At vche warþe oþer water þer þe wyȝe passed 715
He fonde a foo hym byfore, bot ferly hit were,
And þat so foule and so felle þat feȝt hym byhode.
So mony meruayl bi mount þer þe mon fyndez
Hit were to tore for to telle of þe tenþe dole.
Sumwhyle wyth wormez he werrez and with wolues als, 720
Sumwhyle wyth wodwos þat woned in þe knarrez,
Boþe wyth bullez and berez and borez oþerquyle,
And etaynez þat hym anelede of þe heȝe felle;
Nade he ben duȝty and dryȝe and Dryȝtyn had serued
Douteles he hade ben ded and dreped ful ofte. 725
For werre wrathed hym not so much þat wynter nas wors,
When þe colde cler water fro þe cloudez schadde
And fres er hit falle myȝt to þe fale erþe.
Ner slayn wyth þe slete he sleped in his yrnes
Mo nyȝtez þen innoghe in naked rokkez 730
Þer as claterande fro þe crest þe colde borne rennez
And henged heȝe ouer his hede in hard iisseikkles.
Þus in peryl and payne and plytes ful harde
Bi contray caryez þis knyȝt tyl Krystmasse euen
      al one; 735
      Þe knyȝt wel þat tyde
      To Mary made his mone
      Þat ho hym red to ryde
      And wysse hym to sum wone. f. 101ʳ

Bi a mounte on þe morne meryly he rydes 740
Into a forest ful dep þat ferly watz wylde,
Hiȝe hillez on vche a halue and holtwodez vnder
Of hore okez ful hoge, a hundreth togeder;
Þe hasel and þe haȝþorne were harled al samen,
With roȝe raged mosse rayled aywhere, 745
With mony bryddez vnblyþe vpon bare twyges,
Þat pitosly þer piped for pyne of þe colde.
Þe gome vpon Gryngolet glydez hem vnder

---

726 nas] *Davis*; was *MS*
727 schadde] *TG*; schadden *MS*
732 iisseikkles] iisse *changed from* ysse *MS*

Þur3 mony misy and myre, mon al hym one,
Carande for his costes lest he ne keuer schulde   750
To se þe seruyse of þat syre þat on þat self ny3t   .
Of a burde watz borne oure baret to quelle;
And þerfore sykyng he sayde, "I beseche þe, Lorde,
And Mary, þat is myldest moder so dere,
Of sum herber þer he3ly I my3t here masse   755
Ande Þy matynez tomorne, mekely I ask,
And þerto prestly I pray my Pater and Aue
            and Crede."
        He rode in his prayere
        And cryed for his mysdede,   760
        He sayned hym in syþes sere
        And sayde, "Cros Kryst me spede!"

NADE he sayned hymself, segge, bot þrye
Er he watz war in þe wod of a won in a mote
Abof a launde on a lawe, loken vnder bo3ez   765
Of mony borelych bole aboute bi þe diches,
A castel þe comlokest þat euer kny3t a3te,
Pyched on a prayere, a park al aboute,
With a pyked palays pyned ful þik
Þat vmbete3e mony tre mo þen two myle.   770
Þat holde on þat on syde þe haþel aysed
As hit schemered and schon þur3 þe schyre okez.
Þenne hatz he hendly of his helme and he3ly he þonkez
Jesus and Sayn Gilyan, þat gentyle ar boþe,
Þat cortaysly had hym kydde and his cry herkened.   f. 101ᵛ
"Now bone hostel," coþe þe burne, "I beseche yow 3ette!"   776
Þenne gerdez he to Gryngolet with þe gilt helez
And he ful chauncely hatz chosen to þe chef gate,
Þat bro3t bremly þe burne to þe bryge ende
            in haste.   780
        Þe bryge watz breme vpbrayde,
        Þe 3atez wer stoken faste,

Þe wallez were wel arayed,
Hit dut no wyndez blaste.

Þe burne bode on blonk, þat on bonk houed   785
Of þe depe double dich þat drof to þe place.
Þe walle wod in þe water wonderly depe
Ande eft a ful huge he3t hit haled vpon lofte
Of harde hewen ston vp to þe tablez,
Enbaned vnder þe abataylment in þe best lawe;   790
And syþen garytez ful gaye gered bitwene,
Wyth mony luflych loupe þat louked ful clene.
A better barbican þat burne blusched vpon neuer.
And innermore he behelde þat halle ful hy3e,
Towres telded bytwene, trochet ful þik,   795
Fayre fylyolez þat fy3ed and ferlyly long,
With coruon coprounes craftyly sle3e.
Chalkwhyt chymnees þer ches he inno3e
Vpon bastel rouez þat blenked ful quyte.
So mony pynakle payntet watz poudred ayquere   800
Among þe castel carnelez clambred so þik
Þat pared out of papure purely hit semed.
Þe fre freke on þe fole hit fayr innoghe þo3t
If he my3t keuer to com þe cloyster whythinne,
To herber in þat hostel whyl halyday lested,   805
       auinant.
   He calde and sone þer com
   A porter pure plesaunt,
   On þe wal his ernd he nome
   And haylsed þe kny3t erraunt.   810

"Gode sir," quoþ Gawan, "woldez þou go myn ernde
To þe he3 lorde of þis hous, herber to craue?"
"3e, Peter," quoþ þe porter, "and purely I trowoe   f. 102ʳ
Þat 3e be, wy3e, welcum to won quyle yow lykez."

785 blonk . . . bonk] *Davis*; bonk . . . blonk *MS*
795 Towres] towre *MS*
803 innoghe] *originally* inohe, *then* o *changed to* g *MS*
813 trowoe] *TG, Gollancz emend* trowee

Þen 3ede þe wy3e 3erne and com a3ayn swyþe 815
And folke frely hym wyth to fonge þe kny3t.
Þat let doun þe grete dra3t and derely out 3eden
And kneled doun on her knes vpon þe colde erþe
To welcum þis ilk wy3 as worþy hom þo3t.
Þay 3olden hym þe brode 3ate, 3arked vp wyde, 820
And he hem raysed rekenly and rod ouer þe brygge.
Sere segge3 hym sesed by sadel quel he ly3t
And syþen stabeled his stede stif men inno3e.
Kny3tez and swyerez comen doun þenne
For to bryng þis buurne wyth blys into halle. 825
Quen he hef vp his helme þer hi3ed innoghe
For to hent hit at his honde þe hende to seruen;
His bronde and his blasoun boþe þay token.
Þen haylsed he ful hendly þo haþelez vchone
And mony proud mon þer presed þat prynce to honour. 830
Alle hasped in his he3 wede to halle þay hym wonnen,
Þer fayre fyre vpon flet fersly brenned.
Þenne þe lorde of þe lede loutez fro his chambre
For to mete wyth menske þe mon on þe flor.
He sayde, "3e ar welcum to welde as yow lykez 835
Þat here is, al is yowre awen to haue at yowre wylle
            and welde."
        "Graunt mercy," quoþ Gawayn,
        "Þer Kryst hit yow for3elde."
        As frekez þat semed fayn 840
        Ayþer oþer in armez con felde.

Gawayn gly3t on þe gome þat godly hym gret
And þu3t hit a bolde burne þat þe bur3 a3te,
A hoge haþel for þe nonez and of hyghe eldee;
Brode, bry3t watz his berde and al beuer-hwed, 845
Sturne, stif on þe stryþþe on stalworth schonkez,
Felle face as þe fyre and fre of hys speche;
And wel hym semed, for soþe, as þe segge þu3t,

815   3erne and com *supplied Davis*; 3are and com *Gollancz*
832   fersly]   s *corrected from* f MS

To lede a lortschyp in lee of leudez ful gode.
Þe lorde hym charred to a chambre and chefly cumaundez   f. 102ᵛ
To delyuer hym a leude hym loȝly to serue;   851
And þere were boun at his bode burnez innoȝe,
Þat broȝt hym to a bryȝt boure þer beddyng watz noble,
Of cortynes of clene sylk wyth cler golde hemmez
And couertorez ful curious with comlych panez   855
Of bryȝt blaunmer aboue, enbrawded bisydez,
Rudelez rennande on ropez, red golde ryngez,
Tapitez tyȝt to þe woȝe of tuly and tars,
And vnder fete on þe flet of folȝande sute.
Þer he watz dispoyled, wyth spechez of myerþe,   860
Þe burn of his bruny and of his bryȝt wedez.
Ryche robes ful rad renkkez hym broȝten
For to charge and to chaunge and chose of þe best.
Sone as he on hent and happed þerinne
Þat sete on hym semly wyth saylande skyrtez,   865
Þe ver by his uisage verayly hit semed
Welneȝ to vche haþel, alle on hwes
Lowande and lufly alle his lymmez vnder,
Þat a comloker knyȝt neuer Kryst made,
            hem þoȝt.   870
        Wheþen in worlde he were,
        Hit semed as he moȝt
        Be prynce withouten pere
        In felde þer felle men foȝt.

A cheyer byfore þe chemné, þer charcole brenned,   875
Watz grayþed for Sir Gawan grayþely with cloþez,
Whyssynes vpon queldepoyntes þat koynt wer boþe.
And þenne a meré mantyle watz on þat mon cast

850 chefly] clesly MS
856 blaunmer] bla + 7 minims + er-abbreviation MS; blaunner Gollancz and Davis
860 myerþe] er abbreviated MS
862 hym] hem MS
865 hym] hyn MS
872 moȝt] myȝt MS
874 foȝt] fyȝt MS
877 þat] þa MS

Of a broun bleeaunt, enbrauded ful ryche
And fayre furred wythinne with fellez of þe best,   880
Alle of ermyn in erde, his hode of þe same.
And he sete in þat settel semlych ryche
And achaufed hym chefly and þenne his cher mended.
Sone watz telded vp a tabil on trestez ful fayre,
Clad wyth a clene cloþe þat cler quyt schewed,   885
Sanap and salure and syluerin sponez.
Þe wyʒe wesche at his wylle and went to his mete.   f. 103ʳ
Seggez hym serued semly innoʒe
Wyth sere sewes and sete, sesounde of þe best,
Doublefelde, as hit fallez, and fele kyn fischez,   890
Summe baken in bred, summe brad on þe gledez,
Summe soþen, summe in sewe sauered with spyces,
And ay sawses so sleʒe þat þe segge lyked.
Þe freke calde hit a fest ful frely and ofte
Ful hendely quen alle þe haþeles rehayted hym at onez   895
         as hende:
       "Þis penaunce now ʒe take
       And eft hit schal amende."
       Þat mon much merþe con make
       For wyn in his hed þat wende.   900

Þenne watz spyed and spured vpon spare wyse
Bi preué poyntez of þat prynce, put to hymseluen,
Þat he beknew cortaysly of þe court þat he were
Þat aþel Arthure þe hende haldez hym one,
Þat is þe ryche ryal kyng of þe Rounde Table,   905
And hit watz Wawen hymself þat in þat won syttez,
Comen to þat Krystmasse as case hym þen lymped.
When þe lorde hade lerned þat he þe leude hade,
Loude laʒed he þerat so lef hit hym þoʒt
And alle þe men in þat mote maden much joye   910

---

     883   chefly]   cefly *MS*
     884   tabil]   *Gollancz, TG*; tablit *Emerson*; tapit *MS*
     893   sawses so sleʒe]   *TG (note)*, sawses *Gollancz*; sewes (*?*), sleʒeʒ *Morris*; sawes so
sleʒez *MS*

To apere in his presense prestly þat tyme
Þat alle prys and prowes and pured þewes
Apendes to hys persoun and praysed is euer;
Byfore alle men vpon molde his mensk is þe most.
Vch segge ful softly sayde to his fere, 915
"Now schal we semlych se sleȝtez of þewez
And þe teccheles termes of talkyng noble,
Wich spede is in speche vnspurd may we lerne,
Syn we haf fonged þat fyne fader of nurture.
God hatz geuen vus his grace godly for soþe 920
Þat such a gest as Gawan grauntez vus to haue,
When burnez blyþe of his burþe schal sitte
          and synge.
     In menyng of manerez mere
     Þis burne now schal vus bryng, f. 103ᵛ
     I hope þat may hym here 926
     Schal lerne of luf talkyng."

Bi þat þe diner watz done and þe dere vp
Hit watz neȝ at þe niyȝt neȝed þe tyme.
Chaplaynez to þe chapeles chosen þe gate, 930
Rungen ful rychely, ryȝt as þay schulden,
To þe hersum euensong of þe hyȝe tyde.
Þe lorde loutes þerto and þe lady als;
Into a cumly closet coyntly ho entrez.
Gawan glydez ful gay and gos þeder sone. 935
Þe lorde laches hym by þe lappe and ledez hym to sytte
And couþly hym knowez and callez hym his nome
And sayde he watz þe welcomest wyȝe of þe worlde,
And he hym þonkked þroly and ayþer halched oþer
And seten soberly samen þe seruise quyle. 940
Þenne lyst þe lady to loke on þe knyȝt,
Þenne com ho of hir closet with mony cler burdez.
Ho watz þe fayrest in felle, of flesche and of lyre
And of compas and colour and costes, of alle oþer,
And wener þen Wenore, as þe wyȝe þoȝt. 945

930 Chaplaynez] claplaynez *MS*

Ho ches þurȝ þe chaunsel to cheryche þat hende.
An oþer lady hir lad bi þe lyft honde
Þat watz alder þen ho, an auncian hit semed,
And heȝly honowred with haþelez aboute.
Bot vnlyke on to loke þo ladyes were,   950
For if þe ȝonge watz ȝep, ȝolȝe watz þat oþer;
Riche red on þat on rayled ayquere,
Rugh ronkled chekez þat oþer on rolled;
Kerchofes of þat on, wyth mony cler perlez,
Hir brest and hir bryȝt þrote bare displayed,   955
Schon schyrer þen snawe þat schedez on hillez;
Þat oþer wyth a gorger watz gered ouer þe swyre,
Chymbled ouer hir blake chyn with chalkquyte vayles,
Hir frount folden in sylk, enfoubled ayquere,
Toreted and treleted with tryflez aboute,   960
Þat noȝt watz bare of þat burde bot þe blake broȝes,   f. 104ʳ
Þe tweyne yȝen and þe nase, þe naked lyppez,
And þose were soure to se and sellyly blered.
A mensk lady on molde mon may hir calle,
              for Gode!   965
        Hir body watz schort and þik,
        Hir buttokez balȝ and brode;
        More lykkerwys on to lyk
        Watz þat scho hade on lode.

When Gawayn glyȝt on þat gay þat graciously loked   970
Wyth leue laȝt of þe lorde he lent hem aȝaynes.
Þe alder he haylses, heldande ful lowe,
Þe loueloker he lappez a lyttel in armez,
He kysses hir comlyly and knyȝtly he melez.
Þay kallen hym of aquoyntaunce and he hit quyk askez   975
To be her seruaunt sothly if hemself lyked.

946 Ho]   *Wright*; he *MS*
956 schedez]   schedes (?) *Morris*; scheder *MS*
958 chalkquyte]   *Onions*; mylkquyte *MS*
960 Toreted]   *Davis*; toret *MS*
967 balȝ]   *TG*; bay *MS*
971 lent]   *Andrew*; went *MS*   aȝaynes]   y *changed from* u *MS*

Þay tan hym bytwene hem, wyth talkyng hym leden
To chambre to chemné and chefly þay asken
Spycez, þat vnsparely men speded hom to bryng,
And þe wynnelych wyne þerwith vche tyme.   980
Þe lorde luflych aloft lepez ful ofte,
Mynned merthe to be made vpon mony syþez,
Hent heʒly of his hode and on a spere henged
And wayned hom to wynne þe worchip þerof
Þat most myrþe myʒt meue þat Crystenmas whyle: 985
"And I schal fonde, bi my fayth, to fylter wyth þe best
Er me wont þe wede, with help of my frendez."
Þus wyth laʒande lotez þe lorde hit tayt makez
For to glade Sir Gawayn with gomnez in halle
                þat nyʒt,   990
            Til þat hit watz tyme
            Þe lord comaundet lyʒt;
            Sir Gawen his leue con nyme
            And to his bed hym diʒt.

On þe morne, as vch mon mynez þat tyme   995
Þat Dryʒtyn for oure destyné to deʒe watz borne,
Wele waxez in vche a won in worlde for his sake.
So did hit þere on þat day þurʒ dayntés mony;
Boþe at mes and at mele messes ful quaynt   f. 104ᵛ
Derf men vpon dece drest of þe best.   1000
Þe olde auncian wyf heʒest ho syttez,
Þe lorde lufly her by lent, as I trowe.
Gawan and þe gay burde togeder þay seten
Euen inmyddez as þe messe metely come,
And syþen þurʒ al þe sale as hem best semed   1005
Bi vche grome at his degré grayþely watz serued.
Þer watz mete, þer watz myrþe, þer watz much ioye,
Þat for to telle þerof hit me tene were
And to poynte hit ʒet I pyned me parauenture.
Bot ʒet I wot þat Wawen and þe wale burde   1010

987   wede]   *TG*; wedez *MS*
992   lord]   *TG*; kyng *MS*

Such comfort of her compaynye caȝten togeder
Þurȝ her dere dalyaunce of her derne wordez,
Wyth clene cortays carp closed fro fylþe,
Þat hor play watz passande vche prynce gomen,
    in vayres.   1015
   Trumpez and nakerys,
   Much pypyng þer repayres;
   Vche mon tented hys
   And þay two tented þayres.

Much dut watz þer dryuen þat day and þat oþer   1020
And þe þryd as þro þronge in þerafter,
Þe ioye of Sayn Jonez Day watz gentyle to here,
[With moste myrþe and mynstrelsye Childermas sued]   [1022a]
And watz þe last of þe layk, leudez þer þoȝten.
Þer wer gestes to go vpon þe gray morne,
Forþy wonderly þay woke and þe wyn dronken,   1025
Daunsed ful dreȝly wyth dere carolez.
At þe last, when hit watz late, þay lachen her leue,
Vchon to wende on his way þat watz wyȝe stronge.
Gawan gef hym god day, þe godmon hym lachchez,
Ledes hym to his awen chambre þe chymné bysyde   1030
And þere he draȝez hym on dryȝe and derely hym þonkkez
Of þe wynne worschip þat he hym wayued hade
As to honour his hous on þat hyȝe tyde
And enbelyse his burȝ with his bele chere:
"Iwysse, sir, quyl I leue me worþez þe better   1035
Þat Gawayn hatz ben my gest at Goddez awen fest."   f. 105ʳ
"Grant merci, sir," quoþ Gawayn, "in god fayth hit is yowrez,
Al þe honour is your awen—þe Heȝekyng yow ȝelde!
And I am wyȝe at your wylle to worch youre hest,
As I am halden þerto, in hyȝe and in loȝe,   1040
    bi riȝt."

  1014 þat] *TG*; & *MS*
  [1022a] *see explanatory note to this line below*
  1030 þe] þ *MS*
  1032 þat] & *MS*
  1037 merci] *Madden*; nerci *MS*

Þe lorde fast can hym payne
To holde lenger þe kny3t,
To hym answrez Gawayn
Bi non way þat he my3t.   1045

Then frayned þe freke ful fayre at himseluen
Quat derue dede had hym dryuen at þat dere tyme
So kenly fro þe kyngez kourt to kayre al his one
Er þe halidayez holly were halet out of toun.
"For soþe, sir," quoþ þe segge, "3e sayn bot þe trawþe,   1050
A he3e ernde and a hasty me hade fro þo wonez,
For I am sumned myselfe to sech to a place
I not in worlde whederwarde to wende hit to fynde.
I nolde bot if I hit negh my3t on Nw 3eres morne
For alle þe londe inwyth Logres, so me Oure Lorde help!   1055
Forþy, sir, þis enquest I require yow here,
Þat 3e me telle with trawþe if euer 3e tale herde
Of þe Grene Chapel, quere hit on grounde stondez
And of þe kny3t þat hit kepes of colour of grene.
Þer watz stabled bi statut a steuen vus bytwene   1060
To mete þat mon at þat mere, 3if I my3t last.
And of þat ilk Nw 3ere bot neked now wontez
And I wolde loke on þat lede, if God me let wolde,
Gladloker, bi Goddez sun, þen any god welde!
Forþi, iwysse, bi 3owre wylle, wende me bihoues,   1065
Naf I now to busy bot bare þre dayez
And me als fayn to falle feye as fayly of myyn ernde."
Þenne la3ande quoþ þe lorde, "Now leng þe byhoues,
For I schal teche yow to þat terme bi þe tymez ende,
Þe Grene Chapayle vpon grounde greue yow no more,   1070
Bot 3e schal be in yowre bed, burne, at þyn ese,
Quyle forth dayez and ferk on þe fyrst of þe 3ere
And cum to þat merk at mydmorn to make quat yow likez   f. 105ᵛ
            in spenne.
        Dowellez whyle New 3eres Daye   1075

___

1053 not] *Madden*; wot *MS*
1069 þat] *Morris*; þa *MS*

       And rys and raykez þenne.
       Mon schal yow sette in waye,
       Hit is not two myle henne."

Þenne watz Gawan ful glad and gomenly he laȝed:
"Now I þonk yow þryuandely þurȝ alle oþer þynge.   1080
Now acheued is my chaunce, I schal at your wylle
Dowelle and ellez do quat ȝe demen."
Þenne sesed hym þe syre and set hym bysyde,
Let þe ladiez be fette to lyke hem þe better.
Þer watz seme solace by hemself stille,   1085
Þe lorde let for luf lotez so myry
As wyȝ þat wolde of his wyte, ne wyst quat he myȝt.
Þenne he carped to þe knyȝt, criande loude,
"Ȝe han demed to do þe dede þat I bidde,
Wyl ȝe halde þis hes here at þys onez?"   1090
"Ȝe, sir, for soþe," sayd þe segge trwe,
"Whyl I byde in yowre borȝe be bayn to ȝowre hest."
"For ȝe haf trauayled," quoþ þe tulk, "towen fro ferre
And syþen waked me wyth, ȝe arn not wel waryst
Nauþer of sostnaunce ne of slepe, soþly I knowe.   1095
Ȝe schal lenge in your lofte and lyȝe in your ese
Tomorn quyle þe messequyle and to mete wende
When ȝe wyl wyth my wyf, þat wyth yow schal sitte
And comfort yow with compayny til I to cort torne.
          Ȝe lende   1100
       And I schal erly ryse,
       On huntyng wyl I wende."
       Gauayn grantez alle þyse,
       Hym heldande as þe hende.

"Ȝet firre," quoþ þe freke, "a forwarde we make: 1105
Quatsoeuer I wynne in þe wod hit worþez to yourez
And quat chek so ȝe acheue chaunge me þerforne.
Swete, swap we so—sware with trawþe—
Queþer, leude, so lymp lere oþer better."

1092 ȝowre] *Madden*; ȝowe *MS*

"Bi God," quoþ Gawayn þe gode, "I grant þertylle   1110
And þat yow lyst for to layke lef hit me þynkes."   f. 106ʳ
"Who bryngez vus þis beuerage, þis bargayn is maked":
So sayde þe lorde of þat lede. Þay laȝed vchone,
Þay dronken and daylyeden and dalten vntyȝtel,
Þise lordez and ladyez, quyle þat hem lyked,   1115
And syþen with Frenkysch fare and fele fayre lotez
Þay stoden and stemed and stylly speken,
Kysten ful comlyly and kaȝten her leue.
With mony leude ful lyȝt and lemande torches
Vche burne to his bed watz broȝt at þe laste   1120
       ful softe.
      To bed ȝet er þay ȝede,
      Recorded couenauntez ofte;
      Þe olde lorde of þat leude
      Cowþe wel halde layk alofte.   1125

III

Ful erly bifore þe day þe folk vprysen,
Gestes þat go wolde hor gromez þay calden
And þay busken vp bilyue blonkkez to sadel,
Tyffen her takles, trussen her males,
Richen hem þe rychest to ryde alle arayde,   1130
Lepen vp lyȝtly, lachen her brydeles,
Vche wyȝe on his way þer hym wel lyked.
Þe leue lorde of þe londe watz not þe last
Arayed for þe rydyng, with renkkez ful mony,
Ete a sop hastyly when he hade herde masse,   1135
With bugle to bentfelde he buskez bylyue.
By þat any daylyȝt lemed vpon erþe
He with his haþeles on hyȝe horsses weren.
Þenne þise cacheres þat couþe cowpled hor houndez,
Vnclosed þe kenel dore and calde hem þeroute,   1140

1126 Ful] F *rubricated MS; see note l above*
1129 her (*1st*)] *Madden*; he *MS*
1137 þat] þat þat *MS*

Blwe bygly in buglez þre bare mote;
Braches bayed þerfore and breme noyse maked;
And þay chastysed and charred on chasyng þat went,
A hundreth of hunteres, as I haf herde telle,
        of þe best.   1145
    To trystors vewters ʒod,
    Couples huntes of kest,
    Þer ros for blastez gode   f. 106ᵛ
    Gret rurd in þat forest.

At þe fyrst quethe of þe quest quaked þe wylde;   1150
Der drof in þe dale, doted for drede,
Hiʒed to þe hyʒe, bot heterly þay were
Restayed with þe stablye, þat stoutly ascryed.
Þay let þe herttez haf þe gate, with þe hyʒe hedes,
Þe breme bukkez also with hor brode paumez;   1155
For þe fre lorde hade defende in fermysoun tyme
Þat þer schulde no mon meue to þe male dere.
Þe hindez were halden in with hay! and war!
Þe does dryuen with gret dyn to þe depe sladez.
Þer myʒt mon se, as þay slypte, slentyng of arwes—   1160
At vche wende vnder wande wapped a flone
Þat bigly bote on þe broun with ful brode hedez.
What! þay brayen and bleden, bi bonkkez þay deʒen,
And ay rachches in a res radly hem folʒes,
Hunterez wyth hyʒe horne hasted hem after   1165
Wyth such a crakkande kry as klyffes hade brusten.
What wylde so atwaped wyʒes þat schotten
Watz al toraced and rent ryʒt at þe resayt
Bi þay were tened at þe hyʒe and taysed to þe wattrez;
Þe ledez were so lerned at þe loʒe trysteres   1170
And þe grehoundez so grete þat geten hem bylyue
And hem to fylched as fast as frekez myʒt loke
        þerryʒt.
    Þe lorde, for blys abloy,

1166 hade] haden *MS*
1168 ryʒt] *supplied; see explanatory note 1168 below*

Ful oft con launce and ly3t   1175
And drof þat day wyth joy
Thus to þe derk ny3t.

Þus laykez þis lorde by lynde-wodez euez
And Gawayn þe god mon in gay bed lygez,
Lurkkez quyl þe dayly3t lemed on þe wowes   1180
Vnder couertour ful clere, cortyned aboute;
And as in slomeryng he slode sle3ly he herde
A littel dyn at his dor and dernly vpon;
And he heuez vp his hed out of þe cloþes,
A corner of þe cortyn he ca3t vp a lyttel   f. 107ʳ
And waytez warly þiderwarde quat hit be my3t,   1186
Hit watz þe ladi, loflyest to beholde,
Þat dro3 þe dor after hir ful dernly and stylle
And bo3ed towarde þe bed, and þe burne schamed
And layde hym doun lystyly and let as he slepte.   1190
And ho stepped stilly and stel to his bedde,
Kest vp þe cortyn and creped withinne
And set hir ful softly on þe bedsyde
And lenged þere selly longe to loke quen he wakened.
Þe lede lay lurked a ful longe quyle,   1195
Compast in his concience to quat þat cace my3t
Meue oþer amount. To meruayle hym þo3t,
Bot 3et he sayde in hymself, "More semly hit were
To aspye wyth my spelle in space quat ho wolde."
Þen he wakenede and wroth and to hir warde torned   1200
And vnlouked his y3elyddez and let as hym wondered
And sayned hym, as bi his sa3e þe sauer to worthe,
            with hande.
      Wyth chynne and cheke ful swete,
      Boþe quit and red in blande,   1205
      Ful lufly con ho lete
      Wyth lyppez smal la3ande.

1179 Gawayn] G: *MS*
1183 dernly] *Davis; cf. Morris, TG and Gollancz n.*; derfly *MS*
1199 in] *illegible MS, trace of* i *by ultraviolet*

"God moroun, Sir Gawayn," sayde þat gay lady,
"Ʒe ar a sleper vnslyƷe, þat mon may slyde hider.
Nor ar Ʒe tan as tyt! Bot true vus may schape   1210
I schal bynde yow in your bedde, þat be Ʒe trayst."
Al laƷande þe lady lanced þo bourdez.
"Goud moroun, gracios," quoþ Gawayn þe blyþe,
"Me schal worþe at your wille and þat me wel lykez,
For I Ʒelde me Ʒederly and Ʒeʒe after grace,   1215
And þat is þe best, be my dome, for me byhouez nede";
And þus he bourded aƷayn with mony a blyþe laƷter.
"Bot wolde Ʒe, lady louely, þen leue me grante
And deprece your prysoun and pray hym to ryse,
I wolde boƷe of þis bed and busk me better;   1220
I schulde keuer þe more comfort to karp yow wyth."
"Nay for soþe, beau sir," sayd þat swete,   f. 107ᵛ
"Ʒe schal not rise of your bedde, I rych yow better:
I schal happe yow here þat oþer half als
And syþen karp wyth my knyƷt þat I kaƷt haue.   1225
For I wene wel, iwysse, Sir Wowen Ʒe are,
Þat alle þe worlde worchipez; quereso Ʒe ride
Your honour, your hendelayk is hendely praysed
With lordez, wyth ladyes, with alle þat lyf bere.
And now Ʒe ar here, iwysse, and we bot oure one;   1230
My lorde and his ledez ar on lenþe faren,
Oþer burnez in her bedde and my burdez als,
Þe dor drawen and dit with a derf haspe;
And syþen I haue in þis hous hym þat al lykez,
I schal ware my whyle wel, quyl hit lastez,   1235
          with tale.
     Ʒe ar welcum to my cors
     Yowre awen won to wale,

1208   gay] *TG; fayr MS*
1213   gracios] *gᵃos (?) MS; cf. grace, line 1215*
1214   your] *yor or you, y like þ (as frequently throughout), last letter erased and 2-abbrev. for ur written above o MS*   wel] *inserted in another hand MS*
1216   be] *he MS*

Me behouez of fyne force
Your seruaunt be and schale." 1240

"In god fayth," quoþ Gawayn, "gayn hit me þynkkez
Þaȝ I be not now he þat ȝe of speken;
To reche to such reuerence as ȝe reherce here
I am wyȝe vnworþy, I wot wel myseluen.
Bi God, I were glad and yow god þoȝt 1245
At saȝe oþer at seruyce þat I sette myȝt
To þe plesaunce of your prys—hit were a pure ioye."
"In god fayth, Sir Gawayn," quoþ þe gay lady,
"Þe prys and þe prowes þat plesez al oþer
If I hit lakked oþer set at lyȝt, hit were littel daynté; 1250
Bot hit ar ladyes innoȝe þat leuer wer nowþe
Haf þe, hende, in hor holde, as I þe habbe here,
To daly with derely your daynté wordez,
Keuer hem comfort and colen her carez,
Þen much of þe garysoun oþer golde þat þay hauen. 1255
Bot I louye þat ilk lorde þat þe lyfte haldez,
I haf hit holly in my honde þat al desyres
    þurȝe grace."
    Scho made hym so gret chere
    Þat watz so fayr of face, f. 108ʳ
    Þe knyȝt with speches skere 1261
    Answared to vche a cace.

"Madame," quoþ þe myry mon, "Mary yow ȝelde,
For I haf founden, in god fayth, yowre fraunchis nobele,
And oþer ful much of oþer folk fongen bi hor dedez 1265
Bot þe daynté þat þay delen. For my disert nys euen,
Hit is þe worchyp of yourself þat noȝt bot wel connez."
"Bi Mary," quoþ þe menskful, "me þynk hit an oþer,
For were I worth al þe wone of wymmen alyue

1255 þat] þat þᵗ *MS*
1256 louye] louie *Madden*; louie *or* loune *Morris*; louue = "praise" *other eds.*; loyue *MS*
1262 Answared] aswared *MS*
1265 bi] *supplied Davis*
1266 nys euen] *Davis*; nysen *MS*; see explanatory note 1265–67 below

And al þe wele of þe worlde were in my honde   1270
And I schulde chepen and chose to cheue me a lorde,
For þe costes þat I haf knowen vpon þe, knyʒt, here
Of bewté and debonerté and blyþe semblaunt
And þat I haf er herkkened and halde hit here trwee,
Þer schulde no freke vpon folde bifore yow be chosen."   1275
"Iwysse, worþy," quoþ þe wyʒe, "ʒe haf waled wel better,
Bot I am proude of þe prys þat ʒe put on me
And, soberly your seruaunt, my souerayn I holde yow,
And yowre knyʒt I becom and Kryst yow forʒelde."
Þus þay meled of muchquat til mydmorn paste   1280
And ay þe lady let lyk as hym loued mych;
Þe freke ferde with defence and feted ful fayre.
Þaʒ ho were burde bryʒtest, þe burne in mynde hade,
Þe lasse luf in his lode for lur þat he soʒt
　　　　　boute hone—   1285
　　　　Þe dunte þat schulde hym deue,
　　　　And nedez hit most be done.
　　　　Þe lady þenn spek of leue,
　　　　He granted hir ful sone.

Þenne ho gef hym god day and wyth a glent laʒed,   1290
And as ho stod ho stonyed hym wyth ful stor wordez:
"Now he þat spedez vche spech þis disport ʒelde yow!
Bot þat ʒe be Gawan hit gotz in mynde."
"Querfore?" quoþ þe freke and freschly he askez,
Ferde lest he hade fayled in fourme of his castes;   1295
Bot þe burde hym blessed and "Bi þis skyl" sayde:
"So god as Gawayn gaynly is halden   f. 108ᵛ
And cortaysye is closed so clene in hymseluen,
Couth not lyʒtly haf lenged so long wyth a lady
Bot he had craued a cosse, bi his courtaysye,   1300
Bi sum towch of summe tryfle at sum talez ende."

1281　as hym] ahỹ *MS*
1283　ho] *Gollancz*; I *MS*　　　burne] *Gollancz*; burde *MS*; *see explanatory note 1283–*
87 below
1286　schulde] sclulde *MS*

Þen quoþ Wowen: "Iwysse, worþe as yow lykez;
I schal kysse at your comaundement, as a knyȝt fallez,
And fire lest he displese yow, so plede hit no more."
Ho comes nerre with þat and cachez hym in armez, 1305
Loutez luflych adoun and þe leude kyssez.
Þay comly bykennen to Kryst ayþer oþer;
Ho dos hir forth at þe dore withouten dyn more,
And he ryches hym to ryse and rapes hym sone,
Clepes to his chamberlayn, choses his wede, 1310
Goȝez forth quen he watz boun blyþely to masse;
And þenne he meued to his mete, þat menskly hym keped,
And made myry al day til þe mone rysed
     with game.
    Watz neuer freke fayrer fonge 1315
    Bitwene two so dyngne dame,
    Þe alder and þe ȝonge,
    Much solace set þay same.

And ay þe lorde of þe londe is lent on his gamnez,
To hunt in holtez and heþe at hyndez barayne; 1320
Such a sowme he þer slowe bi þat þe sunne heldet
Of dos and of oþer dere, to deme were wonder.
Þenne fersly þay flokked in, folk, at þe laste
And quykly of þe quelled dere a querre þay maked.
Þe best boȝed þerto with burnez innoghe, 1325
Gedered þe grattest of gres þat þer were
And didden hem derely vndo as þe dede askez;
Serched hem at þe asay summe þat þer were,
Two fyngeres þay fonde of þe fowlest of alle.
Syþen þay slyt þe slot, sesed þe erber, 1330
Schaued wyth a scharp knyf and þe schyre knitten;
Syþen rytte þay þe foure lymmes and rent of þe hyde,
Þen brek þay þe balé, þe bowelez out token
Lystily for laucyng þe lere of þe knot. f. 109ʳ

1304 so] fo *MS*
1315 Watz] wᵗ *MS*
1333 bowelez] *Davis*; boueleȝ *Gollancz*; bauleȝ *TG*; balez *MS*
1334 þe *(1st)*] *Gollancz*; & *MS*

Þay gryped to þe gargulun and grayþely departed   1335
Þe wesaunt fro þe wynthole and walt out þe guttez;
Þen scher þay out þe schulderez with her scharp knyuez,
Haled hem by a lyttel hole to haue hole sydes.
Siþen britned þay þe brest and brayden hit in twynne
And eft at þe gargulun bigynez on þenne,   1340
Ryuez hit vp radly ry3t to þe by3t,
Voydez out þe avanters and verayly þerafter
Alle þe rymez by þe rybbez radly þay lance;
So ryde þay of by resoun bi þe rygge bonez,
Euenden to þe haunche, þat henged alle samen,   1345
And heuen hit vp al hole and hwen hit of þere,
And þat þay neme for þe noumbles bi nome, as I trowe,
       bi kynde;
     Bi þe by3t al of þe þy3es
     Þe lappez þay lance bihynde,   1350
     To hewe hit in two þay hy3es
     Bi þe bakbon to vnbynde.

Boþe þe hede and þe hals þay hwen of þenne
And syþen sunder þay þe sydez swyft fro þe chyne
And þe corbeles fee þay kest in a greue.   1355
Þenn þurled þay ayþer þik side þur3 bi þe rybbe
And henged þenne ayþer bi ho3ez of þe fourchez,
Vche freke for his fee as fallez for to haue.
Vpon a felle of þe fayre best fede þay þayr houndes
Wyth þe lyuer and þe ly3tez, þe leþer of þe paunchez   1360
And bred baþed in blod blende þeramongez.
Baldely þay blw prys, bayed þayr rachchez,
Syþen fonge þay her flesche, folden to home,
Strakande ful stoutly mony stif motez.
Bi þat þe dayly3t watz done þe douthe watz al wonen   1365
Into þe comly castel, þer þe kny3t bidez
       ful stille
     Wyth blys and bry3t fyr bette.

1344 So] fo *MS*
1357 ayþer] aþer *MS*

Þe lorde is comen þertylle;
When Gawayn wyth hym mette   1370
Þer watz bot wele at wylle.

Thenne sumned þe lorde in þat sale to samen alle þe
    meny,   f. 109ᵛ
Boþe þe ladyes on loghe to ly3t with her burdes.
Bifore alle þe folk on þe flette frekez he beddez
Verayly his venysoun to fech hym byforne;   1375
And al godly in gomen Gawayn he called,
Techez hym to þe tayles of ful tayt bestes,
Schewez hym þe schyree grece schorne vpon rybbes.
"How payez yow þis play? Haf I prys wonnen?
Haue I þryuandely þonk þur3 my craft serued?"   1380
"3e iwysse," quoþ þat oþer wy3e, "here is wayth fayrest
Þat I se3 þis seuen 3ere in sesoun of wynter."
"And al I gif yow, Gawayn," quoþ þe gome þenne,
"For by acorde of couenaunt 3e craue hit as your awen."
"Þis is soth," quoþ þe segge, "I say yow þat ilke: 1385
Þat I haf worthyly wonnen þis wonez wythinne
Iwysse with as god wylle hit worþez to 3ourez."
He hasppez his fayre hals his armez wythinne
And kysses hym as comlyly as he couþe awyse:
"Tas yow þere my cheuicaunce, I cheued no more;   1390
I wowche hit saf fynly þa3 feler hit were."
"Hit is god," quoþ þe godmon, "grant mercy þerfore.
Hit may be such hit is þe better and þe me breue wolde
Where 3e wan þis ilk wele bi wytte of yorseluen."
"Þat watz not forward," quoþ he, "frayst me no more.   1395
For 3e haf tan þat yow tydez, trawe 3e non oþer
    3e mowe."
    Þay la3ed and made hem blyþe

1369   lorde]   e *partly gone MS*
1372   sumned]   comaunded *MS; see explanatory note 1372 below*
1376   Gawayn]   Gaway *MS*
1386   þat]   *Gollancz*; & *MS*   wonnen]   *supplied TG*
1389   he]   *Madden*; ho *MS*
1394   yorseluen]   *TG*; 3orseluen *Gollancz*; horseluen *MS*

> Wyth lotez þat were to lowe,
> To soper þay ȝede as swyþe,   1400
> Wyth dayntés nwe innowe.

And syþen by þe chymné in chamber þay seten,
Wyȝez þe walle wyn weȝed to hem oft,
And efte in her bourdyng þay bayþen in þe morn
To fylle þe same forwardez þat þay byfore maden: 1405
Wat chaunce so bytydez hor cheuysaunce to chaunge,
What nwez so þay nome, at naȝt quen þay metten.
Þay acorded of þe couenauntez byfore þe court alle;
Þe beuerage watz broȝt forth in bourde at þat tyme,   f. 110^r
Þenne þay louelych leȝten leue at þe last,   1410
Vche burne to his bedde busked bylyue.
Bi þat þe coke hade crowen and cakled bot þryse
Þe lorde watz lopen of his bedde, þe leudez vchone;
So þat þe mete and þe masse watz metely delyuered,
Þe douthe dressed to þe wod er any day sprenged   1415
        to chace;
> Heȝ with hunte and hornez
> Þurȝ playnez þay passe in space,
> Vncoupled among þo þornez
> Rachez þat ran on race.   1420

Sone þay calle of a quest in a ker syde,
Þe hunt rehayted þe houndez þat hit fyrst mynged,
Wylde wordez hym warp wyth a wrast noyce.
Þe howndez þat hit herde hastid þider swyþe
And fellen as fast to þe fuyt, fourty at ones;   1425
Þenne such a glauer ande glam of gedered rachchez
Ros þat þe rocherez rungen aboute,
Hunterez hem hardened with horne and wyth muthe,
Þen al in a semblé sweyed togeder
Bitwene a flosche in þat fryth and a foo cragge.   1430

1406 Wat] *TG*; þat *MS*
1412 crowen] *TG*; crowez *MS*
1426 glauer ande] *Emerson*; glauerande *MS*

In a knot bi a clyffe at þe kerre syde,
Þer as þe rogh rocher vnrydely watz fallen,
Þay ferden to þe fyndyng and frekez hem after.
Þay vmbekesten þe knarre and þe knot boþe,
Wyȝez, whyl þay wysten wel wythinne hem hit were   1435
Þe best þat þer breued watz wyth þe blodhoundez.
Þenne þay beten on þe buskez and bede hym vpryse,
And he vnsoundyly out soȝt, seggez ouerþwert.
On þe sellokest swyn swenged out þere,
Long sythen fro þe sounder þat siȝte for olde,   1440
For he watz bige, bor alþergrattest,
Ful grymme quen he gronyed; þenne greued mony,
For þre at þe fyrst þrast he þryȝt to þe erþe
And sparred forth good sped boute spyt more.
Þise oþer halowed hyghe! ful hyȝe, and hay! hay! cryed,   1445
Haden hornez to mouþe, heterly rechated.   f. 110ᵛ
Mony watz þe myry mouthe of men and of houndez
Þat buskkez after þis bor with bost and wyth noyse
             to quelle.
        Ful oft he bydez þe baye   1450
        And maymez þe mute inn melle.
        He hurtez of þe houndez and þay
        Ful ȝomerly ȝaule and ȝelle.

Schalkez to schote at hym schowen to þenne,
Haled to hym of her arewez, hitten hym oft;   1455
Bot þe poyntez payred at þe pyth þat pyȝt in his scheldez,
And þe barbez of his browe bite non wolde—
Þaȝ þe schauen schaft schyndered in pecez,
Þe hede hypped aȝayn weresoeuer hit hitte.

1433 þay] *legible in facsimile*
1435 wythinne] wytinne *MS*
1440 fro] for *MS*   siȝte] wiȝt *MS*
1441 bige] *MS faded but b and g faintly visible with ultraviolet; see explanatory note*
1441 below bor] *looks like* hor *but* h *originally* b (?) *MS*
1442 ful grymme] (?), *from facsimile*
1443 þre at] *from facsimile*
1444 sparred] *Menner;* sped him *others; MS virtually illegible*
1447 myry] *four minims* + yry

Bot quen þe dyntez hym dered of her dryȝe strokez   1460
Þen, braynwod for bate, on burnez he rasez,
Hurtez hem ful heterly þer he forth hyȝez,
And mony arȝed þerat and on lyte droȝen.
Bot þe lorde on a lyȝt horce launces hym after,
As burne bolde vpon bent his bugle he blowez,   1465
He rechated and rydez þurȝ ronez ful þyk,
Suande þis wylde swyn til þe sunne schafted.
Þis day wyth þis ilk dede þay dryuen on þis wyse
Whyle oure luflych lede lys in his bedde,
Gawayn, grayþely at home in gerez ful ryche   1470
                    of hewe.
                Þe lady noȝt forȝate
                To com hym to salue;
                Ful erly ho watz hym ate
                His mode for to remwe.   1475

Ho commes to þe cortyn and at þe knyȝt totes.
Sir Wawen her welcumed worþy on fyrst
And ho hym ȝeldez aȝayn ful ȝerne of hir wordez,
Settez hir softly by his syde and swyþely ho laȝez
And wyth a luflych loke ho layde hym þyse wordez: 1480
"Sir, ȝif ȝe be Wawen wonder me þynkkez,
Wyȝe þat is so wel wrast alway to god
And connez not of compaynye þe costez vndertake,
And if mon kennes yow hom to knowe ȝe kest hom of your
                    mynde;   f. 111ʳ
Þou hatz forȝeten ȝederly þat ȝisterday I taȝtte   1485
Bi aldertruest token of talk þat I cowþe."
"What is þat?" quoþ þe wyghe, "Iwysse I wot neuer.
If hit be sothe þat ȝe breue þe blame is myn awen."
"ȝet I kende yow of kyssyng," quoþ þe clere þenne,
"Quereso countenaunce is couþe quikly to clayme;   1490

1466   rydez]   rode *other eds.; see explanatory note 1466 below*
1473   To com]   *Waldron;* com to *MS*
1479   softly]   *Morris;* sofly *MS*
1484   *catchword* & if *MS*

Þat bicumes vche a kny3t þat cortaysy vses."
"Do way," quoþ þat derf mon, "my dere, þat speche,
For þat durst I not do lest I deuayed were;
If I were werned I were wrang, iwysse, 3if I profered."
"Ma fay," quoþ þe meré wyf, "3e may not be werned,   1495
3e ar stif innoghe to constrayne wyth strenkþe 3if yow lykez,
3if any were so vilanous þat yow devaye wolde."
"3e, be God," quoþ Gawayn, "good is your speche,
Bot þrete is vnþryuande in þede þer I lende
And vche gift þat is geuen not with goud wylle.   1500
I am at your comaundement to kysse quen yow lykez,
3e may lach quen yow lyst and leue quen yow þynkkez
            in space."
        Þe lady loutez adoun
        And comlyly kysses his face,   1505
        Much speche þay þer expoun
        Of druryes greme and grace.

"I woled wyt at yow, wy3e," þat worþy þer sayde,
"And yow wrathed not þerwyth, what were þe skylle
Þat so 3ong and so 3epe as 3e at þis tyme,   1510
So cortayse, so kny3tyly as 3e ar knowen oute—
And of alle cheualry to chose þe chef þyng alosed
Is þe lel layk of luf, þe lettrure of armes.
For to telle of þis teuelyng of þis trwe kny3tez,
Hit is þe tytelet token and tyxt of her werkkez   1515
How ledes for her lele luf hor lyuez han auntered,
Endured for her drury dulful stoundez
And after wenged with her walour and voyded her care
And bro3t blysse into boure with bountees hor awen—
And 3e ar kny3t comlokest kyd of your elde,   1520
Your worde and your worchip walkez ayquere   f. 111ᵛ
And I haf seten by yourself here sere twyes,
3et herde I neuer of your hed helde no wordez
Þat euer longed to luf, lasse ne more;

1514 For] r blotted and illegible MS
1516 ledes] des blotted and illegible MS   for] blotted and illegible MS

And ȝe þat ar so cortays and coynt of your hetes   1525
Oghe to a ȝonke þynk ȝern to schewe
And teche sum tokenez of trweluf craftes.
Why! ar ȝe lewed þat alle þe los weldez?
Oþer elles ȝe demen me to dille your dalyaunce to herken?
          For schame!   1530
     I com hider sengel and sitte
     To lerne at yow sum game;
     Dos techez me of your wytte
     Whil my lorde is fro hame."

"In goud fayþe," quoþ Gawayn, "God yow forȝelde!   1535
Gret is þe gode gle and gomen to me huge
Þat so worþy as ȝe wolde wynne hidere
And pyne yow with so pouer a mon as play wyth your knyȝt
With anyskynnez countenaunce, hit keuerez me ese.
Bot to take þe toruayle to myself to trwluf expoun   1540
And towche þe temez of tyxt and talez of armez
To yow þat, I wot wel, weldez more slyȝt
Of þat art, bi þe half, or a hundreth of seche
As I am oþer euer schal in erde þer I leue,
Hit were a folé felefolde, my fre, by my trawþe.   1545
I wolde yowre wylnyng worche at my myȝt
As I am hyȝly bihalden and euermore wylle
Be seruaunt to yourseluen, so saue me Dryȝtyn!"
Þus hym frayned þat fre and fondet hym ofte
For to haf wonnen hym to woȝe, whatso scho þoȝt ellez;   1550
Bot he defended hym so fayr þat no faut semed
Ne non euel on nawþer halue, nawþer þay wysten
          bot blysse.
     Þay laȝed and layked longe;
     At þe last scho con hym kysse,   1555
     Hir leue fayre con scho fonge
     And went hir waye, iwysse.

Then ruþes hym þe renk and ryses to þe masse
And siþen hor diner watz dyȝt and derely serued.   f. 112ʳ
Þe lede with þe ladyez layked alle day   1560

Bot þe lorde ouer þe londez launced ful ofte,
Swez his vncely swyn, þat swyngez bi þe bonkkez
And bote þe best of his brachez þe bakkez in sunder
Þer he bode in his bay tel bawemen hit breken
And madee hym mawgref his hed for to mwe vtter,   1565
So felle flonez þer flete when þe folk gedered.
Bot ȝet þe styffest to start bi stoundez he made
Til at þe last he watz so mat he myȝt no more renne
Bot in þe hast þat he myȝt he to a hole wynnez
Of a rasse bi a rokk þer rennez þe boerne.   1570
He gete þe bonk at his bak, bigynez to scrape,
Þe froþe femed at his mouth vnfayre bi þe wykez,
Whettez his whyte tuschez. With hym þen irked
Alle þe burnez so bolde þat hym by stoden
To nye hym on-ferum, bot neȝe hym non durst   1575
          for woþe;
     He hade hurt so mony byforne
     Þat al þuȝt þenne ful loþe
     Be more wyth his tusches torne,
     Þat breme watz and braynwod bothe,   1580

Til þe knyȝt com hymself, kachande his blonk,
Syȝ hym byde at þe bay, his burnez bysyde.
He lyȝtes luflych adoun, leuez his corsour,
Braydez out a bryȝt bront and bigly forth strydez,
Foundez fast þurȝ þe forth þer þe felle bydez.   1585
Þe wylde watz war of þe wyȝe with weppen in honde,
Hef hyȝly þe here, so hetterly he fnast
Þat fele ferde for þe freke lest felle hym þe worre.
Þe swyn settez hym out on þe segge euen
Þat þe burne and þe bor were boþe vpon hepez   1590
In þe wyȝtest of þe water. Þe worre hade þat oþer,
For þe mon merkkez hym wel as þay mette fyrst,

1565 madee MS and most eds.
1580 and] supplied Morris
1583 luflych] luslych MS
1588 freke] Madden; frekez MS

Set sadly þe scharp in þe slot euen,
Hit hym vp to þe hult þat þe hert schyndered
And he ȝarrande hym ȝelde and ȝedoun þe water   1595
       ful tyt.   f. 112ᵛ
    A hundreth houndez hym hent,
    Þat bremely con hym bite;
    Burnez him broȝt to bent
    And doggez to dethe endite.   1600

There watz blawyng of prys in mony breme horne,
Heȝe halowing on hiȝe with haþelez þat myȝt;
Brachetes bayed þat best as bidden þe maysterez
Of þat chargeaunt chace þat were chef huntes.
Þenne a wyȝe þat watz wys vpon wodcraftez   1605
To vnlace þis bor lufly bigynnez.
Fyrst he hewes of his hed and on hiȝe settez
And syþen rendez him al roghe bi þe rygge after,
Braydez out þe boweles, brennez hom on glede,
With bred blent þerwith his braches rewardez.   1610
Syþen he britnez out þe brawen in bryȝt brode cheldez
And hatz out þe hastlettez as hiȝtly bisemez,
And ȝet hem halchez al hole þe haluez togeder
And syþen on a stif stange stoutly hem henges.
Now with þis ilk swyn þay swengen to home.   1615
Þe bores hed watz borne bifore þe burnes seluen
Þat him forferde in þe forþe þurȝ forse of his honde
       so stronge.
    Til he seȝ Sir Gawayne
    In halle hym þoȝt ful longe;   1620
    He calde and he com gayn
    His feez þer for to fonge.

Þe lorde ful lowde with lote laȝed myry
When he seȝe Sir Gawayn, with solace he spekez;
Þe goude ladyez were geten and gedered þe meyny,   1625

1623 laȝed] *Gollancz*; and laȝed *TG*; and laȝter *Davis*; & laȝed *MS*
1624 Gawayn] G: *MS*

He schewez hem þe scheldez and schapes hem þe tale
Of þe largesse and þe lenþe, þe liþernez alse
Of þe were of þe wylde swyn in wod þer he fled.
Þat oþer knyȝt ful comly comended his dedez
And praysed hit as gret prys þat he proued hade,   1630
For suche a brawne of a best, þe bolde burne sayde,
Ne such sydes of a swyn segh he neuer are.
Þenne hondeled þay þe hoge hed, þe hende mon hit praysed
And let lodly þerat þe lorde for to here.   f. 113ʳ
"Now, Gawayn," quoþ þe godmon, "þis gomen is your awen   1635
Bi fyn forwarde and faste, faythely ȝe knowe."
"Hit is sothe," quoþ þe segge, "and as siker trwe
Alle my get I schal yow gif agayn, bi my trawþe."
He hent þe haþel aboute þe halse and hendely hym kysses
And eftersones of þe same he serued hym þere.   1640
"Now ar we euen," quoþ þe haþel, "in þis euentide
Of alle þe couenauntes þat we knyt syþen I com hider,
        bi lawe."
            Þe lorde sayde, "Bi Saynt Gile,
            Ȝe ar þe best þat I knowe!   1645
            Ȝe ben ryche in a whyle
            Such chaffer and ȝe drowe."

Þenne þay teldet tablez trestes alofte,
Kesten cloþez vpon; clere lyȝt þenne
Wakned bi woȝez, waxen torches   1650
Seggez sette and serued in sale al aboute;
Much glam and gle glent vp þerinne
Aboute þe fyre vpon flet, and on fele wyse
At þe soper and after mony aþel songez,
As coundutes of Krystmasse and carolez newe,   1655
With al þe manerly merþe þat mon may of telle,
And euer oure luflych knyȝt þe lady bisyde.
Such semblaunt to þat segge semly ho made
Wyth stille stollen countenaunce þat stalworth to plese

1639   hent]   supplied *TG*; hent *or* hasped *Madden*
1645, 1647   knowe, drowe *MS; Gollancz* knawe, drawe

Þat al forwondered watz þe wyʒe and wroth with hymseluen,   1660
Bot he nolde not for his nurture nurne hir aʒaynez
Bot dalt with hir al in daynté, howseeuer þe dede turned
       towrast.
      Quen þay hade played in halle
      As longe as hor wylle hom last,   1665
      To chambre he con hym calle
      And to þe chemné þay past.

Ande þer þay dronken and dalten and demed eft nwe
To norne on þe same note on Nwe ʒerez Euen;
Bot þe knyʒt craued leue to kayre on þe morn   1670
For hit watz neʒ at þe terme þat he to schulde.
Þe lorde hym letted of þat, to lenge hym resteyed,   f. 113ᵛ
And sayde, "As I am trwe segge, I siker my trawþe
Þou schal cheue to þe Grene Chapel þy charres to make,
Leude, on Nw ʒerez lyʒt longe bifore pryme.   1675
Forþy þow lye in þy loft and lach þyn ese
And I schal hunt in þis holt and halde þe towchez,
Chaunge wyth þe cheuisaunce bi þat I charre hider.
For I haf fraysted þe twys and faythful I fynde þe.
Now 'þrid tyme þrowe best' þenk on þe morne,   1680
Make we mery quyl we may and mynne vpon joye
For þe lur may mon lach whenso mon lykez."
Þis watz grayþely graunted and Gawayn is lenged,
Bliþe broʒt watz hym drynk and þay to bedde ʒeden
       with liʒt.   1685
      Sir Gawayn lis and slepes
      Ful stille and softe al niʒt;
      Þe lorde, þat his craftez kepes,
      Ful erly he watz diʒt.

After messe a morsel he and his men token.   1690
Miry watz þe mornyng, his mounture he askes.
Alle þe haþeles þat on horse schulde helden hym after

1686 Gawayn] G: *MS*
1690 morsel] *four minims* + orsel *MS*

Were boun busked on hor blonkkez bifore þe halle ȝatez.
Ferly fayre watz þe folde for þe forst clenged;
In rede rudede vpon rak rises þe sunne   1695
And ful clere costez þe clowdes of þe welkyn.
Hunteres vnhardeled bi a holt syde,
Rocheres roungen bi rys for rurde of her hornes;
Summe fel in þe fute þer þe fox bade,
Traylez ofte a trayteres bi traunt of her wyles;   1700
A kenet kyres þerof, þe hunt on hym calles;
His felaȝes fallen hym to þat fnasted ful þike,
Runnen forth in a rabel in his ryȝt fare,
And he fyskez hem byfore. Þay founden hym sone
And quen þay seghe hym with syȝt þay sued hym fast,   1705
Wreȝande hym ful weterly with a wroth noyse,
And he trantes and tornayeez þurȝ mony tene greue,
Hauilounez and herkenez bi heggez ful ofte.
At þe last bi a littel dich he lepez ouer a spenne,   f. 114ʳ
Stelez out ful stilly bi a strothe rande,   1710
Went haf wylt of þe wode with wylez fro þe houndes.
Þenne watz he went er he wyst to a wale tryster,
Þer þre þro at a þrich þrat hym at ones,
              al graye.
         He blenched aȝayn bilyue   1715
         And stifly start onstray,
         With alle þe wo on lyue
         To þe wod he went away.

Thenne watz hit list vpon lif to lyþen þe houndez
When alle þe mute hade hym met, menged togeder: 1720
Suche a sorȝe at þat syȝt þay sette on his hede
As alle þe clamberande clyffes hade clatered on hepes.
Here he watz halawed when haþelez hym metten,

1693   bifore] biforere *MS*
1700   a trayteres] *see explanatory note 1700 below*
1706   hym] ym *illegible MS*   weterly] we *illegible MS*, w *from offset*
1710   strothe] ro *rewritten MS*
1712   to] to to *MS*
1719   list vpon lif] *Morris*; lif vpon list *MS*

Loude he watz ȝayned with ȝarande speche;

Þer he watz þreted and ofte þef called   1725

And ay þe titleres at his tayl þat tary he ne myȝt;

Ofte he watz runnen at when he out rayked

And ofte reled in aȝayn, so Reniarde watz wylé.

And ȝe he lad hem bi lagmon, þe lorde and his meyny,

On þis maner bi þe mountes quyle mydouervnder   1730

Whyle þe hende knyȝt at home holsumly slepes

Withinne þe comly cortynes on þe colde morne.

Bot þe lady for luf let not to slepe

Ne þe purpose to payre þat pyȝt in hir hert,

Bot ros hir vp radly, rayked hir þeder   1735

In a mery mantyle mete to þe erþe,

Þat watz furred ful fyne with fellez wel pured,

No hwe gord on hir hede bot þe haȝer stones

Trased aboute hir tressour be twenty in clusteres;

Hir þryuen face and hir þrote þrowen al naked,   1740

Hir brest bare bifore and bihinde eke.

Ho comez withinne þe chambre dore and closes hit hir after,

Wayuez vp a wyndow and on þe wyȝe callez

And radly þus rehayted hym with hir riche wordes

               with chere: 1745

      "A! mon, how may þou slepe,

      Þis morning is so clere?"   f. 114ᵛ

      He watz in drowping depe

      Bot þenne he con hir here.

In dreȝ droupyng of dreme draueled þat noble   1750

As mon þat watz in mornyng of mony þro þoȝtes,

How þat destiné schulde þat day dele hym his wyrde

At þe Grene Chapel when he þe gome metes

And bihoues his buffet abide withoute debate more.

Bot quen þat comly com he keuered his wyttes,   1755

Swenges out of þe sweuenes and swarez with hast.

1738 hwe gord] hwez goud *MS; see explanatory note 1738–39 below*

1752 dele hym] *supplied TG*; dyȝt *Morris*

1755 com] *supplied TG*

Þe lady luflych com laȝande swete,
Felle ouer his fayre face and fetly hym kyssed.
He welcumez hir worþily with a wale chere;
He seȝ hir so glorious and gayly atyred, 1760
So fautles of hir fetures and of so fyne hewes,
Wiȝt wallande joye warmed his hert.
With smoþe smylyng and smolt þay smeten into merþe,
Þat al watz blis and bonchef þat breke hem bitwene
            and wynne. 1765
    Þay lanced wordes gode,
    Much wele þen watz þerinne;
    Gret perile bitwene hem stod
    Nif Maré of hir knyȝt mynne.

For þat prynces of pris depresed hym so þikke, 1770
Nurned hym so neȝe þe þred, þat nede hym bihoued
Oþer lach þer hir luf oþer lodly refuse.
He cared for his cortaysye lest craþayn he were,
And more for his meschef ȝif he schulde make synne
And be traytor to þat tolke þat þat telde aȝt. 1775
"God schylde," quoþ þe schalk, "þat schal not befalle!"
With luf laȝyng a lyt he layd hym bysyde
Alle þe spechez of specialté þat sprange of her mouthe.
Quoþ þat burde to þe burne, "Blame ȝe disserue
ȝif ȝe luf not þat lyf þat ȝe lye nexte, 1780
Bifore alle þe wyȝez in þe worlde wounded in hert,
Bot if ȝe haf a lemman, a leuer þat yow lykez better,
And folden fayth to þat fre, festned so harde
Þat yow lausen ne lyst—and þat I leue nouþe.   f. 115ʳ
And þat ȝe telle me þat now trwly I pray yow, 1785
For alle þe lufez vpon lyue layne not þe soþe
            for gile."
    Þe knyȝt sayde, "Be Sayn Jon,"
    And smeþely con he smyle,
    "In fayth I welde riȝt non 1790
    Ne non wil welde þe quile."

1770 prynces] *Emerson*; prynce *MS*

"Þat is a worde," quoþ þat wy3t, "þat worst is of alle,
Bot I am swared for soþe, þat sore me þinkkez.
Kysse me now comly and I schal cach heþen,
I may bot mourne vpon molde as may þat much louyes."   1795
Sykande ho swe3e doun and semly hym kyssed
And siþen ho seueres hym fro and says as ho stondes,
"Now, dere, at þis departyng do me þis ese,
Gif me sumquat of þy gifte, þi gloue if hit were,
Þat I may mynne on þe, mon, my mournyng to lassen."   1800
"Now iwysse," quoþ þat wy3e, "I wolde I hade here
Þe leuest þing for þy luf þat I in londe welde,
For 3e haf deserued, for soþe, sellyly ofte
More rewarde bi resoun þen I reche my3t;
Bot to dele yow for drurye þat dawed bot neked,   1805
Hit is not your honour to haf at þis tyme
A gloue for a garysoun of Gawaynez giftez.
And I am here an erande in erdez vncouþe
And haue no men wyth no malez with menskful þingez;
Þat mislykez me, ladé, for luf at þis tyme,   1810
Iche tolke mon do as he is tan, tas to non ille
          ne pine."
          "Nay, hende of hy3e honours,"
          Quoþ þat lufsum vnder lyne,
          "Þa3 I nade no3t of yourez,   1815
          3et schulde 3e haue of myne."

Ho ra3t hym a riche rynk of red golde werkez
Wyth a starande ston stondande alofte
Þat bere blusschande bemez as þe bry3t sunne;
Wyt 3e wel, hit watz worth wele ful hoge.   1820
Bot þe renk hit renayed and redyly he sayde,
"I wil no giftez, for Gode, my gay, at þis tyme;   f. 115ᵛ
I haf none yow to norne ne no3t wyl I take."

1799   if] *Madden*; of *MS*
1810   tyme] tyne *MS*
1815   nade no3t] hade o3t *MS*

Ho bede hit hym ful bysily and he hir bode wernes
And swere swyfte by his sothe þat he hit sese nolde, 1825
And ho soré þat he forsoke and sayde þerafter,
"If ȝe renay my rynk, to ryche for hit semez,
ȝe wolde not so hyȝly halden be to me,
I schal gif yow my girdel, þat gaynes yow lasse."
Ho laȝt a lace lyȝtly þat leke vmbe hir sydez, 1830
Knit vpon hir kyrtel vnder þe clere mantyle;
Gered hit watz with grene sylke and with golde schaped,
Noȝt bot arounde brayden, beten with fyngrez;
And þat ho bede to þe burne and blyþely bisoȝt,
Þaȝ hit vnworþi were, þat he hit take wolde. 1835
And he nay þat he nolde neghe in no wyse
Nauþer golde ne garysoun er God hym grace sende
To acheue to þe chaunce þat he hade chosen þere.
"And þerfore, I pray yow, displese yow noȝt
And lettez be your bisinesse, for I bayþe hit yow neuer 1840
       to graunte;
       I am derely to yow biholde
       Bicause of your sembelaunt
       And euer in hot and colde
       To be your trwe seruaunt." 1845

"Now forsake ȝe þis silke," sayde þe burde þenne,
"For hit is symple in hitself? And so hit wel semez.
Lo! so hit is littel and lasse hit is worþy.
Bot whoso knew þe costes þat knit ar þerinne,
He wolde hit prayse at more prys, parauenture; 1850
For quat gome so is gorde with þis grene lace,
While he hit hade hemely halched aboute
Þer is no haþel vnder heuen tohewe hym þat myȝt
For he myȝt not be slayn for slyȝt vpon erþe."
Þen kest þe knyȝt and hit come to his hert 1855
Hit were a juel for þe jopardé þat hym iugged were:

1825 swyfte by] *Emerson*; swyftel *MS*
1830 þat] þat þat *MS*

When he acheued to þe chapel his chek for to fech,
My3t he haf slypped to be vnslayn þe sle3t were noble.
Þenne he þulged with hir þrepe and þoled hir to speke,   f. 116ʳ
And ho bere on hym þe belt and bede hit hym swyþe—   1860
And he granted and hym gafe with a goud wylle—
And biso3t hym, for hir sake, disceuer hit neuer
Bot to lelly layne fro hir lorde. Þe leude hym acordez
Þat neuer wy3e schulde hit wyt, iwysse, bot þay twayne
                for no3te.   1865
        He þonkked hir oft ful swyþe
        Ful þro with hert and þo3t.
        Bi þat on þrynne syþe
        Ho hatz kyst þe kny3t so to3t.

Thenne lachchez ho hir leue and leuez hym þere   1870
For more myrþe of þat mon mo3t ho not gete.
When ho watz gon Sir Gawayn gerez hym sone,
Rises and riches hym in araye noble,
Lays vp þe luf lace þe lady hym ra3t,
Hid hit ful holdely þer he hit eft fonde.   1875
Syþen cheuely to þe chapel choses he þe waye,
Preuély aproched to a prest and prayed hym þere
Þat he wolde lyste his lyf and lern hym better
How his sawle schulde be saued when he schuld seye heþen.
Þere he schrof hym schyrly and schewed his mysdedez,   1880
Of þe more and þe mynne, and merci besechez
And of absolucioun he on þe segge calles;
And he asoyled hym surely and sette hym so clene
As domezday schulde haf ben di3t on þe morn.
And syþen he mace hym as mery among þe fre ladyes   1885
With comlych caroles and alle kynnes ioye
As neuer he did bot þat daye to þe derk ny3t
                with blys.
        Vche mon hade daynté þare

1858   My3t] my3 MS
1863   fro] Morris; for MS
1872   ho] Madden; he MS   Gawayn] G MS
1878   lyste] Burrow; lyfte MS

Of hym and sayde, "Iwysse,   1890
Þus myry he watz neuer are
Syn he com hider, er þis."

Now hym lenge in þat lee, þer luf hym bityde!
Ȝet is þe lorde on þe launde ledande his gomnes.
He hatz forfaren þis fox þat he folȝed longe;   1895
As he sprent ouer a spenne to spye þe schrewe,
Þeras he herd þe howndes þat hasted hym swyþe,   f. 116ᵛ
Renaud com richchande þurȝ a roȝe greue
And alle þe rabel in a res ryȝt at his helez.
Þe wyȝe watz war of þe wylde and warly abides   1900
And braydez out þe bryȝt bronde and at þe best castez.
And he schunt for þe scharp and schulde haf arered;
A rach rapes hym to ryȝt er he myȝt
And ryȝt bifore þe hors fete þay fel on hym alle
And woried me þis wyly wyth a wroth noyse.   1905
Þe lorde lyȝtez bilyue and lachez hym sone,
Rased hym ful radly out of þe rach mouþes,
Haldez heȝe ouer his hede, halowez faste,
And þer bayen hym mony braþ houndez.
Huntes hyȝed hem þeder with hornez ful mony,   1910
Ay rechatande aryȝt til þay þey renk seȝen.
Bi þat watz comen his compeyny noble,
Alle þat euer ber bugle blowed at ones
And alle þise oþer halowed þat hade no hornes.
Hit watz þe myriest mute þat euer men herde,   1915
Þe rich rurd þat þer watz raysed for Renaude saule
           with lote.
      Hor houndez þay þer rewarde,
      Her hedez þay fawne and frote
      And syþen þay tan Reynarde   1920
      And tyruen of his cote.

1906   lachez]   cachez *MS*   hym]   *Morris*; by *MS*
1909   braþ]   *Morris*; bray *MS*
1919   Her]   her her *MS*
1920–21   *written as one line MS*

And þenne þay helden to home, for hit watz nieȝ nyȝt,
Strakande ful stoutly in hor store hornez.
Þe lorde is lyȝt at þe laste at hys lef home,
Fyndez fire vpon flet, þe freke þerbyside,   1925
Sir Gawayn þe gode, þat glad watz withalle,
Among þe ladies for luf he ladde much ioye.
He were a bleaunt of blwe þat bradde to þe erþe,
His surkot semed hym wel þat softe watz forred,
And his hode of þat ilke henged on his schulder,   1930
Blande al of blaunner were boþe al aboute.
He metez me þis godmon inmyddez þe flore
And al with gomen he hym gret and goudly he sayde,
"I schal fylle vpon fyrst oure forwardez nouþe
Þat we spedly han spoken, þer spared watz no drynk."   f. 117ʳ
Þen acoles he þe knyȝt and kysses hym þryes   1936
As sauerly and sadly as he hem sette couþe.
"Bi Kryst," quoþ þat oþer knyȝt, "ȝe cach much sele
In cheuisaunce of þis chaffer, ȝif ȝe hade goud chepez."
"ȝe, of þe chepe no charg," quoþ chefly þat oþer,   1940
"As is pertly payed þe chepez þat I aȝte."
"Mary," quoþ þat oþer mon, "myn is bihynde,
For I haf hunted al þis day and noȝt haf I geten
Bot þis foule fox felle—þe Fende haf þe godez!—
And þat is ful pore for to pay for suche prys þinges   1945
As ȝe haf þryȝt me here þro, suche þre cosses
          so gode."
          "Inoȝ," quoþ Sir Gawayn,
          "I þonk yow, bi þe rode,"
          And how þe fox watz slayn   1950
          He tolde hym as þay stode.

With merþe and mynstralsye, wyth metez at hor wylle,
Þay maden as mery as any men moȝten—
With laȝyng of ladies, with lotez of bordes
Gawayn and þe godemon so glad were þay boþe—   1955

1936   þe]   *supplied Madden*
1941   chepez]   *see explanatory note 1941 below*

Bot if þe douthe had doted oþer dronken ben oþer.
Boþe þe mon and þe meyny maden mony iapez
Til þe sesoun watz seȝen þat þay seuer moste;
Burnez to hor bedde behoued at þe laste.
Þenne loȝly his leue at þe lorde fyrst   1960
Fochchez þis fre mon and fayre he hym þonkkez:
"Of such a selly soiorne as I haf hade here,
Your honour at þis hyȝe fest, þe Hyȝekyng yow ȝelde!
I ȝef yow me for on of yourez, if yowreself lykez,
For I mot nedes, as ȝe wot, meue tomorne   1965
And ȝe me take sum tolke to teche, as ȝe hyȝt,
Þe gate to þe Grene Chapel, as God wyl me suffer
To dele on Nw ȝerez Day þe dome of my wyrdes."
"In god fayþe," quoþ þe godmon, "wyth a goud wylle
Al þat euer I yow hyȝt halde schal I redé."   1970
Þer asyngnes he a seruaunt to sett hym in þe waye
And coundue hym by þe downez þat he no drechch had,   f. 117ᵛ
For to ferk þurȝ þe fryth and fare at þe gaynest
          bi greue.
     Þe lorde Gawayn con þonk,   1975
     Such worchip he wolde hym weue.
     Þen at þo ladyez wlonk
     Þe kynȝt hatz tan his leue.

With care and wyth kyssyng he carppez hem tille
And fele þryuande þonkkez he þrat hom to haue   1980
And þay ȝelden hym aȝayn ȝeply þat ilk.
Þay bikende hym to Kryst with ful colde sykyngez.
Syþen fro þe meyny he menskly departes;
Vche mon þat he mette, he made hem a þonke
For his seruyse and his solace and his sere pyne   1985
Þat þay wyth busynes had ben aboute hym to serue;
And vche segge as soré to seuer with hym þere
As þay hade wonde worþyly with þat wlonk euer.

1962   selly]   *Madden*; sellyly *MS*
1973   ferk]   *Madden*; frk *MS*
1981   aȝayn]   *Madden*; aȝay *MS*

Þen with ledes and ly3t he watz ladde to his chambre
And blyþely bro3t to his bedde to be at his rest.   1990
3if he ne slepe soundyly say ne dar I
For he hade muche on þe morn to mynne, 3if he wolde,
      in þo3t.
    Let hym ly3e þere stille,
    He hatz nere þat he so3t;   1995
    And 3e wyl a whyle be stylle
    I schal telle yow how þay wro3t.

IV

Now ne3ez þe Nw 3ere and þe ny3t passez,
Þe day dryuez to þe derk, as Dry3tyn biddez.
Bot wylde wederez of þe worlde wakned þeroute,   2000
Clowdes kesten kenly þe colde to þe erþe
Wyth ny3e innoghe of þe norþe þe naked to tene.
Þe snawe snitered ful snart þat snayped þe wylde,
Þe werbelande wynde wapped fro þe hy3e
And drof vche dale ful of dryftes ful grete.   2005
Þe leude lystened ful wel þat le3 in his bedde,
Þa3 he lowkez his liddez, ful lyttel he slepes,
Bi vch kok þat crue he knwe wel þe steuen.
Deliuerly he dressed vp er þe day sprenged   f. 118ʳ
For þere watz ly3t of a laumpe þat lemed in his chambre.   2010
He called to his chamberlayn, þat cofly hym swared,
And bede hym bryng hym his bruny and his blonk sadel.
Þat oþer ferkez hym vp and fechez hym his wedez
And grayþez me Sir Gawayn vpon a grett wyse.
Fyrst he clad hym in his cloþez þe colde for to were   2015
And syþen his oþer harnays, þat holdely watz keped,
Boþe his paunce and his platez piked ful clene,
Þe ryngez rokked of þe roust of his riche bruny;
And al watz fresch as vpon fyrst and he watz fayn þenne
      to þonk;   2020

1998 Now] N *rubricated; see note I above*
2010 laumpe] *Madden*; laupe *MS*

He hade vpon vche pece
Wypped ful wel and wlonk.
Þe gayest into Grece,
Þe burne bede bryng his blonk.

Whyle þe wlonkest wedes he warp on hymseluen—   2025
His cote wyth þe conysaunce of þe clere werkez
Ennurned vpon veluet, vertuus stonez
Aboute beten and bounden, enbrauded semez
And fayre furred withinne wyth fayre pelures—
ȝet laft he not þe lace, þe ladiez gifte,   2030
Þat forgat not Gawayn for gode of hymseluen.
Bi he hade belted þe bronde vpon his balȝe haunchez,
Þenn dressed he his drurye double hym aboute,
Swyþe sweþled vmbe his swange swetely, þat knyȝt;
Þe gordel of þe grene silke þat gay wel bisemed   2035
Vpon þat ryol red cloþe þat ryche watz to schewe.
Bot wered not þis ilk wyȝe for wele þis gordel
For pryde of þe pendauntez, þaȝ polyst þay were
And þaȝ þe glyterande golde glent vpon endez,
Bot for to sauen hymself when suffer hym byhoued,   2040
To byde bale withoute dabate of bronde hym to were
          oþer knyffe.
     Bi þat þe bolde mon boun
     Wynnez þeroute bilyue,
     Alle þe meyny of renoun   2045
     He þonkkez ofte ful ryue.

Thenne watz Gryngolet grayþe, þat gret watz and huge   f. 118ᵛ
And hade ben soiourned sauerly and in a siker wyse;
Hym lyst prik for poynt, þat proude hors þenne.
Þe wyȝe wynnez hym to and wytez on his lyre   2050
And sayde soberly hymself and by his soth swerez:
"Here is a meyny in þis mote þat on menske þenkkez.
Þe mon hem maynteines, ioy mot he haue!
Þe leue lady, on lyue luf hir bityde!

2027   vertuus]   vertuu + us-*abbreviation MS*
2053   he]   *Gollancz*; þay *MS*

Ȝif þay for charyté cherysen a gest   2055
And halden honour in her honde, þe Haþel hem ȝelde
Þat haldez þe heuen vpon hyȝe and also yow alle!
And ȝif I myȝt lyf vpon londe lede any quyle
I schuld rech yow sum rewarde redyly, if I myȝt."
Þenn steppez he into stirop and strydez alofte.   2060
His schalk schewed hym his schelde, on schulder he hit laȝt,
Gordez to Gryngolet with his gilt helez,
And he startez on þe ston, stod he no lenger
          to praunce.
     His haþel on hors watz þenne,   2065
     Þat bere his spere and launce.
     "Þis kastel to Kryst I kenne":
     He gef hit ay god chaunce.

The brygge watz brayde doun and þe brode ȝatez
Vnbarred and born open vpon boþe halue.   2070
Þe burne blessed hym bilyue and þe bredez passed,
Prayses þe porter bifore þe prynce kneled—
Gef hym God and goud day, þat Gawayn He saue—
And went on his way with his wyȝe one
Þat schulde teche hym to tourne to þat tene place   2075
Þer þe ruful race he schulde resayue.
Þay boȝen bi bonkkez þer boȝez ar bare,
Þay clomben bi clyffez þer clengez þe colde.
Þe heuen watz vphalt bot vgly þervnder;
Mist muged on þe mor, malt on þe mountez,   2080
Vch hille hade a hatte, a myst-hakel huge.
Brokez byled and breke bi bonkkez aboute,
Schyre schaterande on schorez þer þay doun schowued.
Wela wylle watz þe way þer þay bi wod schulden   f. 119ʳ
Til hit watz sone sesoun þat þe sunne ryses   2085
          þat tyde.
     Þay were on a hille ful hyȝe,
     Þe quyte snaw lay bisyde;
     Þe burne þat rod hym by
     Bede his mayster abide.   2090

"For I haf wonnen yow hider, wy3e, at þis tyme,
And now nar 3e not fer fro þat note place
Þat 3e han spied and spuryed so specially after.
Bot I schal say yow for soþe, syþen I yow knowe
And 3e ar a lede vpon lyue þat I wel louy,   2095
Wolde 3e worch bi my wytte 3e worþed þe better.
Þe place þat 3e prece to ful perelous is halden;
Þer wonez a wy3e in þat waste, þe worst vpon erþe,
For he is stiffe and sturne and to strike louies,
And more he is þen any mon vpon myddelerde   2100
And his body bigger þen þe best fowre
Þat ar in Arþurez hous, Hestor oþer oþer.
He cheuez þat chaunce at þe Chapel Grene,
Þer passes non bi þat place so proude in his armes
Þat he ne dyngez hym to deþe with dynt of his honde;   2105
For he is a mon methles and mercy non vses,
For be hit chorle oþer chaplayn þat bi þe chapel rydes,
Monk oþer masseprest oþer any mon elles,
Hym þynk as queme hym to quelle as quyk go hymseluen.
Forþy I say þe, as soþe as 3e in sadel sitte,   2110
Com 3e þere 3e be kylled, may þe kny3t rede—
Trawe 3e me þat trwely—þa3 3e had twenty lyues
          to spende.
     He hatz wonyd here ful 3ore,
     On bent much baret bende,   2115
     A3ayn his dyntez sore
     3e may not yow defende.

"Forþy, goude Sir Gawayn, let þe gome one
And gotz away sum oþer gate, vpon Goddez halue!
Cayrez bi sum oþer kyth þer Kryst mot yow spede,   2120
And I schal hy3 me hom a3ayn and hete yow fyrre
Þat I schal swere bi God and alle his gode hal3ez,   f. 119ᵛ
As help me God and þe halydam and oþez innoghe,
Þat I schal lelly yow layne and lance neuer tale

2105   dyngez]   *TG*; dynnez *MS*

Þat euer ȝe fondet to fle for freke þat I wyst."   2125
"Grant merci," quoþ Gawayn and gruchyng he sayde:
"Wel worth þe, wyȝe, þat woldez my gode
And þat lelly me layne I leue wel þou woldez.
Bot helde þou hit neuer so holde and I here passed,
Founded for ferde for to fle in fourme þat þou tellez,   2130
I were a knyȝt kowarde, I myȝt not be excused.
Bot I wyl to þe chapel for chaunce þat may falle
And talk wyth þat ilk tulk þe tale þat me lyste,
Worþe hit wele oþer wo, as þe wyrde lykez
                hit hafe.   2135
         Þaȝe he be a sturn knape
         To stiȝtel and stad with staue,
         Ful wel con Dryȝtyn schape
         His seruauntez for to saue."

"Mary!" quoþ þat oþer mon, "now þou so much spellez   2140
Þat þou wylt þyn awen nye nyme to þyseluen
And þe lyst lese þy lyf þe lette I ne kepe.
Haf here þi helme on þy hede, þi spere in þi honde,
And ryde me doun þis ilk rake bi ȝon rokke syde
Til þou be broȝt to þe boþem of þe brem valay;   2145
Þenne loke a littel on þe launde on þi lyfte honde
And þou schal se in þat slade þe self chapel
And þe borelych burne on bent þat hit kepez.
Now farez wel, on Godez half, Gawayn þe noble!
For alle þe golde vpon grounde I nolde go wyth þe   2150
Ne bere þe felaȝschip þurȝ þis fryth on fote fyrre."
Bi þat þe wyȝe in þe wod wendez his brydel,
Hit þe hors with þe helez as harde as he myȝt,
Lepez hym ouer þe launde and leuez þe knyȝt þere
                al one.   2155
         "Bi Goddez self," quoþ Gawayn,
         "I wyl nauþer grete ne grone;

2131   not] *Madden*; mot *MS*
2137   and] & & *MS*
2150   go]   ge *MS*

To Goddez wylle I am ful bayn
And to hym I haf me tone."

Thenne gyrdez he to Gryngolet and gederez þe rake,   f. 120ʳ
Schowuez in bi a schore at a schaʒe syde,   2161
Ridez þurʒ þe roʒe bonk ryʒt to þe dale.
And þenne he wayted hym aboute, and wylde hit hym þoʒt,
And seʒe no syngne of resette bisydez nowhere
Bot hyʒe bonkkez and brent vpon boþe halue   2165
And ruʒe knokled knarrez with knorned stonez;
Þe skwez of þe scowtes skayned hym þoʒt.
Þenne he houed and wythhylde his hors at þat tyde
And ofte chaunged his cher þe chapel to seche:
He seʒ non suche in no syde, and selly hym þoʒt,   2170
Saue a lyttel on a launde a lawe, as hit were,
A balʒ berʒ bi a bonke þe brymme bysyde
Bi a forʒ of a flode þat ferked þare;
Þe borne blubred þerinne as hit boyled hade.
Þe knyʒt kachez his caple and com to þe lawe,   2175
Liʒtez doun luflyly and at a lynde tachez
Þe rayne and hit richez with a roʒe braunche.
Þenne he boʒez to þe berʒe, aboute hit he walkez,
Debatande with hymself quat hit be myʒt.
Hit hade a hole on þe ende and on ayþer syde   2180
And ouergrowen with gresse in glodes aywhere
And al watz holʒ inwith; nobot an olde caue
Or a creuisse of an olde cragge, he couþe hit noʒt deme
                    with spelle.
         "We! Lorde," quoþ þe gentyle knyʒt,   2185
         "Wheþer þis be þe Grene Chapelle?

2171   were]   *Madden*; we *MS*
2177   rayne]   *first letter faded MS*   hit richez]   his riche *MS; see explanatory note*
2177 below
2178   þenne]   *second* n *faded MS*
2179   Debatande]   *first* e *faded MS*
2180   Hit]   *faded but legible MS*
2182   And al]   *faded but legible MS*

Here my3t aboute mydny3t
Þe Dele his matynnes telle!

"Now iwysse," quoþ Wowayn, "wysty is here;
Þis oritore is vgly, with erbez ouergrowen;   2190
Wel bisemez þe wy3e wruxled in grene
Dele here his deuocioun on þe deuelez wyse.
Now I fele hit is þe Fende, in my fyue wyttez,
Þat hatz stoken me þis steuen to strye me here.
Þis is a chapel of meschaunce, þat chekke hit bytyde!   2195
Hit is þe corsedest kyrk þat euer I com inne!"
With he3e helme on his hede, his launce in his honde,   f. 120ᵛ
He romez vp to þe roffe of þe ro3 wonez.
Þene herde he of þat hy3e hil in a harde roche
Bi3onde þe broke in a bonk a wonder breme noyse: 2200
Quat! hit clatered in þe clyff as hit cleue schulde,
As one vpon a gryndelston hade grounden a syþe.
What! hit wharred and whette as water at a mulne;
What! hit rusched and ronge rawþe to here.
Þenne "Bi Godde," quoþ Gawayn, "þat gere, as I trowe,   2205
Is ryched at þe reuerence me, renk, to mete
            bi rote.
        Let God worche! 'We loo'—
        Hit helppez me not a mote.
        My lif þa3 I forgoo,   2210
        Drede dotz me no lote."

Thenne þe kny3t con calle ful hy3e:
"Who sti3tlez in þis sted me steuen to holde?
For now is gode Gawayn goande ry3t here.
If any wy3e o3t wyl, wynne hider fast   2215
Oþer now oþer neuer his nedez to spede."
"Abyde," quoþ on on þe bonke abouen ouer his hede,
"And þou schal haf al in hast þat I þe hy3t ones."
3et he rusched on þat rurde rapely a þrowe
And wyth quettyng awharf er he wolde ly3t;   2220

2187 Here] *TG*; he *MS*   2205 as] *Madden*; at *MS*

And syþen he keuerez bi a cragge and comez of a hole,
Whyrlande out of a wro wyth a felle weppen,
A denez ax nwe dy3t, þe dynt with to 3elde,
With a borelych bytte bende by þe halme,
Fyled in a fylor, fowre fote large— 2225
Hit watz no lasse bi þat lace þat lemed ful bry3t! —
And þe gome in þe grene gered as fyrst,
Boþe þe lyre and þe leggez, lokkez and berde,
Saue þat fayre on his fote he foundez on þe erþe,
Sette þe stele to þe stone and stalked bysyde. 2230
When he wan to þe watter, þer he wade nolde,
He hypped ouer on hys ax and orpedly strydez
Bremly broþe on a bent þat brode watz aboute
      on snawe.
    Sir Gawayn þe kny3t con mete, f. 121ʳ
    He ne lutte hym noþyng lowe; 2236
    Þat oþer sayde, "Now, sir swete,
    Of steuen mon may þe trowe."

"Gawayn," quoþ þat grene gome, "God þe mot loke!
Iwysse þou art welcom, wy3e, to my place, 2240
And þou hatz tymed þi trauayl as truee mon schulde
And þou knowez þe couenauntez kest vus bytwene:
At þis tyme twelmonyth þou toke þat þe falled
And I schulde at þis Nwe 3ere 3eply þe quyte.
And we ar in þis valay verayly oure one; 2245
Here ar no renkes vs to rydde, rele as vus likez.
Haf þou þy helme of þy hede and haf here þy pay.
Busk no more debate þen I þe bede þenne
When þou wypped of my hede at a wap one."
"Nay, bi God," quoþ Gawayn, "þat me gost lante, 2250
I schal gruch þe no grwe for grem þat fallez.
Bot sty3tel þe vpon on strok and I schal stonde stylle

2223   with to] *Madden*; wᵗ o *MS*
2240   welcom] *Madden*; welcon *MS*
2247   Haf þou þy] haf þy þy; *see explanatory note 2247 below and cf. textual note to*
a3aynes, *971*

And warp þe no wernyng to worch as þe lykez
     nowhare."
     He lened with þe nek and lutte   2255
     And schewed þat schyre al bare,
     And lette as he noȝt dutte;
     For drede he wolde not dare.

THEN þe gome in þe grene grayþed hym swyþe,
Gederez vp hys grymme tole Gawayn to smyte;   2260
With alle þe bur in his body he ber hit on lofte,
Munt as maȝtyly as marre hym he wolde.
Hade hit dryuen adoun as dreȝ as he atled
Þer hade ben ded of his dynt þat doȝty watz euer.
Bot Gawayn þat giserne glyfte hym bysyde   2265
As hit com glydande adoun on glode hym to schende,
And schranke a lytel with þe schulderes for þe scharp yrne.
Þat oþer schalk wyth a schunt þe schene wythhaldez
And þenne repreued he þe prynce with mony prowde wordez:
"Þou art not Gawayn," quoþ þe gome, "þat is so goud halden,   2270
Þat neuer arȝed for no here by hylle ne be vale,
And now þou fles for ferde er þou fele harmez!   f. 121ᵛ
Such cowardise of þat knyȝt cowþe I neuer here.
Nawþer fyked I ne flaȝe, freke, quen þou myntes
Ne kest no kauelacion in kyngez hous Arthor.   2275
My hede flaȝ to my fote and ȝet flaȝ I neuer;
And þou, er any harme hent, arȝez in hert;
Wherfore þe better burne me burde be called
     þerfore."
     Quoþ Gawayn, "I schunt onez   2280
     And so wyl I no more;
     Bot þaȝ my hede falle on þe stonez
     I con not hit restore.

"Bot busk, burne, bi þi fayth, and bryng me to þe poynt.
Dele to me my destiné and do hit out of honde,   2285

2274   myntes]   myntest *MS; see explanatory note 2274 below*
2280   Gawayn]   G: *MS*

For I schal stonde þe a strok and start no more
Til þyn ax haue me hitte: haf here my trawþe."
"Haf at þe þenne!" quoþ þat oþer and heuez hit alofte
And waytez as wroþely as he wode were.
He myntez at hym maȝtyly bot not þe mon rynez,   2290
Withhelde heterly his honde er hit hurt myȝt.
Gawayn grayþely hit bydez and glent with no membre
Bot stode stylle as þe ston oþer a stubbe auþer
Þat raþeled is in roché grounde with rotez a hundreth.
Þen muryly efte con he mele, þe mon in þe grene: 2295
"So, now þou hatz þi hert holle, hitte me bihous.
Halde þe now þe hyȝe hode þat Arþur þe raȝt
And kepe þy kanel at þis kest ȝif hit keuer may."
Gawayn ful gryndelly with greme þenne sayde:
"Wy! þresch on, þou þro mon, þou þretez to longe;   2300
I hope þat þi hert arȝe wyth þyn awen seluen."
"For soþe," quoþ þat oþer freke, "so felly þou spekez,
I wyl no lenger on lyte lette þin ernde
          riȝt nowe."
          Þenne tas he hym stryþe to stryke   2305
          And frounsez boþe lyppe and browe;
          No meruayle þaȝ hym myslyke
          Þat hoped of no rescowe.

He lyftes lyȝtly his lome and let hit doun fayre
With þe barbe of þe bitte bi þe bare nek.   f. 122ʳ
Þaȝ he homered heterly, hurt hym no more   2311
Bot snyrt hym on þat on syde, þat seuered þe hyde.
Þe scharp schrank to þe flesche þurȝ þe schyre grece
Þat þe schene blod ouer his schulderes schot to þe erþe.
And quen þe burne seȝ þe blode blenk on þe snawe   2315
He sprit forth spennefote more þen a spere lenþe,
Hent heterly his helme and on his hed cast,
Schot with his schulderez his fayre schelde vnder,

2291 his] *Madden*; hs *MS*
2299 Gawayn] G: *MS*
2305 he] he he *MS*

Braydez out a byrȝt sworde and bremely he spekez—
Neuer syn þat he watz barne borne of his moder   2320
Watz he neuer in þis worlde wyȝe half so blyþe—
"Blynne, burne, of þy bur, bede me no mo!
I haf a stroke in þis sted withoute stryf hent
And if þow rechez me any mo I redyly schal quyte
And ȝelde ȝederly aȝgayn—and þerto ȝe tryst—   2325
          and foo.
     Bot on stroke here me fallez—
     Þe couenaunt schop ryȝt so
     Fermed in Arþurez hallez—
     And þerfore, hende, now hoo!"   2330

The haþel heldet hym fro and on his ax rested,
Sette þe schaft vpon schore and to þe scharp lened
And loked to þe leude þat on þe launde ȝede,
How þat doȝty, dredles, deruely þer stondez,
Armed ful aȝlez: in hert hit hym lykez.   2335
Þenn he melez muryly wyth a much steuen
And wyth a rynkande rurde he to þe renk sayde:
"Bolde burne, on þis bent be not so gryndel.
No mon here vnmanerly þe mysboden habbez
Ne kyd bot as couenaunde at kyngez kort schaped.   2340
I hyȝt þe a strok and þou hit hatz, halde þe wel payed.
I relece þe of þe remnaunt of ryȝtes alle oþer.
Iif I deliuer had bene a boffet paraunter
I couþe wroþeloker haf waret, to þe haf wroȝt anger.
Fyrst I mansed þe muryly with a mynt one   2345
And roue þe wyth no rofsore; with ryȝt I þe profered
For þe forwarde þat we fest in þe fyrst nyȝt   f. 122ᵛ
And þou trystyly þe trawþe and trwly me haldez,

2320 barne] *Andrew*; b + *two minims* + *rne MS*
2329 Fermed in] *Menner from offset; MS and facsimile illegible*   Arthurez] *a
. . . . . ez MS (rest illegible)*
2337 rynkande] *Napier*; rykande *MS*
2339 habbez] *TG*; habbe *MS*
2344 anger] *Madden; uncertain, MS faded*

Al þe gayne þow me gef as god mon schulde.
Þat oþer munt for þe morne, mon, I þe profered.   2350
Þou kyssedes my clere wyf—þe cossez me raȝtez.
For boþe two here I þe bede bot two bare myntes
        boute scaþe.
    Trwe mon trwe restore,
    Þenne þarf mon drede no waþe.   2355
    At þe þrid þou fayled þore
    And þerfor þat tappe ta þe.

"For hit is my wede þat þou werez, þat ilke wouen girdel
Myn owen wyf hit þe weued, I wot wel for soþe.
Now know I wel þy cosses and þy costes als   2360
And þe wowyng of my wyf: I wroȝt hit myseluen.
I sende hir to asay þe and sothly þou me þynkkez
On þe fautlest freke þat euer on fote ȝede;
As perle bi þe quite pese is of prys more,
So is Gawayn, in god fayth, bi oþer gay knyȝtez.   2365
Bot here yow lakked a lyttel, sir, and lewté yow wonted;
Bot þat watz for no wylyde werke ne wowyng nauþer,
Bot for ȝe lufed your lyf; þe lasse I yow blame."
Þat oþer stif mon in study stod a gret whyle,
So agreued for greme he gryed withinne;   2370
Alle þe blode of his brest blende in his face
Þat al he schrank for schome þat þe schalk talked.
Þe forme worde vpon folde þat þe freke meled:
"Corsed worth cowarddyse and couetyse boþe!
In yow is vylany and vyse þat vertue disstryez."   2375
Þenne he kaȝt to þe knot and þe kest lawsez,
Brayde broþely þe belt to þe burne seluen:
"Lo! þer þe falssyng, foule mot hit falle!
For care of þy knokke cowardyse me taȝt
To acorde me with couetyse, my kynde to forsake,   2380
Þat is larges and lewté þat longez to knyȝtez.

2355 þarf] þar *MS*
2362 þou] *supplied*

Now am I fawty and falce and ferde haf ben euer
Of trecherye and vntrawþe: boþe bityde sorȝe
       and care!
     I biknowe yow, knyȝt, here stylle,   f. 123ʳ
     Al fawty is my fare;   2386
     Letez me ouertake your wylle
     And efte I schal be ware."

Thenn loȝe þat oþer leude and luflyly sayde:
"I halde hit hardily hole, þe harme þat I hade.   2390
Þou art confessed so clene, beknowen of þy mysses,
And hatz þe penaunce apert of þe poynt of myn egge,
I halde þe polysed of þat plyȝt and pured as clene
As þou hadez neuer forfeted syþen þou watz fyrst borne.
And I gif þe, sir, þe gurdel þat is golde hemmed;   2395
For hit is grene as my goune, Sir Gawayn, ȝe maye
Þenk vpon þis ilke þrepe þer þou forth þryngez
Among prynces of prys, and þis a pure token
Of þe chaunce of þe Grene Chapel at cheualrous kynȝtez.
And ȝe schal in Þis Nwe ȝer aȝayn to my wonez   2400
And we schyn reuel þe remnaunt of þis ryche fest
       ful bene."
     Þer laþed hym fast þe lorde
     And sayde: "With my wyf, I wene,
     We schal yow wel acorde,   2405
     Þat watz your enmy kene."

"Nay, for soþe," quoþ þe segge and sesed hys helme
And hatz hit of hendely and þe haþel þonkkez,
"I haf soiorned sadly; sele yow bytyde
And He ȝelde hit yow ȝare þat ȝarkkez al menskes!   2410
And comaundez me to þat cortays, your comlych fere,
Boþe þat on and þat oþer, myn honoured ladyez,
Þat þus hor knyȝt wyth hor kest han koyntly bigyled.
Bot hit is no ferly þaȝ a fole madde

2385   *catchword* I beknowe yow knyȝt *MS*
2390   hardily] *Madden*; hardilyly *MS*
2396   Sir Gawayn] Sir G: *MS*

And þur3 wyles of wymmen be wonen to sor3e, 2415
For so watz Adam in erde with one bygyled
And Salamon with fele sere and Samson eftsonez—
Dalyda dalt hym hys wyrde—and Dauyth þerafter
Watz blended with Barsabe, þat much bale þoled.
Now þese were wrathed wyth her wyles, hit were a wynne
     huge 2420
To luf hom wel and leue hem not, a leude þat couþe.
For þes wer forne þe freest þat fol3ed alle þe sele f. 123ᵛ
Exellently of alle þyse oþer vnder heuenryche
       þat mused;
   And alle þay were biwyled 2425
   With wymmen þat þay vsed.
   Þa3 I be now bigyled
   Me þink me burde be excused.

"Bot your gordel," quoþ Gawayn, "God yow for3elde!
Þat wyl I welde wyth guod wylle, not for þe wynne golde 2430
Ne þe saynt ne þe sylk ne þe syde pendaundes,
For wele ne for worchyp ne for þe wlonk werkkez,
Bot in syngne of my surfet I schal se hit ofte
When I ride in renoun, remorde to myseluen
Þe faut and þe fayntyse of þe flesche crabbed, 2435
How tender hit is to entyse teches of fylþe.
And þus, quen pryde schal me pryk for prowes of armes,
Þe loke to þis luf lace schal leþe my hert.
Bot on I wolde yow pray, displeses yow neuer:
Syn 3e be lorde of þe 3onder londe þer I haf lent inne 2440
Wyth yow wyth worschyp—þe Wy3e hit yow 3elde
Þat vphaldez þe heuen and on hy3 sittez—
How norne 3e yowre ry3t nome and þenne no more?"
"Þat schal I telle þe trwly," quoþ þat oþer þenne,
"Bertilak de Hautdesert I hat in þis londe. 2445
Þur3 my3t of Morgne la Faye, þat in my hous lenges

2426 With] with wyth MS
2429 Gawayn] G: MS
2445 Bertilak] See explanatory note 2445

And koyntyse of clergye, bi craftes wel lerned,
Þe maystrés of Merlyn mony hatz taken—
For ho hatz dalt drwry ful dere sumtyme
With þat conable klerk þat knowes alle your kny3tez   2450
          at hame,
          Morgne þe goddes
          Þerfore hit is hir name,
          Weldez non so hy3e hawtesse
          Þat ho ne con make ful tame—   2455

"Ho wayned me vpon þis wyse to your wynne halle
For to assay þe surquidré 3if hit soth were
Þat rennes of þe grete renoun of þe Rounde Table;
Ho wayned me þis wonder your wyttez to reue
For to haf greued Gaynour and gart hir to dy3e   f. 124ʳ
With glopnyng of þat ilke gome þat gostlych speked   2461
With his hede in his honde bifore þe hy3e table.
Þat is ho þat is at home, þe auncian lady;
Ho is euen þy naunt, Arþurez halfsuster,
Þe duches do3ter of Tyntagelle, þat dere Vter after   2465
Hade Arþur vpon, þat aþel is nowþe.
Þerfore I eþe þe, haþel, to com to þy naunt,
Make myry in my hous; my meny þe louies
And I wol þe as wel, wy3e, bi my faythe,
As any gome vnder God for þy grete trauþe."   2470
And he nikked hym naye, he nolde bi no wayes.
Þay acolen and kyssen and kenne ayþer oþer
To þe Prynce of Paradise and parten ry3t þere
          on coolde.
          Gawayn on blonk ful bene   2475
          To þe kyngez bur3 buskez bolde,
          And þe kny3t in þe enker grene
          Whiderwardesoeuer he wolde.

Wylde wayez in þe worlde Wowen now rydez
On Gryngolet, þat þe grace hade geten of his lyue;   2480

2448   hatz]   *Madden*; ho MS
2461   glopnyng]   *Morris*; gopnyng MS   gome]   gomen MS
2472   and kennen]   *supplied TG*

Ofte he herbered in house and ofte al þeroute
And mony aventure in vale and venquyst ofte,
Þat I ne ty3t at þis tyme in tale to remene.
Þe hurt watz hole þat he hade hent in his nek
And þe blykkande belt he bere þeraboute   2485
Abelef as a bauderyk bounden bi his syde,
Loken vnder his lyfte arme, þe lace, with a knot,
In tokenyng he watz tane in tech of a faute.
And þus he commes to þe court, kny3t al in sounde.
Þer wakned wele in þat wone when wyst þe grete   2490
Þat gode Gawayn watz commen; gayn hit hym þo3t.
Þe kyng kyssez þe kny3t and þe whene alce
And syþen mony syker kny3t þat so3t hym to haylce
Of his fare þat hym frayned; and ferlyly he telles,
Biknowez alle þe costes of care þat he hade,   2495
Þe chaunce of þe chapel, þe chere of þe kny3t,
Þe luf of þe ladi, þe lace at þe last.   f. 124ᵛ
Þe nirt in þe nek he naked hem schewed
Þat he la3t for his vnleuté at þe leudes hondes
        for blame.   2500
      He tened quen he schulde telle,
      He groned for gref and grame;
      Þe blod in his face con melle
      When he hit schulde schewe, for schame.

"Lo! lorde," quoþ þe leude, and þe lace hondeled,   2505
"Þis is þe bende of þis blame I bere in my nek,
Þis is þe laþe and þe losse þat I la3t haue
Of couardise and couetyse þat I haf ca3t þare,
Þis is þe token of vntrawþe þat I am tan inne
And I mot nedez hit were wyle I may last;   2510
For mon may hyden his harme bot vnhap ne may hit,
For þer hit onez is tachched twynne wil hit neuer."
Þe kyng comfortez þe kny3t and alle þe court als
La3en loude þerat and luflyly acorden

2491 Gawayn] G:: MS
2506 in] supplied Madden
2511 mon] Andrew; non MS

Þat lordes and ladis þat longed to þe Table, 2515
Vche burne of þe broþerhede a bauderyk schulde haue,
A bende abelef hym aboute of a bryȝt grene,
And þat for sake of þat segge in swete to were.
For þat watz acorded þe renoun of þe Rounde Table
And he honoured þat hit hade euermore after, 2520
As hit is breued in þe best boke of romaunce.
Þus in Arthurus day þis aunter bitidde,
Þe Brutus Bokez þerof beres wyttenesse;
Syþen Brutus þe bolde burne boȝed hider fyrst
After þe segge and þe asaute watz sesed at Troye, 2525
      iwysse,
    Mony aunterez herebiforne
    Haf fallen suche er þis.
    Now þat bere þe croun of þorne
    He bryng vus to his blysse! AMEN. 2530

HONY SOYT QUI MAL PENCE.

Explanatory Notes

A bracketed italic number appearing in each first citation (and also in some further citations for convenience) refers to the section of the select bibliography below where the work in question is listed. Abbreviations for dictionaries, indexes, and serials appear there in section 12.

1–36 The prologue.   Gollancz cites the brief Trojan connection at the beginning of *Wynnere and Wastoure* [*10*] and at the end of *Morte Arthure* [*10*], but the present prologue is unique in Arthurian romance. Its two opening lines, to be sure, employ a widespread formula on Troy's fall and conflagration, its account of the Britons' Trojan descent repeats a medieval commonplace, and the three-part disposition of its subject-matter (ancient deeds, noble genealogy, special theme) parallels *Beowulf* and the thirteenth-century prose *Perlesvaus* [*6*] (1:23–26); still it is shaped to its own formal purpose, giving "magnitude" to the poem yet introducing by a kind of *insinuatio*, or indirection, what will turn out to be high comedy. See Silverstein, "Sir Gawain, Dear Brutus" [*7*], pp. 190–92.

2 *borȝ*   In Middle English this word ranges in meaning from fortified tower to town or borough, and here may be merely a synonym for Troy in line 1. But the distinction which appears in medieval texts between the city, called Troy, and its inner keep or palace, called Ilion, suggests that *borȝ* may be intended to convey that difference now, and reading the line thus makes it stronger. See, e.g., Benoit de Sainte-Maure, *Roman de Troie*, ed. Constans (SATF, 1904–12), 3041ff., esp. 3041–42: "De l'une part sist Ylion / De Troie le maistre donjon . . . / Sor une roche tote entiere"; Guido della Colonna [*8*],

p. 49: "rex Priamus . . . in eminentiori loco urbis ipsius cuiusdam natiue rupis excelse magnum et famosum Ylion formari constituit"; and *Ovide moralisé*, the prose text, ed. de Boer (Verhandel. d. k. Nederl. Akad. v. Wetensch., n.s., LXI.2, Amsterdam, 1954), pp. 111, 302, 322: "le beau chasteau de Ylion," "Ylion le chastel," etc. Lydgate's *Troy Book* [*10*] makes the same distinction (4770–71): "But of þis riche, royal, chefe dongoun, / Þat Ylion in Troye bare þe name"; so does Caxton in his version of Raoul Lefevre's *Recuyell of the Historyes of Troye* (ed. Sommer [1894], p. 508): "In the moste apparaunt place of the cyte vpon a roche / the kynge pryant dide do make hyse ryche palays that was named ylyon." See also Flutre, under *Ilion*; for a MS illumination of the passage in Lefevre, BN, fr. 22552, folio 206ᵛ; and the device displayed at a dinner for Queen Isabella of France described by Froissart, *Chroniques*, iv.1 (ed. J. A. C. Buchon [Paris, 1840], 3:7). The distinction survives in England in a number of examples of a mazelike stone or turf construction, called from an ancient game a Troy, at the center of which lies the place to be achieved, thus giving its name to the whole: Gillian-, Gelyan-, or Julian-Bower (Gilling-Bore, Jul-Laber): see W. H. Matthews, *Mazes and Labyrinths* (London, 1922), esp. pp. 71–78, 173–74; J. Saward, *The Book of British Troy Towns* (Caerdroia Project, 1982), esp. p. 29, items 1, 20, 27, 30; R. Coate and A. Fisher, *A Celebration of Mazes* (Minotaur Designs, 2nd ed., 1983), esp. pp. 8–9; and cf. *EDD*, under *Julian-Bower*. Attempts to relate the name to Iulus, son of Aeneas, are dubious and to Saint Julian the Hospitaler without foundation; Gillian-Bower, Julian-Bower evidently = Ilion-Borȝ.

3 *Þe tulk* A notable crux. Was Aeneas the traitor intended, or Antenor, not named here but known to tradition? Madden picks the former, Gollancz the latter. The preponderant current view seems to be Madden's, as in Davis, who quotes Guido della Colonna [*8*], and, in English, *The Geste Hystoriale* [*10*], 11192ff., 11832ff., esp. 11973, the *Scottish Troy Fragments* [*10*], 830ff., and Lydgate's *Troy Book* [*10*], iv. 4538ff., 6316–469. See also Laud *Troy Book* [*10*], 18589–604. Ultimately based on the ancient accounts ascribed to Dares and Dictys, the traitorous involvement of Aeneas also goes back to Servius's commentary on *Aeneid*, i.242, making explicit what he finds implied in Livy, i.1.

5 *Þe athel* In form this kind of epithet, which appears three further times in *Gawain* (904, 1110, 1926) and regularly in some contemporary alliterative pieces (e.g., *The Wars of Alexander*, *The Parlement of the Thre Ages*, *Mum and the Sothsegger*, *Golagros and Gawan* [all *10*]), is derived from older *chanson de geste* and historical poem, e.g., Laȝamon's *Brut* [*6*]. As here, it normally occurs in the first half-line and is alliterated. But there is another use, unalliterated, in the second half-line (*Gawain*, 405, 553, 1213, 2149) which may be observed, though not frequently, in *The Parlement*,

The Siege of Jerusalem, and *Alexander B* [all *10*], and as a regular feature of the later *Death and Liffe*, 118, 329, 338, 340 (in *SP* 10 [1918]:221–94). Such instances reflect the employment of the device in the unalliterated, short-lined French poetic romances, both as part of proper names (see n. 552, and Flutre [*12*], *passim*) and as *ad hoc* descriptive device (e.g., Yvain li cortois, Hestor li preux). In England, two instances of this sort appear in Robert Mannyng's short-lined *Chronicle* [*6*] (Wawayn þe Curteys) and, among his Anglo-Norman sources and contemporaries, five in Langtoft and one in Wace. No epithets used in either fashion occur in *Patience*, *Pearl*, or *Erkenwald* [all *3*], but two instances of the second kind appear in *Purity* [*3*], 682 and 1372.

7 *west iles* "Western realms." See *MED* [*12*], *ile* n., 2a(a). Genesis 10:5, *insulae gentium, yles of gentylis*, uses *iles* (following the Hebrew) for the lands settled by the sons of Japheth, among whom in the Josephus-Eusebius genealogies of the Middle Ages belonged Antenor, Aeneas, and the Trojans: see *MED*, *ile*, 2b, and *ilond*, 1 (b), and Nennius, *Historia Brittonum* [*6*], cap. 17.

8,11,12 *Romulus, Tuscius, Langaberde* According to tradition the eponymous founders of their respective countries. The appearance of Tuscius, or Tirius (see next note), and Langaberde would here seem to intrude upon a genealogy primarily of Aeneas's descendents, who established Rome and Britain. But the three provinces of Italy making up part of the Carolingian patrimony, i.e., Lombardy, Tuscany, and Rome, came to constitute King Arthur's imperial Italian claim, as in, e.g., the alliterative *Morte Arthure* [*10*], 1583–87, and implied in part by *The Awntyrs off Arthure* and *Kyng Alisaunder* [*10*]; cf. *The Sege off Melayne* [*10*], 10–24. Hence the relevance here of the two additional non-Roman founders. See Silverstein, "Sir Gawain, Dear Brutus" [*7*], pp. 203–5.

11 *Tuscius* Or *Tirius*, MS *Ticius*. Gollancz suggests that the MS reading may be a corruption of Tuscus, Tuscius, whom, we may add, Servius Danielis on *Aeneid* calls the founder of Tuscany; and that suggestion is here adopted in the text. A reading T'cius = Tuscius in the scribe's source, carelessly written or read, could have produced the no-name Ticius. Tirius has also been suggested by the present editor as an alternative: Tyreus, Tyrrus is the name in an early Vergil commentary, paired with Tyrrhenus, after whom it is said the Tyrrhenian (Tuscan) Sea is called, and some Vergil MSS also denote a Latin namesake Tirius, Tirrus. The scribe's c and r are very much alike, and one might have been written for the other. See Silverstein, "Sir Gawain, Dear Brutus," pp. 195–96.

13 *Felix Brutus* Grandson (Nennius) or great-grandson (Geoffrey of Monmouth) of Aeneas and founder of the third Troy, i.e., Britain, as Romulus was founder of the second, Rome. Nowhere else, however, is he called Felix. The name seems to arise from, or be related to, three circumstances: (1) In all the stories a double parricide, Brutus is in fact *infelix* and an outcast. English writers had the motive to reduce the onus, hence a perverted text of the history of Nennius and the accounts of Geoffrey of Monmouth and his followers, develop an *apologia* for this dubious ancestor by emphasizing the felicity of his fated role as a founder. Laȝamon uses the word *sæl*, "fortunate," of him and calls him *Brutus þe sele*, which Madden translates "Brutus the good," in keeping with other uses of the epithet in the poem; but in view of the two following considerations the *Gawain* poet, did he know the *Brut*, might well have thought to take its first meaning, i.e., *felix*. (2) *Felix* in Latin letters and on coins was an epithet for the founder of a city, appropriate, according to Tiberius Donatus in his *interpretatio* of Vergil, even to Antenor, and especially to Aeneas and to the Julian house, which raised Rome to its height of good fortune. (3) In lines 13–14, describing the foundation of Britain, *Gawain*'s phrase *wyth wynne* translates *feliciter*, a conventional term of praise summarizing the reign of a good prince but here also an interpretation of Brutus's epithet *Felix*, to which it turns back as a play on words. See Silverstein, "Sir Gawain, Dear Brutus," pp. 196–202.

18   *blysse and blunder*   An alliterated phrase not found elsewhere in Middle English poetry hence peculiarly *Gawain*'s, intimating, but as a part of the comedy not directly stating, the character of the poem's "theme." See Silverstein, "Sir Gawain, Dear Brutus," p. 191.

26, 31, 32   *as I haf herde telle, as I in toun herde, with tonge*   Conventional phrases found in the contemporary alliterative poetry, vouchsafing the story's truth by means of the authority of an older book or tradition: see 690 and 2521–23, and Oakden [5] 2:247, 306, 340, and 386–87. They also echo a convention of the French romances: see n. 690. Within the second phrase the words *in toun*, meaning "among men, where people are," etc., are also a tag, as TG observes and with further instances in n. 1049. For the phrases and tags found throughout which appear in other related pieces of the time, see Oakden [5] 2, chaps. 10–13.

35–36   There is some question whether these lines refer to the traditional English alliterative meter, as if to be read thus: "linked by correctly echoing words (*lel letteres*, i.e., alliteration) in a manner so long current in this country," hence constitute a comment by the poet on the metrical art of his supposed source as well as on his own practice (see Davis). We would wish it to be so. But *MED* [12], *lel*, 2(c), lists only this instance in *Gawain* for the special sense which the reading requires, and the objections of P. J. Frankis, in *N & Q* 206 (1961):329–30, should give us pause; two fifteenth-century Scottish citations use *lel* with *letteris* to mean "truthful," notably in Henryson's *Age and Youth*. It could be argued that what the poet is saying is simply that he is not making up the story but got it from others, that it is known from older times (see also 2523 below), and that he is reporting it truly.

36 *in londe* Another tag. See Oakden 2:381, 390.

37 As in 1 and 2 this line also embodies a formula for a setting in Arthurian romance often used to start a particular suite of adventures, and, leaving out the prologue, *Gawain* might well have begun directly with it: see, e.g., Chrétien de Troyes's *Erec*, *Yvain*, and *Charrette* [6]; Renaut de Beaujeu's *Le bel inconnu* [6], 11–70; the fabliau *Du mantel mautaillié* (Montaiglon and Raynaud, *Receuil . . . des fabliaux* 3:1); and the English ballad *The Marriage of Sir Gawaine*, st. 3 (Child, no. 31). The Arthurian high court as occasion for entertainments was dealt with by Madden (and Child after him), but though it includes Christmas among the five yearly high courts, it is not confined to that season. Geoffrey of Monmouth's great Pentecost court (*Historia*, ed. Hammer, ix.9; ed. Griscom, ix.12) is the primal source of all the accounts, but from before the fourteenth century Christmas was a special time of festivities in England. The alliterative *Morte Arthure*, indeed, shifts the occasion to Christmas and *Gawain*'s account conveys a comparable contemporaneity.

39 *þe Rounde Table* The conventional name for the association of knights in Arthur's court. The table itself, whether from the secular story of its establishment in Wace (*Brut* [6], 9747–60) or from the Christianizing one, as in the Vulgate *Merlin* (2:53–55) and the prose *Suite du Merlin* (pp. 94ff.) [both 6], plays no part in *Gawain*, as is the case in many other romances, French and English.

43 *caroles* Dances accompanied by song, frequently mentioned in courtly entertainment from Chrétien and *The First Continuation of Perceval* onward, and also in the Vulgate *Lancelot* (3.1:108) and the *Roman de la rose* (331, 335, 726, 741, 775, 792, etc.) [all 6]. They were fashionable in England in the fourteenth century and after. See R. L. Greene, *The Early English Carol* (Oxford, 2nd. ed., 1977), introduction, esp. chaps. 1 and 2, pp. xxiii–xxviii, with references to various Middle English texts, including Chaucer and *Gawain*.

44 "For there the feast was unvaryingly abundant for fifteen days." With Gollancz this reads *ilyche* as adv. and *ful* as adj. modifying *fest*. TG takes *ful* as adv. with *fifteen days*, citing the *Suite du Merlin* (I, 173), "Et dura cele feste quinze jours tous pleniers." This, however, is ambiguous and better support for the case could be found in, among others, *William of Palerne* [10], 5352: "Fulle fiftene daies þat feste was holden"; and *Of Arthour and of Merlin* [10], 3581–82. In the end one might prefer the Vulgate *Merlin* [6]

(2:97): "si fu la feste .viij. iors grans & pleniers," where the modifiers clearly refer to the festival's splendor, not its duration, and may derive from the notion of the high court, *court planiere*: see the 1530 prose *Perceval* [6], folio lxxxvii^v, col. 1, *et passim*, and cf. n. 37 above.

51 *vnder Krystes seluen* Davis reads the phrase as conventional for "on earth, under heaven," quoting Laȝamon [6], 13963 (Madden 27976) and *Morte Arthure* [10], 537. But another Laȝamon passage, 13591–92 (Madden 27230–33), which as here uses the word *seolue*, imparts a further nuance: "ȝe beoð under criste./ cnihten alre kennest / and ich æm rihchest alre kinge./ vnder Gode seolue," which can only mean "I am the mightiest of all kings save God himself." So here in *Gawain* with the fame of Arthur's knights, below that of Christ himself, who is the most famous of all knights.

61 *doubble* A piece of contemporary realism. Usually taken to mean a double portion of food (see *MED*, *doublĕ*, adv., [c]) and that interpretation is supported by line 483. The word can also refer, however, to the formal seating and serving of guests, i.e., in pairs. Emerson (in *SP* 22:181–82) explains 107–13 and 1001–4 so, giving other instances, but without noticing the present line. To his examples may be added three others, the first in John of Garland, *Morale scolarium* (mid thirteenth century), chap. ix, "De curialitatibus in mensa conservandis," 172 (ed. Paetow, in Memoirs of the University of California 4.2 [1927]:203 and n.): "Postea iungantur bini quicumque vocantur"; and a contemporary gloss reads: "bini, homines duo et duo." The second instance is in the *Roman de la rose*, 133365–71: "et quant ele iert a table assise, / face, s'el peut, a touz servise. / . . . / et doit, por grace deservir, / devant le compaignon servir / qui doit mengier en s'escuële." The third instance occurs in John Russell's *Boke of Nurture* [9], 1049–55, which, speaking of a time in England not much more than a generation after *Gawain*, says that "in Chambur or halle at a table . . . Bisshoppes. Marques, Vicount, Erle goodly, / May sytte at .ij. messez yf þey be lovyngely," and that others of honorable estate may sit ".ij. or els .iij. at a messe." That such an arrangement is intended in *Gawain* is supported by 128: "Ay two had disches twelue," an obvious reference to the paired seating and serving.

66–70 Another touch of contemporary realism. The nature of the entertainment is not fully clear. Gollancz conjectures that the gift-giving involves some form of handy-dandy, a game in which a player wins an object by guessing correctly in which hand another player holds it. Emerson (in *JEGP* 21 [1922]:365) suggests of 69–70 that what the ladies lost and the gentlemen won was a kiss, but whether in the same game or another (as Gollancz implies) does not come out.

74–84 *Guenor* Guenever, the very model of courtly beauty; for which see, among others, the Vulgate *Merlin*, chap. 14 (2:157–58, ll. 41–42ff.):

"Car ce estoit la plus bele feme qui fust en toute bertaigne au tans de lors";
and the Vulgate *Lancelot* (3.1:29, esp. ll. 11ff.): "Moult fu la roine genieure
de grant biaute. Mais riens ne monta la biaute a la ualour que ele auoit." See
also the Vulgate *La morte le roi Artus* [6], 6:205. Cf. 945 and its explanatory
note below. All such accounts go back, once again, to Geoffrey of Mon-
mouth [6]: "tocius insule mulieres pulcritudine superabat" (ed. Hammer,
ix.5; ed. Griscom, ix.8). Cf. Laȝamon, 11096−97 (Madden 22235−38).
Mannyng's *Chronicle*, 10418−22, adds descriptive details drawn from Wace,
9646−55, who, however, omits Geoffrey's original superlative. For the
forms of the queen's name itself see *Gawain*, 109, 945 (with explanatory
note), 2460, and Flutre, West, and Ackerman [all *12*]. Add also Langtoft's
Chronicle, pp. 172, 174, 218, 220; and Mannyng's *Chronicle*, 11227.

77   *tolouse*   Cf. 568. A rich red fabric frequently called *tuly* and thought
to come from Toulouse, as this passage states: see *OED*, *tuly*. Gollancz and
Davis note that the term can only doubtfully be identified with the French
city. Indeed, the fourteenth-century Caius text of *Guy of Warwick*, 84,
translates French *Tulette*, meaning Toledo, by *Tholouse*: cf. EETS ES,
42:6−7, with the French *Gui de Warewic*, 68 (ed. Ewert, 1 [1933]:3); and
Purity, 1108, "toles of Tolowse," meaning knives, may also refer to Toledo.
Flutre, under *Tolose*, *Toulose*, etc., lists no instance, however, for French
and Provençal, where Toledo seems to be meant, and one for Tolosa in
Spain.

   tars   Costly stuff, whether tapestries and carpets, as here and in 858,
or materials for clothing, as in 571. Tars, Tarse for Tarsus in Cilicia or for
Tharsia in Turkestan were readily confused. TG, following *OED* and quoting
Mandeville's *Travels*, assumes the second to be correct. But all the French
and Provençal romances are taken to refer to Tarsus in Cilicia by Flutre, un-
der *Tarce* and *Tarsie*, and their variants.

82   *with yȝen gray*   "With lively, sparkling eyes," though some take gray
to mean the color blue-gray. See *MED*, *grei*, 2(b). The French term is *vair*
(see Godefroy) and occurs often in the romances. There are parallels in
meaning in the twelfth- and thirteenth-century *artes poetriae*, e.g., in Faral
[5], Matthew of Vendôme, *Ars versificatoria*, §56, 15, of Helen; and Geoffrey
de Vinsauf, *Poetria nova*, 570. See also D. S. Brewer, in *MLR* 50 (1955):
257−69, *et passim*.

90−102   The Carados adventure in *The First Continuation* of the *Perceval*
uses a form of this "custom," which, in the alternatives expressed, is very
like it here: e.g., *Perceval*, 1530 prose version [6], folio lxxviii^v, col. 1: "ia-
mais ne voullus menger ains que nouuelles ou merueilles ne fussent deuers
moy venues." Cf. the verse versions, ed. Roach, 1:90, and 3.1:142−43; and
contrast Chretien's *Perceval*, ed. Lecoy, 2820−26 (ed. Hilka, 2786−92). For

the origin and frequent occurrence of the "custom" in the romances generally, see Madden and also Child (ballad no. 29, introduction n. ‡). Most of the instances occur at Pentecost and in Carduil or Caerleon, but the prose *Queste* (ed. Pauphilet [1923], pp. 3ff.; ed. Sommer, 6 [1913]:3ff.) sets the scene in Camelot. See n. 37 above.

107–14   Agravain, Gawain, and Yvain sit at the royal table, being of royal blood and Arthur's nephews, and Bishop Baldwin is there in the place of honor at Arthur's right as the ranking ecclesiast. The actual arrangement facing the dais from the hall (Emerson, in *SP* 22:181) is this:

         Yvain–Baldwin   Arthur–Gaynor   Gawain–Agravain

Seating by pairs is not confined to this table only: 128 and its context indicate that all the distinguished guests were so served. The details are drawn from contemporary life and the legendary Round Table plays no part at dinner here. See n. 61 and lines 1001–3.

109   *Gawan*   In older tradition, as in this poem, the noblest of Arthur's knights. Geoffrey of Monmouth's *Historia* early testifies to his reputation as a young warrior, Wace's *Brut* to his role as a courtier, and his greatness in both respects continues widely in the romances. The best known English tribute to his manners, excepting *Gawain* itself, is in Chaucer's Squire's Tale (V[F], 95–97), which praises a stranger knight for such perfection "That Gawayn, with his olde curteisye . . . / Ne koude hym nat amende with a word." In other romances, first French then English, where Lancelot and others replace him as protagonist, Sir Gawain becomes less perfectly admired. The assumption in the present poem of his notable chivalric manners and morals not only suits the taste of its evidently high-bred audience but also is necessary to the working out of the plot. For a general account of Sir Gawain see B. J. Whiting, in *Mediaeval Studies* 9 (1947):189–234. For variants in the name see 398, 463, 559, 838, 906, 1226, 1618, etc., and Flutre, Ackerman, Chapman, Kottler, and Markman [*12*].

110, 112, 113   *Agrauayn, Bawdewyn, Ywan*   Agravain, Sir Gawain's younger brother, and Yvain son of King Urien occur frequently in the romances, but in Middle English the special epithet for the former, *a la Dure Mayn*, has been found only here; see Ackerman [*12*]. The French occasionally call him "li Orgueilleus," and Chrétien's *Perceval*, 8139–40, *The First Continuation*, 5437–38 (Redacs EMQ, 2:159), and the 1530 prose *Perceval*, folio lxxi, col. 1, "li Orgueilleus as [au] dures mains" [all *6*]. See also *Claris et Laris* (ed. Alton [1884]), 13311–12, and *Les merveilles de Rigomer* (ed. Foerster [1908]), 14245–46. Bishop Baldwin appears in *The Turke and Gowin* (*Bishop Percy's Folio Manuscript* 1 [1867]:96; and ed. Madden, p. 249) and both versions of *Sir Gawain and the Carl of Carlyle* [*10*], but not in earlier tradition, whether English or French. Gollancz and TG equate him with a Bishop Bedwini in the Welsh *Mabinogion* and the triads.

114ff. Cf. Baltazar's (Belshazzar's) feast in *Purity*, 1401ff.

126–27 "Each man took, ungrudged, as he himself liked."

130–31 For this formula, the inexpressibility topos, suggesting by his silence (elsewhere the difficulty of stating) the richness of a feast, found also in the French, cf. 165 and its note and 1008–9.

132–33 Some readers find here the musical announcement of the dinner's second course and take *lud* to mean "people, guests." It seems rather better, however, to hear in the passage the sound of the Green Knight's approach on horseback and to read *lud* as "prince, sovereign," i.e., King Arthur, who will soon, on fulfillment of the "custom," be able to have his dinner.

134–36 The interval between the first and second courses as the moment for the entrance of the stranger bringing *nouvelles* or *mervailles*: see *Perlesvaus*, 596–97 (I, 48): "Si com on ot servir du premier mes e on atendoit le secont, atant ez vos .iii. demoiseles o eles entrent en la sale." At English coronation feasts from the fourteenth century on it was at the second course that the royal champion rode in to make his challenge, e.g., *The Chronicle of John Hardyng*, ed. Henry Ellis (London, 1812), p. 518. See also M. F. Johnston, *Coronation of a King*, pp. 8, 83–87, 90, 95–96, 115–16, 120–21, 133, 140–41; Mead, *The Medieval Feast*, p. 188; Sydney Anglo, *Spectacle, Pageantry, and Early Tudor Poetry*, pp. 15–16; and Cosman, *Fabulous Feasts*, p. 33 [all 9 *Feasts*].

136ff. The Green Knight. For his appearance see the introduction p. 4f. above, where relations with *The First Continuation* and *The Parlement* are discussed. See also n. 2111 below. As is frequently the case in folkloristic accounts of figures of this sort, Heinrich Zimmer's association of the Green Knight with Death (*The King and the Corpse* [6], pp. 67ff.) depends on the use of general analogues which smooth away particularities that conflict with it and advances disputable interpretations of some of our poem's details, e.g., his account (pp. 70–71) of the ring offered by the lady to Sir Gawain: contrast Silverstein, "Sir Gawain in a Dilemma" [7], pp. 8–10, 14–15.

140 *etayn* See n. 1773 below.

155 *blaunner* From OFr *blanc* and *neir*, AN **blaunc-ner* = ermine: see Gollancz and Davis. This could have produced the ME variants *blaundenere*, *blaundemere*, and *Gawain*, 856, *blaunmer*.

157 *hewe* The MS reading *grene* (see textual note) leaves the second half-line without an alliteration, which Davis seeks to rectify by omitting it and shifting the caesura to precede *hose*, but this makes a rather limping line. The present emendation *hewe* assumes that a word has been lost from the text and with Davis that the here discarded *grene* was originally a gloss.

It produces a four-stress, four-alliteration line, of which there are some forty other examples in the poem.

160 *scholes* Since he has not come for fighting, the Green Knight is riding in his hose without steel sabatons, hence is shoeless, like other medieval knights engaged on peaceful missions. See Emerson, in *MLN* 36 (1921):212; Cecily Clark, in *RES*, n.s. 6 (1955):174–77; and Marjorie Rigby, in *RES*, n.s. 7 (1956):173–74.

165 *to tor for to telle* An alliterative formula, possibly of Scandinavian origin (TG). But the theme of inexpressibility occurs frequently in the romances and goes back ultimately to Vergil, *Aeneid*, vi. 625–27, and the ancients. Cf. 130–31, 1008–9, and notes.

186 *capados* Evidently a kind of cape with a hood, fastened under the chin. The name has been derived from OFr *cap à dos* and from *Capadoce*, i.e., Cappadocia, it being supposed that the earlier form of the garment was made of Cappadocian leather. See among others G. L. Hamilton, in *MP* 5 (1908):365–76, esp. 368–69, which also cites *cappe de huse* from Russell's *Boke of Nurture*, and quotes the General Wardrobe accounts of 1348: *capedehustes Regis*, i.e., the "kyngez capados."

209 "A cruel axe to describe in words, if anyone could (describe it)."

224 *word þat he warp* A frequently used Middle English alliterative phrase going back to OE poetry: Oakden [5] 2:308.

246–47 Gollancz interprets this as "some from fear and others from courtesy," but Davis is surely right in taking *al* and *sum* as adverbs and reading, "I think it was not entirely owing to fear, but partly out of courtesy." The words are ironic; the guests were scared stiff!

267 *in fere* "In (martial) array." See *MED*, *fēre* n. (5), and Cawley and Waldron. TG reads this as probably "in company," i.e., with a company of fighting men, from OE *gefēra*.

288 *giserne* Technically a long-shafted battle-axe or halberd, with a knifelike point rising from the blade: see *MED*; and Godefroy and Tobler-Lommatzsch, *gisarme*, *guisarme*. No doubt it here means simply battle-axe, as do *axe*, *denes axe*, and *sparþe*, used elsewhere in the poem to support the alliteration.

293 *quitclayme* A law term. For its significance see n. 298.

294 *stonde* The earliest examples of this verb in *OED* (*stand*, 52 a and b) meaning "stand and take (a blow) from (someone)," in a phrase expressing the person withstood, not by a possessive adjective with the direct object ("stand his stroke") but, as here, in the dative (*stonde hym a strok*), are later than in *Gawain*, i.e., mid fifteenth century and after, e.g., Holland, *Howlat*, ca. 1450, and Malory, *Arthur*, 1470–85. Cf. l. 2286.

295 *diʒt me þe dom* Cf. Chaucer, *Troilus*, iv. 1188: "There as þe dom of mynos wolde it dyghte," and *Apology for Lollard Doctrine*, 60: "A iuge is said for he ditiþ right to þe peple"; the latter in *MED*, *dight*, 4a. See n. 298.

296 *barlay* Identified with *barley*, used in children's games to stake a claim by right of first choice (I. and P. Opie, *The Lore and Language of Schoolchildren* [Oxford, 1959], pp. 135, 146–49; and *EDD*); and for its origin variously related to Fr *par loi*, *par lei*, to *bailler* contaminated with "parley," and to a term in seventeenth-century English verse said to mean "blow" (White, in *Neophilologus* 37:114–15). The meaning here may be "(when I claim) my turn" (Davis).

298 *A twelmonyth and a day* I.e., until the same day next year, a time span widespread in fictional compacts, but also common, as Davis observes, in legal agreements, thus continuing the legal touch established by *quit-clayme*, 293, the stranger's appeal to Arthur as judge, 295, and Sir Gawain's bid to turn the peers into an *ad hoc* royal advisory council, 347; and supporting the entire concern for *justitia* and *fides*, the keeping of promises and agreements, on which the central dilemma of the poem will later turn. See nn. 456, 651–53, 1112, and 2508–14 below.

301ff. For the sources and analogues of the challenge, especially its relations with the Carados episode in the French *Continuations* of the *Perceval*, and among those particularly the 1530 prose, see the introduction above, p. 2.

304 *runischly* Cf. 457; *Patience*, 191; *Purity*, 1545; and as *renischche*, *renyschly*, see *Purity*, 96 and 1724, and *The Wars of Alexander*, where it appears four times. In some of those contexts the word may signify "strange," but here "fierce, rough, ferocious" would seem to be the primary meaning. Elsewhere *roi(g)nous*, meaning "scurvy, coarse," occurs, which Davis takes to be of Romance origin and different from *runisch*. Cf. Gollancz.

319 *wroth as wynde* See Oakden 2:312 and 361, to which add stanzaic *Morte Arthur* [10], 1144 and note, and Onions, in *N & Q* 146 (1924):244.

323 *nys* Cf. 358. In the Carados episode in all the versions of *The First Continuation* Sir Kay calls *fol* any knight who would accept the head-chopping challenge.

336–37 About the meaning of the former of these lines the translators are ambiguous and the commentators disagree, raising questions that turn on the antecedent of *hys*, whether it be Arthur or the giant, and whether *dintez* means real blows or practice strokes. If we choose the former alternative for *hys* (i.e., Arthur's) we might render: "no more daunted or dismayed by King Arthur's mighty (practice) strokes than if any knight at table had simply brought him a drink of wine." (Gollancz suggests that we might have expected *mintez* instead of *dintez* here; cf. 2345, 2350, and 2352.) Such a reading is dramatically appropriate and forms a kind of parallel to the Green Chapel scene, 2200–2211, where Sir Gawain fails to be daunted by the giant's axe grinding. A viable alternative is to take *dintez*, plural, as a scribal error for *dinte*, singular, as emended in the present text, and render: "because of the mighty blow he [the giant] was about to receive."

366–71 Though rulers may bless their ambassadors when these set out (implying royal command or consent), as does Charlemagne in *The Song of Roland*, such formality does not generally appear in Arthurian romance at the beginning of quest or adventure. *Libeaus desconus* (ed. Kaluza [Altengl. Bibl., Bd. 5 (1890)], pp. 17–18), like *Gawain*, is an exception. (See also Chrétien's *Erec*, where the queen blesses Eric as he starts out in pursuit of the knight and dwarf who have insulted her.) In actuality a knight might seek the blessing of his king to engage in single combat before a battle with an enemy challenger: George Neilson, *Trial by Combat* (Glasgow, 1890), pp. 211–12 (Halidon Hill, A.D. 1333). The words *his hert and his honde schulde hardi be* seem to be unique with *Gawain* in a context like this, and have failed to provoke the commentator's notice. *MED*, *hond*, 6(a), and *herte*, 2b(b), lists but does not isolate "heart and hand," as meaning "wish and deed, thought and deed," and as "contrasting or combining . . . internal feeling and external expression," and fails to mention *Gawain*. Cf. *OED*: "With will and execution; readily, willingly"—its earliest citation being from the Earl of Surrey, sixteenth century. The phrase in fact represents a topos, hitherto also unobserved, which goes back to ancient Latin poetry, draws the Bible in a special way into its orbit, spreads into medieval epic and romance, and still continues to our day. The story is too complex for a note beyond the recording of some references: *animo manuque* in Ovid, *Metamorphoses* vii. 347; Vergil, *Aeneid* xii.348; *Ilias latina*, 711; Albertus Stadensis, *Troilus* iv.265 (cf. iv.298 and v.731–32). To these may be added instances of the military variant *armis animisque* listed in E. von Wölfflin, *Ausgewahlte Schriften* (Leipzig, 1933), chap. 6, p. 254. In the Bible the formula occurs in Lamentations 3:41, with a difference in meaning which adds the notions of supplication and dependence, and affects such vernacular pieces as Conrad von Wurzburg, *Trojanische Krieg*, 17766; Gottfried von Strassburg, *Tristan*, 4862; *Li vers de le mort*, ed. Windahl (Lund, 1887), p. 253; Amadis de Gaula, *Los libros de caballerias españoles*, ed. Buenida (Madrid, 1960), p. 927a; and Petrarch, Sonnet 25, l. 6. Connected also is the phrase *cuer et cors*, very frequent in French chivalric literature, e.g., Watriquet de Couvin, *Le dis de l'arbre royal*, 108–10 (ed. Scheler [Brussels,

1868], p. 86) and *Comment li peres enseigne au filz*, 110 (ed. Scheler, p. 121); and *cors et corages*: Jean de Meun, *L'art de chevalerie*, chap. 2 (ed. Robert, SATF [1897], p. 6), and Jean Priorat, *Li abregiance de l'ordre de chevalerie*, i.2, 314–18 (ed. Robert, SATF [1897], p. 11), going back to Vegetius, 1.2. (A further variant, to swear with hand on heart, is probably not related originally to the present topos: see DuCange 4:459, col. 3.) For Middle English, to the instances in *MED*, all of the fifteenth century except the *Ormulum*'s must be added the stanzaic *Morte Arthur*, 2838, 3564, but especially 2942–43: Sir Gawain "was full thro / To do batayle with herte and hande"; *Rowlande and Sir Ottuel*, 1004 (ed. Herrtage, EETS ES, no. 35, p. 86), referring to the Saracens "þat hardy were of herte & hande"; and *The Avowis of Alexander*, 2688, describing Porrus as "hardy also of hart and hand" (*The Buik of Alexander* [*10*], 2:175). In *Mum and the Sothsegger* [*10*], 432, the satire depends on its transformation of what is by now a readily recognizable commonplace.

372–74 The turn here in the king's remarks from earnestness to jest recalls Wace's *Brut* [*6*], 9337–44, where Arthur begins a battle by calling for Mary's aid and cutting down an enemy with the "first stroke": "'Miens est,' dist il, 'li premiers cous,'" and then he continues jokingly, "'A cestui ai sun luier sous'"—"'I've paid this fellow's lodgings for the night.'" (Laȝamon [*6*], 10594–600 [Madden 21231–44], keeps the passage but loses the joke.) Cf. the Vulgate *Merlin* [*6*], II, 390, ll. 42–391, line 3. For the theme of the "first stroke," see *La chanson de Roland*, ed. Bedier, II, 316.

379–81, 401–8 To know each other's name is necessary to the agreement between these two adversaries, but it is also a *donné* of the romances, which make a point of the etiquette of naming. Sir Gawain, as here, is normally straightforward and gives his name, when asked, at once. Lancelot sometimes appears in disguise with a temporary *nom de guerre*. For the Green Knight such disguise and the postponement of his actual naming (2445) intensifies mystery and suspense. In Lancelot's case the point involves another romance convention, that a knight is recognized by his deeds. That principle later permits the game of ambiguity ("You're Gawain, you're not Gawain") between hero and hostess at Hautdesert (1293, 1481), hero and giant at the Green Chapel (2270).

405 *Gawan þe hende* For the epithet, unalliterated in the second half-line, see n. 5 above.

409 *frayst my fare* Usually read as a conventional phrase for "call on me," signifying more precisely either "ask how I am getting on" (Gollancz) or "see what I will do" (Davis). But it can also mean "try my entertainment," thus fitting with the moment's witty encounter, and producing perhaps an intended *double entendre*.

423 *ly3tly ly3t* This *double entendre* (*traductio*) depends on the contrast between light and heavy. The axe is heavy, it cuts through bones and flesh and bites into the ground. *Ly3tly* (OE *lĕ[o]htlīce*), "lightly, swiftly, easily," takes on color from *ly3t* (OE *līhtan*), "to come down, land on." The words thus signify "descend lightly," and/or "land landingly," the latter lending support to the weight of the fall. Hence *ly3tly* suggests both "lightly" and "heavily" together, as it were. The phrase is unique with *Gawain* in the surviving alliterative poetry of the time.

425 *scade* Davis emends to *schade*, but see McLaughlin, p. 122, and the introduction above, p. 27.

428 It has been noted that in the folklore background of this episode the kicking of the head by the spectators is an attempt to keep it from rejoining its body, and it does so join the body in the Long version of *The First Continuation* and the 1530 prose, though the kicking itself does not appear in any of the known texts of that romance. See n. 436–39.

435 Cf. 2060. Davis quotes *The Wars of Alexander*, 778: "Stridis into stelebowe, stertis apon loft."

436–39 In the Mixed and Short versions of *The First Continuation* (but in neither the Long nor the 1530 prose) the decapitated knight holds head in hand by the hair and behaves as if in normal health: ed. Roach, 1:92, ll. 3406–9, and 3.1:148, ll. 2310–13, and 147, ll. 2316–19.

440 *bluk* Onions and TG emend to *bulk*, ON *búlki*, "heap, cargo," but cf. Morris and also Gollancz, which relates *bluk* to OFr *bloc*, and see the vocabulary below.

456 *recreaunt* Another of the legal terms used by the Green Knight to make precise the compact: cf. n. 298. Usually read by the editors in its general sense "coward," *recreaunt* in fact has a number of juridical meanings, among them "one who acknowledges defeat in judicial combat, one who is in default": see DuCange, *recredere*, especially VII, 59a ad fin.; Godefroy, *recreant*; and Latham, *recreantia* and *recredentia*, "bail, security," and *recredo*, "pledge, give security for delivery of." *OED, recreant* B2, notes its appearance in the early legal writers Bracton and Glanville and cites the later Levins, which gives the gloss *perfidus*, i.e., one who breaks his word. See also W. von Wartburg, *Französisches Etymologisches Wörterbuch*, 2.2 (1946):1305a, which records *récréant = parjure* (thirteenth century).

460 The "fairy formula" of this disappearance is in keeping with the *merveille* just experienced by the court. Waldron [2] cites *Sir Orfeo*, 288 (ed. Bliss, Oxford, 1954): "No never he nist whider thai bicome," and 296: "Ac never he nist whider thai wolde."

477   A play on words between the statement's literal meaning and its proverbial use to signify "be finished with the matter." See Whiting [*12*], A 251. Davis suggests that *gaynly*, 476, draws attention to the figure. We might thus render it "with a pretty turn," signifying that Arthur is showing off by his manner the aptness of his *jeu d'esprit*.

480   *bi trwe tytel*   "By the authority of its visible presence." This is a kind of legal phrase meaning "the legitimate evidence by which a claim is substantiated": *OED*, *title*, 6, and *true*, 4c. See also 626, and cf. *Beowulf*, 833, where Grendel's arm is fixed on the wall as a *tacen sweotol* of the protagonist's heroic deed.

483   *double*   See n. 61.
      as derrest my3t falle   "In the noblest fashion."

495–535   For the significance to the plot of these verses on the passage of the seasons, the growing apprehension they produce and their contemporary poetic and thematic associations, see the introduction above, p. 6f., and Silverstein, "The Art of Sir Gawain" [7].

496–99   The aphorisms here are discussed in "The Art of Sir Gawain," pp. 259ff., and in the introduction above, p. 7. *Bot þa3 þe ende be heuy* reflects Proverbs 14:13, and *þe forme to þe fynisment foldez ful selden* translates directly a verse from Cato's *Distichs*, i.18. The source of a third aphoristic verse, *For þa3 men ben mery in mynde quen þay han mayn drynk*, is hard to find. The Latin and vernacular collections record nothing strictly like it: see, e.g. Walther *Sprichwörter* [8], esp. nos. 4574 (cf. Psalm 103:15: "vinum laetificat animam"), 4575, 4576a, 23457, and in view of our hero's ominous prospects arising from a "game," no. 6423, which has a special sting in its tail: "Dum bibitur vinum, dum luditur ante caminum, / Tunc surgunt risus, stultis tunc est paradisus." An exact Latin parallel, however, from ancient poetry is recorded by the fourth-century compiler Nonius Marcellus, who was certainly known in the earlier Middle Ages and in the fifteenth century and has recently been found in thirteenth-century annotations to the lexicographer Papias (DuCange, *Ebriolatus*, and Nonius, ed. Onions [Oxford, 1895], p. 132): "Ebriolati mentem hilariam accipiunt." See R. and M. Rous, in *Medieval Scribes, Manuscripts & Libraries, Essays Presented to N. R. Ker*, ed. Parkes and Watson (London, 1978), pp. 354–55. In the Carados incident the 1530 prose *Perceval* also "moralizes" the turn from joy to sorrow, though not with a group of readily recognizable proverbs, as here. See nn. 674ff. and 682–83 below.

503   *flesch, fysche*   A play on the two meanings of *flesch*—meat, body (as opposed to spirit)—producing an ambiguity which permits the joking contrast with *fysche*.

527–28   Cf. *Sir Tristrem* [*10*], 12–19, p. 1: "þis semely somers day, / In winter it is nouȝt sen; / Þis greues waxen al gray, / þat in her time were grene. / So dos þis world, y say. . . ." But for *graye* as verb *OED* and *MED* cite only this instance in *Gawain*, and *OED* gives no further occurrence until 1618.

529   *And þus ȝirnez þe ȝere in ȝisterdayez mony*   The theme of the quick passage of life to death, as if from morning to night, and of the transformation of the living present into so many yesterdays, is discussed in Silverstein, "The Art of Sir Gawain," citing a contemporary poem of the Vernon MS (Silverstein, *Medieval English Lyrics* [*10*], no. 47, pp. 68–71). To that discussion may be added two observations: first, that the theme is based in part on Psalm 89:4 (90:4): "quia mille anni in oculis tuis sicut dies hesterna"; and second, that in Innocent III's use of the passage in the *De miseria humanae conditionis*, or *De contemptu mundi* (I, xxiii), he changes the words so that it is not God (*oculis tuis*) who sees the world's present go hurrying by into yesterday, but the man about to die: "Mille anni *ante oculos morientis* sicut dies hesterna." This lends the theme a special poignancy for Sir Gawain. See the introduction above, p. 6f.

530   The introduction by Day to Gollancz, p. xvii, notes the connection with *The Wars of Alexander* both for the clause *as þe worlde askez* and for association of the course from spring to winter with the turn from human weal to woe: "And eftir wele comys wa, for so þe werd askis."

536   *Al Hal Day*   November 1, All Saints' Day, the time for King Arthur's autumn high court, hence suitable as the setting for the start of a winter adventure (see n. 37 above). Sir Gawain actually departs, 566, on November 2, All Souls', the day when the faithful dead were commemorated, and that may seem appropriate in a particular sense, given Sir Gawain's negative expectations. Among the various tearful departures in French romance, the beginning of Sir Gawain's Grail adventure in *The First Continuation* is noteworthy: "Adont pleurent li cevalier, / Li vaslet et li escuier / Et la roïne et les puceles, / Les dames et les demoiseles; / Molt par demainent grant doleur / Por le bon neveu leur signeur, / Ne sevent dire ne penser / En quel terre il en doit aler. / Lors oire mesire Gavains, / Cil remest mors entre leur mains. / *A cest mot doit dire cascuns / Une Paternostre as defuns*" (ed. Roach, 3.1:452, ll. 7025–36; cf. 2:511–12; MSS *TVD*, 1:353, omit the last two lines).

551–55   For all these knights see Flutre, West, and Ackerman [*12*].

552   *Sir Doddinal de Sauage*   Dodinal (Dodinel, Dodineals, Dodineau, Dodinax, Dodinas, etc.) li Salvage in the French and English romances. Printed by all the editors of *Gawain* from Madden to Moorman as *Dod-*

dinaual de Sauage, a form not only unique in either language, but also barbarous and wrong. In fact, the MS originally seems to have read what looks like *doddinas*, then the scribe wrote *n* over the *s* and added *al*, evidently intending *doddinal*, but failed to cancel the first *na*, thus leaving the erroneous *doddinanal* (not *doddinaual*, n and u often being indistinguishable in the MS). This suggests that the scribe may have had two variant copy texts before him, and we can read equally *Doddinas* or *Doddinal*. The *de* would better be *þe* but is left unaltered, since the MS is clear on the point, there are parallels elsewhere of *de* for *þe*, and *de* supports the line's alliteration.

553 *Lucan þe gode*   This characterization of Lucan is rare. *Claris et Laris*, 14007, calls him "le bon poigneor," and *The First Continuation* (Long version, 5443–44, ed. Roach and Ivy, 2:159) "Lucans li boteillier, / Qui molt estoit bons chevalier," but these phrases are not sufficiently distinctive. For the form of the epithet, unalliterated and in the second half-line, see n. 5 above.

564–65   Cf. the 1530 prose *Perceval*, folio lxxix, col. 1, where king and barons sigh for Carados's trouble: "mais Carados nen prent soussy disant quil en actendra la fortune." The aphoristic lines themselves, which are not listed in Whiting, may reflect, perhaps through some current uses, *Aeneid* v.709–10: "Nate dea, quo fata trahunt retrahuntur sequamur; / Quicquid erit, superanda fortuna ferendo est." Cf. *Aeneid* xii.677: "Quo deus et quo dura vocat fortuna, sequamur," where *dura* suggests *Gawain's derf*. Medieval examples of these verses as proverbs are listed in Walther, nos. 9863, 25276, 25624, 25624a, 25628, 25678, 25724a, 28054b. The difference between Carados's situation and Sir Gawain's is that the former leaves the protagonist at home until the antagonist returns, hence he can *await* what fortune brings; whereas Sir Gawain must actively *seek out* his adversary, hence *follow* fortune: cf. the rather parallel difference as between Chaucer's Wife of Bath's Tale and Gower's Tale of Florent. See Silverstein, "Wife of Bath and the Rhetoric of Enchantment, or How to Make a Hero See in the Dark," *MP* 58 (1961):153–73, esp. 165. For *dere* in combination with *derf* Davis suggests "dear, pleasant," or, alternatively, "fierce, cruel" (from OE *dēor*), but prefers the former as making up an inclusive phrase of a common type, e.g., "young and old," "good and bad" (cf. *prospera adversave*). *Dere* can also mean "high, noble" (see 2465), thus giving the line a rather Senecan ring ("Our destinies harsh and high"). The verb *fonden* is ambiguous, having a range of nuances in Middle English. *MED* lists this instance as signifying "to subject [something] to testing or examination." The Latin parallels indicate that to this may be added a richer content, i.e., "to pursue [adventures, etc.], to experience, to suffer." As to the grammar of the phrase, *destinées* is read by Davis (by implication) as a plural, *derf* and *dere* as modifying adjectives, but Gollancz's reading of these last two as substantives, with *destinées* as genitive singular, is adopted here, i.e., "destiny's bitter and sweet."

568–618 The arming of Sir Gawain. A regular convention of the Arthurian literature from Geoffrey of Monmouth on. As with Sir Gawain here on a rich red carpet, so is Erec formally armed in Chrétien on a *tapit* "Dessus l'image d'un liepart" (2634–35), and in *Perceval le Gallois*, ed. Poitvin, 3 (Mons, 1866):67, 11107–8: "Sour .1. cendal menu freté, / Ont monsigneur Gauvain armé." Characteristically our poet's detailed description of the armor is of his time, especially in the *sabatons*, the *aventail* on Sir Gawain's helmet, and in the trappings of the horse, *payttrure*, 601, and *couertor*, 602. In English, cf. King Arthur's arming in the alliterative *Morte Arthure*, 902ff., and especially in Robert Mannyng's earlier *Chronicle*, 10025–54, where the names for many of the parts are the same, though the hauberk is "wiþ plates y-burnuscht ful wel," but *Gawain*'s byrnie made "of byrȝt stel ryngez" alone. Our hero is thus covered, mail and plate, in fourteenth-century mixed armor. See also *Wynnere and Wastoure*, 111–18, and Lydgate's *Troy Book*, iii.44–108.

568 Cf. n. 77 and l. 858.

571 *Dubbed in a dublet* An obvious piece of wordplay (*traductio*) in an alliterated phrase not easily found elsewhere in the poetry of *Gawain*'s time.

572 *closed aloft* I.e., fastened on top, that is, at the neck.

574 *sabatonz* Steel shoes, but not broad-toed as *OED* describes them: see Brett, in *MLR* 22 (1927):453–54. An innovation of the early fourteenth century, they are first called by this name in English ca. 1330 in Mannyng's *Chronicle*, 10026, for Wace's *chauces de fer* in his *Brut*, 9275. See also Sir Gawain's *chauces de fer* in *The First Continuation* (Long version, 1028, ed. Roach and Ivy, 2:32). Such steel footwear ending in long "pikes" became normal with armor in the century. Armed as he is for combat, Sir Gawain wears his sabatons, in contrast to the Green Knight, who rode *scholes*, since he had not come to King Arthur's court for fighting: see n. 160 above.

597 *Gryngolet* Gringalet, the name frequently given to Sir Gawain's horse in the French romances, e.g., in Chrétien's *Erec*, the *Chevalier à l'épée* and *The First Continuation*, perhaps derived from an original like Welsh *Gwyngalet, "white-hard" (i.e., bony). See R. Bromwich, *Troiedd Ynys Prydein* (Cardiff, 1961), pp. civ–vii, and 106. The Vulgate *Merlin* (2:339–43) gives an account of how Sir Gawain got the horse from Clarions king of the Sesnes.

603–4 "And all was arrayed on red, nails brilliant gold, so that everything glittered," etc.

605ff. The helm. It is stapled for strength and padded against blows. The *auentayle*, a short cape of mail falling from helmet to shoulders as a protection for throat and neck is a feature of fourteenth-century armor: see G. L. Hamilton, in *MP* 3 (1905):541–46; B. White, in *Neophilologus* 37 (1953):113–14; and Sir James Mann, *European Arms and Armor* [9 Costumes] 1 :xxxv. To it is attached the *vrysoun* (OFr *horsoun*), 608, an embroidered silk band: Hamilton, in *MP* 5 (1908):371. The *cercle*, 615, worn around the upper part of the helmet, is a gold band studded with gems, in this case brown and shining diamonds; cf. Wace, *Brut*, 9285 and 9287; Laȝamon, 10550 (Madden 21143–44); and Mannyng's *Chronicle*, 10042.

610–13 *bryddez on semes, papiayez, Tortors* Birds among foliage, particularly parrots and turtledoves, often appear in medieval embroidery, manuscript borders, and elsewhere; Davis notes the covers of gold cups in *Purity*, 1464–66, "al bolled abof wyth braunches and leves, / Pyes and papejayes purtrayed withinne."

peruyng is here written for *peruynk*, "periwinkle." All editors previous to Davis read *pernyng*, "preening," i.e., a present participle modifying *papiayez*; but see his objections. Periwinkles, recognizable by their five-petaled blue flowers and opposed leaves, are frequent in illumination, their trailing stems being readily adaptable to foliated border designs.

trulofez Probably the "trew-loue-flour" (see *OED*, *true-love*, 4), as found, e.g., in *Emaré*, 125, 149, a romance related in other respects to the present passage; cf. 613 and 1382 here with *Emaré*, 118, "Seuen wynter hyt was yn makynge." For seven years (winters) as a conventional term for a long time, see the 1530 prose *Perceval*, "de si grande beaulte estoit Remplie [la belle Guimier] que se nature eust mis .vii. ans a la former"; and *OED*, *winter* 2, signifying, from OE, year. Cf. n. 1382.

618 *broun* The word means either "shining" (as in 426 above) or "brown"; if the former, then it is redundant here. For the latter see the London lapidary in J. Evans and M. Serjeantson, EETS, no. 190 (1933), p. 30, which says that diamonds from India "arne broun of colour & of violet."

619ff. Sir Gawain's shield *þat was of schyr goulez / Wyth þe pentangel depaynt of pure golde hwez*. Sir Gawain bears a variety of blazons in Arthurian literature, among them notably "argent, a canton gules" and (fifteenth–sixteenth century) "purpure, a double-headed eagle or, beaked and membered azure," but also a shield "de sinople a un aigle d'or," alternatively with a lion, also as in the alliterative *Morte Arthure*, 3869, with a "gryffone of golde" (cf. *The Awntyrs of Arthure*, 508–9). Sinople has been read by many as green, but that is a meaning it probably did not have until the later fourteenth century. In the earlier romances it normally signifies red, *gules* (see Godefroy [*12*], Tobler-Lommatzsch [*12*], and Brault, *Early Blazon* [9 Heraldry], p. 275); and in *Perlesvaus* [6], 784–85 and 1185–86 (1:56 and 71), Judas Maccabaeus's shield, which will become Sir Gawain's, is ".i. escu vermeill o avoit escrit .i. aigle d'or," the colors, or tinctures, being those in *Gawain*. As for the eagle, two manuscripts (O and P) of *Perlesvaus* give in its place *angle*, signifying either angel or angle (*angulum*); one may wonder whether such a reading suggested to a fertile mind like our poet's a connection with his particular angle, i.e., the pentangle. In any case, a pentangle as Sir Gawain's device, Madden long ago observed, is to be found nowhere else; nor has any attempt succeeded in associating it, or its supposed heraldic equivalent the mullet, with any contemporary circumstance or patron of the poet. The so-called Seal of Solomon, whether five- or six-pointed, appears in popular use and learned reference throughout the Middle Ages; it is found on churches and in the thirteenth century among seal designs: see W. de Gray Birch, *Seals* (New York and London, 1907), p. 191. But most of the survivals of special interest for *Gawain* originate, to an editor's frustration, well after its time, in the later fifteenth and the sixteenth to seventeenth centuries. They include such items as the Common Seal of the Carmelite Priory, Aberdeen, which carried a pentangle with the letters M A R I A between its points (Birch, p. 227); a pentangle ring with S A L V S like Lucian's Hygeia between the points, illustrated among "medieval" objects in Evans, *Magical Jewels*—but of the sixteenth century; and Pierius Valerianus, *Hieroglyphica*, lib. xlvii (Basle, 1556, folios 351–52) and Cornelius a Lapide, *Comment. in Apoc. s. Johannis* (Antwerp, 1662), p. 23, both of whom associate the device with Christ's Five Wounds on the Cross as in *Gawain*. (The present editor has witnessed a popular continuation of this association by an eighteenth-century devotional plaque in an Upper Austrian church commemorating a miraculous cure of the fever: cf. Erwin Richter, in *Mitteil. d. Anthrop. Gesellsch. in Wien* 88–89 [1959]:116–24.) As for the military use of the pentangle, Cornelius Agrippa (*De occulta philosophia*, III, xxxi, Leiden ed., 1531, p. 321), Pierius and Cornelius a Lapide, bringing together two passages from Lucian, associate the figure in ancient times with Antiochus Soter's victorious troops. In addition, Pierius and Cornelius refer to a Roman unit called *Propugnatores*, who bore the pentagram on their shields. That statement draws on the fourth- to fifth-century *Notitia dignitatum* [9 *Heraldry*] known in England, if C. E. Stevens's speculations are admissible, to Geoffrey of Monmouth and Giraldus Cambrensis in the twelfth and thirteenth centuries; Gelenius's reference (1552) to a MS newly recovered in his day "ex ultimis Britannis" may on this view be to a medieval copy. In the *Notitia* many units are listed as carrying on their *clipei* starlike devices with seven to twelve points; but none of the editors records a five-pointed version. MSS BN lat. 9661 and Bodl. Canon Misc. 378 have six points, and Madrid Res. 36 (Q. olim G. 129), which is now known to have been Pierius's source, is a copy of the Bodley text. See *Notitia*, eds. Basle 1552 (Gelenius), sig. i⁵; Venice 1593 (Panciroli), fol. 126; Leiden 1608 (Rhuardesius), fol. 127; Bonn 1839–53 (Böcking) 2:21*, fig. 9; and Berlin 1876 (Seeck), p. 119, no. 91. See also Stevens, "The Notitia Dignitatum in England," *Aspects of the N.D.*, ed. Goodburn and Bartholomew (British Archeol. Reports, Suppl. Series 15 [1976]), pp. 211–24; and for the MSS and their relations, I. G. Maier, in *Latomus* 27 (1968), esp. 99–102.

The word *pentangel* itself appears in English for the first time here in *Gawain* and not again until 1646 in Browne's *Pseudodoxia epidemica*, nor has its proper source previously been found. Medieval Latin usually names the figure, transliterating the Greek, *pentagon* or *pentagram*. *OED* derives *Gawain*'s word from GR *penta* + Engl *angle*, and adds that as designating the object used in magic it is "perhaps an accommodated form of *pentagle*, in origin a variant of PENTACLE." The independent instances of *pentacle*, as usually cited, are late, however, once again end of the fifteenth century and after, and its connection with OFr *pendacol*, *pentacol* ("something which hangs from the neck") is obscure. The fact is that L *pentangulus* had already appeared, perhaps a thirteenth-century neologism, in the dictionaries of Hugutio of Pisa and Giovanni Balbi, both widely known in England in the fourteenth century, and as It *pentangolo*, describing the human soul, in the *Convivio* (iv.7, ad fin.), probably drawn by Dante from Hugutio, who was his source in many lexical matters. Our poet's *pentangel* may thus be simply an Englishing of that word, now applied to the Solomonic figure. See "Sir Gawain in a Dilemma," p. 4, n. 14.

For other accounts of the shield, from which the present note differs, see especially Davis; J. R. Hulbert, in *MP* 13 (1915–16):721–30; R. H. Green, in *ELH* 29 (1962):121–39; and for the devices of Arthurian knights generally, Brault, *Early Blazon* [9], *passim*, and for Sir Gawain in particular pp. 40–42.

623 *And quy þe pentangel apendez to þat prynce* The account which follows in the poem of a design traditionally magical or mystical, but here used as a moral symbol standing for the hero's personal qualities, discloses something essential to the plot: that is why the poet is "in tent yow to telle" what it means "þof tary hyt [him] schulde." See the introduction above, and nn. 632ff. and 651–53 below. For an opposite view, which sees the meaning as marred by inconsistencies and largely irrelevant to the story, see Davis.

626 *In betoknyng of Trawþe* *Trawþe* = *fides*, both having by *Gawain*'s time a considerable range of meanings, spiritual and secular, one of them related to the *scutum fidei* in Ephesians 6:16. Another meaning particularly appropriate here refers to the virtue which makes a man keep his oaths and agreements and is the foundation of a knight's moral character, that he is just, and of the basic social duty of his order, that it maintain justice. The poet seems to have in mind Cicero, *De officiis*: "Fundamentum autem est iustitiae fides, id est dictorum conventorumque constantia et veritas." (Cf. the "etymology" in *De republica*, IV, preserved by Nonius Marcellus, I, 24M, 12–14, ed. Onions, p. 30, which may be rendered thus: "*Fides* seems to me to get its very name from the fact that what is said is done—*cum fit quod dicitur.*") This reading of *Trawþe*, confirmed in various repetitions of the point throughout the poem and relevant as it is to the climax of the plot where Sir Gawain is tried to the limit in the keeping of a compact, is likewise appropriate to the last set of "fives" for which the pentangle is said to stand (see nn. 651–53 and 653 below), all of them referable to the parts of justice, as they descended, variously, from Cicero and Macrobius, and were lodged in and developed by medieval compends like the *Moralium dogma philosophorum* [8] attributed to Guillaume de Conches (twelfth century) and the moral sections of Brunetto Latini's *Tresor* [8] (thirteenth century), both well known in England in *Gawain*'s time. The famous attack on Gustav Ehrismann's Ciceronianism by Ernst Curtius ("The 'Chivalric System of the Virtues,'" in *European Literature and the Latin Middle Ages*, trans. Trask, Princeton/Bollingen paperback, 1973, pp. 519–37) calls attention to Ehrismann's oversimplification of the medieval development of moral psychology but is itself not free of fault, both historical and analytic. Among other matters Curtius's assertion that nothing about the *Moralium dogma* makes it appear suitable for a "mirror of knighthood" (p. 529) would seem to contradict the view of those medieval writers who quote it in their chivalric romances and of their contemporaries the scribes who include it and its dependent Brunetto Latini in MSS containing also Benoit's *Roman de Troie*, Wace's *Roman de Rou*, the *Roman d'Alexandre*, *La quest del saint graal*, and the *Erec* and the *Cligés* of Chrétien. See n. 653 below and Silverstein, "Sir Gawain in a Dilemma" [7], pp. 2–4 and nn. 4, 12, 13.

    bi tytle þat hit habbez "Rightly," because of its character and tradition. See n. 480 above.

628–30 *vche lyne vmbelappez and loukez in oþer / And ayquere hit is endelez* I.e., it is made by a single thread or filament, as it were, drawn alternately over and under and having no beginning or end. As for the term *þe endeles knot*, which the poet assures us was used for the figure by the English everywhere, no single instance other than his own survives from his time. The Middle Ages knew the Gordian knot, the Herculean knot and the *nodus Salamonis*, as well as what were called lovers' knots. In Italy, Dante and Forese (*Rime*, lxxiv, 8–10, and lxxv. 1) refer to *il nodo (di) Salamone*, no doubt using the term metaphorically for a difficulty hard to unravel. It is also used between 1361 and 1389 for a decoration on clothing and on a gold cup, as recorded in Pietro Sella, *Glossario latino italiano* (Studi e testi, no. 109 [Città del Vaticano, 1944]), pp. 449, 567, under *pluviale*; and Matteo Villani, *Istorie*, 3:53 (Firenze: Giunti, 1581, p. 188), calls *un nodo di Salamone* the pendant or brooch worn by a member of a society called, from that circumstance, the *Compagnia del nodo*, founded in 1352. The great Italian dictionaries, including the della Crusca, all of which draw on Filippo Baldinucci, *Vocabolario toscano* (1681), call it, in language of interest for *Gawain*, "Vn certo lavoro . . . a guisa di nodo, di cui non apparisce nè il capo nè il fine." But there is no evidence in their medieval sources connecting it specifically with the pentangle; and Villani's context suggests that his nodo di Salamone is seen as a lovers' knot, *il nodo del [fraternale] amore*.

632ff. The meaning of the shield, Sir Gawain's virtues. He is virtuous in five ways, each way in five respects; and of these ways the first four concern his five senses, his five fingers, Christ's Five Wounds, and the Virgin's Five Joys. For the five senses, see R. W. Ackerman, in *Anglia* 76 (1958): 254–65; for the five fingers, R. H. Green, in *ELH* 29 (1962): 134, referring to Joannes de sancto Geminiano, who allegorizes them as five moral virtues; and for both, but with a strong caveat, Davis, nn. 640 and 641. The Five Wounds and the Five (Seven, Fifteen) Joys are frequently the subjects of medieval lyric and devotion. See also nn. 651–53 and 653 below.

632–33 *ay faythful . . . , and as golde pured* An ancient commonplace for the testing and fining of virtue, e.g., Ovid, *Tristia*, i.5, 25: "Scilicet ut fulvum spectatur in ignibus aurum / Tempore sic duro est inspicienda fides"; and Hugo Sotovagina, archdeacon of York (twelfth century): "Vasa probat figuli fornax, ignis probat aurum; / Iustos atque probos vita fidesque probat" (ed. Wright, *The Anglo-Latin Satirical Poets and Epigrammatists of the Twelfth Century* (Rolls Series [1872] 2:222). See also Walther, nos. 31249b and 32921, *et passim*; *Ayenbite of Inwyt* [10], p. 106; and the fifteenth-century Scots poem *Ratis Raving*: "Fore men are prewyt be ther wertew3 / As goldsmyth gold in furnas doi3" (ed. Lumly, EETS, no. 43, p. 101).

636 *nwe* Probably not a newly assumed blazon but newly made or painted, as Davis suggests. The point is paralleled in the 1530 prose *Perceval*, folio cxlv, col. 2: on leaving the castle of Beaurepaire Perceval "prent vng escu de gueulles quil auoit nouellement faict faire." See also *The Second Continuation* in verse, ed. Roach, 4:157 [6].

649–50 The image of the Virgin on the inside of the shield reflects a traditional association of her figure with King Arthur that begins with Nennius (chap. 56) and continues especially with the account of Arthur's shield in Geoffrey of Monmouth (ed. Hammer, ix.2; ed. Griscom, ix.4) and his followers. Closely parallel to *Gawain*, as Gollancz observes, is Holkot, *In librum Sapientiae*, lectio 35: "In historia britonum scribitur de Archturo rege quod in interiori parte scuti sui ymaginem virginis gloriose depictum habuit quam quotiens in bello fatigatus aspexit spem recuperauit et vires." A Middle English sermon (EETS, no. 209, pp. 325–26) quotes Holkot in detail.

651–53 The fifth of the sets of five, whose significance has been discussed often, comprises a group of five chivalric virtues, the names for which occur, with the exception of *Clannes*, everywhere in the romances. Gollancz cites *Franchise, Pitié, Largesce, Cortoisie, Compaignie*, and others from the *Roman de la rose* (10422–23) but they do not include *Clannes* (see next note) and in any case make up only a small part of a long and miscellaneous list. The present editor's "Sir Gawain in a Dilemma" [7] argues that the five here in *Gawain* represent the parts of justice, ultimately deriving from Cicero and Macrobius, whose terms are translated by two medieval adaptations—the French version of the *Moralium dogma philosophorum* [8] and Brunetto Latini's *Tresor* [8]—into the French names which the poet here uses, some unchanged, others in their English equivalents. In Latin those parts are, with variations arising from differences in their ancient sources, *liberalitas* (*benevolentia*), *amicitia, innocentia, humanitas* (*affectus*), and *pietas* (*misericordia*); in Brunetto Latini and the vernacular version of the *Moralium dogma* their French equivalents are *franchise, compaignie, innocence, cortoisie*, and *pitiez*: cf. *Gawain*'s *Fraunchyse, Felaȝschip, Clannes, Cortaysye, Pité*. Even Sir Gawain's trust in Christ's Five Wounds and the Five Joys of the Virgin, seen by some as a reference to the theological virtues, might be included under *religio* and *observantia*, which likewise are parts of justice. See n. 626 above.

653 *Clannes* Davis observes that its equivalent is not listed among the virtues of the "baronage of Love" in the *Roman de la rose*, which Gollancz had supposed the *Gawain* poet had in mind here. Davis adds that in Middle English *clannes*, which meant not simply "chastity" but "sinlessness, innocence" generally, glosses *honestas, mundicia, puritas, sinceritas* in the *Catholicum anglicum*. But that, while undeniably so, is to lose some definition by taking the term in isolation from the others in the passage. It can also be a translation of L *innocentia*, OFr *innocence*, one of the parts of justice, which goes back to Cicero, *Tusculanae disputationes*, III.8, 16: "nam est innocentia adfectio talis animi, quae noceat nemini," and V.14, 41: "innocens is dicitur, non qui leviter nocet, sed qui nihil nocet," and which, with psychological intensification, the *Moralium dogma* [8] defines thus: "Innocentia est puritas animi *omnem iniurie illationem abhorrens*" (p. 25); cf. the French, p. 126: "Innocence est vne uertuz de pur coraige *qui doubte a faire toutes torconneries*"; and Brunetto Latini, *Tresor*, II.c, 1, p. 285: "Innocense est purete de corage *ki het a faire tous torsfais*." *Clannes* is a virtue not easily found attributed to Sir Gawain in the romances, certainly not if it is read as signifying chastity (for he has had many loves, as he confesses in a version of *The First Continuation*), but in the 1530 prose *Perceval* (folio xlviiᵛ, col. 1) Sir Gawain's squire says of him that "de tout vice est nect innocent et immacule: *cest celluy qui ne pourroit endurer felonnie ne mechan-*

cete," thus not only pairing *innocent* with *nect, immacule* (cf. English *clene, clannes*), but also giving us another vernacular version of the definition of *innocentia* in the *Moralium dogma philosophorum*. That around the middle of the fourteenth century this particular virtue was known in England as Sir Gawain's is witnessed importantly by *The Parlement of the Thre Ages*, in a phrase, hitherto unremarked, occurring in an account of King Arthur allegedly based on Languyon's *Voeux de paon*; it speaks (475) of Sir Gawain the good "that neuer gome harmede," which means of course that he is *innocens*. Since none of this is found in Languyon its appearance here is patently based on the English author's wider reading in the Arthurian romances, where he found the *Moralium dogma*'s *innocentia* applied as in the 1530 *Perceval* to the character of Sir Gawain. We may add that the very presence in *Gawain* of *clannes* as one of the five virtues supports further the argument that together they represent the parts of justice. See n. 2508–14 below.

656–61 The intertwined and boundless order of these virtues in Sir Gawain is symbolized by the form of the pentangle. Cf. 628–30 and note.

674ff and esp. 682–83 At this juncture in the Carados episode the 1530 prose moralizes on how a piece of foolish pleasantry can bring an end to joy: "O que malheureux est qui par sa couppe ou par une folle plaisance mect tant de monde en dolleur et en peine; et en le fin le plaisir seul est en cent tormens conuerti" (fol. lxxix, col. 1). Davis (n. 674ff.) quotes a lament in *La chevalier à l'épée*, 160–63.

681 *angardez* Genitive of the noun *angard(e)*, *angart*, from OFr *angarde*, "vanguard," but also "height, observation post, high place for advanced defense": see Godefroy and Tobler-Lommatzsch. Here in effect an adjective, "overweening, vainglorious, arrogant." How the English moral-psychological significance arose out of the topographical meanings in French is unclear, but the transformation would perhaps have been aided by ME *overgart*, "arrogance." See Brett, in *MLR* 7 (1913): 160–62; *OED*, *overgart*; and Gollancz and Davis.

684–88 Cf. the 1530 prose *Perceval*, folio cxxi, col. 1, as Gawain rides out to avenge an unknown knight's death: "atant print conge & sen part q'l ne veult en nulle maniere demeurer pour priere quon luy saiche faire . . . demeurent tous en grand douleur pour lamour du cheuallier Gauuain. . . ."

690 See nn. 26, 31, and 2521–23. This is a convention also of the French romances ("com l'estoire le reconte," "Si com raconte l'escripture," "Qui cest rice romans dira") and not necessarily a reference to a particular *bok*.

691ff. Sir Gawain's journey is a mixture of romance and reality typical of the poem. Beginning at a mythical Camelot set somewhere in the south-west, it goes northward to North Wales, then with the islands of Anglesey (Anglesey itself, Holy Island, Puffin Island, etc.) on the left turns east along the coast, fording the Conway and the Clwyd (to whose sea promontories "þe fordez by þe forlondez" may refer), crosses the River Dee into Wirral somewhere between Chester and the estuary, and finally ends at the fictional castle of Hautdesert. TG cites a similar journey by Giraldus Cambrensis through North Wales, with a crossing, however, below Chester (*Itinerarium Kambriae*, in *Opera*, ed. Dimock, Rolls Ser., 6 [1868]:136–39), and this may have been the regular medieval route. More recently Dodgson (in *Early English and Norse Studies Presented to Hugh Smith* [London, 1963], pp. 19–25) has proposed that the Dee crossing was at its mouth from the Point of Air ("þe forlondez") in Flintshire by way of Hilbre Island to the top of the Wirral peninsula near West Kirby, a point at which a crossing would normally not be feasible. But the legend of a miraculous crossing as of the Red Sea connected with Werburgh of Chester was known in the area, and West Kirby may be "þe Holy Hede" here intended by an association of such a form of its name as Kerkby with the Kaerkeby = Castrum Cuby or Caer Gybi which was the Welsh for Holyhead in Anglesey. As for the direction of the journey after Wirral, Madden suggests, and TG agrees, that it goes northward into Cumberland and that the forest in 741ff. is Inglewood. More recent opinion seems to favor a journey eastward ending in northern Staffordshire: see n. 2163–84 below. But topographical legends linking the story with Cumberland and Westmorland (Cumbria) still survive: e.g., G. R. Phillips, in *Country Life*, 13 March 1975, pp. 662–63. For the connection with the question of authorship, see the introduction above, p. 17. As to the danger, loneliness, discomfort, and want which our poet dwells on (691–762) as being Sir Gawain's lot, they illustrate what Cicero and his medieval pendants say of the man who wishes to act justly: "Nemo enim iustus esse potest qui mortem, qui exilium, qui dolorem, qui egestatem timet . . .": *De officiis*, ii. 11, 38; cf. *Moralium dogma* [8], pp. 12, 106, 107; found also in Brunetto Latini. For the knight and justice see nn. 626, 651–53, 653, 2508–14.

691 *Logres* The French form of Welsh Lloegyr (L Loegria), the name of King Arthur's kingdom south of the Humber. Geoffrey of Monmouth (ed. Griscom, ii.1; ed. Hammer, ii.2) says it was named after Locrine, eldest son and heir to British Brutus.

696 Cf. *Perlesvaus*, I, 30, as King Arthur starts his quest: "Dame, fet il, ge n'avré compeignie se Dieu non." See also *The Second Continuation*, 23850, and the 1530 prose, folio cxlviii, col. 2, where the hermit "se leua sans atarger car seruiteur nauoit ne clerc ne compaigniee fors que dieu."

701 *þe wyldrenesse of Wyrale* Made into a forest in the early twelfth century and still wild in the sixteenth. Records indicate the difficulties of citizens and authorities with armed marauders there in the later fourteenth century; see Savage, in *MLN* 46 (1931):455–57.

702 *God oþer gome wyth goud hert* A variant of "God and good men": Onions, in *TLS*, 13 August 1931, p. 621; and cf. Olzewska, in *English and Medieval Studies Presented to J. R. R. Tolkien* (London, 1962), p. 125.

713ff. This summary account of Sir Gawain's wanderings, sufferings, and encounters is a more intense and finally wintry version of what occurs often in the French romances, but there is also a notable heightening of some of its details by touches that coincide remarkably with Seneca's *De beneficiis*, iv.22, 2–4: "Sed illud intuere, an ad istam virtutem, quae saepe tuta ac facili aditur via, etiam per saxa et rupes ['Mony klyf he ouerclambe'] et feris ac serpentibus obsessum ['Sumwhyle wyth wormez he werrez and with wolues als, / . . . wyth wodwos,' etc.] iter fueris iturus." Seneca was widely known in England in *Gawain*'s time: see, among others, *The English Library Before 1700*, ed. Wormald and Wright (London, 1958), p. 98.

717 *so foule and so felle* Oakden [5] notes some parallels in English, but see also in the Vulgate *Merlin* (2:84, line 14) the variant but suggestive "se il est fel e fol."

718–19 See the Long version of *The First Continuation of Perceval*, 97–99 (ed. Roach and Ivy, 2:4), "Gauvains a fet / Tant proësces que il meïsmes / N'am porroit pas dire le disme"; and cf. the 1530 prose, folio xlvii^v, col. 1. For the phrase *of þe tenþe dole* see *Pearl*, 136.

723 *anelede* The earliest recorded survival of the word in English; from L *anhelare*, perhaps by way of OFr *aneler*, meaning "breathe, puff, aspire, strive after," etc.: see Godefroy and Tobler-Lommatzsch. *OED*, *anhele*, cites this instance as meaning "to blow, puff," and *MED* as "?Get wind of; ?puff after, pursue furiously." Craigie, *DOST*, and *OED* note the figurative use, "to aspire (to)," in Wyntoun's *Chronicle*, ca. 1420; and Latham, *anhel/itus*, etc., records other British figurative instances of the Latin from ca. 1160 on: *anhelo* ca. 1160, 1494, *aneleo* 1332, "to strive after": *anhelatio* 1350, "eager pursuit or desire." Davis's suggestion is no doubt correct that all association here with literal panting is gone. 'Tis a pity, all the same, to lose one's puffing ogre.

740 *meryly* Conventional for how a knight looks or behaves in all his splendor; but Sir Gawain could hardly be merry or happy at the moment. "Bravely" would perhaps be a good ambiguous compromise.

763ff. The castle and its surroundings. Its sudden appearance after Sir Gawain's prayer has for the moment something about it of the marvelous as with the Grail Castle and the gleaming fastnesses of the Christian otherworlds. In the end the role it plays has to do, not with magic or allegory, but with moral conduct and social principle, and the details, though no doubt touched by literature and manuscript illumination, are those of the castle architecture of the poet's time. Whether or not he was drawing on any actual fortress he had seen, the castle's setting here parallels (without the vineyards!) the ordered chateau landscapes in French accounts, e.g., *Perlesvaus* and *The First Continuation*, but also others: see H. Doerks, *Haus und Hof in der Epen des Crestien von Trois* (Inaug.-Diss., Greifswald, 1885), and W. Borsdorf, *Die Burg in "Claris und Laris" und im Escanor* (Inaug.-Diss., Berlin, 1890), esp. p. 12. The building itself with its towers, ornamental tops, chalk-white chimneys, "bastel" roofs, and colored pinnacles recalls *The Romance of Alexander* in MS Bodley 264 and especially the *Très riches heures* of Jean Duc de Berry, both virtually contemporary with Gawain [9 Castles]. In England the period knew a number of great castles, among them Pontefract in the West Riding of Yorkshire "floating on its hilltop like a vision of chivalry," and, with its noble façade and many towers, Warwick, where the Duc de Berry may have been entertained when a prisoner of war, 1360 to 1368, and thus passed its influence to France in the design of Mehun-sur-Yèvres as pictured in the *Très riches heures*: see Marcus Binney, in *Country Life*, 16 December 1982, p. 1952. But closer to *Gawain* in that book is the illustration of the fortress of Saumur, which, combining actuality with art, creates a sense of excess that is at once realistic and marvelous: see Paul Durrieu, *Chantilly, Les très riches heures de Jean Duc de Berry*, vol 2, pl. ix; and Christopher Hohler, in *The Flowering of the Middle Ages*, pp. 134–78, esp. 134–35 [both 9 Castles]. It is such an excess that, by grace of the poet's humor, makes our hero think of elaborate table decorations (802): cf. the paper canopies placed over dishes in *Purity*, 1407, "pared out of paper and poynted of golde."

774   *sayn Gilyan*   Julian the Hospitaler, patron saint of travelers, whom knights errant invoke for protection and lodging. The charm of the passage lies in the comforting confirmation that, after all, Jesus and Julian are themselves *gentyle*, as it were, gentlemen, not simply kindly as the editors sometimes aver, hence respond with understanding to the prayer of a weary fellow knight.

785   *blonk, bonk*   For this transposition of MS *bonk, blonk* see Davis.

790   *Enbaned*   "Provided with bantels." These are stepped horizontal courses of masonry set either at the foot of a wall, as in *Pearl*, 992–94, or at the top under the battlements, as here (and in *Purity*, 1458–59), where, reverse-stepped, they form part of the *machicolis*, to impede assault. See Gordon and Onions, in *Medium aevum* 2 (1933): 184–85; and *MED, bantel* n. and *embaned* vb., ppl. For illustrations of this feature of contemporary

castle architecture, see Viollet-le-Duc, *Dictionnaire raisonné de l'architecture* 5:196–213; his *Military Architecture*, trans. M. MacDermott, *passim* (index, *machicoulis*); and, in England, *The History of the King's Works*, ed. H. M. Colvin, vol. 1 (1963), pl. 10 (Carisbrooke Castle gatehouse, A.D. 1380), and vol. 2, pl. 50 (Lancaster Castle, built by Henry IV) [all *9 Castles*]. Cf. MS Bodley 264, esp. fol. 20ᵛ.

in þe best lawe I.e., according to the best canons of castle building of the period.

792 *loupe þat louked* Windows or loopholes with shutters, for which *OED*, *loop* sb. 1, and *MED*, *loup(e)* n. (2a), quote Gregory's *Chronicle*, ca. 1470 (75). There are many instances of such windows with shutters among the illustrations in MS Bodley 264. See also Viollet-le-Duc, *Dictionnaire raisonné* 4:381–82; and *Military Architecture*, pp. 117–18, 129, *et passim*.

806 *auinant* Adverb, "in pleasant surroundings," or "enjoying himself." *MED* records adjective and noun only and not this instance, but see Godefroy, *avenant* adv. On the analogy *aunter* for *auenture* Gollancz prints *auinant*, apparently unattested elsewhere, and Moorman follows suit. The MS itself cannot yield other than *amnant* (Madden) or *auinant* (Morris, etc.); cf. facsimile. *Amnant*, if for *aminant, amenant*, through OFr from Late L *amoenans-antem*, may seem possible, though only *amēne* adj. (L *amoenum*) appears in contemporary texts. For the rhyme with *plesaunt, erraunt* (808, 810) McLaughlin cites Wyld's view that the au/a variants in the writing of such French words represent a genuine distinction between their nasalized (upper class) and unnasalized local pronunciation, then observes (p. 84) that the scribe may not have been so well schooled as the poet hence, assuming that he wrote from dictation, was uncertain what sound he heard in *auinant*, the first of these three words, since in the rhyme the primary stress tended to fall forward of their endings. The point is inconclusive; there is some evidence that the scribe was working from written sources: see the introduction, section 5, "Lengthened Vowels," above, and nn. 552 above and 945 below (Wenore).

813 *Peter* An appropriate oath since Peter was the patron saint of porters and the source of their generic name: see, e.g., the Trentham text of *Floris and Blanchefleur*, 499–500 and 513 (ed. McKnight, EETS, no. 14, pp. 84–85): "'Childe,' he seide, 'to brygge þou shalt come, / The Senpere fynde at hoom,'" and "þe Senperes name was Darys."

845, 847 In *The Awntyres of Arthur*, 357, the king has a "beueren berde"; and the sun-god in *The Wars of Alexander*, 4922, has a "fell face as þe fire." Both cited by TG.

856 *blaunmer* Cf. n. 155.

858 Cf. n. 77 and l. 568.

861 *bry3t* A conventional adjective for the splendid look of what a knight wears (and supportive of the alliteration), though by now Sir Gawain's clothes can hardly seem bright, in contrast to the color of the new robe which he will soon put on, 864ff.

864–70 This passage has seemed difficult, perhaps slightly corrupt, to many: see Davis. It may be read thus: "As soon as he chose one and was clothed in it, (one) with flowing skirts that fitted him well, verily to everyone it seemed almost to be spring by his appearance, glowing (as he was) all in colors, his limbs quite handsome beneath (the robe)." Both instances of *alle* are taken to be adverbial, both being in effect intensives and the one in 867 intended perhaps to suggest a variety of colors. In contrast to the present rendering TG takes *hwes* and *lowande* with *lymmez*. The theme of the hero's beauty when after a long journey or arduous adventure he is freshly dressed is to be found in the romances, e.g., *Perlesvaus*, the 1530 prose *Perceval* (folio ccvi, col. 2) and Chrétien's *Yvain* and *Charrette*. Gollancz cites Chaucer's squire: "Embrouded was he, as it were a mede / Al ful of fresshe floures, whyte and rede." The comparison to spring exploits an old poetic commonplace, the personification of Ver or Flora (or the earth) putting on a multicolored robe of flowers: see, e.g., *Carmina burana*, no. 146, st. 1, and 138, st. 1 (ed. Hilka and Schumann, I.2 [1941], 247, 232); Matthew of Vendôme, in Faral, *Les arts poétiques*, pp. 148, 160; and the opening of the *Roman de la rose*. Cf. Nigel Wireker, *Contra curiales et officiales clericos* (ed. Wright, *Anglo-Latin Satirical Poets*, p. 146): "Ver, caput atque comes aestatis, in otia curas / Laxat, et ablato frigore nitet," where *nitet* (there are instances elsewhere) suggests *Gawain's lowande*, 868. In the present situation the simile is wittily reversed, an actual robing analogized to the figurative coming of spring, a spring made manifest, in the minds of Sir Gawain's hosts, here in the castle in December.

879 *bleeaunt* A rich silk fabric, hence also, as in 1928, the garment itself made of such a fabric: see *MED*. The term *bliaut* (Med L *blialdus*) occurs as early as the twelfth century in French for an over-tunic (see Godefroy and Tobler-Lommatzsch), and J. L. Nevinson (in *Medieval England*, p. 308 [9 *Costumes*]) considers the present instances to be conscious archaizing. In contrast to Nevinson, Davis suggests that in the fourteenth century the word may have meant "robe" in a more general sense. The older ending -aut was replaced in AN by present participle -ant, -aunt.

896 *as hende* Taken, as in TG and Gollancz, with the preceding clause, and as making a rhetorical balance with *hendely*. Davis reads it as a vocative with the following sentence: "Of your courtesy," i.e., "Please."

897 *Þis penaunce*   Sir Gawain's rising joy and the high spirits of his hosts mark this courteous play on fast and feast. It is fish, appropriate to the vigil of Christmas, but fish metamorphosed by an elaborate culinary art, for Christmas Eve's is a *ieiunium* of joy. Contrast "þe crabbed Lentoun / Þat fraystez flesch wyth þe fysche and fode more symple" (502–3). What the art might be is suggested by Russell's *Boke of Nurture* [*9 Feasts*], pp. 166–68, 171–75.

939 That the second half-line does not alliterate properly may indicate scribal corruption, as Gollancz and Davis point out.

945 *wener þen Wenore*   This wordplay with the name of Arthur's queen, capturing the moment's enchantment for our hero, is unique to *Gawain* and has never been noted by editor or commentator. It parallels a device found in Latin poetry and the *artes poetriae* from the twelfth century on: e.g., with ordinary nouns, *saxior saxo*, *ferrior ferro*; with proper names, *codrior Codro*, *ganimedior Ganimede*; with both together and with double entendre, *petrior Petra* (playing on the second meaning of the name, "stone"). In English, permitting an improvement on the Latin, the two unstressed second syllables tend, especially in the presence of r, to fall together in sound and, in addition, the stem derives its meaning, not merely from history and myth, but also, as with Petra, *intrinsically*, from its coincidence with the adjective *wēn*, "lovely." Guenever is the exemplar of courtly beauty (see n. 74–84 above) and that beauty is embodied in her name. The poet evidently intended this exploitation of the coincidence; of the four occurrences in the poem of the queen's name, all the others begin with g, not w. For the Latin see *Carmina burana*, moral.-sat., no. 19; Alexander Neckam, *De natura rerum*, 2:190 (ed. Wright, Rolls Series, 34:344); Walter of Châtillon, 16.17:4 (ed. Strecker, *Mon. lat. Gedichte*, p. 143); Geoffrey de Vinsauf and Everard of Bethûne, in Faral, *Les arts poètiques* [5], pp. 311, 348; Gervaise of Melkley, *Ars poetica*, ed. H. J. Gräbener (Münster, Westfalen, 1965), pp. 96–97; and Walther, nos. 17308a, 28331 and 31547b.

956 A relative clause with the subject pronoun unexpressed, referring to "Hir brest and . . . rote." This is, as Davis notes, good syntax for the period. "White as snow" is widespread in descriptions of feminine beauty, "white as fresh-fallen snow" especially in the French. See Godefroy, adj. *negié*; Tobler-Lommatzsch, v. *negier* (*noif negiee*); Sainte-Palaye, adj. *negée*, *negie*; and add, among other examples, the *Ovide moralisé*, iii. 1783–84 (ed. C. De Boer, Verhandelingen der Koninglijke Akademie van Wetenschappen in Amsterdam, n.s., 15 [1915]:337): "Sa poitrine tendre et deugie, / Qui plus blanche est que noif negie." The figure appears earlier in Geoffrey of Monmouth, in the description of Estreldis, II.ii: "Candorem carnis eius nec inclitum ebur. nec nix recenter cadens. nec lilia ulla uincebant." For English see the *Gest Hystoriale*, vii.3066–67 (describing Helen); cf. 3027–28. (In

Benoit's *Roman de Troie*, 5147–48, the unusual use of the comparison to describe a man, namely Agamemnon, elaborates the simple phrase of Dares Phrygius: "Agamemnon albo corpore.") A closer parallel to *Gawain*'s figure, transformed as it is to "whiter than the snow that falls on the hills," is to be found, though not applied as here with gentle plastic consequence to female throat and breast, in Thomas Chestre's contemporary *Sir Launfal*, 241 (ed. A. J. Bliss [London, 1960], p. 58): "Har faces were whyt as snow on downe."

960 *Toreted and treleted* Adjectives formed on nouns for the "trellised" embroidered edge of a headdress: see Godefroy, *to(u)ret* and *tre(i)llette*. See also Joan Evans, *Dress in Medieval France* [*9 Costumes*], p. 57 and pl. 55. For the representation of this lady as an *auncien* see n. 2460ff. below.

965 *for God!* "by God! as God is my witness!" Cf. 1822 and see examples in *MED, for*, prep. 2(d). From OE *for Gode* = L *praesente* or *audiente Deo*. *For* related to G *vor*, MHG *vor*, *vore*, L *prae*.

967 *bal3* TG's emendation of MS *bay*, which Brett, in *MLR* 8 (1913): 162–63, suggests is the same word as in bay window; but see Davis's objection. The alliterative formula *bal3 and brode*, as here, occurs in *The Parlement of the Thre Ages*, 112, and *The Wars of Alexander*, 4923.

975–76 A statement of their greetings made more sprightly by its being indirect. What they said was something like "We beg to know you better," and "Your willing servant, ladies, if it please you." Cf. Gollancz's note to *Wynnere and Wastoure* [*10*], 108.

977 Davis quotes *The Wars of Alexander*, 353, "takes him betwene þam twa," which is used of the queen's taking Anectanebus aside. Cf. *Shrewesbury Fragments* (EETS ES, no. 104 [1909]), chap. 27: "Ful tenely toke him hom betwen."

999 *at mes and at mele* Gollancz suggests that *mele* refers to the regular repast, *mes* to the less formal serving of food. *Messes* in the same line means the food itself.

1004 *as þe messe metely come* "As the serving came, in keeping with due precedence."

1006 *grome* TG and Davis suggest that this probably means "man," rather than "servant, groom," and indicate that the word became confused in late ME with *gome*, "man" (from OE *guma*), which it eventually replaced. But the point of the passage is that the diners were served, down to the last servant or retainer (*grome*), all according to precedence. See *MED, grǫme* n., esp. 2.

1007 For the connection of this passage with Laȝamon see the introduction above, p. 8, and add 10198 (Madden 20439): "her wes wop & her wes rop." The device, called *repetitio*, is listed among the rhetorical colors (*ornatus facilis*) in the *Artes poetriae*: Faral [5], pp. 167, 177–78, 231, 321, 331, 351.

1008 The inexpressibility topos to indicate the richness of dinner. Cf. 130–31 and 165 and their notes.

1012–13 The first line has been rendered variously, e.g., "In the private exchange of courtly conversation" (Cawley); "With the seemly solace of their secret words" (Borroff); "Through delightful dalliance of dark-whispered words" (Williams), etc. The ambiguity lies in *derne*, which means, not only "private, intimate" or "secret," but also "mysterious, recondite" (see *MED*, *derne* 4[a]), hence marked by hidden or allusive meanings, as with metaphor, aphorism, and *double entendre*; cf. 1661–63. For the moral purity of the conversation, see the injunction to lovers against bawdy talk in the *Roman de la rose*, 2097–102. The relevant term in the French romances is *sans vileinie*, and is applied to the dalliance and love talk, as well as their intention, in which, e.g., Sir Gawain engages in *The First Continuation*: "D'amours, de droit, de cortoisie, / Ont puis ensamble tant parlé / Et boinement ris et jué"; and (MS *L*) "Des gens, d'amors sans vilonie / Ont puis tot ensamble parlé" (ed. Poitvin, 3:106; ed. Roach, 3:110 and 111. Cf. Roach, 2:73–74, and 3:32–33; and the 1530 prose version, folio lxxix, col. 1). Its opposite is illustrated by Mordred's seduction of his host's *demoiselle* in the Vulgate *Lancelot* (4:360–62); and in the dirty wit of the lady's and knight's repartee in Jean de Condé's well-known fourteenth century fabliau, "Li sentiers batus": ed. Scheler, *Dites e contes de Baudoin de de Condé e son fils Jean de Condé* (Brussels, 1867), 3:300–302.

[1022a] Gollancz deduces from the calendar that a verse describing December 28, Holy Innocents' or Childermas, has been omitted from the MS and to supply the loss invents the one printed here.

1028 *stronge* Referring to guests outside the castle and its vicinity, from a distance; OFr *straunge*. Gollancz emends to *strange*. Davis notes, however, that o occurs for au in French words, most frequently in the south but also sometimes elsewhere: see *Sir Gawain and the Carle of Carlisle*, ed. Kurvinen [*10*], n. to 9. It appears again in the present MS in *Purity*, 1494.

1032 *wayued* Others, including Gollancz, print *wayned*, but see TG's citations in support of the present reading, including 1743; and Laȝamon, 9482 (Madden, 19003), *Purity*, 453, and *William of Palerne* [*10*] 2978.

1038 *Heȝekyng* Cf. 1963, and see Emerson, in *JEGP* 21 (1922):379. Treated by the poet as a compound (OE *hēahcyning*) alliterating on h.

1049 *toun* See n. 31 above.

1067 *And me als fayn* This idiom is not recorded by *OED* (*me*, 7.d) before the year 1812. Davis notes less "colloquial" instances with the pronoun in the nominative (I, ye) in *Pearl* and Malory.

1068–78 The appearance together of *þou* and *ȝe* in this passage is notable and reflects an inconsistency found elsewhere in the poem: cf., among others, 1252–53, 1272, 1275. Where use is roughly consistent, *ȝe* appears in addresses to a superior and in the polite talk between social equals (but not between the Green Knight, Arthur, and Sir Gawain at Camelot, where the rougher *þou* is used, as it is also by the guide to the Green Chapel, once Sir Gawain has refused his advice). Throughout the three temptations *ȝe* occurs punctiliously, except when on the first day the lady says that other women would wish to "Haf þe . . . as I þe habbe here," and on the third she wakes Sir Gawain with *þou* and later, after kissing him, asks for *þy gifte, þi gloue*, which he refuses, relapsing as he does so into *þy luf*, but only this once. At the Chapel the Green Knight starts with *þou* but turns to *ȝe* as his tone gets gentler, then goes back and forth between the two, and Sir Gawain in response also vacillates. See Davis, pp. 144–45.

1074 *in spenne* A tag, like *in stedde*, 439.

1110 *Gawayn þe gode* See 1926 and n. 5 above.

1112 *beuerage* The drink which seals an agreement. *MED* cites a number of instances of use in this legal sense from the years 1275 to about 1400. Cf. l. 1409, and for the legalistic nuance elsewhere in the poem see n. 298 above.

1133ff. The three days' hunts and the love temptations. The literal function of these interwoven episodes is clear enough, but to find in them figurative significance has presented difficulties, which a new essay by W. R. J. Barron, *Trawthe and Treason* (1980), seeks to circumvent by applying to the passage the general term metaphor, with no intent to press the details where they will not work, but elsewhere more precisely as particular details can be used to conjure up atmosphere and suggest complex "meaning." See, for example, the allegory boar = devil.

1139ff. The accounts of the hunts themselves combine realistic observation (movement, noise, and the hills, cliffs, valleys, and waters of the dale country) with the technical details and terms to be found in the romances and cynegetic treatises. As for the latter, Twiti's account describes three manners of hunting: (1) The chase of *forloin* (OFr *forloigne*, "separation"), in which you hunt with the hounds that have gone ahead and blow recheat (see 1446, 1466, 1911) for those coming up or far behind. (2) The chase with the pack in order. (3) The *stably*, an ordered roundup, with archers and greyhounds. See Twiti, ed. Danielsson, pp. 48–50. In *Gawain* the deer hunt (1150ff.) follows 3, and the boar (1421ff.) and fox (1690ff.) hunts evidently follow 1. TG notes that the hunting and "undoing," or "breaking," of deer are described in English pieces like *The Parlement of the Thre Ages*, *The Awntyrs off Arthure*, *Sir Tristrem*, *Ipomadon*, *Summer Sunday* [all *10*], and Chaucer's *Book of the Duchess*; and that the insertion of the passages here may have been suggested to our poet by some such incident as that in *Le chevalier à l'épée* [*6*], 372–75: "Li ostes dist apres mengier / Qu'il vialt aler ses bois veior, / Et si rova Gauvain seior / Et deduir o la damoiselle." For medieval hunting generally, texts and studies, see the bibliography, section 9.

1141 *þre bare mote*   Three separate long notes, blown according to custom, as the hounds were released from their common kennel and uncoupled, or unleashed. In Chaucer's *Book of the Duchess* 375–77, it is the *mayster-hunte* who blows the three motes.

1142 *braches*   Cf. *rachchez*, 1362, etc., and *brachetes*, 1603. Small scenting hounds, which hunt in packs and are used, as in the present instance, to find the game. According to Twiti and *The Master of Game* [*9 Hunting*], the buck, doe, and fox are hunted thus and are said to be *enquillez*, or *acquilez*, i.e., "trovez de braches," that is, "hunted up." By a second method the game is said to be *enchacés*, English *enchased*, i.e., started by a *limer*; it is used for the hart, hare, boar, and wolf. But the *Gawain* poet does not make the distinction explicit, since the boar (1419ff.), like deer and fox, is *enquillez*, i.e., found by *rachchez* (*braches*).

1146 *vewters*   Greyhound-keepers: see *MED*, *feut(e)rer*, n. That these men belong with grooms and woodsmen is evident in *The Master of Game*, chap. xxii. OFr instances refer especially to boar-hunting: Godefroy, 1 *veltrier*, s.m., and Tilander, *Glanures lexicographiques* (Lund, 1932), pp. 268–69. The English evidently reflects French influence but Latham lists *veltrarius* and its variants in Anglo-Latin from the year 1100 on. See also DuCange, *vautrarius*.

1150ff.   The deer hunt follows the practice described by *The Master of Game* and the French *Roy Modus* and *Gaston Phébus* [all *9 Hunting*]. In a selected area of woods huntsmen with light greyhounds and other small driving hounds (*taysours*) on leash are placed in a semicircle at some distance from one another but in visual contact. This is the *stably* (1153, called *establi* in Twiti's *Venerie*). As the deer run by, the light greyhounds and other *taysours* are slipped and the game driven toward the boundaries where the archers stand ready to shoot them. Other men prevent the animals from escaping and force them back upon huntsmen waiting at various stations (*trystors*, 1146, etc.) with heavier greyhounds to pull them down. See Tilander, *Essais d'étymologie cynégétique*, p. 84.

1150 *quest* The baying of the hounds while searching after game, as well as the search itself: *OED, quest,* 6.b, and *The Master of Game,* chap. 14: "rennyng houndes, þe whiche moste renne alle þe day questynge and makyng gret melody in her langage."

1156 *fermysoun tyme* *The Master of Game,* appendix, "Seasons of Hunting," lists the dates of the closed season for hart and buck (the red and fallow deer males) as September 14 to June 24, and of the open season for hinds and does (the corresponding females) as September 14 to February 2. See n. 1320 below.

1157 *meue* Usually printed thus, though u and n are hard to distinguish from each other in the MS. TG notes that *meue* is the technical term for starting a hart (Twiti, *meüz; Master of Game, meued*), hence the likelier word to be used here. There was also an OFr verb *mener,* "to chase hard," derived from *menée,* the hunting call blown when the deer was in full flight, but used, according to Twiti, only for the hart, boar, and wolf.

1158 *hay! and war!* Cf. 1445. Both terms were used in hunting deer, the one as a cry of encouragement to the hounds, the other as a warning cry. Both no doubt came directly from the French, and *hay* ultimately from Gmc *hei.* See the vocabulary below; Tilander, Cynegetica 5, pp. 113ff.; Godefroy and Tobler-Lommatzsch, *gar, gare,* interj.; and *Chace dou cerf* [9 *Hunting*], p. 63. *OED, ware* v.¹, 1b, suggests a coalescence with native *ware,* OE *warian.*

1168 Davis observes that the second half-line is metrically incomplete and that evidently something has been lost, perhaps a word like *ryȝt* after *rent,* as added to the present text, the stress being on the first syllable of *resayt.* Contrast Sapora's scansion.

1169 *taysed* For this technical term for the driving of animals see Gascoigne, *The Noble Arte of Venerie* [9], p. 246; and *The Master of Game,* appendix, "Teazer."
    þe wattrez TG cites *The Boke of St Albans* [9 *Hunting*], sig. evij (and ed. Tilander, lines 341–66), which says that a hunted hart will seek a river, and *The Master of Game,* chap. 3, that he will come out of the water the same way he went in "a bowe shoot or more, and þan he shal ruse out of þe way."

1178ff. The contrast of the early rising and vigor of the hunters with Sir Gawain's sleeping late, beginning here and continuing on the two succeeding days, may have recalled to fourteenth-century readers a theme of the preachers, sometimes echoed in the hunting manuals as well, inveighing against idleness abed, which could lead to lechery and license. See *Ayenbite* *of Inwyt*, pp. 47–48, *The Book of Vices and Virtues*, pp. 26–27, and *Jacob's Well*, p. 104 [all *10*]; going back to Friar Lorens's *Somme le roi.*

1224 *þat oþer half* Davis observes that this apparently means she will tuck him up in the bedclothes on the side opposite to that on which she is sitting (cf. 1211), hence on both sides.

1237 *ʒe ar welcum to my cors* Of this Gollancz says: "The lady's bluntness in coming to the point testifies to her inexperience in such a role." But Davis argues, on evidence from contemporary texts, that *cors* with possessive adjectives can in effect be the equivalent of a personal pronoun, and that "to be welcome" used with a pronoun may refer to the person who is pleased. The line here would therefore be read simply as "You are welcome to me, i.e., I am glad to have you here." It is a possible argument. Yet the words can also mean literally what the reader thinks they do, and he is led to think so by the lady's own summary of the circumstances (1230–33): we are alone, my lord and his retainers are gone away, the other men and my damsels are in bed, the door of this chamber is locked, so "ʒe ar welcum to my corse, / Yowre awen won to wale, / Me behouez of fyne force / Your seruaunt be." This is not a "crude" offer "ill suited to this early stage of the lady's courtship of Gawain," rather a quick opening attack to see what our hero will do. Similar offers are made to King Arthur and Sir Gawain in *Perlesvaus* without much in the way of preliminary, and they parry them, and of course to Sir Lancelot in Chrétien's *Charrette*. As for the bluntness, we may recall what is said to Sir Gawain in *The First Continuation*, e.g., the 1530 prose version, folios lxxiiii^v, col. 2–v, col. 1: "Et apres que bien leust regarde et contemple sa contenance luy dist que veritablement il estoit Gauuain . . . & puis luy dist. *Sir la pucelle comme voyez du tout se mect a vostre bandon & de son corps vous faict present tout par amours & en honeur si vous plaist a le recepuoir.*" This was their first and only meeting, and the girl was, no doubt, inexperienced.

1239 *of fyne force* A phrase from the French, signifying either physical force or abstract necessity (Godefroy, 2. *fin*, adj.) but here, evidently, the latter, where context specifies something like "constrained by the laws of courtly behavior." Davis calls attention to the contrast in 1496, "constrayne wyth strenkþe."

1252–53 For the use of *þe* and *your* together see n. 1068–78 above.

1255 *garysoun oþer golde* An alliterative formula found in OE prose and common in ME: see Oakden; and cf. 1837, *golde ne garysoun.* TG notes that the phrase is of Scandinavian origin: "gulli ok gersimum, gull rautt ok gørsimar"; and that in *Gawain* the ON *gersum* has been replaced by *garysoun* from OFr.

1265–67 There is still no agreement on the meaning of this passage, which does not yield clear sense as it stands in the manuscript. Davis attempts to reduce the difficulty by taking (with Ker) *fongen*, 1265, as a past participle parallel to *founden*, 1264, adding *hi* before *hor dedez*, 1265, and emending *nysen*, 1266 (Menner *uysen*, Waldron *nys euer*) to *nys euen*. The present edition adopts the first and third of these points, but punctuates differently, taking *Bot þe daynté þat þay delen*, 1266, as the predicate of *dedez*, and putting *For my disert* with the next sentence. A translation might then go thus: "And received very different (treatment) from other folk, their behavior (being) but the (conventional) honors that they share out. Since my deserving is not equal (to the real honor you do me), it redounds to your high praise, you who know how to behave only well (to others)." But this is still not fully satisfactory. For *wel connez*, a variant of *connen god*, "to know how to behave," see *MED, connen*, 6(e).

1272, 1275 For *þe* and *yow* in these lines see n. 1068–78 above.

1283–87 To read the entire passage as stating the lady's thoughts would be, as Davis observes, to inform the reader prematurely that Sir Gawain's host is in fact the Green Knight. But to divide the passage between what becomes an incomplete statement by the lady and another giving us a supposed authorial explanation, is also not entirely satisfactory. As to the Gollancz emendations, printed in present text, their effect is to attribute the entire statement to Sir Gawain. Davis finds it hard to see how, if original, they could have led to the actual manuscript readings (meaning, no doubt, primarily *I* for *ho*, since *burde* for *burne* could be a carry-over from the earlier *burde* in the line), yet he agrees that they make good sense. With respect to the situation in the story, *Perlesvaus*, 1258–61 (1:74), likewise has Sir Gawain put love aside for duty during a quest: "[Messire Gavains] esgarda la dame maintes foiz por sa grant biauté, e s'il vousist croire son cuer e ses ielz, il eüst tost changiee sa pensee. Mes il avoit si son cuer lié e estraint qu'il ne li lessoit penser chose qui a vilenie tornast, por le haut pelerinage qu'il avoit enprise."

1293 For the romance convention on which this teasing remark depends for its force, see n. 379–81, 401–08 above.

1320 *barayne* See n. 1156. *The Master of Game* [*9 Hunting*], chap. 3, says: "As of þe hyndes some bene barayn and some be þat bere calfes; of þise þat bene barayne here sesoun bygynneþ when þe sesoun of þe hert failleþ, and lasteþ to lenton."

1324 *querre* Or *querré* An orderly assemblage of slain deer and the place where it is made. *The Master of Game*, roughly contemporary (ca. 1410) with *Gawain*, describes the practice in all its formality thus (MS

Digby 182, folio 57ʳ; cf. Baillie-Grohman, chap. 36, p. 109): "And alle þe while that þe huntynge lasteth shulde þe cartes go about fro place to place to brynge deer to þe quirre. And þer shulde þe sewers of þe halke be forto kepe þe quirre and to make by it on a rowe, alle þe heedes one way and euery deeres feete to oþeres backe. And þe hertes shulde be leyde on a rewe, or II, or III, after þat þei beth many or fewe, and þe rascayle in þe same wyse by hemselfe." Accounts of how the word comes to have this meaning have thus far been wanting. *OED, quarry* sb.[1], records *Gawain's* as the first such use in English, and derives the word itself from OFr *cuirée, curée* (cf. *cuir*, "skin"), signifying both the flesh served as a "reward" to the hounds on the hide of a deer and the occasion of the serving. That is the normal meaning in the French texts, whatever the ultimate source of the word (*coriata*, "animal skin"; or *corata*, "entrails," crossed with *curare*, "to gut an animal": contrast Tilander, Cynegetica 8, pp. 211–15ff., with Gamillscheg, *Etymologisches Wörterbuch der französischen Sprache*, 2nd ed., 1969, under *curée*). But no French instances have been adduced signifying "an orderly assemblage of slain deer." How the two meanings are related does not readily appear, nor do the lexicographers or editors raise the question. Elsewhere *Gawain* (1359–61) describes rewarding the hounds "Vpon a felle of the fayre best," without, however, naming it in the French fashion *querré*; the word which he uses here appears only once and in the present meaning. It is tempting to see in this case a contamination in form of ME *quer, quere* (OFr *quer, quere*, L *chorus, chorea*), "an ordered assemblage," with *quyrrey* (*cuirée*), "reward": note Wycliffe, Song of Solomon, 6:13, dated 1382 (ed. Forshall and Madden [Oxford, 1850], 3:81, and ed. Lindberg [Stockholm, 1963], p. 290), "Queres of tentes, querys of tentis," translating *choros castrorum*. Cf. *OED, choir, quire* sb., 6. (Was there also an older Latin verbal noun * *coreata*, from *c[h]oreo–are*, "an arrangement of things," not limited to the chase but paralleling *coriata*, "flesh laid on a hide," recorded by Latham for the year 1205?) *The Master of Game* gives *quirre, quyrrey, enquyrreide*, "reward, rewarded," as a rendering of *Gaston Phébus*, its French original, but also *querre, quirre, quyrrey*, meaning "an ordered assemblage of slain deer" (as if *chorus [coreata] cervum*) in a passage not found in *Gaston Phébus*. The question thus arises whether that special usage, hence the special word, as here in *Gawain*, is particular to English hunting at the end of the fourteenth century.

1325ff.   To know how to "undo" or "break" a deer was a sign of gentlemanly breeding in a knight, as the well-known episode in the Tristram romance illustrates. Cf. also *Ipomadon B*, 409–10, and *The Parlement of the Thre Ages*, 66–96. Davis observes that romances and treatises usually describe the undoing of the stag but that here the animals are hinds, hence that Gollancz's reference to the "coddis" in *The Boke of St Albans* is hardly apposite. Bruce discusses the passage in *Englische Studien* 32 (1903): 23–36.

1328 *þe asay* A test of the thickness of the flesh, done, according to Gascoigne, *The Noble Art*, pp. 133–34, by cutting "a slit drawn alongst the brysket . . . , somewhat lower than the brysket toeards the belly." Gascoigne says this is a specifically English practice. Cf. *The Boke of St Albans*, sig. fii^v (ed. Tilander, ll. 547ff.); and *The Parlement of the Thre Ages*, 70–71: "And I s[clis]te hym at þe assaye to see how me semyde / And he was floreschede full faire of two fyngere brode."

1330–31 For the *erber*, or gullet, see *MED*. It was *schaued* free of the flesh clinging to it and tied to prevent the contents from coming out. TG quotes *La chace dou cerf*, 259–63 (ed. Tilander): "Et les epaules autresi / Dois lever aprés, ce te di. / La souzgorge aprés en levez, / L'erbiere et le josier coupes / Et l'erbiere dever nouer." Cf. *The Jewel for Gentrie*, cited in Bruce.

1333 *bowelez* The erroneous *balez* of the MS is evidently influenced by *balé*, which precedes it. Cf. 1609.

1334 *þe knot* See n. 1330–31.

1342 That portion of the numbles which is found in the deer's forepart. *The Boke of St Albans*, sig. e vij^v (ed. Tilander, ll. 375–77) says: "Oon croke of the Nomblis lyth euermoore / Vnder the throote bolle of the beest be foore / That callid is auaunters." Cited by TG.

1355 *corbeles fee* Also called raven's bone and corbyn bone from OFr *os corbin*. It was cast into the branches of a tree for the crows or ravens who followed the hunters. In *Roy Modus* and *Gaston Phébus* it apparently refers to the pelvic bone, but in English it comes to mean, according to Gascoigne, *The Noble Arte*, p. 135, "a little gristle which is vpon the spoone of the brysket." See Tilander, *Nouveaux mélanges* (Cynegetica 8), pp. 48–50.

1358 *Vche freke for his fee* The fee is that part of the animal that each man at the hunt can claim as his. *The Master of Game* and *The Boke of St Albans* describe the division. The hide of the deer went to the one who killed and marked it; the left shoulder and in addition perhaps the head went to the gentleman who "undid" the animal; the forester usually got the right shoulder and the "cachers" the neck. The lord by right received the numbles, sides, and haunches.

1362 *prys* The call of the horn when the animal has been taken, that is, killed (from AN *prise*), and during the return home from the chase. See Twiti, *Venerie*, p. 96.

1364 *Strakande* Cf. 1923. Blowing a hunting call made up of many single sounds or motes. In *The Master of Game* (pp. 101, 106, 110, 112), where as here they make a kill of deer and the hounds are rewarded and the hunt turns toward home, such calls vary according to whether they are blown by the lord or the other hunters, but the distinction is not observed by *Gawain*. The *OED* lists the word used in this meaning as of obscure origin, though in other senses *strake* and *stroke* are derived from a Gmc radical *strak-*, giving rise to the verb **strakjan*, G *strecken*, Swd *sträcka*, Mod E *stretch*. Tilander (Cynegetica 4, 231) finds no difficulty in relating the present word to the others since they all have in common the notion of extension whether in streaks, strokes, strides, or prolonged or repeated fanfares.

1372 *sumned* This line has evidently suffered scribal corruption, which spoils the alliteration. Gollancz emends *lorde* to *syre*, and Sapora lists the line as problematical. The present emendation of *comaunded* to *sumned* produces a five-stress, three-alliteration pattern, which occurs some seventy-five times elsewhere in the poem.

1382 *seuen 3ere in sesoun of wynter* *Seuen 3ere* here means an indefinite long time, but *wynter* means winter, not year, as in 613: cf. n. 610–13.

1393–94 An oblique indication, says Davis, that the lord knew the kiss was from his wife; cf. TG. But whatever they know or suspect to be the case, these two males are playing a game enriched for each other by a teasing ambiguity.

1396–97 Davis thinks the bob here may be an afterthought, changing the original construction, *trawe 3e non oþer*, which is an imperative and complete, hence he omits *3e* after *trawe*, thus turning it into an infinitive. See also Madden. But the MS reading makes sense as it stands, even preserving the original idiomatic imperative: "Since you have received what is due you, rest assured you can (get) nothing else."

1409 See n. 1112.

1414 *mete, metely* Wordplay, *traductio*.

1427, 1430, 1432 *rocherez, flosche* Cf. 1698. Seeking to identify the actual terrain on which the present scene is based, Elliott, "Sir Gawain in Staffordshire" [4], contends that the hunters started from Swythamley, "within echoing distance of the Roaches (the poet's *rocheres*), . . . crossed the latter, then headed northwards past Flash (the poet's *flosche*) towards the steep banks and narrow valleys of the Wildboarclough country beyond the river Dane. Many of the features the poet mentions in unusual topographical words still bear the same or closely similar names to-day." These two words can be said to be unusual chiefly as they appear together here and in the context of Elliott's argument, for otherwise they occur widely in the North and Northern Midlands both in Middle English and in modern dialects: see *MED, flashe*, n; and *EDD, flash*, sb¹, and *roach*, sb¹, adj, and vb. For the significance of the argument itself for the question of *Gawain*'s authorship and provenience see the introduction above, p. 17.

1441 *For he watz* Following *watz* Waldron adds *borelych and* in order to fill out a short line.

    bige MS *b.ge* (?), all letters blotted and uncertain. Madden reads *b . . . &*, Morris *beste &*, Gollancz *bronde*, Cawley *brothe*, Waldron *brode*. TG gives *breme*, with which cf. the stanzaic *Morte Arthur* (ed. Bruce, p. 181): "Mordred . . . , / Made him breme as any bore at bay." But none is satisfactory. The present solution is aided by ultraviolet and facsimile. For *bige* see *MED, big* adj. 1(b) and (c).

1461 *bate* Probably "baiting, harassment," related to ME verb *baiten*, ON *beita*, corresponding OE *bǽtan*; but TG translates "strife, fighting," shortened from *debat*. Cf. Gollancz and *MED*, which lists this as the only occurrence, and see the vocabulary below.

1466 *rydez* MS partly illegible. Madden prints *r . . .* in text and in note *rydes? rode?* All others print *rode, r[o]de*, and in notes Gollancz adds *One letter illegible*, TG *od illegible*. Ultraviolet seems to show *ryde* plus another illegible letter, hence the reading of the present text.

1467 *til þe sunne schafted* See *OED, shaft*, v.¹, "Of the sun: ?To set," with only this instance in *Gawain*. But *schafted* here probably means "sent out low, or horizontal, beams" and the phrase "until the day was nearing its end," not literally sunset. Cf. Gollancz and *Peblis to the Play*, in *The Maitland Folio Ms.*, ed. Craigie, 1:183 (STS 2.7 [1919]), noted in this connection by Ursula Dronke: "Be þat the sone wes settand schaftis / And neir done wes þe day. . . ." See also Davis.

1481 Cf. n. 1293 above.

1493, 1497 *deuayed, deuaye* Madden and Morris print *denayed* and *denaye* (MS *de vaye*), thus disturbing the alliteration, which in the first instance is on *d*, in the second on *u*. *MED devaien* v., from OFr *deve(i)er*, gives only these occurrences.

1499–1500 This proverbial phrase is neglected by the *Gawain* commentators and not to be found in Whiting. Of it Gollancz remarks, "A courteous way of stating that the manners of Camelot are superior to those of the provinces." No doubt. But at the moment Sir Gawain's defensive strategy is to pose prudence against cavalry tactics, stating that might does not make right ("force n'est droit"), a theme that in aphoristic form has a considerable medieval history: see *Disticha Catonis*, breves no. 48 (also in French, e.g., in the Vernon MS, ed. Furnivall, EETS no. 117, p. 563); Walther, esp. nos. 33278a, 33376, 33648; LeRoux de Lincy, *Proverbes français* (1859) 2:300; and Morawski, *Proverbes français antérieurs au xve siècle* (1925), nos. 758–59. In Arthurian tradition the first line goes back to Geoffrey's *Historia*, ix. 62, appearing there, not as a principle of manners, but of *politics*, in King Arthur's refutation of Lucius's British claim. Variations of it and the conduct it prescribes as applied to love occur in the French romances, e.g., Chrétien's *Charrette*, 1314–22, and their context, among "les costumes et les franchises" of love; Andreas Capellanus, i.2 and ii.8, §v (ed. Trojel, pp. 9, 310); the scene of Mesire Gavains's confession to Bishop Salemon in the R version of *The First Continuation* of the *Perceval*, where God is said to excuse courtly couples but not those who take their love by force (3.1, especially ll. 576–96); and the implications of Marie de France, *Guigemar*, 705–21. In addition, the aphorism appears, if not in connection with love, at least in relation to Perceval's treatment of a frail and aged lady: see, e.g., the Didot *Perceval* (ed. Roach [1941], p. 153): "force n'est mie drois." See also the 1530 prose *Perceval*, folio cxxxv, col. 2 bottom; and *Second Continuation*, 10211–14 (ed. Roach, 4:58). After Geoffrey the political use continues in his followers Wace, Peter Langtoft, and Laȝamon, also in the Vulgate *Merlin* [6] (2:426, ll. 14–16); but the point is made with special relevance in Robert Mannyng's *Chronicle* [6], 11661–64, where the language suggests, not merely the first of *Gawain*'s lines here, but most strikingly the second as well: "Hit is no skile, ne law non makes, / Þyng þat þou þorow force takes; / & swylk giftes men schal furdo, / Þat wyþ wrong was taken so."

1508ff.   This sentence, which breaks off at 1511 and, after a long parenthesis, resumes loosely at 1520, produces something of a lively incoherence that is part of the colloquial charm of the entire stanza.

1516–17   Cf. *The Wars of Alexander*, 7: "How ledis for þaire lemmans has langor endured."

1550   This line has been read in two ways: with *woȝe* as verb meaning "to woo, to make love" (Davis), in which case the subsequent clause implies that she does not really want his advances; or with *woȝe* as noun meaning "wrong, evil," or, as elsewhere in *Gawain*'s time, "harm," the subsequent clause becoming therefore more complex in meaning and referring to the ultimate purpose of the thus far undisclosed scheme of his host and hostess.

1558   *ruþes hym*   Probably "bestirs himself," but the precise meaning and origin of the verb are obscure. The only other occurrences are in *Purity*, 895 and 1208, where they describe rousing up someone from sleep. TG refers to ON *hryðja*, "shake" (cf. MHG *rütten*) and *(h)ryðja*, "toss, clear out." Gollancz calls attention to instances in this dialect of þ for z (cf. *ro-þeled, Purity*, 59) and suggests that *ruþen* is a variant of "rouse"; cf. Swed. *rusa*.

1571–73 Cf. the angry boar in *Seven Sages*, 897–99 (ed. Brunner, EETS, no.191, 34): "He wette his tossches and his fet. / Þe erþe wiȝ his snowte he bet. / Þourh þe mouht þe fom was wiȝt." Cited by Waldron.

1575 *nye, neȝe* Wordplay (*traductio*).

1593 TG notes instances of the bold hunter killing a boar with his sword: Arthur in *The Avowing of Arthur* and Begon in *Garin le Loherain*; and Davis quotes (from Baillie-Grohman, pl. xlvii) *Gaston Phébus* as saying that to kill a boar with the sword when the animal was not "held" by hounds was nobler than to kill him with the spear. The tussle here in the water is heroic indeed, as the poet is at pains to make clear.

1623 The present text follows Gollancz, omitting the *&* of the MS, but Davis's emendation *laȝter* is tempting.

1641 *euen, euentide* In festive mood Sir Gawain indulges in a patent piece of punning.

1644 *Bi saynt Gile* Gollancz observes that this invocation is perhaps particularly appropriate for a hunter like Sir Bertilak, since the saint's legend associates him with a hind: see Saint Aegidius in Jacobus de Varagine, *Legenda aurea*. If the poet here had that association in mind it is unusual in the literature of his time: among some twenty such invocations in the extant French and English romances and in Chaucer (*House of Fame*, 1183, and Canon's Yeoman's Tale, 1185) none involves animals or hunting. See Ackerman, Flutre, and West; *Amis and Amiloun*, ed. Kölbing (Heilbronn, 1884), 952 and n., and 1126; *Englische Studien* 8 (1889):134–35; and Skeat's note to *House of Fame*, 1183.

1652 *glam and gle* For this formula see Oakden.

1655 *coundutes of Krystmasse* Christmas carols. The OFr *condut, conduit*, Med. L *conductum* (*conductus*) was a kind of motet sung as the priest was advancing to the altar, but the term came to be more widely applied to harmonized part-song. See *MED*; Godefroy, *conduit* 2; Tobler-Lommatzsch; DuCange, *conductus* 11 and *condictus*; and Latham, where *conductus*, "harmonized song," is cited for the year 1326 and later. The association with Christmas in England is recorded as early as ca. 1250 in *The Owl and the Nightingale*, 483. For *carolez* see n. 43.

1661–62 Though the precise sense of *nurne* and *towrast* is uncertain in *Gawain*, the passage seems to mean, "But because of his breeding he did not wish to say no to her directly but turned her off with polite indirection, no matter how his behavior went awry [i.e., was turned by her to his disadvantage]." His *dede* and her turning it were of course primarily a game of words.

1671 "For it was near the time of the appointment he was obliged to go to." The verb of motion is, as often in the period, omitted and the preposition *to* bears the stress and carries the alliteration.

1680 "þrid tyme þrowe best" Cf. the tale of a wife's "payment" after three successive misdeeds in *Seven Sages*, the Cotton-Rawlinson redaction, dated ca. 1350, l. 2062 (ed. Killis Campbell [Boston, 1907]): "þe thrid time thraws best." Not in the Latin or French analogues nor in Brunner's Middle English version. There are several proverbs in English on the third time, or day, as lucky or otherwise notable, but the present instance is usually put with "The third time pays for all": see *Oxford Dictionary of English Proverbs*, 3rd ed. rev. F. P. Wilson (1970); G. L. Apperson, *English Proverbs and Proverbial Phrases* (1929); and M. P. Tilley, *A Dictionary of the Proverbs in England in the Sixteenth and Seventeenth Centuries* (Ann Arbor, 1950). Not in Whiting. Whether *þrowe* here is subjunctive or imperative (or even maybe a noun) is doubtful. Perhaps it should be seen as a sort of indeterminate form produced by the aphorism's monosyllabic march. Waldron translates "Third day, throw best," with the first two words adverbial rather than subject, and the meaning of the verb derived from its use in the game of dice. That view of the origin is attractive but no earlier or contemporary evidence seems to be forthcoming; the examples in *OED*, "to make (a cast) at dice," etc., are all late.

1698 *rocheres* See n. 1427, 1430, 1432 above.

1700 *a trayteres* Gollancz and TG emend to *a traueres* (Morris *trayvers*), and TG cites *Purity*, 1473: "So trayled & tryfled a traueres wer alle." The original may, however, represent OFr *a tretours* (var. *trestours*), *al tretour* (var. *trestour*), and there seems to be no need for emendation. See Godefroy and Tobler-Lommatzsch, *trestor, -our, -ur*. Tobler-Lommatzsch quotes the *Bestiaire* of Guillaume le Clerc on the tricky course of the fox: "Mais il i a osiaus plusiours, / Qui les guiches et *les trestours* / *Dou goupil* aperchoivent bien." Cf. DuCange, *trestornatus*.

    trayles For the cynegetic sense of this verb, "to follow a trail," see *Vénerie*, ed. Tilander, p. 98, and *Mélanges d'étymologie*, pp. 165–66.

1701, 1714, 1726 The hounds. A *kenet* is a small "running" hound, also called a harrier (*heirer*), according to *The Master of Game*, chap. 4. Those leashed in threes *all graye* are greyhounds. *Titleres* (from OFr *tiltre*) are hounds kept on leash at hunting stations in the woods and slipped as the quarry runs by: see Godefroy and Cotgrave's seventeenth-century *Dictionary*. Cited by TG.

1725 Though details of the fox hunt are related to the treatises on the chase and no doubt to current practice, some suggest a memory of the Reynard romances, e.g., the phrase *ofte þef called*; see *Roman de Renart*, lx, 1623, ed. Ernest Martin (Strasbourg, 1882), 1:324: "Renart le larron"; and cf. Jacquemart Gielee, *Renart le nouvel*, 2070, ed. Henri Roussel (SATF, Paris, 1961), p. 129, and Balduinus Iuvenis, *Reynardus vulpes*, 829, ed. R. B. C. Huygens (Zwolle, 1968), p. 96: "O fur Reynarde!" Proverbially the fox pelt represented deceit or fraud, a point not irrelevant in *Gawain*, where, as our hero gets caught in a deceit, so the lord and lady are involved in a fraud.

1729 *bi lagmon* I.e., the fox led them cross-country among the hills, but whether *bi lagmon* means astray (back and forth so that they fell behind in the chase) or strung out in a line behind him, is not clear. *MED* lists only two occurrences of the phrase, here and in the fifteenth-century Shropshire poet John Awdelay (ed. E. K. Whiting, EETS no. 184 [1931], poem 54, l. 114): "Lykyng of flesche . . . ledys ʒoue be lagmon be lyus," where "astray" would fit the context. There seems to be a connection with *lag*, perhaps from ON (cf. Norw dial. *lagga*, "to go slowly"), and Western dialects have used *lagman* for the last of a line of reapers. See Morris, side note to *Gawain*'s line; Menner, in *PQ* 10 (1931):163–68; *EDD*, *lag* adj., v.[2] and sb.[6], 4(7); and Gollancz and Davis.

1730 *mydouerunder* See *OED*, *midoverundern*, *midovernoon*, and *undern*, esp. 2.

1733 *for luf* Commentators have found a deliberate ambiguity in these words which allows the reader for the time being to assume inclination on the lady's part. But it also arises from the nature of the love game itself as seen in the French romances. Though we are constantly assured that our hero and the lady are involved with each other *sans vileinie*, there is an equal reminder of the danger that increasingly lies between them. Whatever her other and as yet hidden purpose, we should be mistaken to assume that the lady is unaffected by the love play.

1738–39 The implication is that the lady was attired seductively rather than in the more discreet manner of a *dame*. But there has been disagreement about the reading of the first of these lines (MS *No hwez goud* etc.), which seems to have suffered scribal corruption. What *hwez* means has been at issue and the position of MS *goud* after its noun seen as pointlessly abnormal and metrically awkward. Besides, the definite article in *þe haʒer stones* needs explanation. If the Gollancz suggestion that this last phrase, "the goodly stones," = pearls, then a scribe may have been led to understand an original *hwe*, in contrast to it, as "color" (ME *hew, hewe*, etc. from OE *hīw, hēow*) instead of "coif" (ME *hŏuve, howe*, etc. from OE *hufe*) hence to emend to the plural *hwez* for balance with *stones*, and also perhaps to misread or change an original past part. *gord(e)* to the awkward adjective *goud*. The present emendations follow these assumptions.

1743   For windows in castles see n. 792 above.

1750 ff.   Under sloth, where idleness abed leading to licence belongs, the moral treatises also list cowardice, which makes men dread their dreams: see *Ayenbite of Inwit*, pp. 31−32; *The Book of Vices and Virtues*, p. 27; and *Jacob's Well*, pp. 106−7 [all *10*]. Cf. Caxton's version of Friar Lorens, *The Boke Named the Royal* (1484), cap. 28, sig. [dvᵛ]. Sir Gawain will later accuse himself of cowardice.

1752   *þat day*   I.e., the next day as defined by 1753−54.

1771   *so neȝe þe þred*   "so close to the dividing or boundary line"; see *OED*, *thread*, 10, quoting this passage as earliest example. Another meaning is also possible, though less likely: "so close to the bare thread, the bare meaning"; cf. *OED*, *thread*, 2b, for "threadbare," and Fr *jusque à la corde*.

1772   *lodly*   Not "distastefully, with repugnance," as some have primly thought, but "churlishly, discourteously," as Madden long ago perceived.

1773   *craþayn*   Noun or adjective, "mean (creature)." The source, forms, and relations of this word, which is rare in Middle English and limited to the North and Northern Midlands, have remained problematical. The French look of its ending, *-ayn*, is not a clue to origin since the development of ME stress produced some confusion in the graphics of unaccented syllables and *-ayn* was sometimes unhistorical, as in this instance; cf. *etayn* (140, 723) from OE *eoten*. *MED* lists the word under *crachoun*, with *chrahun, craton, cratha(i)n, crayon* as variants, and with OFr *cracheron* (*crachon*) as its source. The spelling with ch, *crach(o)un*, occurs only in *Cursor mundi*, and in its Cotton MS reading (23778) "Qua herd a caitiuer chrahun crachun," which gives the line an extra word, the scribe apparently intends to cancel *chrahun* or gloss it as a variant. For the French, Godefroy cites only one instance of *crachon* (actually *chrachon*, dated 1522), where it signifies spittle, nor is there any evidence it was ever used in the meaning required here. To attribute to it in the *Cursor* a metaphoric scorn, which is supposed to get us round the difficulty and justify the derivation of the English from the French, is a modern lexicographer's invention. The required meaning *MED* gives as "A worthless person, a slob." *Gawain's* sense, however, is exceptional (even if we reject *MED's* second, tasteless definition) beside the other instances cited, all but one of which occur in the context of battle, literal or figurative, where the subject is seen as behaving like a coward: usually he has run away, sometimes without resistance, and so been overcome. That one varying use is in a passage of the *Cursor* (9013–14) showing how a wicked woman makes a man subservient, not because he has run away but because he has not: "þe man sco has in hir bandom [*sic*], / He es forcasten als crachon." Here *forcasten* echoes those verbs (*casten, casten down, kast vndir*) found regularly in the other, more military, instances. Paraphrases in the variant texts of the *Cursor* and *The Wars of Alexander* give the word a more general and familiar look: *wrecche, caitefe, knaffe*, the worthless, the unfortunate, the menial and the mean. Related to *crathan, craton* (*crayon* in *The Sege off Melayne* [*10*], where y and the y-form of thorn are readily confused) are a large number of somewhat later instances in d, *cradoun(e), craddone, craudo(u)ne, crawdown, craddan, -en, -in, craaden, -on, crad(d)ant, craddently*, all meaning coward, cowardly, and found in Scotland and the English North and Northern Midlands from the fifteenth century on: see Craigie, *DOST*, and *EDD*. As to the source of these forms, *OED* notes the connection in Scots with *craw down*, referring to a cock that will not fight, but that sounds like popular etymology. *EDD*'s suggestion, *cradant*, from L *credentem* and describing one who from fear fails to keep his legal pledge, is attractive but not recorded in French or English, where the relevant terms are *creant* (*craant*), *recreant* (with loss of d), the former producing, even when relatinized, the Anglo-Latin *creantia* (A.D. 1271), "craving for quarter in a duel": see Latham. More troubling still is that it cannot explain the *Cursor*'s ch spelling, which may not be dismissed simply as erroneous, since it occurs six times at widely separate places in a MS, which does not ordinarily miswrite ch for th. A plausible theory of origins is that *crachon*, on the one hand, and the t-, th-, d-forms, on the other, represent two different words of similar meaning developed from a group of similar-sounding items borrowed from Scandinavian or Low German. That theory is supported by the absence of any recorded OE ancestor and their confinement to the North, where such borrowings were very common. The first of these words, significant for the *Cursor*'s *crachon, -un*, appears as Scots *crachan* (*crackan*), used to denote anything diminutive or sorry-looking; cf. Dan *krak(ke)*, "broken-down nag," borrowed from LG, "a weak person" (also Swiss dial. *ein alter chracher*, "an old dodderer"): see Grant, *SND*, and Falk and Torg, *Norwegisches-dänisches Wörterbuch* (Heidelberg, 1910–11), under *krakke*. The second is not a single word but a group, related to such English verbs as *cratch* (ME *cracche*), *scratch, scrat*, and the noun *scrat*, in turn related to Sw *kratta*, OI *kretta*, OHG *krazzôn*, whatever their ultimate source. The verb *scrat*, "to scratch," recorded in English from about 1225, comes also to mean to struggle to make a living, and the noun (*OED, scrat*, sb.²) signifies, in the Northern counties and Scotland, a small part of anything, but also one who scrapes for a living, a mean person. Forms without s occur in Scandinavian: Sw dial. *krate*, "something small," Norw dial. *krota*, "a little" (Falk and Torg, under *krat*); and the Scots *crat* (*crawtt*, *crot*), corresponds to these and signifies feeble, puny, a small insignificant person: see Grant, *SND*. That range of meanings is not out of keeping with the general sense of *craton-crathan* as wretched, insignificant, or menial. A second noun *scrat* (*OED*, sb.¹, in the phrase Old Scrat = the Devil) is also relevant. Related to ON *skratte*, OI *skrati*, "wizard, troll, monster," etc., and in the combination *karl-skrati* "an evil wretch," it becomes confused in Scandinavian dialects with the former noun to mean scrawny beast, fool, woman: see Holthausen, *Vergleichendes und etymologisches Wörterbuch der Altwestnordischen, Altnorwegischen-Isländischen* (Göttingen, 1948), under *skrati* and *skratti*; de Vries, *Altnordisches etymologisches Wörterbuch* (Leiden, 1962), under *skrati*. See also, without s, OI *kratan* (gen.). A ME analogue or derivative *skratt*, "*armifraudita*, hermaphrodite [= sodomite]," is listed in a fifteenth-century MS among the nouns for reprehensible men: Thomas Wright, *Anglo-Saxon and Old English Vocabularies*, ed. Wülcker (London, 1883), 1:695; cf. OE *scritta*, and DuCange under *hermaphroditus*. OE *scrætte*, "whore," which has been connected with this word and could readily have been assimilated to it, rather translates L *scratta* (see *Eranos* [1926], 111–14) and seems to have no distinctive ME descendents. But none of these meanings or uses would appear to imply cowardice or subjection. One surviving instance, however, illustrates how such an application could occur: in the *Havarðar Saga Isfirðings* (sec. 38) the compound *skrattakarl*, usually rendered old devil, wicked churl, is in fact employed as a term of abuse for a man who has yielded without resistance to the threats of a bullying neighbor, and is seen by his angry sons as a coward. As for Sir Gawain, whose reflections here have given us the unusual word and in danger as he is from his hostess, who views him between play and earnest as her captive, we are reminded of the *crachon* in the *Cursor* (9014), overcome and captured by a woman's wiles like Adam, Samson, David and the rest, though the plot is different, and the moral, and our hero's courtly scruple, which would make him *craþayn*, not for yielding to, but escaping from, the lady's firm insistence, with a delicate emphasis on how to do it inoffensively. See 2414ff. and their explanatory note below.

1775 *traytor to þat tolke* This form of the theme of *loiauté* occurs in the French romances, e.g., *Sir Launfal* and *Le chastelaine de Vergi*.

1786 Cf. *Perlesvaus*, 423 (I,40): "Je vos requier . . . seur totes amors. . . ."

1814 *þat lufsum vnder lyne* "that lovely one neath linen," an alliterative tag for a lady. Parallel phrases, for gentlemen as well as ladies, occur in *Sir Tristrem*, 1202, 2816; *Eger and Grime*, 251; *Emaré*, 250, 501, 864; *Harley Lyrics* (ed. Brook), 4.37, 5.38; and *The Green Knight*, 255. Cited by TG.

1832 *schaped* Gollancz defines as "outlined," past participle of *schape* (cf. 2340), from OE *sceppan*; but Davis reads "trimmed" as if from a verb *chape*, *schape*, related to the noun *chape*, *schape*, "a metal mount or trimming," from OFr *chape*. See the vocabulary below and cf. *MED, chape*.

1853 *haþel vnder heuen* Cf. *The Wars of Alexander*, 4937. TG suggests that this phrase descends from OE "hæle under heofonum"; see *Beowulf*, 52, and *Solomon and Saturn* (ed. Menner [1941]), 60.

1878 *lyste* For this emendation of MS *lyfte* see Burrow, *Reading*, p. 105, and Davis.

1881 *þe more and þe mynne* Some commentators have suggested that this phrase alludes to the elaborate classification of sins, as found, for example, in contemporary penitentials, but the words themselves comprise a widely occurring alliterative tag in ME poetry. TG notes its Scandinavian origin, citing *Vǫluspá*, i, and *Fornmanna sǫgur*, viii.250.

1882ff. For the problem raised by Sir Gawain's confession and absolution see the introduction above, p. 12, and cf. ll. 2391–94.

1923 *Strakande* See n. 1364 above.

1926 *Sir Gawayn þe gode* See n. 5 above and l. 1110.

1936ff. The tone of this passage depends on the contrast between the grave formality of 1936 and the play with *chepe*, *chepez*, and the alliteration on c and ch, running through the rest of the lines.

1941 *chepez* Gollancz emends to *pray*, TG suggests *porchaz* or *porchez*. But what is thus gained for the alliteration is lost for the wordplay.

1963 *hyȝe fest, Hyȝekyng* For alliteration see n. 1038.

1979ff. With this elaborate leave-taking TG compares Gerbert de Montreuil's continuation of Chrétien's *Perceval*, 1159ff. (ed. Williams [1922]).

2003 Cf. *The Awntyrs off Arthure*, 82: "For the snyterand snaw, that snaypely hom snellus"; *The Wars of Alexander* (p. 84): "As any snyppand snaw þat in þe snape liȝtis"; and *Wyntre is Gurde Oute and Gone*, 1 and 2 (from the Commonplace Book of Humfrey Newton): "Wyntre that snartely snewes / And snappes vs with mony snartte snawes": see *Medieval English Lyrics*, ed. Silverstein, p. 162.

2004 *wapped* See *OED, wap*, v.¹, which cites this instance as of the wind blowing in gusts; and *The Destruction of Troy*, 9513 (West Midland), as of smoke blowing about in the air; and *Isumbras*, 632 (Northern) as of a cloth flapping in the wind. To these Onions adds from *Liverpool Town Books* (ed. Twemlow [1918]), 1:292: "the snowe dryvyng and wapping to and froe."

2018 *rokked* Chain mail was scoured of rust by rolling in a barrel filled with sand: see Madden's glossary and also Laȝamon, MS Cotton Caligula, 11122 (Madden 22287), "heo ruokeden burnen," glossed by the reading of the later MS Cotton Otho, "hii rollede wepne." The Latin is *rotare loricam*: DuCange, 2. *rotare*, which cites *Monasticum anglicanum* (ed. Dodsworth-Dugdale, II [1673], 384). Madden quotes the *Itinerarium regis Anglorum Richardi in terram hierosolymarum*, attributed to Geoffrey de Vinsauf, among others, from Samuel Meyrick, *A Critical Inquiry into Antient Armour* (London, 1824), 1:85: "Rotantur loricae, ne rubigine squalescunt." Cf. *Historiae anglicanae scriptores quinque*, II (Oxford, 1687), 371.

2023 Cf. *Pearl*, 231: "No gladder gome heþen into Grece." A formula found, with variations, also in the French, e.g., *The Second Continuation* (4:391, 407, 434, 469), 29310, 29732, 30482, 31438: "dusqu'a Limoge," "jusqu'a Pavie," "tant qu'a (tres qu'a) Rome."

2048 The 1530 prose *Perceval* notes (folio cxlv, col. 1), after the knight's three days of pleasure, that his horse has been well cared for and equipped; and so does *The Second Continuation* (4:155), 23054–55: "Puis fait amener son destrier, / Qui ot este molt bien gardez."

2073 An indirect speech rendering of the porter's conventional words of farewell, "Give you God and good day and God save you." Cf. *Cursor mundi*, 8068. See also *MED*, dai, 10(d), where "good day" means "good bye" in all citations but the ambiguous one from Chaucer; and Waldron, who quotes *Le bone Florence*. Only the *Cursor* uses *Gawain*'s verb "give."

2098–120 With the guide's warning about the size of the giant, whose stroke none can withstand, and the exhortation that Sir Gawain go by another way and escape, cf. the 1530 prose *Perceval*, folio cxl, cols. 1 and 2: "Combattre a luy seroit folli quant si tres grand est & si fort quil nest au monde creature qui ait contra son coup duree. Toutesuois beau sire armez vous & hors de ceste tour yssez scauoir se pourrez eschapper." See also *The Second Continuation*, 4:109; *Perlesvaus*, 1:237; and nn. 2111 and 2137 below.

2102 *Hestor* A spelling found in the French romances, usually for Hestor des Mares, son of King Ban, but sometimes, as here, for Hector of Troy, whose bodily strength and prowess, as well as valor, were proverbial in the Middle Ages: e.g., Servius Danielis, on *Aeneid* i.99, which glosses *saevus Hector* "magnus vel fortis vel bellicosus"; Walther, nos. 3504, 11190, 11779a, 12088a, 13935, 19131; Guido delle Colonne [*8*], pp. 44 and 125; Eustache Deschamps, cccxxxviii.42 (ed. SATF, 4:50); and Whiting [*12*], nos. H317, H318. A good illustration of the point occurs in *The Geste Historiale*, 3882–87: "This prinse [Hector] with his pure strenght plainly ouercome /

All Auntres in Armys, þat he euer raght: / Non so stuerne þat withstod a stroke of his honde. / He was massy & mekull, made for þe nonest, / Neuer Troy no tyme soche a tulke bred, / So graithe, ne so good, ne of so gret myght."

2111   *may þe knyȝt rede*   "If the knight have his way." Sisam, *Fourteenth Century Verse and Prose*, pp. 219–20, emends to *may [y] þe, knyȝt, rede*, "I can warn you, sir knight," on the ground that to understand *þe knyȝt*, as in the MS, to refer to the creature whom the guide has been describing seems inappropriate. But the emendation weakens the march of the sentence (making it repeat in effect the opening clause *Forþy I say þe*, 2110), *knyȝt* can mean simply a fighting male, and in any case it is used to support the alliteration. Moreover, though the guide at this moment dwells on his monstrous character in order to intimidate Sir Gawain, the giant is a kind of knight, as all of Arthur's court knows from his pretensions at the opening of the poem. Giants are frequently large-sized knights in late medieval illuminations, e.g., Goliath, as in the Winchester leaf in the Morgan Library (M.619, twelfth century). Cf. Drogenes at his encounter with Hercules in MS Douce 336, fol. 24 (French, fifteenth century), where the giant is in armor, over which he wears a long, tight-waisted tunic with laminate sleeves, and his helmet sports a striped scarf tied in a loop. But his weapon is the conventional rustic monster's spiked club (*massue*). Samson, the "good" giant, is of course usually stylishly dressed.

2137   *stad with staue*   So rough a figure as the guide describes might naturally be thought to carry a club, as Sir Gawain here imagines, though it turns out otherwise in fact. Cf. the giant with his *massue* in the 1530 prose *Perceval*, folio cxl^v, col. 1; and the black man and his club in the *Mabinogion*'s Lady of the Fountain (trans. Jones and Jones, p. 158).

2163–84   The Green Chapel and its setting. See the introduction by Day to Gollancz, p. xx, which suggests that the poet had in mind a cave in the Staffordshire moorland near the conjunction of Hoo Brook and the River Manifold at Wetton Mill. In the seventeenth century this cave was known as Thursehouse or Thursehole, i.e., fiend's hole. See also R. E. Kaske, "Gawain's Green Chapel and the Cave at Wetton Mill" [4]. For a variant view locating the cave in the valley of the River Dane, see Elliott, "Sir Gawain in Staffordshire." The two sites are not far distant from one another. The popular association of the devil with "deserts," meres, caves, and barrows is very old in western Europe, going back in Christian tradition to the legends of the fall of the angels and the Sons of Men to the waste places of the world. For England see, e.g., Grendel's mere in *Beowulf* and the barrow in *Guthlac A*: L. A. Shook, in *MP* 58 (1960):1–10.

2177   The verse is awkward and probably corrupt. The emendation *hit richez*, "draws it to" on a rough branch, modifies the suggestion of TG, which cites *The Destruction of Troy*, 2370–71. Cf. Gollancz, and see *OED*, *rich* v², 1.

2195 *at . . . hit* "which"

2201, 2203, 2204 *Quat, What, What* The repetition of the interjection signals the screech of the axe on the grindstone.

2223 *denez ax* A long-bladed battle-axe ordinarily without a spike on the back, mentioned frequently in the French romances and in fourteenth-century English texts. See Tobler-Lommatzsch, *hache*; and *MED*, *Danish* (a).

2225 *Fyled in a fylor* Apparently an unique alliterated half-line. Not in Oakden.

2230 *stalked* In the sense "to stride," as here, the first occurrence given by *OED* is in 1530.

2247 *Haf þou þy helme* MS *haf þy þy helme*, which Madden and Morris print unchanged. All others drop one *þy* as if an inadvertent scribal repetition, and not, as emended here, a miswriting for *þou*. Throughout the *Gawain* text in the MS *þou* is written *þ*ᵘ and it looks as if with the first *þy* here the scribe also set down *þ*ᵘ, then modified the *u* erroneously to *y*. For the idiom cf. Laȝamon, 15675 (Madden 31401): "hafue þu al þi kine-lond"; cited in *MED*, *hǎven* v., 7a(a).

2259ff. For the poet's evident knowledge of the Carados story in *The First Continuation* of the *Perceval*, see the introduction above, p. 3f. Here may be noted how, after two delays in the delivery of the stroke, Carados urges his opponent to get on with it and, as in the present scene, accuses him of cowardice. Cf. especially 2284–85 and 2300–301 with the 1530 prose *Perceval*, folio lxxix, col. 2: "Et Carados luy dist par yre pourquoy ne frapez vous beau sire de deux mors me faictes mourir que tant vous metez a frapper il semble que couart soiez." See also the *First* and *Second Continuations*, I, 95, 3500–502; II, 216, 7329–33; III.1, 152, 2402–4, and 153, 2408–10.

2270 Cf. n. 379–81, 401–8 above.

2274 *myntes* Past tense second person singular. The MS reading *myntest* is evidently an error. *MED* lists past tense forms *mint(e)*, *munt(e)*, *mente* (Kentish).

2274–76 Cf. the parallel Lancelot scene in *Perlesvaus*, 6699–700 (1:285): "Sire chevalier, aussi ne fist mie mon frere que vos occeïstes, ainz tint le chef e le col tout coi. Autresi vos covient il faire."

2276 *hede, fote, flaȝ, flaȝ* A play with contrast and the use of the same word with different meanings (*traductio*).

2286   *stonde þe a strok*   Cf. 294 and its note.

2316   *spennefote*   An instinctive standing jump (Waldron). The ana-
logues suggest "with feet close together," but also "with feet kicking out":
see J. H. Smith, in *MLN* 49 (1934):62–63; and Gollancz and TG. For *spere
lenþe* as a conventional measure, see *MED*, *length* 2a(b); and for OFr
Tobler-Lommatzsch, *lance*. The situation here recalls *Perceval*, where (1530
Prose, folios lix, col. 1–lx^v, col. 2) Gauuain, bearing the ring the lady has
given him, yet depends, not on its magic to save him when attacked by four
armed knights, but on his own fighting reaction to their violence. So with
our Sir Gawain in the end, whose dauntless courage moves the giant to ad-
miration (2331–35).

2356   *fayled*   Perhaps a scribal error for *fayldez*.

2364   Use of the pearl to denote great worth (the 1530 prose *Perceval*,
folio xlvii^v, col. 1, says of Sir Gawain "de toute chevallerie est la perle") and
the pea little worth is commonplace, and they are brought together ca.
1450 in a variant of the pearls before swine aphorism in an English transla-
tion of Christine de Pisan: see J. D. Gordon, ed., *The Epistle of Othea to Hec-
tor* (Philadelphia, 1942), p. 143, 21–22: "Perles among pesen is foly to
strowe / Before swyn & oþer bestes vnresonable." But the present compari-
son to express excellence has not been found elsewhere in ME nor again in
English until Puttenham ca. 1579: *The Arte of English Poesie by Webster
alias George Puttenham*, ed. J. Haslewood, (London, 1811), 1:xxxiv, 196,
and ed. Willcock and Walker (Cambridge, 1936, repr. 1970), pp. 234–35,
quoting his earlier *Partheniades*: "Sett shallowe brookes to surginge seas, /
An orient pearl to a white pease." See Whiting, P 91 and P 89, and *Gawain*,
ed. Morris, p. [vi].

2367   *wylyde werke*   "skillful work," usually taken to refer to the girdle,
with *werke* having the suggestion of "handiwork." Madden and Morris read
wylyde as "wild, amorous," and TG and Cawley render the phrase "in-
trigue." But see Gollancz and Davis and cf. further vocab. *werk(e)*.

2374–75, 2379–81   Sir Gawain's prime and motivating fault is thus, in
his own view, "cowardyse," which in turn has led to "couetyse." See n.
2508–14 below.

2376   *knot, kest*   *Med, cast* n., 2(c), defines *kest* here as signifying "a sar-
torial device, a belt or girdle," and gives this as the only occurrence. Davis
says it means "fastening," but with a question. *EDD, cast* v., x, notes several
passages from Scottish and Northern dialects where *cast* as a verb is used
with the nouns *knot* and *loup*, meaning "to tie, join together, knit." This
suggests that the present noun *kest* means, not belt or girdle nor merely a
fastening, but more precisely a bow or tie.

2391   Cf. this secular confession and absolution with 1882ff. and see the introduction above, p. 12.

2414ff.   Women as deceivers of the men who loved them. The theme with a list of instances is a medieval commonplace, which appears also in the French romances. See especially the *Roman de la rose*, 16622−76; and the Vulgate *La mort le roi Artus*, 6:244−45: "Iou ne ui onques preudome qui longement amast par amors que al daarain nen fust hounis." Cf. the Vulgate *Lancelot*, 5:456−60, where a deceived Sir Gawain says "que homme soy honnist qui croyt femme ne bonne ne malle."

2444   *þat oþer*   To provide alliteration this must be read as if *þe toþer*; contrast 110 and 2412, where the alliteration is on the vowel. See Davis.

2445   *Bertilak de Hautdesert*   So recent editors, TG *Bercilak*, Madden and Morris *Bernlak*; see TG's and Davis's note. Bertelak appears in the *Merlin* (ed. Wheatly, EETS, nos. 10 and 21, 2nd ed. [1875, 1877]) and seems to be related to OFr Bertolais, Bertelak, e.g., Bertelak le Roux; see Flutre. Some have held Hautdesert to refer to the Green Chapel and to signify "high hermitage," though it lies at the bottom of a valley and the meaning "hermitage" would seem to have to reflect a highly specialized Celtic use: see Davis. Desert, meaning "deserted or solitary place, waste land," is common in French place names: see Dauzat and Rostaing, *Dictionnaire étymologique des noms de lieux en France* (1963); and Haut and Desert, having the same significance as in the French, are each found in combination in England: see A. H. Smith, *English Place-Name Elements*, I, 236 and 131 (English Place Name Society, vol. 25 [1956]); and W. H. Duignan, *Notes on Staffordshire Place Names* (London, 1902), p. 12; both of which list an early Beaudesert in Staffordshire. *Hautdesert* would thus seem to refer to the rough upland area, or the castle in it, from which the knight would take his name.

2446, 2452   *Morgne la Faye, Morgne þe goddes*   In the romances Morgan is the daughter of Duke Hoel and Igerne, half-sister of King Arthur and wife of King Uryens, skilled in marvels and astrology, which she learned from Merlin, whose love she once was. Cf. esp. the Vulgate *Merlin*, 2:338. Giraldus Cambrensis, *Speculum ecclesiae*, dist. ii, cap. 9 (*Opera*, ed. Brewer, Rolls Series, 4 [1873]:49) calls her *dea*; and a variant version of the Vulgate *Lancelot* says of her, "ne disaient mie que ce fust fame, mes il l'apeloient *Morgain-la-déesse*": see W. J. Jonckbloet, *Roman van Lancelot*, 2 ('S Gravenhage, 1849):lxix; and cf. ed. Sommer, 2:116−17.

2448   *Merlyn*   The well-known wizard of the romances, in Geoffrey of Monmouth's *Historia* a combination of the Welsh Myrddin with Nennius's prophet Ambrosius, calling him Merlinus Ambrosius and connecting him with King Arthur: see R. S. Loomis, ed., *Arthurian Literature in the Middle*

Ages (1959); *Trioedd Ynys Prydein*, ed. Bromwich (1961), esp. pp. 469–74; and Davis.

2448–55   This insertion summarizing Morgan's history in brief phrase and clause gives, beyond information, a colloquial quality to Sir Bertilak's speech.

2460ff.   According to the Vulgate romances Guenever feared Morgan and Morgan in turn hated the queen for having revealed Morgan's affair with Guiomar and caused her to flee the court to Merlin. By the magic arts which Merlin taught her she made, in order to irk the queen and her knights, "la chapele Morgain" at the intersection of two roads leading to "le ual sans retor" and "le ual des faus amans": the Vulgate *Lancelot*, 4:116–17; and Jonckbloet, *Roman van Lancelot*, 2:lxix. For *Gawain*'s portrayal of Morgan as an *auncian*, whose misshapen body is well covered with fussy clothing (957ff.), though her half-brother Arthur is still young, see Madden's citation (pp. 325–26) of the *Prophecies of Merlin*, where the Lady of Avalon asks her for all her clothes: "'Ha! dame,' fait Morgain, 'vous m'avez honnye, car l'on cuidoit que je fusse de jeune aage, et ilz on veu ma chair nue et ridée, et mes mamelles pendans, et aussi la peau de mon ventre, dont la nouvelle sera comptée en maint lieu.' 'Morgain,' fait la Dame d'Avallon, 'je sçay certainement que par maintes fois avez esté en vostre lict tout nue avec maint beau chevalier.' 'En nom Dieu,' fait Morgain, 'se je y ay esté, aussi me suys-je baignée, et oings tous mes membres, dont les chevaliers les troverent toutes fresches et dures.'"

2479–83   There is a remarkable echo in these lines summarizing the return journey of a passage in *The First Continuation*, Long and Mixed versions, at the end of Sir Gawain's Grail visit: "Messire Gawains molt erra / Par maint pais et se pena / D'armes. Molt estut longement. / Je vos di bien veraiement, / Ançois qu'il vausist ains aler / En Bretagne ne retorner. / *Les batailles qu'il acieva / Ne les merveilles qu'il trova, / Ne vos puis ore pas retraire; / Por itant m'en covient a taire, / C'au droit conte vel reparier.* . . ." (ed. Roach, and Ivy, 2:496, 7783–93; cf. 3:532, 17849–59).

2494ff.   The requirement that the returned knight recount his adventures to the court is widespread in Arthurian romance. In *The First Continuation* and the 1530 prose *Perceval* Sir Gawain itemizes his Grail adventure detail by precise detail as here: Roach, 1:382, ll. 14089 ff., and 3.1:527, ll. 8281ff.; ed. Roach and Ivy, 2:545, ll. 18337ff.; and the 1530 prose, folio cxxvi, col. 1.

2508–14   The present editor has argued ("Sir Gawain in a Dilemma" [7]) that 2508–9, repeating in part a similar self-accusation in 2374–75, echo statements which appear in several treatises of the twelfth century and later that deal with the themes of justice and trawþe, and go back ultimately to Cicero's *De officiis*, e.g., the *Moralium dogma philosophorum*, p. 8: "Sed eius officium duo affectus, scilicet *timor et cupiditas* . . . prepediunt." Cf.

the French version: "le cui mestier dui tallant destorbent, c'est paors et couoitise"; and Brunetto's *Tresor*, 2:91, sec. 11: "Mais .ii. volontés empechent l'office de justice, ce sont paour et covoitise. . . ." In the moral treatises these words are the statement of a general principle, without the example of a particular case which depends on either of the faults alone, or on both together equally, or on both but with one subordinate to the other. In the poem's plot "cowardyse" is, as Sir Gawain sees it, the prime mover that "me taght / To accorde me with couetyse," thus making him forsake his nature, that includes "larges" and "lewté," and more fundamentally leads him to "vntrawþe"; yet though this states accurately the causal order of the head-chopping and the gift-giving as motivation for our hero, it is these two circumstances side by side in the immediate reality of the climax which make him, following the treatises, single out cowardice and covetousness as the twin sources of the violation of his word. See nn. 651–53 and 653 and the introduction, p. 12, above. The precise meaning of "covetyse" has given the commentators trouble, since the poet makes it amply plain that Sir Gawain did not take the girdle for its own sake, and refused the richer ring. A passage from *Ancren Wisse* (ed. Tolkien), folio 56b.3–5, cited by Davis, and another from Mannyng's *Handling Synne*, adduced by the present editor, provide contemporary definitions which are appropriate to our hero's situation, i.e., keeping for yourself something which, by promise or otherwise, belongs in fact to someone else. Thus Mannyng (p. 68): "Here, y aske at þe bygynnyng, / Ʒyf þou with wrong ʒerned oþer mannys þyng / . . . / Ʒyf þou withholde, and ʒelde hyt noght, / Auaryse [OFr coueitise] to helle haþ þe broght. / Yn þy lyfe, y rede þou ʒelde hit aʒen, / Þy saluacyon ys elles alle veyn. / Ʒyf þou madest euer any delay, / And ledyst one lyte fro day to day / with þy wurdys pryuyly, / Or perauenture al on hy, / For to haue þyng with wrong, / Euyl couetyse þou menges among." See also *Jacob's Well*, chap. 20, "De cupiditate," p. 136, ll. 19–21 [*10*]. As for Sir Gawain's special sensitivity despite the Round Table's loving laughter in the passage which follows, see the *Moralium dogma*'s remark of one whose character is formed by the virtue *innocentia*: "Hanc seruare qui uolet, omnia scelera sua, licet minima, estimet magna: Who thinks to preserve this virtue in himself will hold all his faults to be great, even the tiniest among them." Earlier (2367–68), when the Green Knight excuses our blushing hero for his small fault ("Bot þat watz for no wylyde werke ne wowyng nauþer, / Bot for ʒe lufed your lyf; þe lasse I yow blame"), the appeal is to the *utile*, the expedient, which an *innocens* like Sir Gawain, though tempted, cannot in the end accept, for he is by definition (see n. 653 above) one *non qui leviter nocet sed qui* nihil *nocet*, and it is here precisely that he comes to face in himself the moral scruple engraved on the soul by the knight's special virtue: "Bonum autem animae quod est honestum est praeferendum bono utili et delectabili. . . . Ex hoc infertur quod tres sunt virtutes morales necessariae ad hoc, ut quis dicatur bonus et virtuosus. Vna quae praefigat animum ad praeferendum bonum honestum utile, et haec est iustitia," justice "which turns the heart to the honorable rather than to the expedient." (Johannes de Lignano, *De iure belli*, cap. 25, ed. Holland, p. 104, citing Justinian's *Institutes*). Cf. the Senecan theme, honor preferred to safety and comfort, n. 713ff. above. This also explains, as an aspect of our hero's *innocentia*, why he remains embarrassed by what has been the girdle's temptation, despite two mitigating circumstances: first, the lady has offered as a token of loving service something which in fact is intended to harm Sir Gawain, and nothing could be more insidious than that (*Nulle sunt occultiores insidie quam hee que latent in similitudine offitii*, quoted by the *Moralium dogma*, p. 10, from Cicero's *Verrines*, II, i.15, 39, and available also in the vernacular, e.g., besides the OFr version of the *Moralium* itself, p. 102, Brunetto Latini and, with a particular application to love, *Les diz et proverbes des sages*, ed. J. Morawski [Paris, 1924], pp. 9, 111, and cf. 63: "Ou mont n'a traÿson si grant / Com celle c'on fait en semblant / De servir amoureusement"); second, the girdle, which is said to have the magic to keep its wearer safe from death or injury, evidently has no such power (Sir Gawain, while wearing it, is wounded and for all we know might have been slain). In ancient Roman law, as Cicero's *De officiis* observes, any oath or promise exacted by force, or as in this case fraud, is invalid, but that hardly soothes our hero's prick of conscience.

2513–21 The transformation of the girdle from mark of shame to badge of honor by King Arthur's court recalls the Vulgate *Lancelot*, 4:215–18. In Chrétien's earlier *Chevalier à la charrette* Sir Lancelot had ridden in a cart for Guenever's sake and this deed surmounted its shame. In the Vulgate, Sir Bohors and the Lady of the Lake ride in a cart into King Arthur's court, the lady saying that for Lancelot's sake "deueroient estre toutes charretes honorees a tous iors mais." Shamed in their turn by this example, the queen, the king, and all the knights ride successively in the cart to honor Lancelot.

2522ff. Cf. the alliterative *Morte Arthure*; Langtoft's *Chronicle* (Rolls Series, 47.1:262–65); and Mannyng's *Chronicle*, 16689–93. *Brutus Bokez* are histories of Britain, usually beginning with its founding by Brutus, but, as here, not necessarily concerned further with his story; and the name for such a book is *Brut*. These lines constitute a brief informal epilogue, which gentles down high comedy by turning back to the poem's *prohemium* and reminding us that all this is "history," far away in the past, then ends with a conventional prayer found in other contemporary narratives. HONI SOYT QUI MAL PENCE: Apparently added by another hand at end of page, this motto, associated with the Order of the Garter, has been used to argue a special view of the poem's origins. See I. Jackson, in *Anglia* 37:393–423.

Select Bibliography

1. Manuscript

British Library, MS Cotton Nero A.x, fols. 91^r–124^v.

Facsimile: *Pearl, Cleanness, Patience and Sir Gawain Reproduced in Facsimile from the Unique MS. Cotton Nero A.x. in the British Museum.* With introduction by Sir I. Gollancz. EETS, no. 162, 1923.

Handwriting: Wright, C. E. *English Vernacular Hands from the Twelfth to the Fifteenth Centuries.* Oxford, 1960. P. 15. Cf. facsimile, p. 8.

History: Watson, A. G. *The Manuscripts of Henry Savile of Banke.* London, 1969. See esp. p. 68, item 274, and cf. facsimile, p. 7.

2. Editions, with Abbreviations

Madden: *Syr Gawayne: A Collection of Ancient Romance-Poems.* Edited by Sir Frederic Madden. London: Bannatyne Club, 1839. Pp. 3–92. Reprint New York: AMS Press, 1971.

Morris: *Sir Gawayne and the Green Knight: An Alliterative Romance-Poem.* Edited by Richard Morris. EETS, no. 4, 1864. 2d edition revised, 1869. Revised by Gollancz, 1897 and 1912.

TG: *Sir Gawain and the Green Knight.* Edited by J. R. R. Tolkien and E. V. Gordon. Oxford, 1925.

Davis: TG, 2d edition by Norman Davis. Oxford, 1967.

Gollancz: *Sir Gawain and the Green Knight.* Edited by Sir I. Gollancz, with introductory essays by Mabel Day and Mary S. Serjeantson. EETS, no. 210, 1940 for 1938.

Pons: *Sire Gauvain et le chevalier vert*. Edited and with French translation by Emile Pons. Paris, 1946.

Cawley: *Pearl and Sir Gawain and the Green Knight*. Edited by A. C. Cawley. Everyman's Library, London, 1962. New edition by Cawley and J. J. Anderson, 1976.

Waldron: *Sir Gawain and the Green Knight*. Edited by R. A. Waldron. London, 1970. New edition in *The Poems of the Pearl Manuscript*, edited by Malcolm Andrew and Ronald Waldron. London: Arnold, and Berkeley and Los Angeles: University of California Press, 1978. Pp. 207–300.

Burrow: *Sir Gawain and the Green Knight*. Edited by J. A. Burrow. Harmondsworth, 1972.

Barron: *Sir Gawain and the Green Knight*. Edited and translated by W. R. J. Barron. Manchester, England, and New York, 1974.

Moorman: *The Works of the Gawain-Poet*. Edited by Charles Moorman. Jackson, Miss., 1977. Pp. 281–444.

3. Editions of Related Texts

Pearl

Morris: EETS, no. 1, 1864.
Gollancz: London, 1891. Revised 1897, new editions 1921, 1966.
Osgood, C. G.: Boston, 1906.
Chase, S. P.: and Others, Boston, 1932.
Gordon, E. V.: Oxford, 1953.
Hillmann, Sister M. V.: New York, 1961.
Ford, Sara de: New York, 1967.
See also Cawley, Moorman, (Andrew and) Waldron in section 2 above.

Purity

Morris: EETS, no. 1, 1864.
Menner, R. J.: New Haven, 1920.
Gollancz: London, 1921, 1933 (as *Cleanness*).
See also Moorman, (Andrew and) Waldron in section 2 above.

Patience

Morris: EETS, no. 1, 1864.
Bateson, H.: Manchester, England, 1912. 2d edition, 1918.
Gollancz: London, 1913. 2d edition, 1924.
Anderson, J. J.: Manchester, England, 1969.
See also Moorman, (Andrew and) Waldron in section 2 above.

Saint Erkenwald

Horstmann, C.: in *Altenglische Legenden*, N.F., Heilbronn, 1881.
Gollancz: London, 1922.
Savage, H. L.: New Haven, 1926. Reprint Archon Books, 1972.
Morse, Ruth: Cambridge, England, and Totowa, N.J., 1975.
Peterson, Clifford: Philadelphia, 1977.

4. Author and Provenience

Day, Mabel. In *Sir Gawain*, ed. Gollancz. Pp. xviii–xx, lxxi.
Elliott, Ralph W. V. "Sir Gawain in Staffordshire: A Detective Essay in Literary Geography." *The Times*, 21 May 1958. P. 12, cols. 6, 7.
Greenwood, Ormerod, translator. *Sir Gawain and the Green Knight: A Fourteenth-Century Alliterative Poem Now Attributed to Hugh Mascy.* London, 1956.
Kaske, R. E. "Gawain's Green Chapel and the Cave at Wetton Mill." In *Medieval Literature and Folklore Studies: Essays in Honor of Francis Lee Utley.* Edited by Jerome Mandel and Bruce A. Rosenberg. Brunswick, N.J., 1970. Pp. 111–21.
Peterson, C., editor. In *Saint Erkenwald.* Pp. 21–23.
Savage, H. L. *The Gawain-Poet: Studies in His Personality and Background.* Chapel Hill, 1956.

5. Language, Meter, Ornaments, Style

Borroff, Marie. *Sir Gawain and the Green Knight: A Stylistic and Metrical Study.* New Haven, 1962. Reprint Archon Books, 1973.
Faral, E. *Les arts poétiques du xiie et du xiiie siècle.* Paris, 1923.
McIntosh, Angus. "Word Geography in the Lexicography of Medieval English." *Annals of the New York Academy of Sciences* 211 (1973):55–66.
McLaughlin, J. C. *A Graphemic-Phonemic Study of a Middle English Manuscript (Cotton Nero A.x).* The Hague, 1963.
Oakden, J. P. *Alliterative Poetry in Middle English.* Manchester, England. Vol. 1, 1930, vol. 2, 1935.
Peterson, C., editor. *Saint Erkenwald.* Pp. 23–26.
Sapora, R. W., Jr. *A Theory of Middle English Alliterative Meter with Critical Applications.* Cambridge, Mass., 1977.
See also *Sir Gawain*, ed. Gollancz, pp. xli–lxvi, ed. Davis pp. 132–52; *Pearl*, ed. Gordon, pp. xliv–lii, 87–116.

6. Sources, Analogues, Arthurian Background

Texts

Bricriu's Feast: Fled Bricrand. Edited and translated by G. Henderson. Irish Texts Society, 2, 1899. Pp. 97–101, 117–29.

Le chevalier à l'épée. Edited by E. C. Armstrong. Baltimore, 1900.

Chrétien de Troyes: *Charrette, Erec and Enid, Ivain.* In *Sämtliche Werke.* Edited by W. Foerster. Halle, 1884–1932. Translated by W. W. Comfort, *Arthurian Romances.* Everyman's Library, 1928.

———. *Perceval.* Editions by Hilka and Lecoy: see *Perceval* below.

———. *Continuations* of the *Perceval:* see *Perceval* below.

Diu Crône. Edited by G. H. F. Scholl. Stuttgart, 1852.

Geoffrey of Monmouth, *Historia regum Britanniae.* Edited by Acton Griscom. London and New York, 1929. Edited by J. Hammer. Cambridge, Mass., 1951. Translated by Sebastian Evans, 1903; revised by C. W. Dunn. Everyman's Library, 1958.

Hunbaut. Edited by J. Sturzinger and H. Breuer. Dresden, 1914.

Peter Langtoft, *The Chronicle.* Edited by Thomas Wright. Rolls Series, no. 47. London, 1866–68.

Lanzelet. Edited and translated by K. G. T. Webster and R. S. Loomis. New York, 1951.

Laȝamon, *Brut.* Edited by G. L. Brook and R. F. Leslie, EETS, nos. 250 and 277, 1963, 1978. Edited by Frederic Madden. London, 1847.

The Mabinogion. Translated by G. Jones and T. Jones. Everyman's Library, 1949.

Robert Mannyng of Brunne, *Chronicle.* Edited by F. J. Furnivall. Rolls Series, no. 87. London, 1887.

———. *Handlyng Synne.* Edited by F. J. Furnivall. EETS, nos. 119 and 123, 1901, 1903.

La mule sans frein. Edited by B. Orlowski. Paris, 1911. Edited by R. T. Hill. Baltimore, 1911.

Nennius, *Historia Brittonum.* Edited by Joseph Stevenson, London, 1838. Edited by E. Faral, *Le légende Arthurienne,* vol. 3. Paris, 1929. Edited by F. Lot. Paris, 1934.

Perceval. Chrétien de Troyes. *Le conte du graal (Perceval) d'apres la copie de Guiot.* Edited by Felix Lecoy. Paris, 1972, 1975. Edited by Alfons Hilka. Halle, 1935.

———. *The First Continuation,* in *The Continuations of the Old French Perceval of Chretien de Troyes.* Vol. 1: edited by W. Roach, Philadelphia, 1949 (the Mixed version); vol. 2: edited by W. Roach and Robert Ivy, 1950 (the Long version); vol. 3.1: edited by W. Roach, 1952 (the Short version).

————. *The Second Continuation*, in *The Continuations of the Old French Perceval*, vol. 4: edited by W. Roach, 1971.

————. The 1530 prose version: ¶*Tresplaisante et Recreative Hystoire du Trespreulx et Vaillant Cheuallier Perceual le galloys Jadis cheuallier de la Table ronde. Lequel acheua les aduentures du sainct Graal. Auec aulchuns faictz belliquelx du noble cheuallier Gauuain Et aultres Chevalliers estans au temps du noble Roy Arthus non au parauant Imprime.* ¶*Auec priuilege.* ¶*On les vend au Pallais a Paris En la boutique de Jehan longis. Jehan sainct denis et Galliot du pre marchans libraires demourent au dict lieu* [Paris, 1530]. Designated *G* in *The Continuations of the Old French Perceval*, 1:xxxii and 4:xiv, and 2:vii and xi.

Perlesvaus: Le haut livre du graal. Edited by W. A. Nitze and T. A. Jenkins. Chicago, 1932–37. Translated by Sebastian Evans, *High History of the Holy Grail*. Everyman's Library. London, 1910.

Renaut de Beaujeu, *Le bel inconnu*. Edited by G. P. Williams. Paris, 1929.

Guillaume de Lorris and Jean de Meun, *La roman de la rose*. Edited by Félix Lecoy. Paris, 1965–70. Translated by C. Dahlberg. Princeton, N.J., 1971.

Suite du Merlin: Merlin, roman en prose du xiiie siècle. Edited by G. Paris and J. Ulrich. SATF, 1886.

The Vulgate *Lancelot: Le livre de Lancelot del Lac*. In *The Vulgate Version of the Arthurian Romances*. Edited by H. Oskar Sommer, vols. 3–5. Washington, D.C., 1910–12.

The Vulgate *Merlin: Lestoire de Merlin*. In *The Vulgate Version of the Arthurian Romances*. Edited by H. Oskar Sommer, vol. 2, 1908. See also *Le roman de Merlin*. Edited by H. Oskar Sommer. London, 1894.

The Vulgate *La morte le roi Artus*. In *The Vulgate Version of the Arthurian Romances*. Edited by H. Oskar Sommer, vol. 6, 1913.

Wace, *Roman de Brut*. Edited by I. Arnold. SATF, 1938–40.

Yder: Der Iderroman. Edited by H. Gelzer. Dresden, 1913.

Studies

Benson, L. D. "The Source of the Beheading Episode in *Sir Gawain and the Green Knight.*" *Modern Philology* 59 (1961):1–12.

Brewer, Elizabeth. *From Cuchulainn to Gawain: Sources and Analogues of Sir Gawain and the Green Knight*. Totowa, N.J., 1974.

Bruce, J. D. *The Evolution of the Arthurian Romance*, 2d ed., Göttingen and Baltimore, 1928.

Coomaraswamy, A. K. "Sir Gawain and the Green Knight, Indra and Namucci." *Speculum* 19 (1944):104–25.

Faral, E. *La légende Arthurienne*. Paris, 1929.

Fierz-Monnier, A. *Initiation and Wandlung*. Bern, 1951.

Graves, Robert. *The White Goddess: A Historical Grammar of Poetic Myth.* London and New York, 1948. Revised edition 1959, 1966, 1972.

Kittredge, G. L. *A Study of Gawain and the Green Knight.* Cambridge, Mass., 1916.

Loomis, R. S. *Arthurian Tradition and Chrétien de Troyes.* New York, 1949.

―――. *Celtic Myth and Arthurian Romance.* New York, 1927.

―――. *The Development of Arthurian Romance.* London, 1963.

―――. *Wales and the Arthurian Legend.* Cardiff, 1956.

Hulbert, J. R. "Syr Gawayn and the Grene Knyȝt." *Modern Philology* 13 (1915–16):433–62, 689–730.

Von Schaubert, Else. "Der englische Ursprung von *Syr Gawayn and the Grene Knyȝt*," *Englische Studien* 57 (1923):330–446.

Thomas, Martha C. *Sir Gawain and the Green Knight: A Comparison with the French Perceval.* Zürich, 1883.

Zimmer, Heinrich. *The King and the Corpse.* Edited by J. Campbell. Bollingen Series 11. New York: Pantheon Books, 1948. See esp. pp. 67–131.

7. Criticism and Interpretation

Barron, W. R. J. *Trawthe and Treason.* Manchester, England, 1980.

Benson, L. D. *Art and Tradition in Sir Gawain and the Green Knight.* New Brunswick, N.J., 1965.

Blanch, R. J., editor. *Sir Gawain and Pearl: Critical Essays.* Bloomington and London, 1966.

Burrow, J. A. *A Reading of Sir Gawain and the Green Knight.* London, 1965.

Cook, R. G. "The Play-Element in Sir Gawain and the Green Knight." *Tulane Studies in English* 13 (1963):5–31.

Davenport, W. A. *The Art of the Gawain-Poet.* London, 1978.

Howard, D. R., and Christian Zacher, editors. *Critical Studies of Sir Gawain and the Green Knight.* Notre Dame, Ind., 1968.

Pearsall, Derek A. "Rhetorical 'Descriptio' in 'Sir Gawain and the Green Knight.'" *Modern Language Review* 50 (1955):129–34.

Silverstein, T. "The Art of Sir Gawain and the Green Knight." *Toronto Quarterly* 33 (1964):258–78.

―――. "Sir Gawain, Dear Brutus and Britain's Fortunate Founding: A Study of Comedy and Convention." *Modern Philology* 62 (1965):189–206.

―――. "Sir Gawain in a Dilemma, or Keeping Faith with Marcus Tullius Cicero." *Modern Philology* 79 (1977):1–17.

Spearing, A. C. *The Gawain-Poet: A Critical Study.* Cambridge, England, 1970.

Wilson, Edward. *The Gawain-Poet.* Leiden, 1976.

For further items see Malcolm Andrew, section 11 below.

8. Latin Texts and Traditions

Brunetto Latini, *Li livres dou tresor de Brunetto Latini*. Edited by F. J. Carmody. University of California Publications in Modern Philology 22, 1948.

Cato, *Distichs*. Edited by M. Boas. Amsterdam, 1952. See also *Vernon MS. Poems* in section 10 below.

Cicero, *De officiis*.

Geoffrey of Monmouth: see section 6 above.

Geoffrey de Vinsauf, *Poetria nova*. In E. Faral, *Les arts poètiques*: see section 5 above.

Giovanni Balbi, *Summa que Catholicon appellatur . . . emendata per magistrum Petrum Egidium*. Leiden, 1520. Based on Hugutio of Pisa.

Guido della Colonna, *Historia destructionis Troiae*. Edited by N. Griffin. Cambridge, Mass., 1936.

Hugutio of Pisa. As yet unprinted, but see Giovanni Balbi above.

Innocent III, Pope, *De contemptu mundi* or *De miseria humanae conditionis*. Edited by M. Maccarone. Verona, 1955.

Matthew of Vendôme, *Ars versificatoria*. In E. Faral, *Les arts poètiques*: see section 5 above.

Moralium dogma philosophorum de Guillaume de Conches. Edited by John Holmberg. Uppsala, 1929. Contains Latin, Old French, and Middle Low Franconian texts. See Alard de Cambrai in section 9 below.

Nennius: see section 6 above.

Nonius Marcellus, *De compendiosa doctrina*. Edited by J. H. Onions. Oxford, 1895.

Notitia dignitatum: see section 9 below.

Seneca, *De beneficiis*.

Servius on Vergil: *Servii grammatici qui feruntur in Vergilii carmina commentarii*. Edited by G. Thilo and H. Hagen. Hildesheim, 1961.

The Vulgate Bible.

Walther, *Sprichwörter*. H. Walther, *Proverbia sententiaeque Latinitatis medii aevi*. Göttingen, 1963–67.

9. Chivalry: Its Character and Customs

Virtues, Duties, Oaths

Alard de Cambrai. *Le livre de philosophie et de moralité*. Edited by J. C. Payen. Paris, 1970. See also section 8 above, *Moralium dogma philosophorum*.

Bonet, Honoré. *L'arbre des batailles*. Edited by Ernest Nys. Brussels and Leipzig, 1883. English translation by G. W. Coopland. Cambridge, Mass., 1949.

Johannes di Lignano. *De iure belli: De bello, de represaliis et de duello.* Edited by T. E. Holland. Oxford, 1917.

Frère Lorens. *La somme des vices et vertues.* English translation by William Caxton as *The Boke Called the Royall.* See also section 10 below, *Ayenbite of Inwyt* and *The Book of Vices and Virtues.*

Lull, Ramon. *Libre del orde de Cavalleria.* In *Obras de Ramon Lull.* Edited by M. Obrador y Bennassar, vol. 1. Mallorca, 1906, pp. 201–47. Old French version, pp. 249–91.

John of Salisbury. *Policraticus*, book vi, and especially chap. 8. Edited by C. C. J. Webb. Cambridge, England, 1909, volume 2, pp. 1–89, and especially 21–23.

Vegetius, *Epitoma rei militaris.* Old French translation in prose by Jean de Meun as *L'art de chevalerie.* Edited by Ulysse Robert, SATF. Paris, 1897. In verse by Jean Priorat as *Li abrejance de l'ordre de chevalerie.* Edited by Ulysse Robert, SATF. Paris, 1897.

Castles

The History of the King's Works. General editor H. M. Colvin, vols. 1 and 2. London, 1963.

Hohler, Christopher. In *The Flowering of the Middle Ages*, pp. 134–78. See *The Flowering . . .* below.

The Romance of Alexander: A Collotype Facsimile of MS. Bodley 264. With introduction by M. R. James. Oxford, 1932.

The *Très riches heures* [of the Duc de Berry]. Paul Durrieu, *Chantilly: Les très riches heures de Jean de France Duc de Berry.* Paris, 1904. See also Henri Malo, editor. Paris, 1945. English translation by J. Longnon and R. Cazalles. New York, 1969.

Viollet-le-Duc, E. E. *Dictionnaire raisonné de l'architecture française du xi⁰ au xvi⁰ siècle*, vol. 5. Paris, 1861. Translation by M. MacDermott as *Military Architecture*, 3d edition. Oxford and London, 1907.

Costumes and Armor

Evans, Joan. *Dress in Medieval France.* Oxford, 1952.

The Flowering of the Middle Ages. Edited by Joan Evans. London, 1966.

Kelly, F. M., and R. Schwabe. *A Short History of Costume and Armour Chiefly in England 1066–1800.* London, 1931.

Mann, Sir James. *European Arms and Armour*, Wallace Collection Catalogues. London, 1962.

Nevinson, J. L. In *Medieval England.* Edited by A. L. Poole. New edition, Oxford, 1958, chap. 9.

Feasts and Festivals

Anglo, S. *Spectacle, Pageantry and Early Tudor Poetry.* Oxford, 1969.

Cosman, M. P. *Fabulous Feasts, Medieval Cookery and Ceremony.* New York, 1976.

Johnston, M. F. *Coronation of a King.* London, 1902.

Mead, W. E. *The English Medieval Feast.* London, 1931.

Russell, John. *The Boke of Nurture Folowyng Englondis Gise.* Edited by F. J. Furnivall. In *The Babees Book*, EETS, no. 32, 1868.

Heraldry

Brault, G. J. *Early Blazon.* Oxford, 1972.

Notitia dignitatum. Edited by O. Seeck. Berlin, 1876. Facsimile edition, Frankfurt am Main, 1962.

Hunting

The Boke of Saint Albans. Facsimile of the 1486 edition, with an introduction by W. Blades. London, 1901. The hunt only, edited by G. Tilander, *Julians Barnes Boke of Hunting.* Karlshamn, 1964.

La chace dou cerf. Edited by G. Tilander, Stockholm, 1960.

Gascoigne, George. *The Noble Arte of Venerie or Hunting.* London, 1575. Reprint Oxford, 1908. Formerly ascribed to George Turbervile.

Gaston Phébus. Edited by G. Tilander. *Cynegetica* 18 (1971).

Henry Duke of Lancaster. *Le livre des saintes médecines.* In E. J. Arnould, *Étude sur le livre des saintes médecines.* Paris, 1948.

The Master of Game by Edward Duke of York. Edited by W. A. and F. Baillie-Grohman. London, 1904. Modernized edition, London and New York, 1909.

Les livres du roy Modus et de la royne Ratio. Edited by G. Tilander. Paris, 1932.

Thiébaux, Marcelle. "Sir Gawain, the Fox Hunt and Henry of Lancaster." *Neuphilologische Mitteilungen* 71 (1970):469–79.

———. *The Stag of Love.* Ithaca, N.Y., 1974.

Tilander, G. *Essais d'étymologie cynégétique. Cynegetica* 1. Lund, 1953.

———. *Mélanges d'étymologie cynégétique. Cynegetica* 5. Lund, 1958.

———. *Nouveaux mélanges d'étymologie cynégétique. Cynegetica* 8. Lund, 1961.

Twiti, William. *La vénerie de Twiti.* Edited by G. Tilander. Uppsala, 1956. Middle English version, *The Art of Hunting.* Edited by Bror Danielsson. Stockholm, 1977.

Love

Andreas Capellanus. *De amore libri tres.* Edited by E. Trojel. Copenhagen, 1892. 2d edition, Munich, 1964. English translation as *The Art of Courtly Love* by J. J. Parry. New York, 1941; reprinted 1964.
Roman de la rose: see section 6 above.

10. Contemporary English and Scottish Texts

Alexander B: see *Kyng Alisaunder* below.
Ancrene Wisse. Edited by J. R. R. Tolkien. EETS, no. 249, 1962. Modern English version by M. B. Salu, *The Ancrene Riwle.* London, 1955.
Of Arthour and of Merlin. Edited by O. D. Macrae-Gibson. EETS, no. 268, 1973.
The Avowynge of King Arther. Edited by J. Robson. In *Three Early English Metrical Romances.* Camden Society, no. xviii, 1842.
The Awntyrs off Arthure at the Terne Wathelyne: A Critical Edition. R. J. Cates. Philadelphia, 1969. See also the edition by F. J. Amours, in *Scottish Alliterative Poems*, STS, 1897, pp. 115–71.
Dan Michel's Ayenbite of Inwyt, or, Remorse of Conscience. Edited by Richard Morris. EETS, no. 23, 1866.
The Buik of Alexander, II. Edited by R. L. Graeme Ritchie. STS, no. 12, 1921. Contains *The Avowis of Alexander* and Languyon's *Les voeux du paon*, pp. 107–248.
Emaré. Edited by E. Rickert. EETS ES, no. 99, 1908.
Sir Gawain and the Carl of Carlisle. Edited by A. Kurvinen. Helsinki, 1951. See also the edition by R. Ackerman. Ann Arbor, 1947.
The Gest Hystoriale of the Destruction of Troy. Edited by G. A. Panton and D. Donaldson. EETS, nos. 39 and 56, 1869–74.
The Knightly Tale of Golagros and Gawane. Edited by F. J. Amours. In *Scottish Alliterative Poems*, pp. 1–46.
The Harley Lyrics. Edited by G. L. Brook. 2d edition. Manchester, England, 1956.
Ipomadon. Edited by E. Kölbing. Breslau, 1889.
Jacob's Well, an Englisht Treatise on the Cleansing of Man's Conscience. Edited by A. Brandeis. Part 1. EETS, no. 115, 1900.
Kyng Alisaunder. Edited by G. V. Smithers. EETS, no. 227, 1952. Contains *Alexander A, B, L, M.*
Laud Troy Book. Edited by J. E. Wülfing. EETS, nos. 121–22, 1902–3.
Lydgate's Troy Book. Edited by H. Bergen. EETS ES, nos. 97, 103, 106, and 126, 1906–35.
Mandeville's Travels Translated from the French of Jean d'Outremeuse. Edited by P. Hamelius. EETS, nos. 153–54, 1916.

Medieval English Lyrics. Edited by T. Silverstein. London, 1971. U.S. title *English Lyrics Before 1500.* Evanston, Ill., 1971.

Morte Arthur (stanzaic). Edited by J. D. Bruce. EETS ES, no. 88, 1903. Another edition by P. F. Hissinger, The Hague and Paris, 1975.

Morte Arthure (alliterative). Edited by E. Björkman. Heidelberg, 1915. See also the editions by J. Finlayson (London and Evanston, Ill., 1967) and V. Krishna (New York, 1976).

Mum and the Sothsegger. Edited by M. Day and R. Steele. EETS, no. 199, 1936.

The Parlement of the Thre Ages. Edited by M. Y. Offord. EETS, no. 246, 1959.

The Quatrefoil of Love. Edited by Sir I. Gollancz and M. Weale. EETS, no. 195, 1935.

Scottish Troy Fragments. Edited by C. Horstmann. In Barbour's *Legendensammlung,* vol. 2. Heilbronn, 1882.

The Sege off Melayne. Edited by S. J. Herrtage. EETS ES, no. 35, 1880.

The Siege of Jerusalem. Edited by E. Kölbing and M. Day. EETS, no. 188, 1931.

Summer Sunday. In *Historical Poems of the XIVth and XVth Centuries.* Edited by R. H. Robbins. New York, 1959.

Sir Tristrem. Edited by G. P. McNeill. STS, 1886.

Vernon Manuscript Poems: The Minor Poems of the Vernon Ms. Edited by C. Horstmann and F. J. Furnivall. EETS, nos. 98 and 117, 1892–1901. Contains Cato's *Distichs* in Latin, Old French, and Middle English (part 2, pp. 553–609) and *Think on Yesterday* (pp. 675–80).

The Book of Vices and Virtues. Edited by W. Nelson Francis. EETS, no. 217, 1942.

The Wars of Alexander. Edited by W. W. Skeat. EETS ES, no. 47, 1886.

William of Palerne. Edited by W. W. Skeat. EETS ES, no. 1, 1867.

Wynnere and Wastour. Edited by Sir I. Gollancz. *Select Early English Poems in Alliterative Verse,* no. 3. London, 1920. Revised edition by M. Day, 1931.

11. Bibliography

Andrew, M. *The Gawain-Poet: An Annotated Bibliography, 1839–1977.* New York, 1979.

12. Dictionaries, Indexes, Journals, Series, with Abbreviations

Dictionaries

Craigie, *DOST: A Dictionary of the Older Scottish Tongue.* Edited by Sir William Craigie. Chicago, 1931–.

Du Cange: *Glossarium mediae et infimae latinitatis.* Edited by C. du Fresne du Cange. Niort, n.d.

EDD: *The English Dialect Dictionary*. Edited by J. Wright. London, Oxford, New York, 1898–1905.

Godefroy: *Dictionnaire de l'ancienne langue française et de tous ses dialectes du ix* *and xv* *siècle*. Edited by F. Godefroy. Paris, 1880–1902. Reprint, SPE and Kraus. Vaduz and New York, 1961.

Grant, *SND*: *The Scottish National Dictionary*. Edited by William Grant. Edinburgh, 1931–76.

Latham: *Revised Medieval Word-List from British and Irish Sources*. Edited by R. E. Latham. London, 1965.

MED: *Middle English Dictionary*. Edited by Kurath, Kuhn, and Reidy. Ann Arbor, Mich. and London, 1956–1979. Incomplete.

OED: *A New English Dictionary on Historical Principles*. Edited by J. A. H. Murray, H. Bradley, W. A. Craigie, and C. T. Onions. Oxford and New York, 1888–1933.

Sainte-Palaye: *Dictionnaire historique de l'ancien langage françoise depuis son origine jusqu'au siècle de Louis XIV*. Edited by La Curne de Sainte-Palaye. Niort, n.d.

Tobler-Lommatzsch: *Altfranzösisches Wörterbuch*. Edited by A. Tobler and E. Lommatzsch. Berlin, 1925–76. Incomplete.

Walther: see section 8 above.

Whiting: *Proverbs, Sentences and Proverbial Phrases from English Writings Mainly Before 1500*. Compiled by B. J. Whiting and H. W. Whiting. Cambridge, Mass., 1968.

Indexes

Ackerman: R. W. Ackerman, *An Index of the Arthurian Names in Middle English*. Stanford University Publications, Language and Literature, vol. 10, 1952.

Chapman: C. O. Chapman, *An Index of Names in Pearl, Purity, Patience and Gawain*. Ithaca, N.Y., 1951.

Flutre: L.-F. Flutre, *Table des noms propres avec toutes leurs variantes figurant dans les romans du moyen age écrits en Français ou en Provençal et actuellement publiés ou analysés*. Poitiers, 1962.

Kottler and Markman: B. Kottler and A. M. Markman, *A Concordance to Five Middle English Poems: Cleanness, St. Erkenwald, Sir Gawain and the Green Knight, Patience, Pearl*. Pittsburgh, 1966.

West: G. D. West, *An Index of Proper Names in French Arthurian Verse Romances 1150–1300*. Toronto, 1969.

Journals

ELH: *English Literary History*.
ES: *Englische Studien*.

JEGP: *Journal of English and Germanic Philology*.
MLN: *Modern Language Notes*.
MLR: *Modern Language Review*.
MP: *Modern Philology*.
N & Q: *Notes and Queries*.
RES: *Review of English Studies*.
SP: *Studies in Philology*.
TLS: *The Times Literary Supplement*.

Series

EETS: Early English Text Society, Original Series.
EETS ES: Early English Text Society, Extra Series.
SATF: Société des Anciens Textes Français.
STS: Scottish Text Society.

Vocabulary

Words that appear more than four times with the same or similar meaning are listed here without line reference; otherwise reference is normally given for each particular use.

A

a *interj.* 1746.

a, an *indef. art.* [OE *ān*]

abataylment *n.* battlement 790. [From OFr *abataill(i)er v.*]

abelef *adv.* slantwise 2486, 2517. [OFr *a be(s)lif*]

abide *v. intr.* to stop, 2090; *imper.* wait! 2217; *trans.* await 1900; bear 1754. [OE *abīdan*]

abloy *adj.* carried away 1174. [OFr *e(s)bloi* pp.]

abode *n.* delay 687. See ABIDE

abof, aboue(n) *adv.* above 2217; upon it 153, 166, 856; in a higher seat 73; in the highest place 112; *prep.* above 184, 478, 765. [OE *abufan*]

about(t)e *adv.* about, round about; *ben a.* to be attentive 1986; *prep.* about, around; concerning 68. [OE *abūtan*]

absolucioun *n.* absolution 1882. [OFr *absolucio(u)n*]

achaufed *v. pa. t.* warmed 883. [OFr *eschaufer*]

acheue *v.* to attain 1081, 1107; *acheue to* reach 1838, 1857. [OFr *achever*]

acole *v.* to embrace 1936, 2472. [OFr *acoler*]

acorde *n.* agreement 1384. [OFr *acorde*]

acorde *v.* to reconcile 2405; *refl.* consent 1863; come to terms 2380; *pp.* accorded 2519; resolved that 2514; *a. wyth* match 602; *a. to* suit 631; *a. of* agree to 1408. [OFr *acorder*]

adoun *adv.* down; downwards 2263. [OE *ofdūne*]

afyaunce *n.* trust 642. [OFr *afia(u)nce*]

aft(t)er *prep.* after, behind, in pursuit of; for 1215, 2093; along 218; *adv.* afterwards; after the same fashion 171; along 1608. [OE *æfter*]

after *conj.* after 2525. [From OE *æfter þam þe*]

agayn, aȝayn *adv.* in return, back, again; *prep.* against 2116. [ON *í gegn*, OE *ongegn*]

age *n.* age; *in her first a.*, in the flower of their youth 54. [OFr *aage*]

aghlich *adj.* terrible 136. [ON *agi* + OE *-lic*]

agreued *v. pp.* weighed down, overcome 2370. [OFr *agreuer*]

aȝaynez *prep.* to meet 971; against 1661. AȜAYN + adv. *-es*]

aȝlez *adj.* without fear 2335. [ON *agi* + OE *-lēas*]

aȝt(e). See OGHE

ay *adv.* always, ever; in each case 73, 128, 190. [ON *ei*]

ayled *v. pp.* troubled 438. [OE *eglan*]

ayquere, aywhere *adv.* everywhere. [OE *æghwǣr*]

ayþer *adj.* each, both 1356, 2180; *pron.* 1357; *ayþer . . . oþer*, each (the) other 841, 939, 1307, 2472. [OE *ǣgþer*]

al. See AL(LE)

alce. See ALS(E)

alder *adj. compar.* older 948; elder 972, 1317. [OE *ældra*]

alder-, alþer- *intensive prefix in* **aldertruest, alþergrattest,** truest, greatest, of all 1486, 1441. [OE *alra*, gen. pl.]

alderes *n. pl.* men of old 95. [OE *ældra*]

algate *adv.* nevertheless 141. [Cf. ON *alla gǫtu*, all along]

Al Hal Day *n.* All Saints' Day (1 NOV.) 536. [OE *alra hǎlgena dæg*]

alyue *adj.* living 1269. [OE *on life*]

al (le) *adj.* all; *adv.* entirely, quite, everywhere; *al peroute* outside altogether 2481; right by 1349; although 143; *pron.* all, everything, everybody. [OE *al(l)* adj. and adv.]

aloft(e) *adv.* up, above, at the top; on horseback 435, 2060; *prep.* on 1648. [ON *á loft*] See LOFT(E)

alosed *v. pp.* praised 1512. [OFr *aloser*]

als(e) *adv.* also, as well; as 1067; **alce** 2492. [OE *alswā*]

also *adv.* also, as well. [OE *alswā*]

alþergrattest. See ALDER-/

aluisch *adj.* elvish 681. [OE *ælf* + ME ending]

alway *adv.* always 1482. [OE *alne weg*]

am *I sg. pres.* am [OE *eam, am*]

amende *v. intr.* to improve 898. [OFr *amender*]

among *prep.* among. [OE *on mong*]

amount (*to*) *v.* to amount to, 1197. [OFr *amo(u)nter*]

anamayld *v. pp.* enamelled 169. [OFr *enamaill(i)er*]

and, ande *or abbrev. throughout,* *conj.* and; if 1009, 1245, 1271, 1393, 1509, 1647, 1966, 1996, 2129; *and ȝet* even if 1009. [OE *and*]

anelede *v. pa. t.* pursued 723. [OFr *aneler*] See expl. n. 723

angardez *n. gen. as adj.* overweening 681. [OFr *angarde*] See expl. n. 681

anger *n.* injury, harm 2344. [ON *angr*]

any, ani *adj.* any, some; *pron.* anyone, any people; **anyskynnez** of any kind 1539 [OE *ænig,* *ǣniges cynnes*]

anious *adj.* troublesome 535. [OFr *anoio(u)s*]

anoþer *adj.* a second (of two) 295, 383. [OE *an* + *oper*]

answare, onsware *v.* to answer. [OE *an(d)swarian*]

apende *v.* to belong 623, 913. [OFr *apendre*]

apere *v.* to appear 911. [OFr *aper-,* accented variant of *apareir*]

apert *adj.* evident 2392; exposed to view 154. [OFr *apert*]

apparayl *n.* ornamental settings 601. [OFr *apareil*]

aproched *v. pa. t.* approached 1877. [OFr *aproch(i)er*]

aquoyntaunce *n. kallen hym of a.* beg to know him better 975. [OFr *acointa(u)nce*]

aray(e) *n.* array, dress 163, 1873. [OFr *arei*]

arayed, arayde *v. pp.* arrayed, dressed 1130, 1134; constructed 783. [OFr *areier*]

are *adv. neuer a.* never before 239, 1632, 1891. [OE *ǣr,* late Nth *ar*; ON *ár*]

arered *v. pp.* drawn back 1902. [OFr *arerer*]

ar(e)wes *n. pl.* arrows 1160, 1455. [OE *ar(e)we*]

arȝe *adj.* afraid 241. [OE *earg*]

arȝe *v.* to be terrified 1463, 2271, 2277, 2301. [OE *eargian*]

aryȝt, oryȝt *adv.* fittingly 40, 1911. [OE *on riht, ariht*]

arme *n.* arm [OE *earm*]

armed *v. pp.* armed 2335. [OFr *armer*]

armes, -ez *n. pl.* arms, armor 281, 567, 590, 2104; knightly warfare, the knightly occupation 95, 204, 1513, 1541, 2437; heraldic arms 631. [OFr *armes*]

ar(n) *v. pres. pl.* are; **are** 1226. [OE *aron*]

arounde *adv.* at the edges 1833. [*a-*, OE *on* + ROUNDE *adj.*]

arsoun(e)z *n. pl.* saddle-bows 171, 602. [OFr *arso(u)n*]

art *n.* art 1543. [OFr *art*]

art *v.* 2 *sg. pres.* art, are 675, 2240, 2270, 2391. [OE *eart*]

as *conj.* as, like, in the way that, according as, as if, as though; as far as 193; so as 1033; as one who, as being 321, 638, 896, 1104; *with oaths* so 256, 2123; while, when 703, 995, 1592; since 324, 1547, 1941; *adv.* (just) as; *correl. with conj.* 437, 2393. [From ALS, OE *alswā*] See TIT, SWYÞE

asay *n.* trial of the thickness of a deer's flesh, "assay" 1328. [AN; OFr *essai*]

asay *v.* See AS(S)AY

ascryed *v. pa. t.* shouted 1153. [OFr *escrier*]

asyngne *v.* to assign 1971. [OFr *asign(i)er*]

ask(e) *v.* to ask for, request; *absol.* require 530, 1327. [OE *ǎxian*]

askez *n. pl.* ashes 2. [ON *aska*; OE *ascan,* pl.]

askyng *n.* request 323, 349. [OE *ǎcsung*]

asoyled *v. pa. t.* absolved 1883. [OFr *assoiler*]

aspye *v.* to discover 1199. [OFr *espier*]

as(s)ay *v.* to make trial of 2362, 2457. [OFr *essayer*]

as(s)aute *n.* assault 1, 2525. [OFr *as(s)aut*]

at(e) *prep.* at, of, from; to 929, 1671; in 467, 557; according to 1006, 1546; between 2399, *watz hym ate* was "at" him 1474; *adv.* at 1727. [OE *æt*]

atyred *v. pp.* attired 1760. [OFr *atir(i)er*]

at(t)le *v.* to intend 27, 2263. [ON *ætla*]

atwaped *v. pa. t.* escaped 1167. [OE *æt* + WAPPE]

athel, aþel *adj.* noble, glorious splendid. [OE *æþele*]

avanters *n. pl.* part of a deer's numbles 1342. [AN *avanter*, from *avant*]

Aue *n.* the Ave Maria 757.

auen. See OWEN

auentayle *n.* mail neck-guard on helmet, 608. [OFr *aventaille*]

auenture, aventure, awenture *n.* adventure, strange doings 29, 250, 489, 2482; **aunter** 27, 2522, 2527; **auenturus** *pl.* 95, 491. [OFr *aventure*]

auenturus *adj.* perilous 93. [OFr *aventuro(u)s, -us*]

auinant *adv.* pleasurably, enjoying (himself) 806. [OFr *avenant*] See expl. n. 806

auyse, awyse *v.* to devise 45, 1389; to scrutinize 771. [OFr *aviser*]

aumayl *n.* enamel 236. [AN *a(u)mail*, OFr *esmail*]

auncian *adj.* aged 1001, 2463; *sb.* 948. [OFr *a(u)ncien*]

aune 10. See OWEN

aunt *n.* aunt 2464, *þy naunt* 2467. [OFr *a(u)nte*]

aunter *n.* See AUENTURE

auntered *v. pp.* ventured 1516. [OFr *aventurer*]

auter *n.* altar 593. [OFr *auter*]

auþer. See OÞER *conj.*

away *adv.* away 1718, 2119. [OE *on weg*]

awen. See OWEN

awharf *v. pa. t.* turned aside 2220. [OE *ahweorfan*]

ax(e) *n. axe* 208, 330, 2223, 2331. [OE *æx*]

B

bade. See BIDE

bay(e) *n.* the hounds' baying about a cornered animal 1450, 1582; the animal's defensive stand 1564. [OFr *(a)bai*]

baye *v.* to bay, bark 1142, 1362; bay at 1603, 1909. [OFr *baier*]

bayn *adj.* obedient 1092, 2158. [ON *beinn*, direct]

bayst *v. pa. t.* was dismayed 376. [AN *(a)baiss-*, OFr *esbaïr*, *esbaïss-*]

bayþe(n) *v.* to grant 327; agree 1404; consent 1840. [ON *beiða*]

bak *n.* back 143, 1563; *at his bak* behind him 1571. [OE *bæc*]

bakbon *n.* backbone 1352. [OE *bæc* + *bān*]

baken *v. pp.* baked 891. [OE *bacan*]

bald(e)ly *adv.* boldly 376, 1362. [OE *baldlīce*] See BOLD

bale *n.* death 2041; misery 2419. [OE *balu*]

balé *n.* belly 1333. [OE *bæl(i)g*]

balȝ(e) *adj.* smooth round swelling 967, 2032, 2172. [OE *balg*]

bande *n.* band 192. [OFr *bande*]

baner *n.* banner 117. [OFr *ban(i)ere*]

barayne *adj.* not pregnant 1320.
[AN *barain(e)*, OFr *baraigne*]

barbe *n.* barb 1457; cutting edge
2310. [OFr *barbe*, beard, barb]

barbican *n.* outer fortification of a
castle 793. [OFr *barbacane*]

bare *adj.* bare; without armor 290;
mere, simple, actual 277, 2352;
þre b. mote three separate notes
1141; *adv.* fully 465; barely
1066. [OE *bær*]

barely *adv.* without fail 548. [OE
bærlice]

baret *n.* fighting 21, 353, 2115;
trouble 752. [OFr *barat*]

bargayn *n.* agreement 1112. [OFr
bargaine]

barlay *adv.* in (my) turn 296. See
expl. n. 296

barne *n.* baby 2320. [ON *barn*, OE
bearn]

barred *v. pp.* marked with parallel
stripes 159, 600. [From OFr
barre]

barres *n. pl.* transverse bars on a
belt 162. [OFr *barre*]

bastel *n.* castle tower; *bastel rouez*
tower roofs 799. [OFr *bastille*]

batayl *n.* fight 277. [OFr *bataille*]

bate *n.* baiting 1461. [ON *beit*, rel.
to OE *bætan*]

baþed *v. pp.* steeped 1361. [OE
baþian]

bauderyk *n.* baldric 621, 2486,
2516. [Cf. OFr *baudrei*, MHG
balderich]

bawe *n. attrib., stele b.* stirrup iron
435. [OE *boga*] See STEL(E) n.[1]

bawemen *n. pl.* archers 1564. [OE
boga + mann]

be-. See also BI-, BY-

be *prep.* See BI

be *v.* to be; *lettez be*, cease from

1840; to **bene** 141 (OE *to
bēonne*); **be(n)** *future 2 pl.* will
be 1646, 2111; **be** *imper.* 1211,
2338; **be** *subj. pres. sg.*; *wheþer
this be?* can this be? 2186; **be(n)**
pl.; **ben(e)** *pp.* [OE *bēon*]

beau *adj.* fair; *beau sir* 1222 [OFr
beau sire]

becom *v.* to become 1279; **bi-
cumes, bycommes** is fitting
471, 1491; **becom** *pa. t. sg.*
came, got to 460; **bicome** *pl.* be-
came 6. [OE *becuman*]

bed(de) *n.* bed [OE *bedd*]

bedde. See BID(DE)

beddyng *n.* bedclothes 853. [OE
bedding]

bede *v.* to offer 374, 382, 2322;
bede *pa. t.*; bade 1437 (*pl.*),
2012, 2024, 2090. [OE *bēodan*,
confused with *biddan*] See BIDDE

bedsyde *n.* bedside 1193. [EME
beddes side] See SIDE

befalle, bifalle *v.* to happen 382,
1776. [OE *befall*]

before adv., **begynne** *v.*, **beholde**
v., **behoue** *v.*, **beknowe** *v.* See
BIFOR(N)E, BEGYNNE etc.

belde *n.* courage 650. [OE (Angl.)
beldo]

bele *adj.* gracious 1034. [OFr *bele*,
fem.] See BEAU and CHERE

bellez *n. pl.* bells 195. [OE *belle*]

belt *n.* belt 162, 1860, 2377, 2485.
[OE *belt*]

belted *v. pp.* belted 2032. [From
ME *belt* n.]

bemez *n. pl.* rays 1819. [OE *bēam*]

bench(e) *n.* bench 280, 344; *vpon
b.* at table 337, 351. [OE *benc*]

bende *n.* band 2506, 2517. [OE
bend]

bende *v. pa. t.* bent; lowered 305;

pp. in *b. by* curved back in line
with 2224; *hatz much baret b.*
has brought about much strife
2115. [OE *béndan*]

bene *adj.* fair 2475; *adv.* pleasantly
2402. [AN *ben*, OFr *bien*]

bent *n.* grassy ground 2233, 2338;
bank 1599; *on b.* on the field
353, 2115; *burne (vp) on b.*
huntsman, warrior 1465, 2148.
[OE *beonet*]

bentfelde *n.* the hunting field
1136. [ME *bent* + *feld(e)*]

ber *n.* beer 129. [OE *bēor*]

berd(e) *n.* beard. [OE *béard*]

berdlez *adj.* beardless 280. [OE
beardlēas]

bere *v.* to bear, carry, wear, lift;
have 1229; cast from within
1819; *b. fela3schip* accompany
2151; **beres** *pres. pl.* 2523;
ber(e) *pa. t.*; *b. on hym* pressed
on him 1860; **born(e)** *pp.* born
752, 996, 2320, 2349; *b. open*
laid open 2070. [OE *beran*]

berez *n. pl.* bears 722. [OE *bera*]

ber3(e) *n.* mound, barrow 2172,
2178. [OE *be(o)rg*]

beseche *v.* to beg 341, 753, 776,
1881; **biso3t** *pa. t.* 96, 1834,
1862. [OE *be-* + *sēcan*]

best *adj. superl., freq. as sb.* best,
noble; *þe best* the best man
1645; those of highest rank 550,
1325; the best thing to do 1216;
wyth þe b. as well as any 986; *of
þe b.* of the best quality 38, 863,
880, 1145; in the best way 889,
1000; *adv.* 73, 1005, 1680. [OE
betst]

best *n.* beast. [OFr *beste*]

beten *v. pa. t. pl.* beat 1437; *pp.*

set, embroidered 78, 1833, 2028.
[OE *bēatan*]

bette *v. pp.* kindled 1368. [OE
bētan]

better *adj. compar.* better 353,
793, 2278; *sb.* 1109; *þe b.* 1393;
adv. better; *þe b.* 410, 1035,
1084, 2096. [OE *betera,
bet(t)ra*, adj.]

beuerage *n.* drink sealing an agree-
ment 1112, 1409. [OFr *bevrage*]

beuerhwed *adj.* beaver-colored,
reddish brown 845. [OE *beofor*
+ *-hiwede*]

bewté *n.* beauty 1273. [OFr
beauté]

bi, by, be *prep.* by, beside, along,
over, according to; at 41; near
1574; towards 2310; measured
by 2226; (in oaths); *be twenty*
twenty at a time 1739; *conj.* by
the time that 1169; when 1006,
2032; **bi þat** *adv.* by that time
597, 1868; thereupon 2152; *conj.*
by the time that; when 1678,
1912, 2043. [OE *bĭ, be*]

bicause of *prep.* because of 1843.
[ME *bi* + *cause*]

bicom(m)e, bicume. See BECOM

bid(de), bedde *v.* to exhort, com-
mand; request 1089; **beddez**
pres. 3 sg. 1374; **bede** *pa. t.* (see
BEDE); **boden** (form influenced
by BEDE) *pp.* asked 327. [OE
biddan]

bide, byde(n) *v. trans.* to wait for
376, 520, 2292; stand and face,
withstand, survive 290, 374,
1450, 2041; *intr.* stay, stand firm
1092, 1366, 1582, 1585; **bode**
pa. t. 785, 1564; **bade** 1699. [OE
bidan]

bye *v.* to buy 79. [OE *bycgan*]
bifalle. See BEFALLE
bi-, byfor(n)e, biforen *prep.* before 1126, 1675; in front, ahead, in the presence of; above 914; in preference to 1275, 1781; **before, byfor(n)e** *adv.* in front 422, 1741; earlier 1405, 1577. [OE *beforan*]
big *adj.* strong 554; full-grown, fierce, courageous 1441; **bigger** *compar.* 2101; **bigly** *adv.* mightily 1141, 1162, 1584. [Origin uncertain; cf. Norw *bugge* strong man]
big(g)e *v.* to found 9, 20. [ON *byggva*]
bigyle *v.* to deceive 2413, 2416, 2427. [OE *be-* + OFr *guiler*]
bigyn(n)e, begynne *v. intr.* to begin 1340, 1571, 1606; *trans.* 495; found 11; *b. þe table* has place of honor at table 112; **bygan** *pa. t.* 661. [OE *beginnan*]
bigog *interj.* 390. [corruption of *bi God*]
bigrauen *v. pp.* engraved 216. [OE *begrafan*]
biȝonde *prep.* beyond 2200. [OE *begeondan*]
byȝt *n.* fork of the legs 1341, 1349. [OE *byht*]
bihynde *adv.* behind 607, 1350; at the back 1741; inferior 1942. [OE *behindan*]
byholde, beholde *v.* to behold 232, 250, 1187; **behelde** *pa. t.* 794; **bihalden, -holde** *pp.* beholden 1842; in duty bound 1547. [OE *behaldan*]
bihoue, by-, be- *v. impers.* to behove; as in *me (þe, he) bihoues* I

am obliged, must; **bihous** *pres. sg.* 2296; **bihoued** *pa. t.* 1771, 2040; **byhode** 717; *burnes behoued to* it was time for people to go 1959. [OE *behōfian*]
bikenne *v.* to commend 1307; **bikende** *pa. t.* 596, 1982. [OE *be-* + KENNE]
biknowe *v.* to confess 2385, 2495; **beknew** *pa. t.* 903; **beknowen** *pp.* cleared by confession 2391. [LOE *becnāwan* to know. For shift of sense to "acknowledge" cf. OE *gecnǣwe* adj. (*is gecnǣwe* = *L confessus est*) and ME *he biknoweþ* and *he is biknowe(n)*, *biknewen*, both occuring with same meaning]
bylde *v.* to build 509; **bult** *pa. t.* 25. [OE **byldan*, pp. *gebyld*]
byled. See BOYLE
biliue, bylyue *adv.* quickly [OE **be life*]
bynde *v.* to bind 1211; **bounden** *pp.* bound, trimmed. [OE *bindan.*]
bischop *n.* bishop 112. [OE *biscop*]
bisemez *v. impers.* it is fitting 1612, 2191; **bisemed** *pa. t.* suited 622, 2035. [OE *be* + SEME]
bisyde *prep.*; *hym b.* sideways 2265; *adv.* alongside, round about 1083, 1582, 2088, 2230; **bisides, bisydez** *adv.* round about 76, 856, 2164. [OE *be sīdan*] See SIDE
bisied, bysily, bisinesse. See BUSY, BUSYLY, BUSYNES
bisoȝt. See BESECHE
bit(te), bytte *n.* blade, cutting edge 212, 426, 2224, 2310. [ON *bit*]

bite *v.* to bite, cut into, pierce 426, 1162, 1457, 1598; **bot(e)** *pa. t.* 426, 1162, 1563. [OE *bītan*]

bityde *v.* to happen 1406; **bitidde** *pa. t.* 2522. [OE *be-* + TYDE]

bytoknyng *n.* sign; *in b. of* as a symbol of 626. [From OE *tācnian* + pref. BI + *-yng*]

bitwene *prep.* between; *adv.* at intervals 791, 795. [OE *betwēon(an)*]

biwyled *v. pp.* deluded 2425. [OE *be-* + *wīglian*]

blake *adj.* black 958, 961. [OE *blæc*]

blame *n.* blame 361, 1779; fault, 1488, 2506; *for b.* as a rebuke 2500. [OFr *bla(s)me*]

blame *v.* to blame 2368. [OFr *bla(s)-mer*]

blande *n.* mingling; *in b.* mingled together 1205. [ON *i bland*]

blande *v. pp.* adorned 1931. [ON, OI *blanda*]

blasoun *n.* shield 828. [OFr *blaso(u)n*]

blaste *n.* blast 784, 1148. [OE *blæst*]

blaunner, blaunmer *n.* a fur, perhaps ermine 155, 573, 856, 1931. [OFr *blanc, neir*, AN *blaunc-ner*]

blawyng *n.* blowing 1601. [OE *blāwung*]

ble(e)aunt *n.* a rich fabric 879; a mantle made of it 1928. [OFr *bliaut*, AN. *bliaunt*]

blede *v.* to bleed 441, 1163. [OE *blēdan*]

blenche *v.* to dodge, twist 1715. [OE *blencan* (rare) deceive]

blende, blent *v. pp.* mingled 1361, 1610; *pa. t.* flowed together 2371. [OE *blendan*]

blended *v. pp.* deluded 2419. [OE *blendan* to blind]

blenk(e) *v.* to gleam 799, 2315. [ON *blekkja*, **blenkja*]

blered *v. pp.* bleared 963. [Cf. OE **blerian*; cf. LG *bleer-oged* bleareyed; MHG *blēren* to weep]

blesse *v.* to call a blessing upon 1296; *refl.* cross oneself 2071. [OE *blētsian*]

blessyng *n.* blessing 370. [OE *blētsung*]

blykke *v.* to shine, gleam 429, 2485; **blycande** *pres. p.* 305. [OE *blīcan, blician*]

blynne *v.* to cease 2322. [OE *blinnan*]

blysful *adj.* delightful 520. [OE *bliss* + *full*]

blys(se) *n.* happiness, joy. [OE *bliss*]

blyþe *adj.* merry, glad; bright, gay 155, 162; *adv.* 1684; **blyþely** *adv.* gaily, merrily 1311, 1834, 1990. [OE *blīþe, blīþelīce*]

blod(e) *n.* blood kinship 357; mettle 286. [OE *blōd*]

blodhoundez *n. pl.* bloodhounds 1436. [OE *blōd* + *hund*]

blonk *n.* horse, steed; *pl.* **blonk-kez** 1128, 1693. [OE (poetic) *blanca*]

blossumez *n. pl.* blossoms 512. [OE *blŏsma*]

blowe *v.*[1] to bloom 512. [OE *blōwan*]

blowe *v.*[2] to blow 1465; **blw(e)** *pa. t.* 1141, 1362; **blowed** 1913. [OE *blāwan, blēow*]

blubred *v. pa. t.* bubbled 2174. [From ME *bluber, blober* n., mimetic]

bluk *n.* the headless body of a man 440. [OFr *bloc*; cf. M Du *bloc*]

blunder *n.* turmoil, blundering 18. [See ME *blundren* daze, be dazed, rel. to *blind*. Cf. ON *blunda*, Norw *blundra* doze]

blusch *n.* gleam 520. [From BLUSCHE *v.*]

blusche *v.* to glance, look 650, 793; **blusschande** *pres. p.* gleaming 1819. [OE *blyscan*]

blwe *n.* blue 1928. [OFr *bleu*]

blwe *v. pa. t.* See BLOWE *v.*²

bobbaunce *n.* pomp, swank 9. [OFr *boba(u)nce*]

bobbe *n.* cluster 206. [Origin unknown, but cf. Ir *baban* cluster; Gael *baban, babag*]

bode *n.* command 852; offer 1824. [OE *bod*]

bode(n). See BIDE, BID(DE)

bodi, body, bodé *n.* body; *pl.* men 353. [OE *bodig*]

boerne, boffet. See BORNE, BUFFET

boȝe *v.* to turn, go; **boȝed** *pa. t.*; **boȝen** *pres.* or *pa. t. pl.* 2077; *boȝe fro* (*of*) leave 344, 1220. [OE *būgan*, str.]

boȝez *n. pl.* boughs, branches 765, 2077. [OE *bōg*]

boyle, byle *v.* to boil, bubble, 2082, 2174. [OFr *boillir*]

bok(e) *n.* book 690, 2521, 2523. [OE *bōc*]

bold(e) *adj.* bold, valiant; *as sb.* bold men 21, 351; *adv. boldly* 2476. [OA *bald, balde*]

bole *n.* tree-trunk 766. [ON *bolr*]

bolne *v.* to swell 512. [ON *bolgna*]

bonchef *n.* happiness 1764. [OFr *bonch(i)ef*]

bone *adj.: bone hostel* a good lodging 776. [OFr *bon hostel*]

bone *n.* boon 327. [ON *bón*]

bones, -ez *n. pl.* bones 424, 1344. [OE *bān*]

bonk(e) *n.* hill-side, slope; **bonkkes, -ez** *pl.*; *bi b.* on the slopes, 511; shore, bank 700, 785. [ON *bakki, *banke*]

bor *n.* boar. [OE *bār*]

borde *n.*¹ table 481. [OE *bord*]

borde *n.*² band, embroidered strip 159, 610. [OE *borda*]

bordez. See BOURDE

borelych *adj.* strong, massive 766, 2148, 2224. [Cf. OE *borlīce* excellently]

borȝ(e). See BURȜ(E)

borne, boerne *n.* stream 731, 1570, 2174. [OE *burna*]

borne, bornyst. See BERE, BURNYST

bost *n.* outcry, clamor 1448. [? cf. AN *bost* boasting, MHG *būs* swelling, Norw *baus* haughty]

bot *adv.* only, but; *b. oure* one alone by ourselves 1230; *conj.* (i) except, other than; *noȝt b.* only 1267, 1833; *no more b.* no more than 2312; (ii) unless 716, 1210, 1300; *b. if*, unless 1782, 1956; (iii) but, however, yet. [OE *būtan, būte*] See BOUTE

bot(e). See BITE

botounz *n. pl.* buttons, bosses 220. [OFr *bo(u)to(u)n*]

boþe, both(e) *adj. and pron.* both; either 2070, 2165; *adv.* as well, too, both. [ON *báðir*]

boþem *n.* bottom 2145. [OE *botm* *boþm* (cf. Mod. NWM)]

boun *adj.* ready 852, 1311, 1693; dressed 2043; *b. to* bound, on the way 548. [ON *búinn, bún-*]

bounté *n.* excellence 357, 1519. [OFr *bo(u)nté*]

bourde, borde *n.* jest 1212, 1409, 1954. [OFr *bo(u)rde*]

bourded *v. pa. t.* jested 1217 [OFr *bo(u)rder*]

bourdyng *n.* jesting 1404. [From stem of OFr *bo(u)rder* + *-yng*]

boure *n.* bedroom 853; ladies' bower 1519. [OE *būr*]

bout(e) *prep.* without 361, 1285, 1444, 2353. [OE *būtan*]

boweles *n. pl.* bowels 1333, 1609. [OFr *bo(u)el*]

brace *n.* collective pair of arm-pieces 582. [OFr *brace*]

braches, -ez *n. pl.* hounds 1142, 1563, 1610; **brachetes** 1603. [OFr *brachet*] See RACH

brad *v. pp.* grilled 891. [OE *brǣdan, brēdan*]

bradde *v. pa. t. intr.* reached 1928. [OE *brǣdan*]

brayde *v.* to draw, pull 1584, 1609, 1901, 2319; sling 621; **brayd(e)** *pa. t.* pulled 1339; flung 2377; jerked, 440; spurted *pa. t. intr.* 429; **brayde** *pp.* lowered 2069; **brayden, brawden** linked 580; embroidered 177, 220; set 1833. [OE *bregdan*, pp. *brogden, bregden*]

brayen *v.* to bray 1163. [OFr *braire*]

brayn *n.* brain 89. [OE *brǣgn*]

brayn *adj.* (?) mad, reckless 286. [?Shortened from BRAYNWOD adj. and the like]

braynwod *adj.* frenzied 1461, 1580. [OE *brǣg(e)n* + *wōd*]

braþ. See BROÞE

braunch(e) *n.* branch 265, 2177. [OFr *bra(u)nche*]

brawden. See BRAYDE

brawen, brawne *n.* brawn 1611;

such a b. of a best such a quantity of flesh on any boar 1631. [OFr *brao(u)n*]

bred *n.* bread 891, 1361, 1610. [OE *brēad*]

bredden *v. pa. t. pl.* bred 21. [OE *brēdan*]

bredez *n. pl.* planks 2071. [OE *bred*]

brek, breke(n) *v. pa. t.* broke, cut open 1333; broke down, over-came 1564; *intr.* burst forth 1764; foamed 2082. [OE *brecan*]

brem(e) *adj.* brave, stout 1155; fierce 1142, 1580; wild 2145; loud 1601, 2200; *adv.* stoutly 781; **bremlych** *adv.* gloriously 509; **brem(e)ly** fiercely 1598, 2233, 2319; quickly 779. [OE *brēme* adj. and adv.]

brenne *v.* to burn 832, 875; *trans.* broil 1609; **brent** *pp.* 2; **brende** refined, bright 195. [ON *brenna*]

brent *adj.* steep 2165. [Cf. OE *brant* ON *brettr, brent-*.]

bresed *adj.* bristling 305. [?Akin to OE *byrst*, ME *bristel*]

brest *n.* breast. [OE *brēost*]

breþer *n. pl.* brothers-in-arms 39. [ON *brœðr*, OMerc *broeþre*, pl.]

breue *v.* to write down 2521; de-clare 465, 1393, 1488; signal the presence of game by giving tongue 1436. [Med L *breviāre*, OE *gebrēfan*]

bryddes, -ez *n. pl.* birds 166, 509, 610, 746. [OE *bridd, briddas* young bird]

brydel *n.* bridle. [OE *brīdel*]

bryg(g)e *n.* drawbridge 781, 821, 2069; *gen.* 779. [OE *brycg*]

bryȝt *adj. and adv.* bright, brightly colored; pure white 155, 573,

856, 955; *compar.* 236; *superl.*
fairest 1283. [OE *berht*]

brymme *n.* water's edge 2172. [Cf.
MHG *brem* border]

bryné. See BRUNY

bryng *v.* to bring; **broʒt** *pa. t. and
pp.* [OE *bringan*]

brit(t)en *v.* to break up, destroy 2,
680; cut (up) 1339, 1611. [OE
brytnian]

brod(e) *adj.* broad, wide; long
212; *adv.* with eyes wide open
446. [OE *brād; brāde*, adv.]

broʒez, broʒt. See BROWE, BRING

broke *n.* stream 2082, 2200. [OE
brōc]

bronde *n.* burnt wood fragment 2;
sword; **bront** 588, 1584. [OE
brand, brond]

broþe *adj.* fierce; grim 2233; **braþ**
1909; **broþely** *adv.* 2377. [ON
bráðr, bráðliga]

broþerhede *n.* brotherhood 2516.
[OE *brōþor* + *-hede*]

broun *adj.* brown 618, 879; *sb.*
brown hide 1162; bright, shining
426. [OE *brūn*]

browe *n.* brow, forehead 1457,
2306; *pl.* **broʒes, -ez** eyebrows
305, 961. [OE *brū*]

bruny *n.* mail-shirt 861, 2012,
2018; **bryné** 580. [ON *brynja*,
OFr *brunie*]

brusten *v. pp.* broken 1166. [ON
bresta, OE *berstan*]

buffet, boffet *n.* blow 382, 1754,
2343. [OFr *buffet*]

bugle *n.* bugle 1136, 1141, 1465,
1913. [OFr *bugle*]

bukkez *n. pl.* bucks 1155. [OE
bucca]

bullez *n. pl.* wild bulls 722. [Cf.
ODan *bul*, OE *bula, bulluc*]

bult. See BYLDE

bur *n.* onslaught, blow 290, 374,
548; strength 2261; violence
2322. [ON *byrr* a following wind]

burde *n.* maiden, damsel, lady;
burdes, -ez *pl.* 942, 1232, 1373.
[OE **byrde* embroideress; cf.
byrdistre, ON. *byrða*]

burde *v. pa. t. subj. impers.*; *me
burde*, I ought to 2278, 2428.
[OE *gebyrian*]

burʒ(e), borʒ(e) *n.* keep = Ilion;
city 9. [OE *burg*] See expl. n. 2

burn(e), buurne (825) *n.* war-
rior, knight, man *voc.* 1071,
2284, 2322. [OE *beorn*] See BENT

burnyst, bornyst *v. pp.* polished
212, 582. [OFr *brunir, burnir,
burniss-*]

burþe *n.* birth 922. [OE *gebyrd,
byrþ-*]

busy *v. intr.* to be busy, bestir one-
self 1066; **bisied,** *pa. t. trans.*
stirred 89. [OE *bysigian*]

busyly, busily *adv.* earnestly, ea-
gerly 68, 1824. [From OE *bysig*]

busynes *n.* solicitude 1986;
bisinesse importunity 1840. [OE
bysignes]

busk *n.* bush 182, 1437. [ODan
buske]

busk(ke) *v. intr.* to get ready, ar-
ray, dress 1220, 1693; *intr.* make
haste; *busken vp* hasten 1128;
trans. make 2248. [ON *búask,*
refl.]

buttokez *n. pl.* buttocks 967. [OE
buttuc]

C

cace, case *n.* chance 907; oc-
currence -1196; circumstances,
affair 546; *to vche a c.* to every-

thing she brought forward 1262.
[OFr *cas*]

cach(che), kach *v.* to catch; **ka-
chande,** *pres. part.* 1581; **ca3t,
ka3t** *pa. t.* 643, 1011, 1118; *pp.*
1225, 2508; to chase, spur on
1581, 2175; catch, seize 368,
434, 1225, 2508; take 133, 1118,
1305; receive, get 643, 1011,
1938; **ca3t vp** lifted 1185; *intr.,*
ka3t to laid hold of 2376; *cach*
hasten, go 1794. [ONFr
cach(i)er, infl. by LACH(CHE)]

cacheres, *n. pl.* huntsmen 1139.
[ONFr *cach(i)ere*]

cayre, kayre *v.* to ride 43, 1048,
1670, 2120. [ON *keyra*]

cakled *v. pp.* cackled 1412. [Cf.
Dan *kagle*]

calle, kalle *v. intr.* to call out,
shout; *c. on* call to 1701, 1743; *c.
of* crave 975, 1882; cry out 1421;
trans. to call, name, summon.
[ON *kalla,* OE (late) *ceallian*]

can. See CON *auxil.*

capados *n.* a kind of hood 186,
572. [? OFr *Capadoce*] See expl.
n. 186

caple *n.* horse 2175. [Cf. ON *ka-
pall,* L *caballus*]

care *n.* sorrow, grief 557, 1254,
1979, 2384; trouble 2495; *care of*
concern about 2379. [OE *caru*]

care *v.* to grieve for 674; be con-
cerned 750, 1773; **carande** *pres.
p.* 674, 750. [OE *carian*]

carye *v.* ride 734. [AN *carier*] See
CAYRE

carnelez *n. pl.* embrasures in bat-
tlements 801. [OFr *carnel, crenel*
infl. by *cornel* corner, angle]

carole *n.* dance accompanied by
song. [OFr *carole*]

carp *n.* talk, conversation 307,
1013; **karp** mention 704. [ON
karp, bragging]

carp(p)e, karp *v.* to speak, say;
converse 696; discuss 1225. [ON
karpa, brag]

case. See CACE

cast, kest *n.* stroke 2298; trick
2413; bow, tie, fastening 2376;
pl. speech, utterances 1295.
[ON *kast*] See expl. n. 2376

cast, kest *v.* to cast, throw, put;
cast, kest *pa. t. and pp.;* lift
1192; *kest . . . to* cast (his eye)
on 228; *of k.* cast off 1147; to
utter 64; offer, make 2242, 2275;
intr. or absol. aim 1901; con-
sider 1855; *c. vnto* speak to, ad-
dress 249. [ON *kasta*]

castel *n.* castle 767, 801 (*attrib.*),
1366; **kastel** 2067. [ONFr *castel*]

caue *n.* cave 2182. [OFr *cave*]

cauelaciounz. See KAUELACION

cause *n.* cause; *at pis c.* for this
reason 648. [OFr *cause*]

cemmed *v. pp.* combed 188. [OE
cemban]

cercle *n.* circlet 615. [OFr *cercle*]

chace *n.* hunt 1416, 1604. [OFr
chace]

chaffer *n.* trade 1647; merchandise
1939. [OE *ceap* + *faru;* cf. ON
kaupfor]

chalkwhyt, -quyte *adj.* white as
chalk 798, 958. [OE *cealc* + *hwit*]

chamber, chambre *n.* private
sitting-room or bedroom. [OFr
chambre]

chamberlayn *n.* chamber atten-
dant or servant 1310, 2011. [OFr
chamberlain]

chapel(le), chapayle *n.* chapel;

capitalized = Green Chapel.
[OFr *chapele*]

chaplayn *n.* priest serving a chapel
930, 2107. [OFr *chapelain*]

charcole *n.* charcoal 875. [OE col;
char rel. to ME *charen* to change,
vary character or condition]

charg *n.* importance; *no charg*, it
does not matter 1940. [OFr
charge.]

charge *v.* to put on 863; charge
451. [OFr *charg(i)er*]

chargeaunt *adj.* laborious, toil-
some 1604. [OFr *chargea(u)nt*]

charyté *n.* charity 2055. [OFr
charité]

charre *v. trans.* to turn back 1143;
take 850; *intr.* bring back 1678.
[OE *cerran, cærran*]

charres *n. pl.* affairs, business
1674. [OE *cerr, cærr*]

chasyng *n.* chasing, straying 1143.
[From OFr *chac(i)er* + *-yng*]

chastysed *v. pa. t.* rebuked 1143.
[OFr *chastiser*, extended stem of
chastiier]

chaunce *n.* chance, fortune 1406,
2068; adventure, quest 1081,
1838, 2399, 2496; *cheuez þat
ch.*, brings it to pass 2103; *for ch.*
in spite of anything 2132. [OFr
ch(e)a(u)nce]

chauncely *adv.* by chance 778.
[From OFr *ch(e)a(u)nce* +
ME *-ly*]

chaunge *v.* to exchange 863,
1107, 1406, 1678; turn 711,
2169 (see CHER(E)). [OFr
cha(u)ng(i)er]

chaunsel *n.* chancel 946. [OFr
cha(u)ncel]

chauntré *n.* singing of mass 63.
[OFr *cha(u)nterie*]

chef *adj.* chief, principal 1512,
1604; main 778; **chefly** *adv.* par-
ticularly 978; quickly 850, 883,
1940; **cheuely** 1876. [OFr
ch(i)ef]

cheyer *n.* chair 875. [OFr *chaiere*]

cheke *n.* cheek 953, 1204. [OE
cē(a)c]

chek(k)e *n.* checkmate; ill luck
2195; fortune (good or bad)
1107, 1857. [OFr *esch(i)ec*]

cheldez. See SCHELDE

chemné *n.* fireplace 875, 978,
1667; **chymné** 1030, 1402;
chymnees *pl.* chimneys 798.
[OFr *cheminée*]

chepe *n.* trade; price 1940; *pl.*
goods got in trade 1941; *hade
goud chepez* had good bargains
1939. [OE *cēap*]

chepen *v.* to bargain 1271. [OE
cēapian]

cher(e), schere *n.* facial expres-
sion 334; *chaunge ch.* turn this
way and that 711, 2169; de-
meanour, behaviour 1759, 2496;
made gret ch. behaved so warmly
1259; *bele ch.* gracious behavior,
charming company 1034; mood,
frame of mind 883; *mad ay god
ch.* remained cheerful 562; *with
ch.* merrily 1745. [OFr *ch(i)ere*]

cheryche *v.* to salute graciously
946; **cherysen** *pres. pl.* treat
kindly 2055. [OFr *cherir, cheriss-*]

ches. See CHOSE

cheualry *n.* system of knightly
conduct 1512. [OFr *chevalerie*]

cheualrous *adj.* chivalrous 2399.
[OFr *chevalero(u)s*]

cheue *v.* to acquire, get 1271,
1390; bring about 2103; *intr.*
come to an end 63; *cheue to*

make your way to 1674. [OFr *chevir* and *achever*]

cheuely. See CHEF

cheuisaunce, cheuicaunce *n.* takings, gain 1390, 1406, 1678; *ch. of* obtaining 1939. [OFr *chevissa(u)nce*]

chylde *n.* child 647; **chylder** *pl.* 280. [OE *cild*, pl. *cildru*]

childgered *adj.* boyish, lively 86 [OE *cild* + *gere*, mood; cf. ON *gere*, MDu *gere*, *gaer*]

chymbled *v. pp.* bound, wrapped up 958. [Rel. to ME *chimbe* and OE *cimbing* joint. Cf. ON *kimbla*]

chymne(es). See CHEMNÉ

chyne *n.* chine, backbone 1354. [OFr *eschine*]

chyn(ne) *n.* chin 958, 1204. [OE *cinn*]

chorle *n.* ordinary man 2107. [OE *ceorl*]

chose *v.* to choose, select 863, 1271, 1310; pick out, descry 798, 1512; *choses þe waye* takes his way 1876; *chosen þe gate* make their way 930; *hence intr.* make one's way, go 451, 778, 946; *subj.* (that) you go 451; **ches** *pa. t. sg.* 798, 946; **chosen** *pl.* 930; **chosen** *pp.* chosen 1275; set about 1838; made his way 778. [OE *cēosan*]

clad *pa. t.* clothed, dressed 2015; *pp.* covered 885. [From OE *clǣþan*, pa. t. *clǣdde (rare); or ME *clōth* n.]

clayme *v.* to claim 1490. [OFr *clamer*, 3 sg. *claime*]

clamberande *v. pres. p.* clustering 1722; **clambred** *pp.* 801. [ON *klambra*]

clanly *adv.* completely 393. [OE *cl ǽnlīce*] See CLENE

clannes *n.* innocence, special sensitivity to one's guilt or fault (= OFr *innocence*, L *innocentia*) 653. [OE *clǽn-nes*] See expl. n. 653

clatered *v. pa. t.* clattered, re-echoed 2201; *pp.* come clattering down 1722; **claterande** *pres. p.* splashing 731. [Cf. OE *clatrung*]

clene *adj.* clean, pure 885, 1013, 1883, 2393; bright 158, 161; elegant, fair 154, 163, 854; *adv.* clean, 2391; bright 576, 2017; neatly 792; completely 146, 1298. [OE *clǣne*]

clenge *v.* to cling (to the earth) 1694, 2078; *c. adoun* shrink down 505. [OE *clingan*]

clepe *v.* to call 1310. [OE *cleopian*]

cler(e) *adj.* clear, bright, fair; *sb.* fair lady 1489; *adv.* in *cler quyt* pure white 885. [OFr *cler*]

clergye *n.* (magical) learning 2447. [OFr *clergie*]

clerk *n.* priest 64; **klerk** sage 2450. [OE *cler(i)c*; OFr *clerc*]

cleue *v. intr.* to split 2201. [OE *clēofan*]

clyff(e), klyf(fe) *n.* cliff, rock. [OE *clif*]

cloyster *n.* enclosure 804. [OFr *cloistre*]

clomben *v. pa. t. pl.* climbed 2078. [OE *climban*, pa. t. pl. *clumbon*]

close *v.* to close, fasten 572, 1742; enclose, cover 186, 578; *pp.* embodied 1298; *closed fro* free from 1013. [From OFr *clos*]

closet *n.* closed private pew 934, 942. [OFr *closet*]

cloþe *n.* cloth 2036; table-cloth 885; *on clothe* on the table 125; **cloþes, -ez** *pl.* clothes 2015; coverings 876; bedclothes 1184; tablecloths 1649. [OE *cláþ*]

cloudez *n. pl.* clouds 505, 727; **clowdes** 1696, 2001. [Cf. OE *clūd* mass of earth or rock]

clusteres *n. pl.* clusters 1739. [OE *cluster*]

cnokez *v. 2 sg.* deal a blow 414. [OE *cnocian*]

cofly *adv.* promptly 2011. [OE *cáflíce*]

coȝed *v. pa. t.* cleared throat (to attract attention) 307. [OE *cohhetan*]

coynt, coyntly(ch). See KOYNT

coke *n.* cock 1412; **kok** 2008. [OE *cocc*]

colde *adj.* cold; sad 1982; **colde** *n.* the cold 505, 747, 2001, 2015, 2078; **coolde** 2474. [OE (Angl.) *cald* n. and adj.]

colen *v.* to assuage 1254. [OE *cōlian*, intr.]

colour *n.* color 944, 1059. [OFr *colo(u)r*]

com(me), cum *v.* to come, arrive; *c. ȝe* if you go 2111; **com(e)** *pa. t.*; **com(en)** *pl.* 556, 824; *c. to* entered into 1855; **com(m)en** *pp.*, **cum(m)en** 60, 62, 533. [OE *cuman*]

comaunded, cumaunde *v.* to bid, command 366, 850; order 992; **comaundez** *imper.* commend 2411. [OFr *co(u)ma(u)nder*]

comaundement *n.* orders, bidding 1303, 1501. [OFr *coma(u)ndement*]

comended *v. pa. t.* praised 1629. [OFr *com(m)ender*]

comfort *n.* solace, pleasure 1011, 1221, 1254. [OFr *confort*]

comfort *v.* to comfort 2513; solace, amuse 1099. [OFr *conforter*]

comly, comlych, cumly *adj.* fair, beautiful, noble; *sb.* fair knight 674; lovely lady 1755; **comloker** *compar.* 869; **comlokest** *superl.* 53, 767, 1520; *sb.* fairest lady 81; **comly(che), comlyly** *adv.* fittingly, graciously. [OE *cȳmlic*, *cȳmlíce* infl. by ME *becomen*, *becomelích*]

commen, -es, cummen. See COM

compayny(e), companye *n.* company 556, companionship 1099, 1011; lady's company 1483; **compeyny** retinue 1912. [OFr *compai(g)nie*]

compas *n.* figure 944. [OFr *compas*]

compast *v. pa. t.* considered 1196. [OFr *compasser*]

con *v.¹* I know how to, can 2283; *3 sg.* 2138, 2455; **connez** *2 sg.* 1483, *2 pl.* 1267; **couth, couþe, cowþe** *pa. t.* could; knew their craft 1139. [OE *can, cūþe*]

con *v.²* *auxil. with infin. for pa. t.* = did; **can** 340, 1042. [OE *can* confused with ME *gan*, did]

conable *adj.* fitting, excellent 2450. [Reduction of OFr *covenable*]

concience *n.* mind 1196. [OFr *conscience*]

confessed *v. pp.*, *c. clene*, made clean by confession 2391. [OFr *confesser*]

conysaunce *n.* cognisance 2026. [OFr *conissa(u)nce*]

connez. See CON

conquestes *n. pl.* conquests 311.
[OFr *conqueste*]

constrayne *v.* to force 1496. [OFr
constreindre, constreign-]

contray *n.* region 713; *bi. c.* over
the land 734. [OFr *contrée*]

conueyed *v. pa. t.* escorted 596
[OFr *conveier*]

coolde. See COLDE

coprounes *n. pl.* ornamental tops
797. [OFr *co(u)pero(u)n*]

corbel *n.* raven 1355. [OFr *corbel*]

corner *n.* corner 1185. [OFr
corn(i)er]

cors *n.*[1] body 1237. [OFr *cors*]

cors *n.*[2] course 116; **cource** 135.
[OFr *co(u)rs*, L *cursus*]

corsed *v. pp. and adj.* cursed
2374; **corsedest** *superl.* 2196.
[OE *cŭrsian*, from *curs* n.]

corsour *n.* courser 1583. [OFr *cor-
sier* with "French" suffix]

co(u)rt *n.* court, members of a no-
ble household; **ko(u)rt** 1048,
2340; *to c.* home 1099; *attrib.*,
c. ferez 594. [OFr *co(u)rt*]
See FERE n.[1]

cortays(e) *adj.* chivalrous, cour-
teous, gracious; *sb.* gracious lady
2411. **cortaysly** *adv.* cour-
teously, graciously 775, 903. [OFr
co(u)rteis]

cortaysy(e) *n.* courtesy, the man-
ners and virtues of courts. [OFr
co(u)rteisie]

cort ferez. See CO(U)RT and FERE n.

cortyn *n.* curtain, bed-hanging 854,
1185, 1192, 1732; **cortayn** 1476.
[OFr *co(u)rtine*]

cortyned *v. pp.* curtained 1181.
[From OFr *co(u)rtine*]

coruon *v. pp.* carved 797. [OE
ceorfan, pp. *corfen*]

cosyn *n.* kinsman 372. [OFr
co(u)sin]

cosse *n.* kiss 1300, 1946, 2351,
2360. [OE *coss*] See KYSSE

cost *n.* nature, quality 1272, 1849,
2360; terms 546; *pl.* movements
944; ways 1483; condition, plight
750; *c. of care* hardships 2495.
[LOE *cost*, from ON *kostr*]

costez *v. 3 sg.* coasts, passes by the
side of 1696. [From OFr *coste*; cf.
AN *costeier*]

cote *n.* coat, skin 1921; tunic 152,
335; coat-armor (see next item)
637, 2026. [OFr *cote*]

cote-armure *n.* coat armor = an
embroidered coat bearing the
knight's blazon and worn over his
armor 586. [OFr *cote* + *armeüre*;
cf. OFr *cote a armer*]

coþe *v. pa. t. sg.* quoth, said 776;
quoþ. [OE *cwæþ*]

couardise *n.* cowardice 2508;
cowardise 2273; **coward(d)yse**
2374, 2379. [OFr *couardise*]

couenaunt, couenaunde *n.*
agreement, compact 393, 1384,
2328, 2340; *pl.* terms of a com-
pact 1123, 1408, 1642, 2242.
[OFr *covena(u)nt*]

couerto(u)r *n.* coverlet 855,
1181; horse-cloth 602. [OFr
co(u)verto(u)r]

couetyse *n.* covetousness 2374,
2380, 2508. [OFr *coveitise*]

coundue *v.* to conduct 1972. [OFr
co(u)nduire]

coundutes *n. pl.* "conductus"; *c.
of Krystmasse* Christmas carols
1655. [OFr *co(u)nduite*]

counse(y)l *n.* counsel 682; *to
your c.* to advise you 347. [OFr
co(u)nseil]

counseyl *v.* to advise 557. [OFr *co(u)nseill(i)er*]

countenaunce *n.* expression of face 335; custom 100, 1490; favour, 1539; looks 1659. [OFr *co(u)ntena(u)nce*]

couples *n. pl.* leashes 1147. [OFr *co(u)ple*]

cource, court. See CORS *n.*² CORT

couþ(e), cowþe. See CON

couþe *adj.* evident 1490. [OE *cūþ*]

couþly *adv.* familiarly 937. [OE *cūþlīce*]

cowardise, coward(d)yse. See COUARDISE

cowpled *v. pa. t.* leashed together in pairs 1139. [OFr *co(u)pler*] See COUPLES

cowters *n. pl.* elbow-pieces 583. [OFr *co(u)t(i)ere* from *co(u)te* elbow]

crabbed *adj.* crabbed 502; perverse 2435. [From ME *crabbe* n., OE *crabba*]

craft *n.* skill 1380; doings 471; *pl.* magic crafts 2447; arts 1527; pursuits 1688. [OE *cræft*]

crafty *adj.* skilfully made 572. [OE *cræftig*]

craftyly *adv.* craftsmanly 797. [OE *cræftiglīce*]

cragge *n.* crag 1430, 2183, 2221. [MWelsh *crag*; cf. MBreton *cragg*]

crakkande *v. pres. p.* echoing, ringing 1166; **crakkyng** *n.* blaring 116. [OE *cracian*]

craþayn *n. and adj.* 1773. See expl. n. 1773

craue *v.* to claim 1384; ask for 277 (*subj.*), 283; crave, beg for 812, 1300, 1670. [OE *crafian*]

Crede *n.* Creed 643, 758. [OE *crēda*]

creped *v. pa. t.* crept 1192. [OE *crēopan*, str.]

cresped *v. pp.* curled 188. [OE *cirpsian*, OFr *crespe*]

crest *n.* mountain-top 731. [OFr *creste*]

creuisse *n.* fissure 2183. [OFr **creveïz, crevaice*]

cry(e) *n.* shouting 64; **kry** 1166; appeal 775. [OFr *cri*]

crye, cri(e) *v.* to shout, call 1088, 1445; lament 760; *kryes þerof* gives tongue at it 1701. [OFr *crier*]

Crystenmas(se) *n.* Christmas 502; *adj.* 985; **Krystmasse** 37, 1655; **Crystemas** 283; **Cristmasse, Crystmasse** 471, 683; *þat Krystmasse* that Chr. celebration 907; *Krystmasse euen* Chr. Eve 734. [OE *crĭsten*, adj. + *mæsse*; cf. LOE *crĭstmæsse*]

croys *n.* cross 643. [OFr *crois*]

croked *adj.* crooked; *were neuer croked*, never went wrong 653. [From ON *krókr*, n.]

cropure, cropore *n.* crupper 168, 602. [OFr *crop(i)ere*, with ME suffix]

cros *n.* cross 762. [ON *kross*, from OIr *cros*]

croun *n.* crown 364; *þat bere þe c. of þorne* = Christ 2529; crown of the head 419, 616. [OFr *co(u)ro(u)ne*; cf. ON *krúna*]

crowen *v. pp.* crowed 1412; **crue** *pa. t.* 2008. [OE *crāwan*]

cum, cum-. See COM, COM-

curious *adj.* of elaborate design 855. [OFr *curio(u)s*]

D

dabate 2041. See DEBATE *n.*

day(e) *n.* day, daylight; life time

2522; *vpon d.* by day 47; *in d.*
ever 80; [OE *dæg*]
daylyeden. See DALY
dayly3t *n.* daylight 1137, 1365.
[DAY + LY3T; cf. OE *dæges līht*]
daynté, daynte *n.* courtesy, cour-
teous behavior 1250, 1662;
honor 1266; *hade d. of* admired
1889; *pl.* delicacies 121, 483,
998, 1401. [OFr *deint(i)é*]
daynté *adj.* charming 1253. [Attrib.
use of DAYNTÉ]
dale *n.* bottom of a valley 1151,
2005, 2162. [OE *dæl*]
daly *v.* to trifle, play at love 1253;
daylyeden *pa. t. pl.* 1114. [OFr
dalier]
dalyaunce *n.* courtly conversation
1012, 1529. [OFr **dalia(u)nce*]
dalt(en). See DELE
dame *n.* lady 470; *pl.* 1316. [OFr
dame]
dar *v. pres. t.* dare 287, 300, 1991;
durst *pa. t.* 1493, 1575. [OE
dearr, dorste]
dare *v.* to cower 315, 2258. [OE
darian]
daunsed *v. pa. t.* danced 1026.
[OFr *da(u)ncer*]
daunsyng *n.* dansing 47. [Stem of
OFr *dauncer* + *-yng*]
dawed *v. pa. t. subj.* would be
worth 1805. [OE *dugan*]
debate, dabate *n.* dispute 1754,
2041, 2248. [OFr *debat*]
debate *v.* to debate, dispute 68;
debatande *pres. p.* deliberating
2179. [OFr *debatre*]
debonerté *n.* courtesy 1273. [OFr
deboneret(i)é, from *de bon(e)
aire*]
dece, des *n.* raised platform, dais.
[OFr *deis*]

ded *adj.* dead; slain 725, 2264. [OE
dēad]
dede *n.* deed, act 1047, 1089,
1265, 1629; *as the d. askez* as
the craft requires 1327; occupa-
tion 1468; affair, what (he) did
1662. [OE *dēd*]
defence *n.* defence; *with d.* defen-
sively 1282. [OFr *defense*]
defende *v.* to defend 1551, 2117;
pp. forbidden 1156. [OFr
defendre]
degré *n.* rank 1006. [OFr *degré*]
de3e *v.* to die 996, 1163; **dy3e**
2460. [ON *deyja*]
dele 2188. See DEUEL
dele *v.* to deal, mete out; give
1805; perform 2192; partake of
1968; **dalt(en)** *pa. t.* and *pp.*
452, 2418, 2449; (? affected by
OFr *dalier*) exchanged pleasan-
tries 1668; *d. vntytel* engaged in
lighthearted repartee 1114; *d.
with* behaved to 1662. [OE
dǣlan]
delful, dulful *adj.* grievous 560,
1517. [From DOEL + *-ful*]
deliuer *adj.* nimble 2343; **de-
liuerly** *adv.* quickly 2009. [OFr
de(s)livre]
delyuer *v.* to assign 851; *pp.* dealt
with 1414. [OFr *de(s)livrer*]
demay *v. imper. refl.* be dis-
turbed 470; **dismayd** (*for*)
pp. dismayed (at) 336. [OFr
de(s)maier]
deme *v.* to judge, consider 240,
246, 1529; think fit, decide 1082,
1089, 1668; tell, say 1322, 2183.
[OE *dēman*]
denez *adj.* Danish 2223, [OE *de-
nisc;* OFr *daneis*]
dep(e) *adj.* deep, profound 741,

786, 1159, 1748; *adv.* 787. [OE
dēop, dēope, adv.]

depaynt(ed) *v. pp.* painted 620;
depicted 649. [OFr *depeindre,* 3
sg. pres. and pp. *depeint*]

departe *v.* to separate 1335; *intr.*
part 1983. [OFr *departir*]

departyng *n.* parting. [From stem
of OFr *departir* + *-yng*]

deprece *v.*¹ to subjugate 6; **deprese**
pressed 1770. [OFr *depresser*]

deprece *v.*² to release 1219. [OFr
de(s)presser, free from pressure;
de(s)priser free from prison]

der(e) *n. pl.* deer 1151, 1157,
1322, 1324. [OE *dēor*]

dere *adj.* costly, precious 75, 121,
193, 571; pleasant 47, 564, 1012,
1026, 2449; beloved, dear 470,
754; noble 2465; festal 92, 1047;
sb. dear 1492, 1798; noble 678,
928; (*the*) **derrest** *superl.* the
most noble = Gawain 445; *adv.*
483. [OE *dēore;* compar. *dēorra*]

dered *v. pa. t.* injured, hurt 1460.
[OE *derian*]

derely *adv.* splendidly 1559; pleas-
antly 1253; courteously 817,
1031; neatly 1327; deeply 1842.
[OE *dēorlīce*]

derf, derue *adj.* doughty 1000,
1492; stout, 1233; grievous, se-
vere 558, 564, 1047. [ON *derf-;*
cf. OI *djarfr,* infl. by OE *deorfan,
derfan*]

derk *adj.* dark 1177, 1887; *sb.*
darkness 1999. [OE *de(o)rc*]

derne *adj.* private, ambiguous,
with hidden meaning 1012;
dernly *adv.* stealthily 1183,
1188. [OE *derne, dernlīce*]

derrest *adv. superl.* See DERE
adj., adv.

deruely *adv.* boldly 2334. [ON
djarfliga]

derworþly, *adv.* sumptuously 114.
[OE *dēorwurplīce*]

des. See DECE

deserue, disserue *v.* to deserve
452, 1779, 1803. [OFr *deservir*]

desyre *v.* to desire 1257. [OFr
desirer]

destiné *n.* fate, destiny 564, 996,
1752; evil destiny, death 2285.
[OFr *destinée*]

deþe, dethe *n.* death 1600, 2105.
[OE *dēaþ*]

deuaye *v.* to deny, refuse 1493,
1497. [OFr *deve(i)er*]

deue *v.* to stun, to strike down
1286. [OE *dēafian*]

deuel, dele *n.* Devil 2188, 2192.
[OE *dēofol*]

deuys *n. a deuys* = OFr *a devis* at
one's desire, of the best 617. [OFr
devis]

deuise *v.* to relate 92. [OFr
deviser]

deuocioun *n.* devotions 2192.
[OFr *devocio(u)n*]

dewe *n.* dew 519. [OE *dēaw*]

diamauntez *n. pl.* diamonds 617.
[OFr *diamant*]

dich, -es *n.* ditch 1709; moat 766,
786. [OE *dīc*]

dyʒe. See DEʒE

diʒt, dyʒt *v.* to appoint; *d. me þe
dom* concede me the right 295; *d.
hym,* went 994; *pp.* set 114; ap-
pointed 678, 1884; dressed 1689;
prepared 1559; made 2223. [OE
dihtan]

dille *adj.* stupid 1529. [OE **dylle,*
rel. to *dol*]

dyn *n.* noise, merrymaking 47,
1159, 1183, 1308. [OE *dyne*]

diner *n.* dinner 928, 1559. [OFr *di(s)ner*]

dyngez *pres. t.* smites 2105. [ON *dengja*]

dyngne *adj.* worthy 1316. [OFr *digne*]

dynt *n.* blow; **dinte** 336; **dunt(e)** 452, 1286. [OE *dynt*]

disceuer, discouer *v.* to uncover, reveal 418, 1862. [OFr *descovrir*, 3 sg. *descuevre*]

disches *n. pl.* dishes 122, 128. [OE *disc*]

discrye *v.* to behold 81. [OFr *descrire, descrivre*]

disert *n.* merit 1266. [OFr *desert*]

dismayd 336. See DEMAY

displayed *v. pa. t.* displayed, left uncovered 955. [OFr *despleier*]

displese *v.* to displease 1304; *impers. subj.* let it displease 1839; *imper. pl. refl.* take offence 2439. [OFr *desplaisir, -plesir*]

dispoyled *v. pp.* stripped 860. [OFr *despoill(i)er*]

disport *n.* entertainment 1292. [OFr *desport*]

disserue See DESERUE

disstrye *v.* to destroy 2375. [OFr *destruire*]

dit *v. pp.* locked 1233. [OE. *dyttan.*]

do *v.* to do, perform, make; **dos, dotz** *3 sg.* 1308, 2211; *imper. pl.* 1533; **did(de)** *pa. t.*; **don(e)** *pp.*; *do me* afford me 1798; *dotz me drede* frightens me 2211; *didden hem vndo* had them cut up 1327; to put, set 478; *do way* cease from 1492; *dos hir* goes 1308; *dos* do! 1533; *pp.* ended 928, 1365. [OE *dōn*]

doel *n.* lament 558. [OFr *doel*]

doggez *n. pl.* dogs 1600. [LOE *docga*]

doȝter *n.* daughter 2465. [OE *dohtor*]

doȝty *adj.*, doughty, brave 2264; *sb.* hero 2334. [OE *dohtig*] See DUȜTY

dok *n.* tail 193. [Cf. Icel *dokkur*]

dole *n.* part 719. [OE *dāl*]

dom(e) *n.* judgement, doom 295, 1216, 1968. [OE *dōm*]

domezday *n.* doomsday 1884. [OE *dōmes dæg*]

donkande *v. pres. p.* moistening 519. [Cf. ON *dǫkk* pool; Swed dial. *dänka* to moisten]

dor(e) *n.* door. [OE *duru, dor*]

do(e)s *n. pl.* does 1159, 1322. [OE *dā*]

doser *n.* wall-tapestry 478. [OFr *doss(i)er*]

dote *v.* to lose one's wits 1956; **doted** *pp.* stupid 1151. [Cf. MDu *doten*]

double *adj.* double (-channelled) 786. **doub(b)le** *adv.* double 2033; (?) in pairs 61; with twice the usual amount 483. [OFr *do(u)ble*]

doublefelde *adv.* with twice the usual amount 890. [OFr *do(u)ble* + OE *-feld*, pp.]

doun *adv.* down; *prep.* 1595, 2144. [OE *of dūne, adūne*]

dounez, downez *n. pl.* hills 695, 1972. [OE *dūn*]

doute *n.* fear 246; *had doute* was afraid 442. [OFr *do(u)te*]

douteles *adv.* doubtless 725. [DOUTE + OE *-lēas*]

douth(e) *n.* assembled company. [OE *duguþ*]

dowelle *v.* to remain 566, 1075, 1082. [OE *dwellan*]

dra3e *v.* to lead 1031; **drowe** *pres.* *subj.* carry on 1647; **dro3(en)** *pa. t.* drew 335; closed 1188; *intr.* withdrew 1463; **drawen** *pp.* 1233. [OE *dragan*]

dra3t *n.* drawbridge 817. [OE *drœht*; ON *dráttr*, **draht-*]

draueled *v. pa. t.* muttered 1750. [Cf. ON *drafl* tattle; *drafa* to talk nonsense]

drechch *n.* delay 1972. [ME *dreccben* v., OE *dreccan*]

drede *v.* to fear 2355; *intr.* be afraid 2211. [From ME *adrēden*; cf. OE *ondrǣdan*, LWS *drǣdan*]

drede *n.* fear 315, 2258. [From DREDE v.]

dredles *adj.* fearless 2334. [From DREDE + OE *-lēas*]

dre3, dry3e *adj.* unmoved 335; enduring 724; unceasing 1460; heavy 1750; *sb.* in *dragez on d.*, holds back 1031; *adv.* forcibly 2263; **dre3ly** *adv.* unceasingly 1026. [ON *drjúgr*, **dréug-*]

dreme *n.* dreaming 1750. [ON *draumr*, dream; OE *drēam*, music]

dreped *v. pp.* slain, killed 725. [OE *drepan*, smite; ON *drepa*, kill]

dres(se) *v.* to arrange, array 75, 1000, 2033; direct 445; *dresses bym vpon grounde* takes his stand 417; *dres me to* proceed to 474; *intr.* get ready 566; repair to 1415; *dressed vp* got up 2009. [OFr *drec(i)er*]

dryftes *n. pl.* snowdrifts 2005. [ON *drift*]

dry3e *adj.* See DRE3

dry3e *v.* to endure 560; *d. vnder* withstand 202. [OE *drē(o)gan*]

Dry3tyn *n.* God. [OE *dryhten*]

drynk *n.* drink 497, 1684, 1935. [OE *drinc*]

drynk *v.* to drink 337; **dronken** *pa. t. pl.* 1025, 1114, 1668; *pp.* as *adj.* drunk 1956. [OE *drincan*]

dryue *v.* to drive; **drof** *pa. t.*; **dryuen, driuen** *pp.*; *trans.* to drive, strike; pass 1176, 1468; to make 558, 1020; *drof to* enclosed 786; *intr.* come, make one's way 121, 222; rush 1151; plunge 2263; *dryuez to* follows on, 1999. [OE *drífan*]

dro3(en). See DRA3E

dro3t *n.* drought 523. [OE *drūgoþ*, **drūhþ-*]

dronken. See DRYNK

dropez *v. 3 sg.* drops 519. [OE *dropian*]

droupyng, drowping *n.* torpor, uneasy slumber 1748, 1750. [ON *drúpa*, v.]

drowe. See DRA3E

drury(e), drwry *n.* love 1507, 1517, 1805; love-token 2033; *dalt d.* had love relations 2449. [OFr *druerie*]

dubbed *v. pp.* adorned 75, 193; arrayed 571. [OFr *ado(u)ber*, *aduber*]

dublet *n.* doublet 571. [OFr *do(u)blet*, *dublet*]

duches *n.* duchess 2465 (*gen.*). [OFr *ducbesse*]

du3ty *adj.* doughty 724. [OE *dyhtig*] See DO3TY

duk *n.* duke 552, 678. [OFr *duc*]

dulful, dunt(e), durst. See DEL-, DYNT, DAR

dure *adj.*; in *Agrauayn a la Dure Mayn* 110
dust *n.* dust 523. [OE *dŭst*]
dut *n.* joy 1020. [OFr *dedu(i)t*]
dut(te) *v. pa. t.* feared 222, 784, *subj.* 2257. [OFr *do(u)ter, duter*]

E

eft(e) *adv.* again; afterwards 898, 2388; then 788; besides 641. [OE *eft*]
eftersones, eftsonez *adv.* again, a second time 1640, 2417. [OE *eftsōna* infl. by *æfter*]
egge *n.* edge 212; weapon 2392. [OE *ecg* edge, (poetic) weapon]
eke *adv.* also, as well 90, 1741. [OE *ēac*; cf. *tōēacan*]
elbowes *n. pl.* elbows 184. [OE *el(n)boga*]
elde *n.* age; generation 1520; **eldee** *of hyghe e.* in the prime of life 844. [OE *eldo*]
elles, ellez *adv.* else, besides 384, 1550, 2108; otherwise 1082; *oþer elles*, or else 1529; *conj.* provided that 295. [OE *elles*]
eln3erde *n.* measuring-rod an ell (45 in.) long 210. [OE *eln* + *gérd*]
em(e) *n.* maternal uncle 356, 543. [OE *ēam*]
enbaned *v. pp.* fortified with projecting horizontal coursings 790. [OProv *enbanar*]
enbelyse *v.* to adorn 1034. [OFr *embelir, embeliss-*]
enbrauded *v. pp.* embroidered 166, 879, 2028; **enbrawded** 78, 856; **enbrawden** 609. [OE *gebrogden* infl. by OFr *broder*]
enclyne *v. intr.* to bow 340. [OFr *encliner*]

ende *n.* end; result 496; *vpon endez* at the ends 2039. [OE *ende*]
endeles *adj.* endless 630; **endelez** 629. [OE *endelēas*]
endite *v.* to direct; *to dethe e.* do to death 1600. [OFr *enditer*, affected by *di3t* in *di3t to deþe*]
endured *v. pp.* endured 1517. [OFr *endurer*]
enfoubled *v. pp.* muffled up 959. [OFr *enfubler*]
Englych *adj.*; *as n. pl.* the English 629. [OE *englisc*, adj.]
enker grene *adj.* bright green 150, 2477. [ON *einkar* + GRENE]
enmy *n.* enemy 2406. [OFr *enemi*]
enn(o)urned *v. pp.* adorned, graced 634; set as decoration 2027. [From stem of OFr *ao(u)rner, aürner* + -*ed*]
enquest *n.* inquiry 1056. [OFr *enqueste*]
entayled *v. pp.* carved; embroidered 612. [OFr *entaill(i)er*]
enterludez *n. pl.* dramatic performances 472. [OFr **entrelude*, MedL *interludium.*]
entyse *v.*; *e. teches* catch the infection 2436. [OFr *entic(i)er*]
entre *v.* to enter 221 (*trans.*), 934. [OFr *entrer*]
er(e) *adv.* before 527, 1274; **er** *prep.* before 197; *er þis* before now 1892, 2528; *conj.* [OE *ǣr*]
erande. See ERNDE
erber *n.* gullet 1330. [OFr *erb(i)ere*]
erbez *n. pl.* herbs, green plants 517, 2190. [OFr *erbe*]
erde *n.* land, region 1808; *in erde* (word tag) in the world, actual(ly) 27. [OE *eard*]

erly *adv.* early. [OE *ǣrlīce*]

ermyn *n.* ermine 881. [OFr *ermine*]

ernd(e) *n.* business, mission, errand; *go myn ernde* go as my messenger 811; *an erande* on a mission 1808. [OE *ǣrende*, ON *erendi*]

erraunt *adj.* errant; *kny3t erraunt*, knight journeying on a quest 810. [OFr *errer*, travel]

erþe *n.* earth, ground. [OE *eorþe*]

ese *n.* ease 1676; *at þyn e., in your e.* at your ease 1071, 1096; consolation 1798; delight 1539. [OFr *aise, eise*]

etayn *n.* ogre, giant 140, 723. [OE *eoten*, ending infl. by Fr loan-words in *-ayn*]

ete *v.* to eat, dine 85, 91; **et(t)e** *pa. t.* 113, 1135. [OE *etan*]

eþe *adj.* easy 676. [OE *ē(a)þe*]

eþe *v.* to conjure 379, 2467. [OE *geǣþan* from *āþ*, oath]

euel *n.* evil 1552. [OE *yfel*]

euen *adj.* even; *even of* fairly quit of 1641; equal 1266; *adv.* just, right, straight 444, 1004, 1589, 1593; actually 2464. [OE *efen, efne*]

euen *n.* eve of a festival 734, 1669; **euensong** vespers 932; **euentide** evening 1641. [OE *ēfen, ēfensong, -tīd*]

euenden *v. pa. t. pl.* trimmed 1345. [OE *geefnan*]

euer *adv.* ever, always, at any time; continually 172, 1657; *for e.* 293; **euermore** *adv.* evermore 1547, 2520; *for e.* 669. [OE *ǣfre*, + *māre*, neut.]

euesed *v. pp.* trimmed 184. [OE *efsian*]

euez *n. sg.* edge 1178. [OE *efes*]

excused *v. pp.* excused 2131, 2428. [OFr *excuser*]

exellently (*of*) *adv.* pre-eminently above 2423. [OFr *excellent*]

expoun *v.* to expound 1540; describe 209; *e. much speche of* have much discussion concerning 1506. [OFr *espo(u)ndre*]

F

face *n.* face, mien; surface 524. [OFr *face*]

fade *adj.* (?)bold 149. [In Northern texts based on *fā, fō* n. enemy]

fader *n.* father 919. [OE *fæder*]

fage *n.* deceit; *no fage* in truth 531. [Origin obscure; cf. fāgen *v.*; *fage* survives in dialects]

fay *n.* faith; *ma fay* on my word 1495. [OFr *fei*]

faye *n.* fairy 2446. [AN *feie*, OFr *fée*]

fayly *v.* to fail, be at fault 455, 641, 1067, 1295, 2356; lack opportunity 278; *fayld neuer* was nowhere wanting 658. [OFr *faillir*]

fayn *adj.* glad 388, 840; fain, desirous 1067, 2019. [OE *fægen*]

fayntyse *n.* frailty 2435. [OFr *faintise*]

fayr(e) *adj.* fair, comely, good(ly); courteous 1116; *þe fayrer* (*comparative*) the better 99. [OE *fæger*]

fayr(e) *adv.* fairly, gracefully, courteously, well; deftly 2309; *compar.* 1315. [OE *fægre*]

fayry3e *n.* magic 240. [OFr *faierie*]

fayþ(e) *n.* faith, plighted word 1783; *in god f.* in truth; *bi my* (*þi*) *f.* on my (thy) honor 2284, 2469. [OFr *feid*]

faythely *adj.* truly 1636. [OFr *feid* + ME -*ly*]

faythful *adj.* trustworthy 632, 1679. [From OFr *feid* + -*ly*]

falce *adj.* untrue, dishonest 2382. [OE *fals*, from L *falsus*]

fale *adj.* faded 728. [OE *fealu*]

falle *v.*; **fel(le)** *pa. t.*; **falled** 2243; **fallen** *pp.* 1432, 2528; to fall down; bend down 1758; *f. to* join, to rush towards 1425, 1702; *f. on* fall on 1904; *f. in* hit on 1699; to happen 23, 2132, 2251, 2528; *pa. subj.* might befall 1588; was coming to 2243, 2327, *foule mot hit f.* bad luck to it 2378; be fitting, right (for) 358, 483, 890, 1303, 1358. [OE *fallan*]

falssyng *n.* breaking of faith 2378. [From OE *fals* + -*yng.* Cf. ME *falsie* v.] See FALCE

faltered *v. pa. t.* staggered 430. [ON *faltrask* be cumbered]

fange. See FONGE

fannand *v. pres. p.* fanning 181. [From OE *fann*, n.]

fantoum *n.* illusion 240. [OFr *fanto(s)me*]

farand *adj.* splendid 101. [ON *farandi*, fitting]

fare *n.* track 1703; faring 2494; *his f.* what had happened to him 694; feast 537; behaviour 409, 2386; observances 1116. [OE *faru*]

fare *v.* to go, proceed 699, 1973; *farez wel* farewell 2149; **ferde(n)** *pa. t.* 149, 703, 1282, 1433; **faren** *pp.* 1231. [OE *faran*, str., pa. t. from *fēran*] See FORFERDE

faste *adj.* binding 1636. [OE *fæst*]

fast(e) *adv.* securely 782; pressingly 2403; earnestly 1042; vigorously, loudly 1425, 1908; quickly 1585, 1705, 2215. [OE *fæste*]

faut(e) *n.* fault, faultiness 1551, 2435, 2488. [OFr *faute*]

fautles, -lez *adj.* faultless, flawless 640, 1761; **fautlest** *superl.*, *on þe f.* the most faultless 2363. [OFr *faute* + OE -*lēas*]

fawne *v.* to stroke 1919. [OE *fagnian*]

fawty *adj.* faulty 2382, 2386. [From FAUTE]

fax *n.* hair 181. [OE *feax*]

feblest *adj. superl.* feeblest 354. [OFr *feble*]

fech *v.* to bring 1375, 2013; obtain 1857; **fette** *pp.* 1084. [OE *fetian*, *feccan*] See FOCH, FOTTE

fede *v.* to feed 1359. [OE *fēdan*]

fee *n.* payment 1622; (hunting) portion of the game to which the huntsman is entitled 1358; *corbeles fee* the raven's fee 1355. [OFr *f(i)e*, *fieu*]

fe(e)rsly *adv.* proudly 329, 1323; fiercely 832. [From OFr *f(i)ers* + -*ly*] See FERE *adj.*

fe3tyng *n. in f. wyse* in warlike fashion 267. [From OE *fe(o)htan*] See FY3T

feye *adj.* doomed to die; *falle f.* die 1067. [OE *fæge*]

fela3es *n. pl.* companions 1702. [OE *fēolaga* from ON *félagi*]

fela3schip *n.* love of fellow men = OFr *compaignie*, L *amicitia* 652; company 2151. [From OE *fēolaga* + ME *schip*]

felde *n.* field 874. [OE *feld*]

felde *v.* to fold, embrace 841. [OE **feldan*; cf. *-feldan*]

fele *adj.* many; **felle** 1566; *sb.* many (people) 428, 1588; **feler** *compar.* more 1391. [OE *fela*]

fele *v.* to feel, perceive 2193, 2272. [OE *fēlan*]

felefolde *adj.* manifold 1545. [OE *felafald*]

felle *adj.* bold, fierce, formidable; *sb.* wild beast 1585; **felly** *adv.* fiercely 2302. [OFr *fel*]

felle *n.*¹ skin. [OE *fell*]

felle *n.*² fell 723. [ON *fjall*, *fell*]

felle(n). See FALLE, FELE

femed *v. pa. t.* foamed 1572. [OE *fǣman*]

fende *n.* fiend; *þe F.* the Devil 1944, 2193. [OE *fēond*]

feng. See FONGE

fer *adv.* far, afar 13, 714, 2092; **ferre** 1093; **fyrre, fire** *compar.* further, moreover, besides; *fyrre passe* proceed 378. [OE *feorr(an)*, *firr*, compar.]

ferde *n.* fear; *for f.* in fear 2130, 2272. [Prob. from *for fer(e)d*] See FERDE *v.* and FOR (cf. *for olde*

ferde *v. pa. t.* feared 1588; *pp.* afraid 1295, 2382. [OE *fǣran*, *fēran*]

ferde(n). See FARE *v.*

fere *adj.* proud, bold 103. [OFr *f(i)er*]

fere *n.*¹ companion 695, 915; wife 2411; equal 676; *cort ferez pl.* companions at court 594. [OE *gefēra*]

fere *n.*² appearance; *in f.* in array 267. [From *afere*, OFr *afaire*]

ferk(ke) *v.* to go, ride 173, 1072, 1973; flow 2173; *ferkez hym vp* gets up 2013. [OE *fer(e)cian*]

ferly *adj.* extraordinary 716; *n.* a marvel, wonder 23, 2414. [ON *ferligr* monstrous; OE. **feorlic* strange]

ferly *adv.* exceedingly 388, 741, 1694; **ferlyly** 796; *his strange tale* 2494. [ON *ferliga*, OE **feorlīce*]

fermed *v. pp.* confirmed 2329. [OFr *fermer*]

fermysoun *n.* closed season 1156. [OFr *fermiso(u)n*]

fest *n.* feast, festival. [OFr *feste*]

fest *v. pa. t.* made fast 2347. [OE *fæstan*, ON *festa*]

festned *v. pp.* bound 1783. [OE *fæstnian*]

fete. See FOTE

feted *v. pa. t.* behaved 1282. [OFr *faitier* prepare]

fetled *v. pp.* set, fixed 656. [From OE *fetel*, girdle]

fetly *adv.* gracefully 1758. [From OFr *fait*, *fet*, adj. + *-ly*]

fette 1084. See FECH

fetures *n. pl.* parts of the body 145, 1761. [OFr *faiture*, *feture*]

fyched *v. pp.* fixed 658. [OFr *fich(i)er*]

fyft *adj.* fifth 651. [OE *fīfta*]

fiften *adj.* fifteen 44. [OE *fīftēne*]

figure *n.* figure 627. [OFr *figure*]

fyȝed *v. pa. t.* fitted 796. [OE *fēgan*]

fyȝt *n.* fight 279. [OE *fe(o)hte*]

fyȝt, feȝt *v.* to fight 278, 717; **foȝt** *pa. t. pl.* 874. [OE *fe(o)htan*]

fyked *v. pa. t.* flinched 2274. [OE **fician*; cf. *befician*]

fylched *v. pa. t.*, *hem to f.* attacked or grabbed them 1172. [Origin uncertain]

fildore *n.* gold thread or cord 189. [OFr *fil d'or*]

fyled *pp.* sharpened 2225. [OE *filian* file, or OFr *affiler*]

fylyolez *n. pl.* pinnacles 796. [OFr *filloele*]

fylle *v.* to fulfil, carry out 1405, 1934. [OE *fyllan*]

fylor *n.* sharpening tool 2225. [Cf. OFr *affilé* sharpened] See FYLED

fylter *v.* to crowd together; contend 986. [OFr *feltrer* press (felt)]

fylþe *n.* impurity, sin 1013, 2436. [OE *fȳlþ*]

fynde *v.* to find; obtain 324; **fonde** *pa. t. sg.* 694 (had served), 716, 1875 (*subj.*); *pl.* 1329; **founden** *pl.* (hunting) started 1704; **funde(n)** *pp.* 396, 640; **founden** 1264. [OE *findan*]

fyndyng *n.* finding and starting game 1433. [From OE *findan* + *-yng*]

fyn(e) *adj.* perfected; fully ratified 1636; fine, superb, perfect 919, 1761; pure, sheer 1239; *adv.* completely 173; superbly 1737; **fynly** *adv.* completely 1391. [OFr *fin.*]

fyng(e)res, fyngrez *n. pl.* fingers 641, 1833; finger's breadths 1329. [OE *finger*]

fynisment *n.* end 499. [OFr *finissement*]

fyr(e), fire *n.* fire; sparks 459. [OE *fȳr*] See STONFYR

fire, fyrre. See FER

fyrst *adj. superl.* first; *(vp)on f.* at first, in the beginning 301, 528, 2019; first of all 9, 491, 1477, 1934; *sb.* first day 1072; *adv.*; before 2227. [OE *fyr(e)st*]

fische *n.* fish 503, 890. [OE *fisc*]

fyskez *v. pres. t.* scampers 1704. [(?)ON **fjaska*; cf. Swed *fjäska*]

fyue *adj. and n.* five; group of five 651. [OE *fīf(e)*]

flaʒ(e). See FLE, FLYʒE

flat *n.* plain 507. [From ME *flat* adj.; cf. OI *flat-r* and ON *flǫt* in English placenames]

fle *v.* to flee 2125, 2130; flinch 2272; **flaʒ(e)** *pa. t.* 2274, 2276 (*second*); **fled** 1628. [OE. *flēon* pa. t. *flēah*]

flesch(e) *n.* flesh 943, 2313; (opposed to spirit) 503, 2435; venison 1363. [OE *flǣsc*]

flet(te) *n.* floor 568, 859; *on þe (þis) f.* 294, 1374, *vpon f.* 832, 1653, 1925 in the (this) hall. [OE *flett*]

flete *v.* to fly swiftly; *pa. t. pl.* (*sg. form*) 1566; **floten** *pp.* having wandered 714. [OE *flēotan*]

flyʒe *n.* fly, butterfly 166. [OE *flē(o)ge*]

flyʒe *v.* to fly 524; **flaʒ(e)** *pa. t.* 459, 2276 (*first*). [OE *flē(o)gan*] See FLE

flynt *n.* flint 459. [OE *flint*]

flod(e) *n.* flood, stream 2173; sea 13. [OE *flōd*]

flokked *v. pa. t.* assembled 1323. [From OE *flocc*, n.]

flone *n.* arrow 1161, 1566. [OE *flān*]

flor(e) *n.* floor (= hall) 834, 1932. [OE *flōr*]

flosche *n.* pool 1430. [Cf. OFr *flache*]

floten. See FLETE

flowrez *n. pl.* flowers 507. [OFr *flo(u)r*]

fnast(ed) *v. pa. t.* snorted, panted 1587, 1702. [OE *fnæstian*]

foch(che) *v.* to get, take 396, 1961. [Var. of FECH; cf. OE *feotian* or *fatian*] See FOTTE

fode *n.* food 503. [OE *fōda*]

foyned *v. pa. t.* struck at; kicked 428. [From ME *foine*, OFr *foi(s)ne*, fish-spear, hay fork]

foysoun *n.* abundance 122. [OFr *foiso(u)n*]

folde *n.* earth, land 23, 524, 1694; ground 422; *vpon f.* (word tag) on earth, living. [OE *folde*]

folde *v.* to fold; *f. to*, match, be like 499; befit, be suitable 359; turn, go 1363; **folden** *pp.* plaited; enfolded 959; plighted 1783. [OE *fealdan, faldan*; evidently representing both ME *plihten* (plight) and *plīten* (fold)]

fole *n.*[1] horse. [OE *fola*]

fole *n.*[2] fool 2414. [OFr *fol*]

folé *n.* folly 1545; **foly** 324. [OFr *folie*]

folȝe *v.* to follow, pursue 1164, 1895; *þat f. alle þe sele*, to whom all prosperity came 2422; **folȝande** *pres. p.* in keeping 145; *of f. sute* of similar kind 859. [OE *folgian*]

folk(e) *n.* people, men; throng 1323. [OE *folc*]

fonde *v.* to try 291, 986; test, tempt 1549; experience, endure, pursue 565. [OE *fondian*]

fonde(t). See FYNDE, FOUNDE

fonge, fange *v.* to take, receive, get 391, 1363, 1556, 1622; welcome, entertain 816, 919, 1315; **feng** *pa. t.* obtained 646; **fonge(d)** *pp.* 919, 1315; **fongen** 1265. [OE *fōn*, str., ON *fanga*, wk.]

foo *adj.* hostile; forbidding 1430; *adv.* fiercely 2326. [OE *fāh, fā-*]

foo *n.* foe 716. [OE *gefā*]

for *conj.* for, because, since. [OE *for þam (þe)*]

for *prep.*[1] for, to be, as, because of, through, in return, exchange for; to prevent 1334; in spite of 1854, 2132, 2251; *for olde* because of age 1440; *for to* in order to; *for as much as* in so far as 356. [OE *for*; cf. G *für*, MHG *vür, vüre*, L *prō*]

for *prep.*[2], in *f. God* 965. See expl. n. 965.

forbe *prep.* beyond 652. [OE *for(a)n + be*]

force, forse *n.* necessity 1239; strength 1617. [OFr *force*]

forde. See FORÞE

forest *n.* forest 741, 1149. [OFr *forest*]

forfaren *v. pp.* headed off 1895. [OE *forfaran*[2]]

forferde *v. pa. t.* killed 1617 [OE *forfaran*[1]] See FARE *v.*

forfeted *v. pp.* transgressed 2394. [OFr *forfait, -fet*, n.]

forgat *v. pa. t.* forgot 2031. [OE *forgetan*, affected by ON *geta*] Cf. FORȜATE

forgoo *v.* to give up 2210. [OE *forgān*]

forȝ *n.* channel 2173. [OE *furh*]

forȝate *v. pa. t.* forgot 1472; **forȝeten** *pp.* 1485. [OE *forgetan*]

forȝelde *pres. subj.* repay, reward 839, 1279, 1535, 2429. [OE *forgeldan*]

forlond *n.* promontory 699. [OE *for(e)- + lond*]

forme *adj.* first 2373; *sb.* beginning 499. [OE *forma*]

forme. See FOURME

forne *adv.* of old 2422. [OE *forne*]

forred. See FURRED

forsake *v.* to deny, refuse 475, 1826, 1846; forsake 2380; **forsoke** *pa. t.* 1826. [OE *forsacan*]

forsnes *n.* fortitude 646. [From FORCE + *nes*]

forst *n.* frost 1694. [OE *forst*]

fortune *n.* fortune 99. [OFr *fortune*]

forth *adv.* forth, forward, away, out; *forth dayez* (= OE *forþ dæges*) late in the morning 1072. [OE *forþ*]

forþ(e), forde *n.* ford 699, 1585, 1617. [OE *ford*, **forþ*]

forþi, -þy *conj.* for this reason, and so. [OE *forþī, -þȳ*]

forward(e) *n.* agreement, covenant 1105, 1636, 2347; *watz not f.* was not in our agreement 1395; *pl.* details of our (their) agreement 378, 409, 1405, 1934. [OE *foreweard*]

forwondered *pp.* astonished 1660. [*for-*(intensive) + WONDER]

fot(e) *n.* foot 422; (*measurement*) 2151, 2225; **fete** *pl.* 428, 1904; *vnder f.* under foot 859; **fotez** *d. pl.* 574. **fote** (*orig. gen. pl.*) *fowre f.* large 2225; *dat. pl. (vp)on (his), to my f.* 329, 2229, 2276, 2363. [OE *fōt*]

fotte *v.* to get 451. [OE *fettan*, var. of *feccan*, affected by FOCH]

foule, fowle *adj.* evil 717; poor in quality (*superl.*) 1329; vile 1944; *adv.* badly 2378. [OE *fūl, fūle*]

founde *v.* to hasten 1585, 2229; **founded, fondet** *pa. t.* 2125, 2130; *pp.* journeyed 267. [OE *fundian*]

founden. See FYNDE

fourchez *n. pl.* fork of body; legs 1357. [OFr *fo(u)rche*]

fo(u)rme *n.* figure 145; manner, fashion 1295, 2130. [OFr *fo(u)rme*]

fourty *adj.* forty 1425. [OE *fēowertig*]

fowre, foure *adj.* four 1332, 2225; *sb.* 2101. [OE *fēower*]

fox *n.* fox 1699, 1895, 1944 (*attrib.*), 1950. [OE *fox*]

frayn (at) *v.* to ask 359, 703, 1046, 2494; to make trial of 489, 1549. [OE *(ge)frægnian*]

frayst *v.* to ask 1395; ask for, seek 279, 324, 391, 455; make trial of 409, 1679; try 503; **frayst(ed)** *pp.* 324, 391, 1679. [ON *freista*]

fraunchis(e) *n.* generosity 1264; = L *liberalitas, benevolentia* 652. [OFr *fra(u)nchise*] See expl. n. 651–53

fre *adj.* noble, generous, good; *sb.* noble lady 1545, 1549, 1783; **freest** *superl.* noblest 2422. [OE *frēo* free, noble (poetic); lady (poetic)]

frek(e) *n.* man, knight. [OE *freca*]

frely *adv.* readily, willingly 816, 894. [OE *frēolīce*]

fremedly *adv.* as a stranger 714. [From OE *fremede* + *ly*]

French *adj.* French; *F. flod* the English Channel 13; **Frenkysch** in *F. fare* French courtly manners 1116. [OE *Frencisc*]

frendez *n. pl.* friends 714, 987. [OE *frēond*]

frenges *n. pl.* fringes 598. [OFr *frenge*]

Frenkysch. See FRENCH

fres *v. pa. t.* froze 728. [OE *frēosan*, pa. t. *frēas*]

fresch(e) *adj.* fresh, clean 2019;
sb. fresh food 122; **freschly** *adv.*
quickly 1294. [OFr *freis*, fem.
fresche; cf. OE *fersc*]

fryth *n.* woods, woodland 695,
1430, 1973, 2151. [OE *fyr(h)þ*,
gefyrþe]

fro *prep.* away from, from. [ON
frá]

fro *conj.* after the time when, after
8, 62. [From *fro þat*]

from *prep.* from 461. [OE *fram*]

frote *v.* to rub 1919. [OFr *froter*]

froþe *n.* froth 1572. [ON *froða*]

frounse *v.* to pucker 2306. [OFr
fro(u)nc(i)er]

frount *n.* forehead 959. [OFr
fro(u)nt]

fuyt. See FUTE

ful *adj.* full 44, 2005. [OE *full*]

ful *adv.* very, quite, fully. [OE *full*]

fulsun *v.* to help 99. [ME *fülstnen*;
cf. OE *fylstan*]

funde(n). See FYNDE

furred *v. pp.* lined with fur 880,
1737, 2029; **forred** 1929. [OFr
fo(u)rrer, *fur-*]

fust *n.* fist, hand 391. [OE *fȳst*]

fute, fuyt *n.* trail of a hunted ani-
mal 1425, 1699. [OFr *fuite*]

G

gafe. See GIF

gay(e) *adj.* gay, bright, fair; *adv. or
predic. adj.* 179, 935; *sb.* fair lady
970, 1822; fair knight 2035;
gayest *superl.* 2023; **gayly** *adv.*
gaily 598, 1760. [OFr *gai*]

gayn *adj.* ready, prompt; obedient
178; *at þe gaynest* by the short-
est way 1973; *adv.* promptly
1621; *n.* an advantage 1241,
2491. [ON *gegn*, adj.]

gayn(e) *v.* be of use to, benefit
584, 1829. [ON *gegna*]

gayne *n.* winnings 2349. [OFr
gaaigne]

gaynly *adv.* with an appropriate
flourish 476; rightly 1297. [From
GAYN, adj.]

game. See GOMEN

gargulun *n.* throat of deer with
gullet and wind-pipe 1335, 1340.
[OFr *garguillun*]

garysoun *n.* keepsake 1807; trea-
sure 1255, 1837. [OFr *gari-
so(u)n*, infl. by ON *gersumi*]

garytez *n. pl.* turrets along the
walls 791. [OFr *garite*]

gart *v. pp.* made, caused 2460.
[ON *gøra*, *gǫrva*; neut. adj. as
pp. *gǫrt*]

gast *v. pp.* afraid 325. [OE *gǣstan*]

gate *n.* way, road; *bi g.* on the way
696; *haf þe g.* go by 1154. [ON
gata]

gaudi *n.* beadwork 167. [OFr
gaudie]

geder(e) *v.* to collect, assemble
1326, 1426, 1566, 1625; lift with
both hands 421, 2260; *g. þe rake*
pick up the path 2160. [OE
gæderian]

gef. See GIF

gemme *n.* gem 78, 609. [OFr
gemme]

gentyle, ientyle *adj.* of gentle
birth, noble 42, 639, 2185; ex-
cellent 1022; *sb.* gentle knight
542; *pl.* of noble condition [OFr
gentil]

gerdez. See GORDEZ

gere *n.* gear; armor 260, 569, 584;
that contrivance 2205; *pl.* bed-
clothes 1470. [ON *gervi*] See
STEL(E) *n.*[1]

gere *v.* to clothe, attire 1872; *pp.* 179, 957, 2227; fashioned 791, 1832. [From GERE n.]

geserne. See GISERNE

gest *n.* guest. [ON *gestr*]

get *n.*: *my get* my take 1638. [From GETE v.]

gete *v.* to get 1871; *pa. t.* 1571; **geten** *pl.* seized 1171; **geten** *pp.* 1943; fetched 1625. [ON *geta*]

gif *v.* to give, grant; **gafe** *pa. t. refl.* surrender 1861; **gef** 370, 2349; *g. goud day* 668, 1029, 2073; **geuen** *pp.* 920, 1500. [ON *gefa, gifa*] See ƷEF

gift(e), gyft, ƷIFT *n.* gift 68, 1500, 1822, 2030; *of (my) g.* as (my) gift 288, 1799, 1807 (*pl.*); *ƷEREZ Ʒ.* New Year's gifts 67. [ON *gift*]

gyld, gilt *v. pp.* gilded, gilt 569, 777, 2062. [OE *gyldan*]

gile *n.* guile 1787. [OFr *guile*]

gyng *n.* company 225. [ON *gengi*]

gyrdez, girdel. See GORDEZ, GORDEL

giserne *n.* battle-axe 288, 375, 2265; **geserne** 326. [OFr *guiserne*]

glad *adj.* merry, glad 495, 1079, 1926, 1955. [OE *glæd*]

glade *v.* to gladden, cheer 989. [OE *gladian*]

gladly *adv.* gladly, with pleasure 225, 370, 415; **gladloker** *compar.* 1064. [OE *glædlīce, -lucor*]

glam *n.* din 1426; noise of conviviality 1652. [ON *glam(m)*]

glauer *n.* babble 1426. [Cf. ME, mod. dial. *glaver(en)*, chatter]

glaum *n.* noise of conviviality 46. [ON *glaumr*]

gle *n.* merriment 46, 1652; gladness 1536. [OE *glēo*]

gled(e) *n.* red-hot charcoal 891, 1609. [OE *glēd*]

glem *n.* beam, ray 604. [OE *glǣm*]

gleme *v.* to shine 598. [From GLEM n.]

glemered *v. pa. t.* gleamed 172. [OE *glimerian*, related to *glǣm* n.; cf. G. *glimmern*]

glent *v. pa. t.* glanced; flinched 2292; sprang 1652; glinted 172, 569, 604, 2039; looked 82, 476. [ON *glenta*; cf. Norw *glenta*]

glent *n.* glance 1290. [From GLENT v.]

glyde *v.* to glide 2266; hasten 748, 935; **glod** *pa. t.* came 661. [OE *glīdan*]

glyfte *v. pa. t.* glanced (sidelong) 2265. [See GLYƷT]

glyƷt, *v. pa. t.* glanced, looked 842, 970. [Rel. to ME *glis(t)en, gliƷ(t)en, glif(t)en,* assoc. with GLENT; cf. OE *glisian*, ON *gljá*]

glyter *v.* to glitter 604, 2039. [ON *glitra*]

glod. See GLYDE

glode *n.* an open space 2181; *on glode* on the ground 2266. [? OE *glǣd, *glād*]

glopnyng (*of*) *n.* dismay (at) 2461. [ON *glúpna*]

glorious *adj.* glorious 46, 1760. [OFr *glorio(u)s*]

gloue *n.* gauntlet, glove 583, 1799, 1807. [OE *glōf(e)*]

glowande *v. pres. p.* shining 236. [OE *glōwan*]

go *v.* to go 448, 2150; depart 1024, 1127; be (alive), 2109; *trans.* 811; **gos** *3 sq.* goes 935; **gotz** 375, 1293; **gotz** *imper. pl.* 2119;

goande *pres. p.* walking, 2214; **gon** *pp.* 1872. [OE *gān*] See ȝEDE

God(e), Godde *n.* God; *for G.* as God is my witness 965, 1822; *gef hym G.* wished him Godspeed 2073; *vnder G.*, on earth 2470. [OE *god*] But cf. expl. n. 51

god(e), good(e), goud(e) *adj.* good; **guod** 2430; *for gode* as a good knight 633; *go(u)d day* "good day," "goodbye" 668, 1029, 1290, 2073; *go(u)d moroun*, "good morning" 1208, 1213. **go(u)dly** *adv.* courteously, graciously [OE *gōd*, adj.]

god(e) *n.* possession 1064; goodness 1482; advantage 2031, 2127; *pl.* stuff 1944. [OE *gōd*, n.]

goddes *n.* goddess 2452. [OE. *god* + OFr *-esse*]

godlych *adj.* fine 584. [OE *gōdlic*]

godmon *n.* master of the house 1029,.1392, 1635, 1932; **godemon** 1955. [GOD(E) + MON]

gold(e) *n.* gold; *attrib.* 587, 620, 2395; *red g.* 663, 857, 1817. [OE *gold*]

gome *n.* knight, man. [OE *guma* (poetic)]

gomen *n.* game, sport, pleasure; **game** 365, 1314, 1532; **gamnez, gomnez, -es** *pl.*; quarry 1635; process 661; *in* or *with g.* merrily, jestingly 1376, 1933. [OE *gamen, gomen*]

gomenly *adv.* merrily 1079. [OE *gomenlīce*]

gord(e) *v. pp.* girt 1738, 1851; **gurde** 588, 597. [OE *gyrdan*]

gordel *n.* girdle 2035, 2037, 2429; **girdel** 1829, 2358; **gurdel** 2395. [OE *gyrdel*]

gordez (*to*) *v.* kicks with spurs

2062; **gerdez** 777; **gyrdez** 2160. [? OE *gyrdan*]

gorger *n.* gorget 957. [OFr *gorg(i)ere*]

gost *n.* soul 2250. [OE *gāst*]

gostlych *adv.* like a phantom 2461. [OE *gāstlīce*]

gotz, gos. See GO

goud(e), goudly. See GOD(E)

gouernour *n.* lord 225. [OFr *go(u)verneo(u)r*]

goulez, gowlez *n.* gules, red in heraldry 619; *red g.* 663. [OFr *goules*; Med L *gulæ*, ermine dyed red]

goune *n.* gown 2396. [OFr *go(u)ne*]

grace *n.* favour, mercy, gracious gift; *druryes greme and g.* the grief and joy of love 1507. [OFr *grace*]

gracios *adj.* beautiful 216; *sb.* lovely one, charming lady 1213; **graciously** *adv.* graciously 970. [OFr *gracio(u)s*]

gray(e) *adj.* grey 82, 1024, 1714. [OE *grǣg*]

grayes *v.* withers 527. [From GRAY adj.]

grayn *n.* blade of axe 211. [ON *grein*, branch, division]

grayþ(e) *adj.* ready 448, 597, 2047. [ON *greiðr*]

grayþe *v.* to get ready (*refl.*) 2259; dress 2014; *pp.* arrayed, prepared 151, 666, 876; set 74, 109. [ON *greiða*]

grayþely *adv.* readily, fittingly, at once 417, 1006, 1335, 1683; duly 2292; pleasantly 876, 1470. [ON *greiðiliga*]

grame *n.* wrath; mortification 2502. [OE *grama*] See GREME

grant merci, graunt mercy, gramercy *n.* many thanks 838, 1037, 1392, 2126. [OFr]

gra(u)nte *v.* to consent 1110, 1861; *trans.* grant. [AN *graa(u)nter*, OFr *creanter*]

grattest. See GRET

grece, gres *n.* fat, flesh 425, 1326, 1378, 2313. [OFr *graisse, gresse*]

gref *n.* grief 2502 [OFr *gr(i)ef*]

grehoundez *n. pl.* greyhounds 1171. [OE *grīg-, greihund*]

grem(e) *n.* wrath 312; grief 1507; humiliation 2370; hurt 2251; *with g.* wrathfully 2299. [ON *gremi*]

grene *adj.* green; *sb.* green man 464; (*compar.*) 235; **grene** *n.* green; verdure 207. [OE *grēne*] See ENKER GRENE

grenne *v.* to grin 464. [OE *grennian*]

gres(se) *n.* grass 235, 527, 2181. [OE *græs, gres*]

gres. See GRECE

gret(e) *adj.* great, large, big; **grett** magnificent 2014; *g. wordes* boasts, threats 312, 325; *sb. pl.* nobles 2490; **grattest** *superl.* 1441; *þe g. of gres* the fattest ones 1326; *adv.* most 207. [OE *grēat*]

gret *v. pa. t.* greeted 842, 1933. [OE *grētan*, wk.]

grete *v.* to weep 2157. [OE *grētan*, str.]

greue *n.* grove, woods. [OE *grǣfa*]

greue *v.* to afflict; to dismay 2460; *intr.* be daunted 1442; take offence 316. [OFr *grever*]

greuez *n. pl.* greaves 575. [OFr *greves*]

gryed *v. pa. t.* shuddered 2370.

[Akin to ME *grūen* v. and rel. to North dial. *grue*]

grymme *adj.* grim, fierce 413, 1442, 2260 [OE *grimm*]

gryndel *adj.* fierce 2338; **gryndelly** *adv.* wrathfully 2299. [From ON *grindill* storm; cf. OE *Grendel*]

gryndellayk *n.* fierceness 312. [ON *grindill*, storm + *-leikr*]

gryndelston *n.* grindstone 2202. [ME *grind*, from ME *grinden* v. (OE *grindan*) + stōn (OE *stān*)]

gryp(p)e *v.* to grasp 330; *g.* to lay hold of 421, 1335; *hit bi grypte* by which he gripped it 214. [OE *grīpan, grippan*]

grome *n.* lackey, servant, retainer 1006, 1127. [Cf. MDu. *grom*, OFr *gromet*]

grone *v.* to groan, lament 2157, 2502. [OE *grānian*]

gronyed *v. pa. t.* grunted 1442. [? OFr *grognir* + OE *grunian*]

grounde *n.* ground 426, 526, 2294; region 705; open field 508; (*vp)on g.* on earth 1058, 1070, 2150; *dresses hym vpon g.* takes his stand 417. [OE *grund*]

grounden *v. pp.* ground 2202. [From GROUNDE n.; cf. OE *gryndan*]

growe *v.* to grow 235. [OE *grōwan*]

gruch *v.* to bear ill will 2251; **gruchyng** *pres. p.* with reluctance 2126. [ONFr *gro(u)ch(i)er*]

grwe *n.* grain; *no grwe* not a bit 2251. [OFr *gru*]

guod, gurde(l). See GODE(E), GORDE(L)

guttez *n. pl.* guts 1336. [OE *guttas*]

3

ȝayned *v. pp.* met, greeted 1724.
[OE *gegegnian*, ON *gegna*]

ȝare *adv.* fully 2410. [OE *gear(w)e*]

ȝark(k)e *v.* to ordain 2410; set
820. [OE *gearcian*]

ȝar(r)ande *v. pres. p.* snarling
1595; chiding 1724. [OE *gyrran*,
*georran]

ȝate *n.* gate 782, 820, 1693, 2069.
[OE *gæt*]

ȝaule *v.* to yowl 1453. [Cf. ON
gaula]

ȝe *adv.* yes, indeed. [OE *gǣ*,
gē(a)]

ȝe *pron. sg.* you; **yow** *acc. and
dat.*; *reflex.* 470, 1390, 2117;
your(e), yowre, ȝowre *poss.
adj.*; **yourez** *pron.*; **yowrez**
1037; **ȝourez** 1387; **ȝourself**
pron. 350, **yourself** 1267; *by y.*
beside you 1522; **yowreself** in *if
y. lykez* if you like 1964; **your-
seluen** you 1548; *to y* upon
yourself 350; **yorseluen** in *of y.*
of your own 1394. [OE *gē, ēow*,
etc.] See also ÞOU and expl. n.
1068–78

ȝede(n) *v. pa. t.* went; **ȝedoun** =
ȝed doun 1595; **ȝod** 1146; *on þe
launde ȝ.* stood there 2333; *on
fote ȝ.* lived 2363. [OE *ēode*]

ȝederly *adv.* promptly 453, 1215,
1485, 2325. [From OE *ēdre*,
ǣdre]

ȝef *v.* to give 1964 [OE. *gefan*]

ȝeȝe *v.* to cry (as wares) 67; *ȝ.
after* cry for 1215. [OE *gēgan,
rel. to ON *geyja*]

ȝelde *v.* to yield; **ȝelde(n)** *pa. t.*
67, 1595, 1981; **ȝolden** *pl.* 820;
pp. 453; to give back, return, re-
ply 2325, 1478; bring back 498;

give 67; repay; *refl.* surrender
1215, 1595. [OE *geldan*]

ȝelle *v.* to yell 1453. [OE *gellan*]

ȝelpyng *n.* vaunting 492. [OE
gylpincg, *gelping]

ȝep(e) *adj.* valiant 105, 284,
1510; fresh 60, 951; **ȝeply** *adv.*
instantly 1981, 2244. [OE *gēap*,
cunning]

ȝer(e) *n.* year; *þis seuen ȝ.* for a
long time 1382; *ȝonge ȝ.* New
Year's tide 492; *ȝeres ȝiftes* New
Year's gifts 67. [OE *gē(a)r*] See
GIFTE, NW(E) ȝER(E) and WYNTER

ȝern(e) *adv.* eagerly 1478, 1526;
swiftly 498. [OE *géorne*]

ȝerne *v.* to long 492. [OE *geornan*]

ȝernes *v.* runs 498; **ȝirnez** 529.
[OE *(ge-)éornan, ge-irnan*]

ȝet *adv.* yet, still, all the same, nev-
ertheless; *ȝet firre* moreover
1105; *and ȝ.* even if 1009. [OE
gēt]

ȝette *v.* to grant 776. [LOE
gē(a)tan from ON *játta*]

ȝif, if *conj.* if; **iif** 2343; if only
1799; whether, if 704, 1057,
2457; *bot if* unless 1054, 1782,
1956. [OE *gif*]

ȝiftes. See ȝER(E)

ȝirnez. See ȝERNES

ȝisterday *adv.* yesterday 1485;
n. pl. passing days 529. [OE
gestrandæg]

ȝod. See ȝED

ȝol *n.* Yule, Christmas 284, 500.
[OE *gēol*, ON *jól*, n. pl.]

ȝolden. See ȝELDE

ȝolȝe *adj.* yellow, withered 951.
[OE *geolu, geolw-*]

ȝomerly *adv.* piteously 1453. [OE
geōmerlīce]

ȝon *adj.* that 2144. [OE *geon*]

ȝonder *adv. as adj.* that 678, 2440. [Cf. OE *geond* and MLG *gender*]

ȝong(e), ȝonke *adj.* young, youthful 89, 1526; *ȝ. ȝer,* New Year 492; *sb.* young(er) one 951, 1317. [OE *geong*]

ȝore *adv.* for a long time 2114. [OE *geāra*]

ȝour-, ȝow(re). See ȝE

H

habbe(z), haf(e). See HAUE

hadet *v. pp.* beheaded 681. [OE *hĕafdian*]

haȝer *adj.* well-wrought 1738; *compar.* fitter, readier 352. [ON *hag-r*]

haȝþorne *n.* hawthorn 744. [OE *haguþorn*]

hay *interj.* (hunting) cry of encouragement to hounds 1158, 1445 [OFr *hai,* Gmc *hei*]

haylse, haylce *v.* to greet. [ON *heilsa*]

hal, halle *n.* castle, hall; *h. dor* hall-door 136, 458; *h. ȝatez* main entrance (within the curtain wall) 1693. [OE *hall*]

halce. See HALS

halche *v.* to salute 939; enclose 185; loop, bound round 218, 1852; fasten 1613; *h. in* join to 657. [OE *halsian*]

halde, holde *v.* to keep, fulfill, hold (up); rule 53, 904, 2056; *h. alofte* uphold 1125; contain 124, 627; restrain 1043, 1158; consider, esteem; **helde** *pa. t. subj.* 2129; **halden, holden** *pp.;* bound 1040; beholden 1828. [OE *háldan*]

hale, halle *v.* to draw 1338; loose 1455; *pp.* in *wel-haled* pulled tight 157; *intr.* rise 788; come, go, pass 136, 458, 1049. [OFr *haler,* from Gmc]

half, halue *adj.* half 185; *sb.* 165, 1543; *adv.* 140, 2321. [OE *half*]

half, halue (*dat. and pl.*) *n.* direction; side 649; **haluez** sides of boar 1613; *(vp)on Godez h.* for God's sake 326, 692, 2119, 2149. [OE *half*]

halfsuster *n.* half-sister 2464. [OE *half- + swustor*] See SISTERSUNES

halȝe *n.* saint 2122. [OE *hǎlga*]

haliday *n.* religious festival, holiday season 805, 1049. [OE *hālig dæg*]

halydam *n.* holy relic (part of a conventional oath-swearing phrase) 2123. [OE *hāligdōm*]

halle(d). See HAL, HALE

halme *n.* shaft, handle 218, 330, 2224. [OE *halm*]

halowe, halawe *v.* to shout 1445, 1908, 1914; shout at 1723. [OFr *halloer*]

halowing *n.* shouting 1602. [From stem of OFr *halloer + -ing*]

hals(e), halce *n.* neck. [OE *hals*]

hame, han, han(de)-. See HOME, HAUE, HONDE(SELLE)

hap *n.* happiness 48. [ON *happ*]

hapnest *adj.* most fortunate 56. [ON *heppinn,* infl. by HAP]

happe *v.* to wrap, enclose 655, 864, 1224. [? Rel. to HASPE]

hard(e) *adj.* hard 732, 733, 789, 2199; *adv.* 2153; firmly 1783; **harder** more firmly 655. [OE *heard, hearde*]

harden *v.* to encourage, hearten 521, 1428. [ON *harðna*]

hardy *adj.* bold 59, 285, 371;

hardily *adv.* assuredly 2390.
  [OFr *hardi*]
harled *v. pp.* tangled 744. [Cf.
  HERLE]
harme *n.* injury, misfortune 2272,
  2277, 2390, 2511. [OE *bearm*]
harnays *n.* armor, gear, 590, 2016.
  [OFr *harneis*]
harnayst *v. pp.* clad in armor 592.
  [From HARNAYS]
hasel *n.* hazel 744. [OE *bæsel*]
haspe *n.* door-pin 1233. [OE
  bæpse]
hasp(p)e *v.* to clasp, buckle. [OE
  bæpsian]
hast(e) *n.* speed 1569; *in b.*
  quickly 780, 2218, *with b.* 1756.
  [OFr *baste*]
haste *v.* to hasten 1165, 1424; *refl.*
  1897. [OFr *baster*]
hasty *adj.* pressing 1051; **hastyly**
  adv. hastily 1135; quickly 605.
  [OFr *basti*]
hastlettez *n. pl.* edible entrails
  1612. [OFr *bastelet*]
hat(t)e *v.* am (is) called 10, 253,
  381, 2445; **hattes** *2 sg.* 379, 401.
  [OE *bătte*, passive of HETE]
hatte *n.* hat 2081. [OE *bætt*]
hatz. See HAUE
haþel *n.* knight; master 2065; Lord
  (= God) 2056. [OE *bæleþ*, infl.
  by *æþele*]
hauberghe, hawbrgh *n.* hauberk
  203, 268. [OFr *bauberc*, infl. by
  OE *balsbeorg*, Med L *balsberga*]
haue, haf(e) *v.* to have; **habbe**
  1252; **habbez, -es, hatz** *2 and 3
  sg.*; **hatz, hauen, haf, han** *pl.*;
  haue, haf *subj.* 2287; 1944; *im-
  per.* 496, 2143, 2287, 2288;
  had(e) *pa. t.*; **had(e), hadez**
  subj.; **hade** *pp.* 1962; to take; ac-

cept 1980, put 1446; reach 700;
beget 2466; *auxil.* have; *pa.
subj.* would have; if . . had; *baf at
þe* let me get at you 2288. [OE
habban, baf-] See NAF
hauilounez *v.* doubles back 1708.
  [From ME *baviloun* n., OFr
  bavilon]
haunche *n.* haunch 1345, 2032.
  [OFr *ba(u)nche*]
hawtesse *n.* pride 2454. [OFr
  bautesse]
he *pron.* he, the one **him, hym**
  acc. and dat.; *refl.*; *pleonastic*
  1464, 2013, 2154; **hymself,
  hym-, hisselue(n)** *refl.*; **his,
  hys** *adj. þat . . bys* whose 913;
  pron. his own affairs 1018. [OE
  bē; bim, dat.; *bis*, gen.]
hed(e) *n.* head; mouth 1523; ar-
  rowhead 1162, 1459; axe head
  210, 217; antlered head 1154;
  lord 253. [OE *bēafod*]
hedlez *adj.* headless 438. [OE
  bēafodlēas]
hef, he3-. See HEUE, HI3-, HY3T
hegge *n.* hedge 1708. [OE **becg*]
He3ekyng, Hy3ekyng *n.* God
  1038, 1963 [OE *bēachcyning*]
helde *v. intr. and refl.* go down,
  sink to the west 1321; bow 972,
  1104; turn 2331; go (ahead),
  come 221, 1523, 1692, 1922.
  [OE *béldan*]
helde 2129. See HALDE
helder *adv.* rather; *þe b.* the more
  for that 376, 430. [ON *beldr*]
helez *n.* heels 1899; spurred heels
  777, 2062, 2153. [OE *bēla*]
helme *n.* helmet [OE *belm*]
help *n.* aid 987. [OE *belp*]
help(p)e *v. to help* 2209; *subj.*
  256, 1055, 2123. [OE *belpan*]

hem, him, hym, hom *pron. dat. and acc. pl.* to, for them; *refl.* **hemself** them 976; *refl.* 1085; **her, hor** *adj.* their [OE *heom, heora*]

heme *adj.* proper 157; **hemely** *adv.* 1852. [OE *gehǣme, customary*]

hemme *n.* border 854. [OE *hemm*]

hemmed *adj.* bordered 2395 [From HEMME]

hende *adj.* courteous, gracious, noble; *superl.* noblest 26; *as sb.* courteous, gracious one 827, 946; *voc.* 1252, 1813; good sir 2330; *as þe h.* 896 (see n.), courteously 1104. **hend(e)ly** *adv.* [OE *gehende*, convenient]

hendelayk *n.* courtliness 1228. [OE *gehende* + ON *-leikr*]

heng(e) *v. wk. tr. and intr.* to hang. [ON *hengja*, trans.]

henne *adv.* hence 1078. [OE *heonane*]

hent *v.* to take, to seize, receive 605, 827; *pa. t. and pp.* [OE *hentan*]

hepes, -ez *n. pl.* heaps; *on h.* in a heap 1722; *vpon h.* fallen in confusion 1590. [OE *hēap*]

her. See HO, HEM

herber *n.* lodging 755, 812. [OE *herebeorg*]

herber *v.* to lodge 805, 2481. [OE *herebeorgian*]

here *adv.* here, now, at this point; **herebiforne** before now 2527; **herinne** in this place 300. [OE *hēr, hērbeforan, -inne*]

here *n.*² company of warriors, host 59, 2271. [OE *here*]

here *n.*² hair. [OE *hǣr, hēr*]

here *v.*¹ to hear (of); be told 630; **herd(e)** *pa. t. and pp.*; *h. telle, h. carp* 26, 263, 1144; **herande** *pres. p.* in the hearing of 450. [OE *hēran*]

here *v.*² to praise 1634. [OE *herian*]

heredmen *n. pl.* courtiers 302. [OE *hēord-, hīredmann*]

herk(k)en *v.* to hear, listen (to). [OE *hercnian*]

herle *n.* strand 190. [MLG *herle*]

herre See HI3(E)

hersum *adj.* devout 932. [OE *hērsum*]

hert *n.* heart 1594; inward feelings, courage. [OE *heorte*] See HOND

hertte *n.* hart, stag 1154. [OE *heor(o)t*]

heruest *n.* autumn 521. [OE *hærfest*]

hes *n.* promise 1090. [OE *hǣs* order, *behǣs* promise]

hest *n.* bidding, behest 1039, 1092. [OE *hǣs* + *-t* (infl. by nn. like *yifte, might*)]

hete *v.* to promise 2121; **hy3t** *pa. t.* 1966, 1970, 2218, 2341; **hette** 448; *pp.* 450. [OE *hātan, hēt, hēht*]

hetes *n. pl.* vows, promises of courtly service 1525. [From HETE v.]

het(t)erly *adv.* fiercely, vigorously, suddenly. [Cf. OE *hetol*, MLG *hetter*]

heþe *n.* heath 1320. [OE *hæþ*]

heþen *adv.* hence, away 1794, 1879. [ON *héðan*]

heue *v.* to lift 1184, 2288; **hef** *pa. t.* 826; made bristle 1587; *intr.* raised up 120; **heuen** *pl.* 1346. [OE *hebban, hef-*]

heuen *n.* heaven(s), sky; 2079, 2442; *vnder h.* on earth 56, 352, 1853. [OE *heofon(e)*]

heuened *v. pp.* raised 349. [OE *hafenian*, infl. by HEUE]

heuenquene *n.* queen of heaven 647. [HEUEN + QUENE, cf. OE *heofoncyning*]

heuenryche *n.* heaven; *vnder h.* on earth 2423. [OE *heofonrīce*]

heuy, heué *adj.* heavy, grievous 289, 496. [OE *hefig*]

hewe *n.* See HWE

hewe *v.* to hew, cut 1351, 1607; **hwen** *pa. t. pl.* 1346, 1353; **hewen** *pp.* cut 477; hammered 211; shaped 789. [OE *hēawan*]

hyde *n.* skin 1332, 2312. [OE *hӯd*]

hyden *v.* to hide, conceal 2511; **hid** *pa. t.* 1875. [OE *hӯdan*]

hider(e) *adv.* hither, here. [OE *hider*]

hyghe *interj.* hi! 1445.

hyȝe *n.* haste; *in h.* suddenly 245. [From HYȜ(E) v.]

hiȝe, hyȝ(e) *v.* to hasten, speed; *refl.* 1910, 2121. [OE *hīgian*]

hiȝ(e), hyȝ(e), heȝ(e) *adj.* tall, high, of special dignity or rank; *h. tyde* festival 932, 1033; important 1051; loud 1165, 1417; mature 844; *sb.* height, high ground 1152, 1169, 2004; *(vp)on h.* on high 1607, 2057; in heaven 256, 2442; loudly 67, 1602; to a high degree 48; *h. and loȝe* great and small 302; all matters 1040; *adv.* high, loudly 307, 468, 1445, 2212; openly 349; **herre** *compar.* taller 333; **hyȝest, heȝest** greatest 57; *adv.* at the highest place at table 1001. [OE *hēh, hěrra*] See also HEȜEKYNG

hyȝly, heȝly *adv.* erect 1587; highly, deeply 949, 1547, 1828; devoutly 755, 773; gaily 983. [From HYȜ(E), HEȜ(E) + *-ly*]

hiȝlich *adj.* impressive 183. [OE *hēalic*, infl. by *hēh*]

hyȝt *v. pa. t.* See HETE

hyȝt, heȝt *n.* height 788; *(vp)on h.* lofty 332, aloft 421. [OE *hēhþo*]

hiȝtly *adv.* fitly 1612. [OE *hyhtlīce*]

hil(le) *n.* hill; *on h.* (word tag) = in a castle 59. [OE *hyll*]

hym(self). See HE, HEM

hind *n.* hind 1158, 1320. [OE *hind*]

hypped *v. pa. t.* hopped 2232; *hypped aȝayn* rebounded 1459. [OE *hyppan*; cf. *hoppian*]

hir, his(seluen). See HO, HE

hit, hyt *pron.* it, *freq. impers.*; he 843, she 988; *hit ar(n)*, there are 280, 1251. **hitself** *refl.* itself 1847. [OE *hit*]

hit(te) *v.* to hit, strike 2296; *pa. t.* 1455, 1459, 1594, 2153; *pp.* 2287; *h. to*, fell to 427. [ON *hitta*]

ho *pron.* she; **her, hir** *acc. and dat.*; *refl.* 1193, 1735; **hir** *adj.* her; **her** 1778. [OE *hēo, heō, heore, hire*]

hod(e) *n.* hood. [OE *hōd*]

hode *n.* degree 2297. [OE *hād*]

hoge. See HUGE

hoȝez *n. pl.* hocks 1357. [OE *hōh*]

holde *v.* See HALDE

holde *n.* stronghold 771; possession 1252. [OE *gehald*]

holde *adv.* loyally 2129. [OE *holde*]

holdely *adv.* carefully 1875, 2016. [OE *holdlīce*]

hole *n.* hole 1338, 1569, 2180, 2221. [OE *hol*]

holȝ *adj.* hollow 2182. [OE *holh*]

holyn *n.* holly; *h. bobbe* holly branch 206. [OE *hole(g)n*]

hol(l)e *adj.* whole, intact, healed; amended 2390; **holly** *adv.* completely 1049, 1257. [OE *hāl*]

holsumly *adv.* healthfully 1731. [OE *hāl* + *-sum*; cf. ON *heilsamr*]

holt *n.* wood 1320, 1677; *attrib.* 1697. [OE *holt*]

holtwode *n.* wood 742. [OE *holtwudu*]

hom. See HEM

hom(e), hame *n.* home, dwelling 12, 408, 1924; *adv.* 2121; *to h.* homewards 1615, 1922; *at h.*; *fro hame* away 1534. [OE *hām*]

homered *v. pa. t.* hammered; struck 2311. [From OE *homor*, *hamor*]

hond(e) *n.* hand; **hande** 458, 1203; possession 1270; *bi h.* in person 67; *tan on h.* undertaken 490; *out of h.* immediately 2285; *holden in h.* dispense 2056; *hert and h.*: see expl. n. 366–71. [OE *hand*, *hond*]

hondele *v.* to handle, take hold of 289, 570, 1633, 2505. [OE *hondlian*]

hondeselle, hanselle *n.* gift(s) 66, 491. [OE *handselen*]

hone *n.* delay 1285. [Prob. Celt; cf. OIr *ón*, *óin*, *huan* loan; Mod Ir *uain* time allowed for repayment; Mod Sc Gael *on*, *oin* loan, laziness]

honour *n.* honor 1038, 1228; honor shown, hospitality 1963, 2056; *your h.* worthy of you 1806; **honours** *pl.* 1813. [OFr *hono(u)r*]

honour, honowr *v.* to honor; celebrate 593. [OFr *hono(u)rer*]

hoo *imper.* stop 2330. [ME *hō*, *v.* from *ho!* interj.; cf. Mod E *whoa!*]

hope *v.* to expect, think, believe; to hope 2308. [OE *hopian*]

hor. See HEM

hore *adj.* hoar, grey 743. [OE *hār*]

horne *n.* (hunting) horn. [OE *horn*]

hors(s)e *n.* horse; **horce** 1464; *on hors(e)* 1692, mounted 2065. [OE *hors*]

hose *n. pl.* hose 157. [OE *hosa*]

hostel *n.* lodging, dwelling 776, 805; **ostel** 253. [OFr *(h)ostel*]

hot *adj.*; *in h. and colde* in all circumstances 1844. [OE *hāt*]

houe *v.* to tarry, halt 785, 2168. [?OE **hofian* or (?) a new ME form from *hōf(on)*, pr. of OE *hebban*]

houes *n. pl.* hoofs 459. [OE *hōf*]

hound, hownd *n.* hound. [OE *hund*]

hous(e) *n.* house; *in house* under a roof 2481. [OE *hūs*]

how(e) *adv.* how, in what way, what; *how þat* how 379, 1752; **howseeuer** *adv.* however 1662. [OE *hū*]

huge, hoge *adj.* great, huge. [OFr *ahoge*, *ahuge*]

hult *n.* hilt 1594. [OE *hilt*]

hundreth *adj. and n.* hundred. [ON *hundrað*]

hunt *v.* to hunt 1320, 1677, 1943. [OE *huntian*]

hunte *n.*¹ hunting array 1417. [From HUNT v.]

hunt(e) *n.*² huntsman. [OE *hunta*]

hunter *n.* hunter 1144, 1165, 1428, 1697. [From HUNT *v.*]

huntyng *n.* hunting 1102. [OE *huntung*]

hurt *n.* wound 2484. [OFr *hurt*]

hurt *v.* to hurt, wound 1452, 1462, 2291; *pa. t.* 2311; *pp.* 1577. [OFr *hurter*]

hwe, hewe *n.*¹ hue, color, shade. [OE *hīw, hēow*]

hwe *n.*² head cover, coif 1738 [OE *hūfe*]

hwen. See HEWE

I

I *pron.*; **me** *acc. and dat.*; *ethic dat.*; *dat. absol.* 1067; *freq. refl.*; **my** *adj.* **my(y)n** (*before vowels*); **myn(e)** *pron.* 342, 1816, 1942; **myself(e), -seluen** myself. [OE *ic, mē, min, mē selfan*]

iapez *n. pl.* jests 542, 1957. [From ME *japen* v., (?) OFr *japer*; cf. OFr *gaber, jabeir*]

iche. See VCHE

ientyle, i(i)f. See GENTYLE, ʒIF

iisseikkles *n. pl.* icicles 732. [OE *īs* + *gicel*; cf. *īses gicel*]

iles *n. pl.* islands 698; realms 7. [OFr *i(s)le*]

ilyche *adv.* unvaryingly 44. [OE *gelīc*]

ilk(e) *adj.* same, very; *pron.* 173, 1385, 1930, 1981. [OE *ilca*]

ille *adv.* ill 346; *n.* in *tas to i.* take amiss 1811. [ON *illa, illr,* adj.]

in *prep.* in, on, at, within; **inn** 1451; (in)to 924, 1699; *adv.* [OE *in, inn*]

inmyddes, -ez *adv. and prep.* in the middle (of) 167, 1004, 1932. [From OE *on middan*]

inne *adv.* in; *þer* (*þat*) . . *inne* in which 2196, 2440, 2509. [OE *inne*]

innermore *adv. compar.* further in 794. [OE *innor* + *māre*]

innogh(e), i(n)noʒ(e), innowe *adj.* many, in plenty; enough 404, 730; say no more! 1948; *adv.* enough 477, 803, 1496; exceedingly 289, 888. [OE *genōh, genōg-*]

inore *adj. compar.* inner 649. [OE *innerra*]

into *prep.* into; from here to 2023. [OE *inn tō*]

inwyth *adv.* within 2182; *prep.* 1055. [OE *in* + *wiþ*]

ioy(e) *n.* joy, gladness; *maden i.* acted joyously 910. [OFr *joie*]

ioyfnes *n.* youth 86. [OFr *joefnesse*]

ioylez *adj.* joyless 542. [From IOY]

ioyne *v.* to join 97. [OFr *joindre, joign-*]

ioly *adj.* gay 86; **iolilé** *adv.* gallantly 42. [OFr *joli(f)*]

iopardé *n.* peril 1856; *in i. to lay* to hazard 97. [OFr *ju (jeu) parti*]

irke *v. impers.*: *irked burnez to nye* men tired of hurting 1573. [Cf. OIr *arcoat* (fut. *-irchoi*) he injures, and *erchoat* harm, injury]

is *3 sg.* is. [OE *is*]

iuel *n.* jewel; *fig.* 1856. [OFr *joel*]

iugged *v. pp.* adjudged, assigned 1856. [OFr *jug(i)er*]

iuste *v.* to joust 42. [OFr *jo(u)ster, juster*]

iustyng *n.* 97. [From OFr *jou(s)ter, juster* + *-yng*]

iwysse *adv.* indeed, certainly; **iwy(i)s** 252, 264. [OE *mid* (or *tō*) *gewisse*]

K

K. See also C

kay *adj.* left 422. [ODan *kei*]

kanel *n.* neck 2298. [ONFr *canel*, channel]

kauelacion *n.* cavilling 2275; **cauelaciounz** *pl.* disputes 683. [OFr *cavillacio(u)n*]

kene *adj.* bold 321, 482; bitter 2406; **kenly** *adv.* daringly 1048; bitterly 2001. [OE *cēne*, *cēnlīce*]

kenel *n.* kennel; *attrib.* 1140. [ONFr **kenil*; cf. OFr *chenil*]

kenet *n.* (hunting) small "running" hound 1701. [ONFr *kenet*; cf. OFr *chenet*]

kenne *v.* to teach 1484; entrust, commend (See BIKENNE) 2067, 2472; **kende** *pa. t.* taught 1489. [OE *cennan*; ON *kenna*]

kepe *v.* to keep, hold, preserve 1059, 2148; *subj.* 2298; let him keep 293; to await 1312; attend to 1688; care for 2016; care 546, 2142; *k. hym with carp* engage in conversation with him 307; *kepe þe* take care 372. [OE *cēpan*]

ker(re) *n.* bushes on marshy ground; *ker(re) syde* edge of a marsh 1421, 1431. [ON *kjarr*, **ke(a)rr*]

kerchofes *n. pl.* kerchiefs for the head and neck 954. [OFr *cuevrech(i)ef*, AN *kevre-*]

kest(en). See CAST *n.* and *v.*

keuer *v.* to recover 1755; obtain 1221, 1254; afford 1539; *intr.* manage (to) 750, 804, 2298; *keuerez* takes his way 2221. [OE *acofrian*, intr.; OFr (*re-*)*couvrer*, AN *-kevre*, trans.]

kyd, kydde *v. pp.* made known, shown 263; *k. hym cortaysly* shown him courtesy 775; behaved 2340; *adj.* renowned 51, 1520. [OE *cȳþan*, pp. *ge-cȳdd*]

kylled *v. pp.* killed 2111. [From OE **cyllan*, rel. to *cwellan*]

kyn *n.* kind; *gen. sg.*, in *alle kynnes* of every kind, every kind of 1886; *fele kyn* (from orig. gen. pl) many kinds of 890. [OE *cynn*]

kynde *n.* natural character 321, 2380; race 5; *of þe worldes k.* among men 261; *bi k.* properly 1348. [OE *cynd*]

kynde *adj.* natural, proper; courtly 473. [OE *gecynde*]

kyndely *adv.* duly, properly 135. [OE *gecyndelīce*]

kyng(e) *n.* king; the king, Arthur 57, 2340; *kynges hous Arthor k.* Arthur's house 2275. [OE *cyning*, *cyng*]

kyrf *n.* cut 372. [OE *cyrf*]

kyrk *n.* church 2196. [ON *kirkja*]

kyrtel *n.* kirtle, a knee-length tunic 1831. [OE *cyrtel*]

kysse *v.* to kiss, exchange kisses; **kyssed, kyst** *pa. t.*; *pp.* 1869. [OE *cyssan*]

kyssyng *n.* kissing 1489, 1979. [From OE *cyssan* + *-ing*]

kyth *n.* (native) land 2120. [OE *cȳþþu*]

knaged *v. pp.* fastened 577. [From ME *knagg*, peg; cf. Swed *knagg*]

knape *n.* fellow 2136. [OE *cnapa*]

knarre *n.* rugged rock, crag 721, 1434, 2166. [? OE **cnear*; cf. LG *knarre* knot]

knawen. See KNOWE

kneled *v. pa. t.* knelt 368, 818, 2072. [OE *cnēowlian*]

knez *n. pl.* knees 577; **knes** 818. [OE *cnēo*]

knyf *n.* knife 1331; **knyffe** *dat.* 2042; **knyuez** *pl.* 1337. [LOE *cnīf*, from ON *knífr*]

kny3t, kni3t *n.* knight; [OE *cniht*]

kny3tyly *adj.* knightly, chivalrous 1511; **kny3tly** *adv.* 974. [From OE *cniht* + *-ly*]

knitte, knyt *v. pa. t.* tied 1331; made fast 1642; **knit** *pp.* knotted, tied 1831; woven 1849. [OE *cnyttan*]

knokke *n.* blow 2379. [From OE *cnocian*] See CNOKEZ

knokled *adj.* knobbed 2166. [From ME *knokel* knob; cf. MDu *cnokel* and OFris *knokele*]

knorned *adj.* craggy 2166. [Cf. KNARRE]

knot *n.* knot; rocky wooded knoll 1431, 1434; *endeles k.* the pentangle 630, 662. [OE *cnotta*, ON *knǫttr*]

know(e), knawe *v.* to acknowledge, recognize, know; **knew** *pa. t.* 682, 1849; **knwe** 460, 2008; **knawen, knowen** *pp.* discovered 1272; acknowledged to be 348, 1511; *k. for* known to be 633. [OE *cnāwan*]

koynt *adj.* skilful; skilfully worked, beautiful 877; **coynt** gracious 1525; **quaynt** finely prepared 999; **coyntly(ch)** *adv.* skillfully 578; gracefully 934; **koyntly** cleverly 2413. [OFr *cointe*, AN *queinte*]

koyntyse, *n.* skill 2447. [OFr *cointise*]

kort, kourt. See CORT

kowarde *adj.* cowardly 2131. [OFr *co(u)ard*]

L

lace *n.* belt, girdle; thong 217, 2226; *luf l.* girdle as love token 1874, 2438. [OFr *laz, las*]

lach(che) *v.* to catch; **la3t, laght** *pa. t.*; **le3ten** *pl.* 1410; *pp.* **la3t**; thrown back 156; to take hold of, receive; accept 1772; *l. at* to seize 328, 433. [OE *læccan*]

lachet *n.* latchet 591. [ONFr *lachet*]

lad(de). See LEDE *v.*

lady, ladi *n.* lady; **ladé** 1810. [OE *hlǣfdige*]

laft. See LEUE *v.*[1]

lagmon *n.*; *lad hem bi l.* led them astray (or lagging behind) 1729. [?From ON; cf. Norw dial. *lagga* go slowly]

la3e *v.* to laugh, smile; *pa. t. wk.* **la3ed**, but **lo3e** 2389. [OE *hlæhhan*]

la3yng *n.* laughing 1954; *luf l.* loving laughter 1774. [From OE *hlæhhan* + *-yng*]

la3ter *n.* laugh 1217; laughter 1623. [OE *hlæhtor*]

lay *v.* to lay, stake 97, 156, 419; utter 1480; *l. vp* put away safe 1874; *l. hym bysyde*, push aside, parry 1777; *refl.* lie down 1190. [OE *lecgan*]

laye *n.* lay 30. [OFr *lai*]

layk *n.* sport, entertainment 262, 1023, 1125, 1513. [ON *leikr*]

layke *v.* play, amuse oneself 1111, 1178, 1554, 1560. [ON *leika*]

laykyng *n.* playing 472. [From ON *leika* + *-yng*]

layne *v.* to conceal 1786, 1863; *layne yow* (*me*) keep your (my) secret 2124, 2128. [ON *leyna*]

layt *n.* lightning 199. [OE *lēget*]

layt(e) *v.* to seek 411, 449; wish to know 355. [ON *leita*]

lakked *v. pa. t.* found fault with 1250; *impers.* in *yow l.* you were at fault 2366. [? From ME *lak* n.; cf. OE *læc* adj. weak, failing, and ON *lakr* lacking, defective]

lance. See LAUNCE *v.*

lante *v. pa. t.* gave 2250. [OE *lænan*]

lappe *n.* loose end, fold 936, 1350. [OE *læppa*]

lappe *v.* enfold, wrap, embrace 217, 575, 973. [From LAPPE n.]

large *adj.* broad, wide 210, 2225. [OFr *large*]

larges(se) *n.* great size 1627; generosity 2381. [OFr *largece, -esse*]

lasse *adj. compar.* less, smaller 1284, 1524, 2226; *adv.* 87, 1829, 1848, 2368; **lece** *see* NEUER. **lest** *adj. superl.* smallest 355, 591. [OE *lǣssa, lǣs(es)t*]

lassen *v.* to ease 1800. [From LASSE]

last(e) *adj. superl.* last 1133; *sb.* 1023; *at þe l.* at last, finally. [OE *lætest*]

last(e) *v.* to survive, last, live 1061, 1235, 2510; **last** *pa. t.* 1665; **lested** 805; **lasted** extended 193. [OE *lǣstan*]

late *adj.* late 1027; **later** *adv. compar.* the later 541. [OE *læt*]

laþe *v.* to invite 2403. [OE *laþian*]

laþen. See LOÞE

laucyng *n.* loosening 1334. [From ME *laus,* lōs adj. + -*yng;* cf. ON lauss] See LAUSEN

laumpe, *n.* lamp 2010. [OFr *la(u)mpe*]

launce *n.* lance 667, 2066, 2197. [OFr *la(u)nce*]

la(u)nce *v.* to cut 1343, 1350; cast, utter 1212, 1766, 2124; *intr.* fly 526; dash, gallop 1175, 1464, 1561. [OFr *la(u)ncer*]

launde *n.* glade, lawn, field. [OFr *la(u)nde*]

lausen, lawse *v.* to undo 2376; break 1784. [From ON *lauss*]

lawe *n.*[1] law; *bi. l.* duly 1643; *in þe best l.* in keeping with the best principles (of castle building) 790. [OE *lagu* from ON]

lawe *n.*[2] mound, knoll 765, 2171, 2175. [OE *hlāw*]

lece, lede *n.* See NEUER, LEUDE

lede *v.* to lead, conduct 936, 947, 977; pursue 1894; hold 849; experience, have 1927, 2058; **lad(de)** *pa. t.; pp.* 1989. [OE *lædan*]

leder *n.* leader 679. [OE *lædere*]

lee *n.* protection, shelter; *in l.* in a castle 849; comfortable nest 1893. [OE *hlēo*]

lef, leue (*wk.*) *adj.* dear, beloved, delightful, 909, 1111, 1133, 1924, 2054; affable, obliging; **leuer** *compar.* dearer 1782; *þat l. wer* whom it would please more 1251; **leuest** *superl.* 49, 1802. [OE *lēof*]

leg(g)e *adj.* entitled to feudal allegiance; sovereign 346, 545. [OFr *l(i)ege*]

leg(g)e *n.* leg 575, 2228. [ON *leggr*]

leȝten 1410; **leke.** See LACH, LOUKE

lel(e) *adj.* loyal, faithful 1513,

1516; true 35; **lelly** *adv.* 449, 1863, 2124, 2128. [OFr *leal*, AN *leël*]

leme *v.* to shine. [ON *ljóma*]

lemman *n.* loved one 1782. [OE *léofman*, EME *leofmon*]

lende *v.* to arrive; dwell, stay 1100, 1499; **lent** *pa. t.* went 971; took his place 1002; *pp.* 2440; *is l. on* is occupied in 1319. [OE *lendan*]

lene *v.*; *l. with* incline 2255; *l. to* lean on 2332. [OE *hleonian*]

leng(e) *v.* to make stay, keep 1683; *hym l.* let him stay 1893; *intr.* stay [OE *lengan*]

lenger. See LONGE *adv.*

len(k)þe *n.* length 210, 1627, 2316; *on lenþe* far away 1231; for a long time 232. [OE *lengþu*]

Lentoun *n.* Lent 502. [OE *lencten*]

lepe *v.* to leap, run 292 (*subj.*), 328, 981, 1131, 1709; **lopen** *pp.* 1413; *lepez hym* gallops 2154. [OE *hléapan*]

lere *adj.* empty; *sb.* something worthless 1109. [OE *gelǽr*]

lere *n.* ¹ ligature 1334 [OFr *lieure*]

lere *n.*², *n.*³ See LYRE *n.*¹ and *n.*²

lern(e) *v.* to learn 908, 918, 927, 1532; teach 1878; *pp.* well taught, skilful 1170, 2447. [OE *léornian*]

lese *v.* to lose 2142; **lost** *pp.* 69, 675. [OE *(for)léosan, losian*]

lest *conj.* (*with subj.*) lest. [OE *þe lǽs þe*]

lest. See LASSE

let(e), lette *v.*¹ to let, allow; let be 360; *imper.* 1994; *l. se* show (me) 299, 414; *l. be* cease from 1840; *l. one* let be 2118; cause to 1084; utter 1086; look and speak,

behave 1206, 1634; *l. as lyk* behave as if, pretend 1190, 1201, 1281, 2257. [OE *lǽtan, létan*, str.]

lette *v.*² to stop 2142, 2303; dissuade 1672. [OE *lettan*, wk.]

letteres *n. pl.* letters 35. [OFr *lettre*]

lettrure *n.* learning 1513. [OFr *lettreüre*]

leþe *v.* to make humble 2438. [OE *geliþian, -leoþian*]

leþer *n.* skin; *l. of þe paunchez* tripes 1360. [OE *leþer*]

leude, lede, lude *n.*¹ man, knight, prince. [OE *léod* (poetic)]

leude *n.*², **lede** people, company 833, 1113, 1124. [OE *léod, léode* pl.]

leudlez *adj.* companionless 693. [From LEUDE *n.*¹]

leue *adj.* See LEF

leue *v.*¹ to leave 1583, 1870, 2154; leave off 1502; **laft** *pa. t.* gave up 369; left behind 2030. [OE *lǽfan*]

leue *v.*² to allow 98. [OE *léfan*]

leue *v.*³ to believe 1784, 2128, 2421. [OE *geléfan*]

leue *v.*⁴ to live 1035, 1544. [OE *lifian, leofian*]

leue *n.* leave 133, 971, 1218, 1670; leave to go 545; leave-taking 1288; *take (etc.) l.* take leave. [OE. *léaf*, f.]

leuez *n. pl.* leaves 519, 526. [OE *léaf* neut.]

lewed *adj.* ignorant 1528. [OE *lǽwede*]

lewté *n.* loyalty, fidelity 2366, 2381. [OFr *leauté*, AN *leuté*]

liddez *n. pl.* eyelids 2007. [OE *hlid*] See Y3LYDDEZ

lyf, lif *n.* lifetime; person 1780; **lyue** *dat.*; **lyues** *pl.* 1516, 2112; *l. haden* lived 52; *(vp)on l.* alive, here on earth (word tag) 385, 1719, 1786, 2054, 2095. [OE *līf*]

liflode *n.* food 133. [OE *līflād*]

lyft(e) *adj.* left 698, 947, 2146, 2487. [OE *lyft*]

lyft(e) *v.* to lift, raise, 12, 2309; *pa. t.* 369, 433, 446; *pp.* raised up 258. [ON *lyfta*]

lyfte *n.* heaven 1256. [OE *lyft*]

ly(3)e *v.* to lie 1780, 1994; lie idle 88, 1096; *imper.* 1676; **lygez** *3 sg. pres.* 1179; **lys, lis** 1469, 1686; **le3** *pa. t.* 2006; **lay** 1195; was in residence 37. [OE *licgan, lig-*; *lygez* from ON *liggja?*]

ly3t *adj.*[1] bright 199; cheerful 87; gay 1119. [OE *lĕ(o)ht* adj.[1]]

ly3t *adj.*[2] light, active 1119, 1464; *set at l.* think light of 1250. [OE *lĕ(o)ht,* adj.[2]]

ly3t *n.* light(s); dawn 1675. [OE *lĕ(o)ht*]

ly3t(e), li3t(e) *v.* to dismount; come down 1373, 2220; land (on) 423, 526; *pa. t.* 822; *pp.* is *l.* has lighted 1924. [OE *līhtan*]

ly3tez *n. pl.* lights, lungs 1360. [LY3T *adj.*[2] as *sb.*]

ly3tly *adj.* gleaming, fine 608. [OE. *lĕ(o)htlic,* shining, light]

ly3tly *adv.* swiftly; easily 1299. [OE *lĕ(o)htlīce*]

lyk *v.* to taste 968. [OE *liccian*]

lyke *adj.* like 187; *sb.* the like 498, *adv.* in *lyk as* as if 1281. [OE *gelīc, gelīce* adv.]

lyke *v.* to please; *impers.*; *lyked ille* it might displease 346; *pers.* like 694 (*also* 893, 1682, 2134?). [OE *līcian*]

lykkerwys *adj.* delicious, sweet 968. [ONFr * *lekerous* (OFr *lecheros*) with ending reformed to ME *wys,* OE *wīse* n.]

lym(m)es, -z *n. pl.* limbs; 139, 868, 1332. [OE *lim*]

lymp(e) *v.* to befall 907; *subj.* falls to our lot 1109. [OE *limpan*]

lynde *n.* lime-tree; (*allit.*) tree 526, 2176; **lynde-wodez** woods (*allit.*) 1178. [OE *linde*]

lyndes *n. pl.* loins 139. [OE pl. *lendenu, lenden*; ON *lendir*]

lyne *n.*[1] line 628. [OFr *ligne*]

lyne *n.*[2] linen attire; *lufsum vnder l.* fair lady 1814. [OE *līn*]

lyppe *n.* lip 962, 1207, 2306. [OE *lippa*]

lyre *n.*[1] cheek, face 943, 2228; **lere** 318. [ME *lēr,* from OE *hlēor,* ON *hlȳr*; forms with *ī* perh. confused with LYRE n.[2]]

lyre *n.*[2] flesh 2050 (coat); **lere** 418. [OE *līra,* confused with LYRE n.[1] (LERE)]

list *n.* joy 1719. [ON *lyst*]

lyst(e) *pres. sg. impers.* it pleases (*me, þe, yow l*); *pa. t.* 941, 2049. [OE *lystan*]

lyste *v.* to hear; *l. his lyf* hear his confession 1878. [OE *hlystan*]

lysten *v.* to listen to 30; *intr.* 2006. [OE *hlysnan*; cf. LYSTE]

lystyly *adv.* craftily 1190; deftly 1334. [OE *listelīce*]

lyt(e) *adj.* little 1777; *pl.* few 701. [OE *lȳt*]

lyte *n.* expectation; *on l.* in delay 2303; in hesitation 1463. [From ME *līten* v., ON *hlíta* to trust]

littel, lyt(t)el *adj.* little, small; *adv.* 2007; *a littel* a little; distance away 2146, 2171. [OE *lȳtel*, adj.]

lyþen *v.* to hear 1719. [ON *hlýða*]

liþernez *n.* ferocity 1627. [OE *lȳþernes*]

lyuer *n.* liver 1360. [OE *lifer*]

lo, loo *interj.* lo! look 1848, 2378, 2505; *we loo* ah well! 2208. [OE *lā*]

lode *n.* leading; *on l.* in tow 969; journey 1284. [OE *lād*]

lodly *adv.* horribly: *let l.* affected horror 1634; offensively 1772. [OE *lāþlīce*]

lofden. See LUF *v.*

loft(e) *n.* upper room 1096, 1676; *(vp)on l.* aloft 788, 2261. [ON (*á*) *loft*] See ALOFTE

loȝe, loghe *adj.* low lying 1170; *sb.* 302, 1040 (*see* HIȜE); *on l.* downstairs 1373; **lowe** *adv.* low 972, 2236; **loȝly** *adv.* with deference 851, 1960. [ON *lágr*]

loȝe 2389. See LAȜE

loke *n.* look 1480; *þe l. to* a glance at 2438. [From LOKE v.]

loke *v.* to look; (*with subj.*) see to it that 448; seem 199; *l. on* (*at, to*) look at, see *trans.;* look after, guard 2239. [OE *lōcian*]

loken. See LOUKE.

lokyng *n.* staring 232. [From OE *lōcian* + *-yng*]

lokkez *n. pl.* locks of hair 156, 419, 2228. [OE *locc*]

lome *n.* tool, weapon 2309. [OE *lōma*]

londe *n.* land, ground, country; *pl.* countryside 1561; *in* (*vpon*) *londe* (word tag) in the land, on earth. [OE *lond*]

long(e) *adj.* long 139, 419, 796,

1195; *hym þoȝt l.* seemed long to h. 1620. [OE *lang, long*]

long(e) *adv.* a long while; **lenger** *compar.* 1043, 2063, 2303. [OE *lónge*; compar. adj. *lengra*]

longe *v.* to belong to, befit 1524, 2381, 2515. [From OE *gelang*, adj.]

longynge *n.* grief 540. [OE *lóngung*]

lopen. See LEPE

lord(e) *n.* lord, noble, ruler; Lord (= God) 753, 1055, 2185; husband 1231, 1271, 1534, 1863. [OE *hlāford*]

lore *n.* learning; *with l.*, learned 665. [OE *lār*]

lortschyp *n.* lordship, command 849. [OE *hlāfordscipe*]

los *n.* renown 258, 1528. [OFr *los*]

losse *n.* damage 2507. [OE *los*]

lost. See LESE

lote *n.* sound, noise 119, 1917, 2211; noise of talk 244, word, saying, speech; bearing 639. [ON *lát*(*pl.*)]

loþe *adj.* hateful; *þuȝt l.* felt loath 1578. [OE *lāþ*]

loþe, laþe *n.* injury 2507; grudge 127. [OE *lāþ*]

loude *adj.* loud 64. [OE *hlūd*]

loude, lowde *adv.* loudly, aloud. [OE *hlūde*]

loue-, louy(e). See LUF, LUFLYCH

louke, lowke *v.* to shut 2007; *intr.* be fastened 628; *pa. t. wk.* 217, 792; *str.* **leke** 1830; **loken** *pp.* fastened 35, 2487; shut 765. [OE *lūcan*]

loupe *n.*[1] loop 591. [Origin obscure; ? blend of ON for form (cf. OI *hlaup*, a leap) and Celt for meaning (cf. Gael *lūb*, a loop)]

loupe *n.*² loop-hole, window 792.
[Med L *lūpa, loupa* from Gmc]

loute *v. intr.* to bend 1306, 1504;
turn, go 833, 933; *trans.* bow to
248; **lut(te)** *pa. t.* 2255; saluted
2236; *l. with* bent 418. [OE
lūtan, str.]

lowande *v. pres. p.* brilliant 679;
glowing 868. [ON *loga*]

lowe *v.* to praise; *to l.* praiseworthy
1399. [OFr *lo(u)er*] See also LOƷE

lowkez; lude. See LOUKE, LEUDE

luf *n.* love, affection, regard; ami-
ability 1086; attrib. in *l. lace*
girdle as love token 1874, 2438;
l. laƷyng loving laughter 1777; *l.
talkyng* art of lovers' conversa-
tion 927; *for l.* because of (my)
love 1733, 1810; *for þy l.* out of
regard for you, for your sake
1802; *for alle lufez vpon lyue*
for all loves there are 1786. [OE
lufu]

luf, louy(e) *v.* to love; *pr. sg.*
1256; be in love 1795; **lou(i)ed**
pa. t. 87, 702, 1281, liked 126;
lufed 2368; **lofden** *pl.* 21. [OE
lufian]

luf lace *n.* See LACE n.

luf laƷyng *n.* See LAƷYNG n.

lufly(ch), louely(ch) *adj.* pleas-
ing, gracious, fair; **loueloker**
compar. 973; **louelokkest,
loflyest** *superl.* 52, 1187;
lufly(ch) *adv.* graciously, cour-
teously, willingly, gladly. [OE.
luflic, -līce]

luflyly *adv.* graciously, amiably, in
eager manner 369, 2176, 2389,
2514. [From LUFLY + -*ly*]

lufsum *adj.* lovely 1814. [OE
lufsum]

luf talkyng *n.* See LUF n.

lur *n.* loss, penalty 355, 1284; sor-
row 1682. [OE *lyre*]

lurk(k)e *v.* to lie snug 1180; *pp.*
lurking 1195. [Cf. Scand dials.
lúrka]

lut(te). See LOUTE

M

ma fay by my faith 1495. [OFr
ma fei]

mace. See MAKE

mach *v.* to match 282. [OE
gemæcca, n.]

madame *n.* (*voc.*) my lady 1263.
[OFr *ma dame*]

madde *v.* to act madly 2414. [From
OE *gemǣdd* adj.]

madee. See MAKE

maƷtyly *adv.* powerfully, forcibly
2262, 2290. [OE *mæhtiglīce*]

may *n.* woman 1795. [ON *mær,
meyj*-; OE *mǣg* (poetic)]

may(e) *v.* can, may; *pl.* 70, 2396;
mowe *pl.* 1397; **myƷt** *pa. t.*; if . .
might 1858; *quat he m.* what he
was doing 1087; **moƷt(en)** 84,
872, 1871, 1953. [OE *mæg*]

mayme *v.* to injure 1451. [From
ME *maym*, OFr *mahaym, may-
hem, mahaigne*]

mayn *adj.* great, strong 94, 187,
336, 497. [ON *megn*, OE
mægen]

mayne *n.* See DURE adj.

maynteine *v.* to support 2053.
[OFr *maintenir, maint(i)en*]

mayster *n.* master 1603, 2090;
lord 136. [OFr *maistre*]

maystrés *n. pl.* arts 2448. [OFr
maistrise, maistrie]

make *v.* to make, do perform; com-
mit 1774; cause to be 2455; **mas**
3 sg. 106; **mace** 1885; **make**

subj. 1 pl. let us make 1105,
1681; **mad(e)** *pa. t.*; created
869; **madee** forced 1565;
maked 1142, 1324; *pp.* 1112;
made 982. [OE *macian*]

male *adj.* male 1157. [OFr
ma(s)le]

male *n.* bag 1129, 1809. [OFr
male]

malt *v. pa. t.* melted 2080. [OE
mieltan, mæltan]

mane *n.* mane 187. [OE *manu*]

maner *n.* custom 90; kinds 484;
way 1730; *pl.* manners 924. [OFr
maniere, AN *manere*]

manerly *adj.* seemly 1656. [From
MANER + *-ly*]

mansed *v. pa. t.* threatened 2345.
[OFr *manec(i)er, manac(i)er*]

mantyle *n.* mantle, robe 153, 878,
1736, 1831. [OFr *mantel*]

marre *v.* to destroy 2262. [OE
merran]

mas, masse. See MAKE, MESSE

masseprest *n.* priest 2108. [OE
mæsseprēost.] See MESSE

mat(e) *adj.* daunted 336; exhausted
1568. [OFr *mat*]

matynez, matynnes *n. pl.* matins
(first of the canonical hours) 756,
2188. [OFr *matines*]

mawgref *prep.*; *m. his hed* do what
he might 1565. [From OFr
**malgred, maugré*, infl. by GREF]

Meȝelmas *n.* Michaelmas (Sept.
29); *M. mone* harvest moon 532.
[Cf. OE *Michaeles mæsse*]

me(y)ny *n.* company, household,
court. [OFr *mai(s)n(i)ee,
me(s)nie*]

mekely *adv.* humbly 756. [Cf. ON
mjúkliga, **mēuk-*]

mele *n.* mealtime 999. [OE *mēl*]

mele *v.* to speak, say. [OE *mǣlan*]

melle *n.*; *inn melle* in the midst,
surrounding him 1451. [ON *i
millum*, OI *i milli*, ODan *i
melle*]

melle *v.* to flow together 2503.
[OFr *me(s)ler*]

melly *n.* contest, battle 342, 644.
[OFr *me(s)lée*]

membre *n.* limb 2292. [OFr
membre]

men. See MON

mended *v. pa. t.* improved 883.
[From AMENDE]

mene *v.* to mean 233. [OE *mǣnan*]

menged *v. pp.* mingled 1720. [OE
mengan]

menyng *n.* understanding 924.
[From MENE + *-yng*]

mensk *adj.* honored 964. [ON
mennskr]

mensk(e) *n.* honor (given) 834,
2052; honor, fame 914; *pl.* 2410.
[ON *mennska*]

mensked *v. pp.* adorned 153.
[From MENSK(E) n.]

menskful *adj.* of worth 1809;
sb. noble (knights) 555; (lady)
1268. [From MENSK(E) + FUL
adj.]

menskly *adv.* courteously 1983; in
his honor 1312. [From MENSK(E)
+ *-ly*]

merci, mercy *n.* mercy 1881,
2106. [OFr *merci*] See GRANT

mere *adj.* noble 924. [OE *mǣre,
mēre*]

mere *n.* appointed place 1061. [OE
gemǣre]

mery, meré, miry, myry *adj.*
merry, joyful, cheerful, gay, fair;
fine 1691; *make m.* enjoy one-
self; **meryly, muryly** *adv.* gaily,

playfully 2295, 2336, 2345; 740:
see expl. n. [OE *myrge*]

merk *n.* appointed place 1073.
[ON *merki*, OE *gemerce*]

merkke *v.* to aim at 1592. [ON
merkja, OE. *me(a)rcian*]

merþe, mirþe, myrþe *n.* joy, plea-
sure, amusement; **myerþe** 860;
meue m. provide amusement
985; *make m.* make merry 71,
106, 899, 982. [OE *myrgþ*]

meruayl(e) *n.* wonder, marvel; *to
m.* marvellous 1197; *had m.*
wondered 233. [OFr *merveille*]

meschaunce *n.* disaster 2195.
[OFr *mesch(e)a(u)nce*]

meschef *n.* harm; *his m.* injury to
himself 1774. [OFr *mesch(i)ef*]

mes(se) *n.* buffet 999; food 1004;
pl. dishes of food 999. [OFr
mes]

messe, masse *n.* mass. [OE *messe,
mæsse*, OFr *messe*]

messequyle *n.* time for mass 1097.
[MESSE + WHYLE]

mesure *n.* height 137. [OFr
mesure]

metail *n.* metal 169. [OFr *metail*]

mete *adj.* equal; extending 1736;
metely *adv.* duly 1004, 1414.
[OE *gemēte*; cf. *gemetlice*]

mete *n.* food, meal; *attrib.* dinner
71; *pl.* dishes 121, 1952. [OE
mete]

mete *v.* to meet 1061, 1753, 1932;
greet 834, 2206, 2235; **met(te)**
pa. t. 703, 1723, 1984; *m. wyth*
1370; *intr.* 1407, 1592; *pp.* come
upon 1720. [OE *mētan*]

methles *adj.* without restraint,
"*desmesuré*" 2106. [OE
mǣþlēas]

meue *v.* to move; arouse 985; influ-

ence 90; *intr.* move, pass (on)
1312, 1965, **mwe** 1565; *m. to* re-
sult in 1197; (hunting) start 1157.
[OFr *mo(u)veir, muev-*, AN
mev-]

mych, miche. See MUCH(E)

myddelerde *n.* the world 2100.
[Cf. EME *middelerd* from OE
middeneard affect. by *middel*
adj. as in *middelȝard, middel-
wereld,* etc; or from OE **mid-
deleard,* corresp. to OS
mittilgard, OHG *mittilgart*]

myddes: *in þe m.* in the midst 74.
See INMYDDES

mydmorn *n.* midmorning, nine
a.m. 1073, 1280. [OE *midd +
morgen*]

mydnyȝt *n.* midnight 2187. [OE
midniht]

mydouerunder *n.* mid-afternoon
1730. [OE *mid + ofer undern*]

myȝt *n.* power 2446; *at my m.* as
far as I can 1546; *for myȝtez so
wayke* because of their powers
that are so feeble 282. [OE *miht*]

myȝt. See MAY

myldest *adj. superl.* gentlest 754.
[OE *milde*]

myle *n. pl.* miles 770, 1078. [OE
mil]

mynde *n.* mind, memory 497,
1484; *in m. hade* reflected 1283;
gotz in m. is a matter of doubt
1293. [OE *gemynd*]

mynge *v.* to draw attention to
1422. [OE *myndgian*]

myn(n)e *v.* to declare 141; urges
982; remember, recall 995, 1992;
m. (vp)on give one's mind to
1681; be reminded of 1800; *m.
of* have in mind 1769. [ON
minna, minnask]

mynne *adj.* less; *þe more and þe*
m. all 1881 [ON *minni*]

mynstralsye, mynstralcie *n.* min-
strelsy 484, 1952. [OFr
menestralsie]

mynt, munt *n.* aim; feint, pre-
tended blow 2345, 2350, 2352.
[From MYNTE v.]

mynte *v.* to aim, swing (axe) 2290;
myntes *pa. t.* 2274; **munt** 2262.
[OE *myntan*]

myre *n.* mire 749. [ON *mýrr*]

miry, mirþe. See MERY, MERÞE

mysboden *v. pp.* misused 2339.
[OE *misbēodan*, pp. *misboden*]

mysdede *n.* sin 760, 1880. [OE
misdēd]

misy *n.* bog 749. [Cf. Mod. Lancs.
dial. *mizzy*; (?)OE **mysig*, adj.]
See MOSSE

mislyke *v.* to displease 1810;
impers. (*subj.*) 2307. [OE
mislīcian]

mysses *n. pl.* faults 2391. [OE
miss; cf. *mis-* pref.]

mist *n.* mist 2080. [OE *mist*]

mysthakel *n.* cloak of mist 2081.
[OE *mist* + *hacele*]

mo *adj.* more 23, 730, 2322, 2324;
adv. 770. [OE *mā*]

mode *n.* mind 1475. [OE *mōd*]

moder *n.* mother 754, 2320. [OE
mōdor]

moȝt(en). See MAY

molaynes *n. pl.* ornamented
bosses on a horse's bit 169. [OFr
molein]

molde *n.* earth; *on* (*þe*) *m.*, *vpon*
m. (word tags) on earth 137,
914, 964; in life 1795. [OE
molde]

mon *n.* man; *pron.* one; *vche* (*no*)
m. everybody, nobody; **men** *pl.*

men, people; **menne** 466. [OE
mon(n)]

mon *3 sg.* must 1811, 2354. [ON
mun]

mone *n.*[1] moon 532, 1313. [OE
mōna]

mone *n.*[2] complaint 737. [OE
*mān, rel. to *mǣnan*, v.]

moni, mony *adj. and pron.* many;
mony a many, many a 710, 1217
(frequently without *a*). [OE
monig]

monk *n.* monk 2108. [OE *munuc*]

mor *n.* moor 2080. [OE *mōr*]

more *adj. compar.* greater, larger,
more, further; *sb.* 130; *lasse ne*
m. at all 1524; *adv.* more, fur-
ther; *no m.* not in return, no
further, not again; none the more
for that 2311; **most** *superl.* great-
est, most; *adv.* 51, 638. [OE
māra, mǣst, LNth *māst*]

morn(e), moroun *n.* next day;
morning 453, 740, 1024, 1208.
[OE *morgen*, dat. sg. *morne*]

mornyng *n.*[1] morning 1691, 1747.
[From MORN(E) v. + -*yng*]

mornyng *n.*[2] See MOURNE v.

morsel *n.* a bite 1690. [OFr *morcel*]

mosse *n.* moss, lichen 745. [OE
mos]

most(e). See MORE and MOT

mot *v. pres. t.* may 342; (frequently
in wishes); must 1965, 2510;
most(e) *pa. t.* had to 1287,
1958. [OE *mōt*, pa. t. *mōste*]

mote *n.*[1] speck 2209. [OE *mot*]

mote *n.*[2] castle 635, 910, 2052;
moat 764. [OFr *mot(t)e*, Med L
mota from Gmc]

mote *n.*[3] moot, (hunting) note on
horn 1364; *pl.* 1141. [OFr *mot*]

mount(e) *n.* hill 740, 2080; *bi m.*,

bi þe mountes among the hills 718, 1730. [OFr *mo(u)nt*, OE *munt*]

mounture *n.* mount, horse 1691. [OFr *mo(u)nteüre*]

mourne *v.* to sorrow 1795; **mo(u)rnyng** *n.* sorrow 543, 1800; *in m. of* troubled with 1751. [OE *múrnan*]

mouþ(e), muthe *n.* mouth; voice 1428, 1447. [OE *mūþ*]

mowe. See MAY(E)

much(e) *adj.* great, powerful 182, 2336; much, abundant; **miche** 569; *sb.* much 1255, 1265, 1992; *þus m.* to this purpose 447; *so m. spellez* you say as much as 2140; *adv.* much, greatly, to a great extent 187, 726, 1795; **mych** 1281; *for as m. as* in so far as 356. [OE *mycel, micel*]

muchquat *n.* many things 1280. [MUCH(E) adj. + WHAT]

muckel *n.* size 142. [OE *myc(e)lu*]

muged *v. pa. t.* drizzled, dripped 2080. [ON; cf. OI *mugga*]

mulne *n.* mill 2203. [OE *mylen*]

munt, muryly. See MYNT(E), MERY

mused *v. pa. t.* had thoughts, i.e. were alive 2424. [OFr *muser*]

mute *n.* hunting-pack 1451, 1720; baying of hounds 1915. [OFr *muete*]

muthe, mwe. See MOUÞ, MEUE

N

naf *v.* have not 1066; **nade** *pa. t.* 763; *subj.* 724. [OE *nabban*] See HAUE

naȝt. See NYȜT

nay *v. pa. t.* denied 1836. [OFr *nier*]

nay(e) *adv.* nay, no. [ON *nei*]

naylet *adj.* studded with nails 599. [OE *nægled*]

naylez *n. pl.* nails 603. [OE *nægel*]

nayted *v. pp.* named 65 [ON *neyta*]

naked *adj.* naked, bare; *sb.* bare flesh 423; the ill-clad 2002. [OE *nacod*]

nakerys *n. pl.* kettledrums 1016; **nakryn** *adj.* 118. [? AN *nacarie; cf. OFr *nacaire*]

name. See NOME

nar *v.* are not 2092. [OE *naron*]

nas *v.* was not 726. [OE *næs*]

nase *n.* nose 962. [OE *nasu*]

nauþer, nawþer, nouþer *adj.* (n)either 1552; *adv. ne . . . nauþer* nor . . . either 203, 659, 2367; *conj.* nor 1552; *nauþer . . . ne*, neither . . . nor. [OE *nāwþer*]

ne *adv.* not; *with other neg.* 1991, 2236; *conj.* nor. [OE *ne*]

nede *adv.* of necessity 1216, 1771; **nedes, -ez** needs 1287, 1965, 2510. [OE *nēde, nēdes*]

nedes *v. impers.* in *hit n.* there is need of 404. [From NED(EZ) n.]

nedez *n. pl.* needs, affairs 2216. [OE *nēd*]

neȝ(e), neghe, nieȝ *adv.* near, close 697, 929, 1671; nearly 1922; *prep.* 1771. [OE *nēh*] See NER

neȝe, negh(e) *v. intr.* to approach 132, 697, 1998; *watz neȝed* had come near 929; *trans.* 1575; reach 1054; touch 1836. [From NEȜ(E) adv.]

nek, nec *n.* neck. [OE *hnecca*]

neked *n.* little 1062, 1805. [ON *nekkvat*]

neme *v.* to name 1347. [OE *nemnan*]

ner(e), nerre *adv.* (*compar.*)
nearer 1305; very close by 1995;
nearly 729; *prep.* nearer to, near
237, 322; *com n.* approached
556. **nexte** *superl. prep.* next,
beside 1780. [OE *nēr* (*nĕrra*,
adj.), compar., ON *nær* compar.
and positive, OE *nĕxt*]

neuen *v.* to name, call, mention
10, 58, 65, 541. [ON *nefna*]

neuer *adv.* never, not at all; none
376, 430; *n. one* no one 223; *n.
bot* only 547; *n. so* no matter
how 2129; *n. þe lece* none the
less 474, 541. [OE *nǽfre*; cf. *nā
þe lǽs*]

newe, nexte. See NWE, NER

nye, ny3e *n.* harm 2141; bitterness
2002; *hit were n.* it would be dif-
ficult 58. [OFr *anui*]

nye *v.* to annoy 1575. [OFr *anuier*]

nie3. See NE3(E)

nif *conj.* unless 1769. [NE + (3)IF]

ny3t *n.* night; **ni(y)3t** 929, 1687;
na3t 1407; *on ny3tez*, at night
47, 693. [OE *niht, nœht*]

nikked, nykked *v. pa. t.* in *n.
hym* (*wyth*) *nay* said no to him
706, 2471. [OE *niccan* from I *nic*
not]

nyme *v.* to take 993; *n. to
þyseluen* bring upon yourself
2141; **nome** *pa. t.* 809; obtained
1407; **nomen** *pp.* taken on 91.
[OE *niman*]

nirt *n.* nick, slight cut 2498. [Cf.
Norw dial. *nerta*, v. and SNYRT]

nys *adj.* foolish 323, 358. [OFr
nice]

nys *v.* is not 1266. [OE *nis*]

no *adj.* no; any 1157; **non** 438,
657, 1552, 2106. See OÞER, WAY
[OE *nān*]

no *adv.* no. See MO, MORE [OE *nā*]

nobelay *n.* nobility; *þur3 n.* as a
matter of honor 91. [OFr *nobleie*]

nob(e)le *adj.* noble, glorious,
splendid; *sb.* 1750. [OFr *noble*]

nobot *conj.* only 2182. [NO3T +
BOT]

no3t, not *adv.* not at all, by no
means; *no3t bot* only 1833. [OE
nāht, nōht]

no3t(e) *n.* nothing 680, 961, 1815,
1823, 1943; *neuer... for n.*
never for any reason 1865; *n.
bot* nothing but 1267. [As OE
nāht, nōht n.]

noyce, noyse *n.* noise. [OFr *noise*]

noke *n.* angle, point 660. [Cf.
Norw dial *nōk*]

nolde *v. pa. t.* would not; *n. bot if*
would not have it happen that
... not 1054. [OE *nolde*] See WIL

nome, name *n.* name. [OE *noma,
nama*]

nome(n). See NYME

non(e) *pron.* none, no one. [OE
nān]

nonez; *for þe nonez* for the nonce,
indeed 844. [ME (*to,* *for*) *þan
anes*; cf. OE *for þan ānum*]

norne, nurne *v.* to announce, pro-
pose; offer 1823; urge, press
1771; *n. hir a3aynez* refuse her
1661; *n. on þe same note*
propose same terms 1669; call
2443. [Cf. Swed dial. *norna,
nyrna*]

norþe *n.* north 2002. [OE *norþ*,
adv.]

not. See NO3T

note *n.*[1] business 358; *to þe n.* for
business 420; *for þat n.* for the
purpose, specially 599. [OE
notu]

note *n.*² musical note 514; "tune" 1669. [OFr *note*]

note *v. pp.* noted 2092. [OFr *noter*]

noþyng *n. as adv.* not at all 2236. [OE *nā(n)þing*]

noumbles *n. pl.* numbles, offal of the slain deer 1347. [OFr *no(u)mbles*]

nouþe, nowþe *adv.* now 1251, 1784, 1934, 2466. [OE *nū þā*]

nouþer. See NAUÞER

now(e) *adv.* now, still, moreover; nowadays 58; *oþer n. oþer neuer* 2216; *conj.* now that 2296; since 2420. [OE *nū*]

nowel *n.* Christmas 65. [OFr *noel*]

nowhere *adv.* nowhere 2164; **nowhare** in no case, not at all 2254. [OE *nāhwǣr, -hwǎra*]

nurne. See NORNE

nurture *n.* good breeding 919, 1661. [OFr *no(u)rreture*]

nwe *adj.* new, fresh, exotic 118, 636, 1401; **newe** 132, 1655; *adv.* newly, anew, 60, 599, 1668, 2223; **nwez** *as sb. gen.* in *what n.* whatever new things 1407. [OE *nēowe, hwæt nēowes*]

Nw(e) ʒer(e), New ʒere *n.* New Year's tide, New Year's day. [NWE adj. + ʒER(E); cf. ON *nýjár.*]

O

of *adv.* off. [OE *of*]

of, o *prep.* of, from, out of (consisting, made) of, by, with, about, concerning; *equiv. of gen. and partitive*; in, on (confused with *on*) 1329, 1457 [OE *of*]

offre *v.* to offer 593. [OE *offrian* or OFr *offrir*]

oft(e) *adv.* often [OE *oft*]

oghe *v.* to have, owe; ought 1526; **aʒt(e)** *pa. t.* owned 767, 843, 1775; owed 1941. [OE *āgan, āhte*]

oʒt *n.* anything 300, 2215. [OE *ā(wi)ht, ō(wi)ht*]

okez *n. pl.* oaks 743, 772. [OE *āc*]

olde *adj.* old 1001, 1124, 2182, 2183. [OE *ald*]

on *adj.* one, a single; one (as opposed to the other) 206, 771, 2312. [OE *ān*]

on *adv.* on, away 2219, 2300; (with *infin.* or *rel.*) on 170, 173, 950, 968. [OE *on*]

on *prep.* (up)on, to, (think) of, at, in(to); (*of time*) on, in, by; = a-, *as in* alive, ahunting. [OE *on*]

on(e) *pron.* one (individual); *with superl.* 137, 1439, 2363; some one 2202, 2217; *þat on* the one 952, 954, 2412. [OE *ān*]

one *adj.* alone, only 2074; *a . . . one* a single 2249, 2345; *al one, al hym (his) one* alone 749, 1048, 2155; *hym one* 904; *oure one* by ourselves 1230, 2245. [OE *āna*]

ones, onez *adv.* once 2280, 2512; formerly 2218; *at onez* at the same time, together 895, 1425, 1913; *at þys o.* right this very moment 1090. [OE *ānes*]

onewe *adv.* anew 65. [OE *on + niwan*]

onferum *adv.* from a distance 1575 [OE *on + feorran*]

only *adv.* only 356. [OE *ānlic,* adj.]

onstray *adv.* out of his course, on another course 1716. [OFr *estraié,* ME *astraie,* infl. by *a-, on-.*]

onsware. See ANSWARE

open *adj.* open 2070. [OE *open*]

oquere *adv.* anywhere 660. [OE
  ōhwǣr]
or *conj.*¹ or 88, 661, 2183. [From
  OÞER conj.]
or *conj.*² than 1543. [Originally
  from ARE]
ory3t. See ARY3T
oritore *n.* oratory 2190. [OFr
  oratur]
orpedly *adv.* boldly 2232. [OE
  orpedlīce]
ostel. See HOSTEL
oþer *adj. and pron.* other (one),
  others (*pl.*), other kinds; dif-
  ferent 132; one another 673;
  an o. otherwise 1268; *non o.*
  nothing else 396; *þat o.* the
  other; second 1020, 2350; *of
  alle o.* than any other 944;
  ayþer o. each the other 841, 939,
  1307, 2472; *vch(on) . . . oþer*
  each . . . the other 98, 501, 628.
  [OE *ōþer*]
oþer, auþer *adv. and conj.* or, or
  else; either (foll. by *oþer, or*) 88,
  702, 1772, 2216; else (foll. by
  oþer) 1956, 2293; *oþer oþer* or
  any one else 2102. [OE *āhwæþer,
  ā(w)þer, ō-*]
oþerquyle *adv.* at other times 722.
  [OÞER *adj.* + WHYLE *n.*]
oþez *n. pl.* oaths 2123. [OE *āþ*]
ouer *adv.* above (them) 223;
  across 2232; over there 700.
  prep. above, over, across. [OE
  ofer]
oueral *adv.* all over 150; every-
  where 630. [OE *ofer all*]
ouerclambe *v. pa. t.* climbed over
  713. [OE *oferclimban*]
ouergrowen *v. pp.* overgrown
  2181, 2190. [OE *ofer* + *grōwen*,
  pp.]

ouer3ede *v. pa. t.* passed by 500.
  [OUER + 3EDE; cf. OE *oferēode*]
ouertake *v.* understand 2387. [OE
  ofer + ON *taka*]
ouerþwert *prep.* through a line of
  1438. [OE *ofer* + ON *þvert*]
ouerwalt *v. pp.* overthrown 314.
  [OE *ofer* + *wæltan*]
oure. See WE
out *adv.* out; *hatz out* removeş
  1612. [OE *ūt*]
oute *adv.* far and wide 1511. [OE
  ūte]
outtrage *n.* excess; *adj.* exceed-
  ingly strange 29. [OFr *outrage*]
owen, awen *adj. and pron.* own;
  auen 293; **aune** 10. [OE *āgen*]

P

pay *n.* pay 2247. [OFr *paie*]
paye *v.* to please 1379; well paid
  2341; paid up 1941. [OFr *payer*]
payne *n.* hardship 733. [OFr *peine*]
payne *v. refl.* to take pains; en-
  deavor 1042. [OFr *se pener*]
paynte *v.* to paint 800; depict 611.
  [OFr *peindre; peint*, 3 sg., pp., sb.]
payre *v.* to be impaired, fail 650,
  1456, 1734. [OFr *empeir(i)er*]
payttrure *n.* breast-trappings of a
  horse 168, 601. [OFr *peitreüre*;
  cf. *peitrel*]
palays *n.* a fence of pales 769. [OFr
  paleïs]
pane *n.* fur edging, facing 154, 855.
  [OFr *pan(n)e*]
papiayez *n. pl.* parrots 611. [OFr
  papegai, papejaye]
papure *n.* paper 802. [OFr
  pap(i)er]
paradise *n.* paradise 2473. [OFr
  paradis]
paraunter, parauenture *adv.* per-

haps 1009, 1850, 2343. [OFr *par aventure*]

pared *v. pp.* cut 802. [OFr *parer*]

park *n.* park 768. [OFr *parc*]

parte *v.* to part 2473. [OFr *partir*]

passage *n.* journey 544. [OFr *passage*]

passe *v.* to pass (by, away), proceed; *trans.* cross 2071; surpass 654; *watz passande* surpassed 1014; **passed** *pa. t.*; **past(e)** 1667, 1280. [OFr *passer*]

Pater *n.* the Pater Noster, 757.

patrounes *n. pl.* lords 6. [OFr *patro(u)n*]

paumez *n. pl.* "palms," broad parts of fallow deer's antlers 1155. [OFr *paume*]

paunce *n.* armor covering abdomen (= *pauncer*) 2017. [OFr *pa(u)nc(i)er*] See next

paunchez *n. pl.* stomachs 1360. [ONFr *pa(u)nche*]

pece *n.* piece 1458; (of armor) 2021. [OFr *p(i)ece*]

pelure *n.* fur 154, 2029. [OFr *pelure*]

penaunce *n.* penance 2392; penitential fare 897. [OFr *pen(e)a(u)nce*]

pendauntes, -aund- *n. pl.* pendants 168, 2038, 2431. [OFr *penda(u)nt* v. pres: p.]

penyes *n. pl.* pennies, money 79. [OE *peni(n)g*]

penta(u)ngel *n.* five-pointed star 620, 623, 636, 664. [From Med L *pentangulus, -a, -um*] See expl. n. 619ff.

pented *v. pa. t.* belonged 204. [OFr *apent* 3 sg., APENDE]

peple *n.* people 123, 664. [OFr *pueple*]

pere *n.* peer 873. [OFr *per*]

perelous *adj.* perilous 2097. [OFr *perillo(u)s*]

perile, peryl *n.* peril 733, 1768. [OFr *peril*]

perle *n.* pearl 954, 2364. [OFr *perle*]

persoun *n.* person 913. [OFr *perso(u)ne*]

pertly *adv.* plainly 544, 1941. [From OFr *apert*]

peruyng *n.* periwinkle 611. [OE *peruince*, L *pervinca*]

pes *n.* peace 266. [OFr *pais, pes*]

pese *n.* pea 2364. [OE *pise, peose*]

piched *v. pp.* attached 576; **pyched** set up 768; **py3t** *pa. t.* struck 1456; was fixed 1734. [OE *piccan*; cf. LOE *pícan*]

pyked *adj.* with spikes 769. [From OE *píc*]

piked *v. pp.* polished 2017. [? OE *pĭcian* or *pícan*; but see *OED*, *pick*, v.¹]

pynakle *n.* pinnacle 800. [OFr *pinacle*]

pine, pyne *n.* pain, grief, trouble 747, 1812, 1985; *pine to* it was difficult to 123. [OE *pín, pínian*] See PAYNE n.

pyne *v. refl.* to trouble oneself 1009, 1538. [OE *pínian*] See PAYNE

pyned *v. pp.* enclosed 769. [OE *pyndan*, ME *pinden* and *pin(n)en*, infl. by *pinnen*, pin]

pipes *n. pl.* pipes 118. [OE *pípe*]

pipe *v.* to pipe 747. [OE *pípian*]

pypyng *n.* music of pipes 1017. [OE *pipian* + *-yng*]

pysan *n.* armor for upper breast and neck 204. [OFr *pisa(i)ne*, L *pisanum* of Pisa]

pité *n.* pity, compassion 654. [OFr *pit(i)é*] See expl. n.

pyth *n.* toughness 1456. [OE *piþa*]

pitosly *adv.* piteously 747. [OFr *pito(u)s* + ME *-ly*]

place *n.* room 123; place, dwelling; [OFr *place*]

play *n.* play, sport 1014, 1379. [OE *plega*]

play *v.* to sport, amuse oneself 262, 1538, 1664. [OE *pleg(i)an*]

playnez *n. pl.* level lands, fields 1418. [OFr *plaine*]

plate *n.* steel plate, piece of plate armor 204, 583, 2017. [OFr *plate*]

plede *v.* to plead 1304. [OFr *plaid(i)er*, *pled-*]

plesaunce *n.* pleasure 1247. [OFr *plaisa(u)nce*, *ples-*]

plesaunt *adj.* obliging 808. [OFr *plaisa(u)nt*, *ples-*]

plese *v.* to please 1249, 1659. [OFr *plaisir*, *ples-*]

ply3t *n.* offence 266, 2393. [OE *pliht*]

plytes *n. pl.* evil conditions 733. [AN *plit*, OFr *pleit*]

poynt *n.* (i) (physical) point of a weapon 1456, 2392; point of angle 627, 658: (ii) (abstract); quality 654; question 902; *bryng me to þe p.* come to the point with me 2284; *for p.* because of his excellent condition. [OFr (i) *pointe*, (ii) *point*]

poynte *v.* to describe item by item 1009. [OFr *point(i)er*]

polaynez *n. pl.* pieces of armor for the knees 576. [OFr *polain*]

policed, polyst *v. pp.* polished 576, 2038; **polysed** cleansed 2393. [OFr *polir*, *poliss-*]

pore, pouer *adj.* poor 1538, 1945. [OFr *povre*, AN *poure*]

porter *n.* porter 808, 813, 2072. [OFr *port(i)er*]

poudred *v. pp.* powdered, scattered 800. [OFr *poudrer*]

pray(e) *v.* to pray, beg. [OFr *preier*]

prayere *n.*[1] prayer 759. [OFr *preiere*]

prayere *n.*[2] meadow 768. [OFr *praiere*, Med L *prātāria* adj. fem. sg.]

prayse *v.* to praise; esteem 1850; *only to p.*, (one) only to praise 356. [OFr *preis(i)er*]

praunce *v.* to prance 2064. [Origin obscure]

prece, prese *v.* to press forward, hasten 830, 2097. [OFr *presser*]

presence *n.* presence 911. [OFr *presence*]

prest *n.* priest 1877. [OE *prēost*]

prestly *adv.* promptly 757, 911. [OFr *prest* + *-ly*]

preue *adj.* valiant 262. [OFr *preu*]

preué *adj.* discreet 902; **preuély** *adv.* privately 1877. [OFr *privé*]

preued, proued *v. pp.* proved 79; given proof of 1630. [OFr *pro(u)ver*, *pruev-*, AN *prev-*]

pryde *n.* pride 681, 2038, 2437; *with p.* splendidly 587. [OE *prȳdo*]

prik, pryk *v.* to pierce, stir 2437; *intr.* to spur, prance 2049. [OE *prician*]

pryme *n.* prime, first division of the day, 6–9 a.m. 1675. [OE *prīm*, L *prīma* (*hōra*)]

prynce *n.* prince; *attrib.* princely 1014; *p. of paradise* Christ 2473. [OFr *prince*]

prynces *n.* princess 1770. [OFr *princesse*]

pris, prys *n.*[1] value 79, 1277, 1850;
  excellence 912, 1249, 1630;
  praise 1379; *your p.* you (cour-
  teously) 1247; *o(f) prys* precious
  615, 2364; noble 1770; 2398;
  prys *adj.* precious 1945. [OFr
  pris]
prys *n.*[2] capture; (hunting) blast on
  a horn when the quarry is taken
  1362, 1601. [OFr *prise*, pp. of
  prendre]
prysoun *n.* prisoner 1219. [OFr
  priso(u)n]
profered *v. pa. t.* offered 1494,
  2350; made the offer 2346. [OFr
  parofrir, AN *prof(e)rir*]
proude, prowde *adj.* proud,
  haughty; splendid 168, 601. [OE
  prūt, prūd, from OFr *prout*,
  prou(d)]
proued 1630. See PREUED
prouinces *n. pl.* provinces 6. [OFr
  province]
prowes *n.* prowess 912, 1249,
  2437. [OFr *pro(u)ece*]
pure *adj.* pure 620; faultless, fair,
  noble 262, 654, 664, 2398; sheer
  1247; *adv.* completely 808;
  purely *adv.* entirely, certainly
  802, 813. [OFr *pur*]
pured *v. pp.* purified, refined 633,
  912, 2393; trimmed to show a
  single color 154, 1737. [OFr
  purer]
purpose *n.* purpose 1734. [OFr
  po(u)rpos]
put *v.* to set, put 1277; *pp.* 902.
  [OE *pūtian, pȳtan*]

Q
qu-. See also WH-
quaynt. See KOYNT

quaked *v. pa. t.* trembled 1150.
  [OE *cwacian*]
quel. See WHIL(E)
queldepoyntes *n. pl.* quilted
  coverings 877. [OFr *coiltepointe*]
quelle *v.* to quell 752; kill 1324,
  1449, 2109. [OE *cwellan*]
queme *adj.* pleasant 2109; fine
  578. [OE *cwēme*]
quene *n.* queen 339, 469; **whene**
  74, 2492. [OE *cwēn*]
querre (querré) *n.* (hunting) or-
  derly assemblage of slain deer
  1324. See expl. n.
quest *n.* (hunting) hounds' search
  after game; baying of hounds on
  scenting or viewing 1150; *calle
  of a q.* give tongue 1421. [OFr
  queste]
quethe *n.* utterance 1150. [From
  OE *cweðan* v.]
queþer *pron.* which of two 1109.
  [OE *hwæþer*] See WHEÞER
quik, quyk *adj.* alive 2109; balky,
  restive 177; *adv.* quickly 975;
  quikly, quykly *adv.* 1324, 1490.
  [OE *cwic(u), cwiclīce*]
quyssewes *n. pl.* thigh-pieces 578.
  [OFr *cuissel*, pl. *cuisseus*]
quitclayme *v.* (law) to renounce
  293. [Pp. of QUYTE + CLAYME]
quyte *v.* to requite, repay 2244,
  2324. [OFr *quiter*]
quoþ. See COÞE

R
rabel *n.* rabble 1703, 1899. [Cf.
  OFr *rabler* v.]
race *n.* stroke 2076; *on r.* headlong
  1420. [ON *ras, rás*]
rach *n.* hound that hunts by scent
  1903, 1907 *gen. pl.*; **rach(ch)ez**

pl. 1164, 1362, 1420, 1426. [OE *ræcc*]

rad *adj.* afraid 251. [ON *hræddr*]

rad *adv.* promptly 862. [OE *hrade*]

radly *adv.* swiftly, promptly. [OE *hrædlīce*]

raged *adj.* ragged 745. [ON *raggaðr*, OE *raggig*]

raȝt. See RECH(E)

rayke *v.* to wander; depart 1076; *out r.*, make for the open 1727; *rayked hir* went 1735. [ON *reika*]

rayled *v. pp.* set 163, 603, 745, 952. [OFr *reill(i)er*]

rayn *n.* rain 506. [OE *regn*]

rayne *n.* rein 457, 2177. [OFr *re(s)ne*]

rayse *v.* to raise 1916; bid rise 821. [ON *reisa*]

raysoun. See RESOUN

rak *n.* drifting clouds 1695. [Cf. ON *rek(i)*, Norw dial. *rak*]

rake *n.* path 2144, 2160. [Cf. ON *rák* stripe, Norw dial. *raak* path, but cf. also OE *racu* watercourse]

ran. See RENNE

rande *n.* edge 1710. [OE *rand*]

rape *v. refl.* to hasten 1309, 1903. [ON *hrapa*]

rapely *adv.* hastily, quickly 2219. [ON *hrapalliga*]

rase *v.*¹ to rush 1461. [ON *rasa*]

rase *v.*² to snatch 1907. [From ONFr *arac(i)er*, OFr *esrach(i)er*]

rasor *n.* razor 213. [OFr *rasor*]

rasse *n.* ledge 1570. [OFr *ras*]

raþeled *v. pp.* entwined 2294. [Rel. to *raddle* n. rod, wattle, from OFr *reddalle*, *ridelle*, *rudelle*. See OED, *raddle* v.¹ *ratheled*]

rawez *n. pl.* hedgerows 513. [OE *rāw*]

rawþe *n.* ruth, grief; *r. to here*, grievous to hear 2204. [OE *hrēow* + suff. *-þ(u)*]

rech(e) *v.* to reach; offer, give 66, 1804, 2059, 2324; *intr.* extend 183; achieve, attain 1243; **raȝt** *pa. t.* offered, gave 1817, 1874, 2297, 2351; *r. out* reached out 432. [OE *rǣcan*]

rechate *v.* (hunting) to blow the recall of the hunters 1446, 1466, 1911. [OFr *rechater*]

rechles *adj.* care-free 40. [OE *recelēas*]

recorded *v. pa. t.* recalled, mentioned 1123. [OFr *recorder*]

recreaunt *adj.* (law) guilty of breaking word or compact 456. [OFr *recrea(u)nt*]

red(e) *adj.* red 304, 663, 1205, 2036; *n.* 952, 1695; *on red* against red background 603. [OE *rēad.*] See GOLD

red(e) *v.* to advise; direct 738 (*subj.*); manage, deal with 373, 2111; **redde** *pa. t.* advised 363; *pp.* explained 443. [OE *rǣdan*, *rēdan*]

redé *adj.* ready 1970. [OE *gerǣde*]

redly *adv.* fully 373; **redyly** promptly 1821, 2324; willingly 2059; rightly 392. [OE *gerǣdelice*]

refourme *v.* to restate 378. [OFr *refo(u)rmer*]

refuse *v.* to refuse 1772. [OFr *refuser*]

rehayte *v.* to encourage 1422; exhort 895; rally 1744. [OFr *rehait(i)er*]

reherce, reherse *v.* to repeat 392; go through, describe 1243. [OFr *reherc(i)er*]

rekenly *adv.* courteously 251, 821; worthily 39. [OE *recenlīce*]

rele *v.* to roll 229, 304; *intr.* turn suddenly 1728; dance or spar about 2246 (*subj.*). [From OE *hrēol*, a reel]

relece *v.* to release 2342. [OFr *relaiss(i)er, reless-*]

remene *v.* to recount 2483. [OFr *remener*]

remnaunt *n.* remainder 2342, 2401. [OFr *remena(u)nt*]

remorde *v.* to call to mind with remorse 2434. [OFr *remordre*]

remwe *v.* to change, alter 1475. [OFr *remuer*]

renay(e) *v.* to refuse 1821, 1827. [OFr *reneier*]

rende *v.* to rend 1608; **rent** *pa. t.* 1332; *pp.* 1168. [OE *rendan*]

renk *n.* knight, man; **renkes** *pl.* 2246, **renkkez** 432, 862, 1134. [OE *rinc*, ON *rekkr,* **renk-*]

renne *v.* to run, be current; **ran** *pa. t. pl.* 1420; **runnen** 66, 1703; *pp.* 1727. [ON *renna*]

renoun *n.* renown, glory; *of renoun* noble 2045. [OFr *reno(u)n*]

repayre *v.* to resort; be present 1017. [OFr *repair(i)er*]

repreued *v. pa. t.* rebuked 2269. [OFr *repro(u)ver, repruev-*, AN *-prev-*]

require *v.* to ask 1056. [OFr *requerre*, 3 sg. *requ(i)er*, L. *requir-*]

rered *v. pp.* raised 353. [OE *rǣran*]

res *n.* rush 1164, 1899. [OE *rǣs*]

resayt *n.* receiving stations 1168 [OFr *receite*]

resayue *v.* to receive 2076. [OFr *receivre*]

rescowe *n.* rescue 2308. [From OFr *rescourre*, v.]

resette *n.* shelter 2164. [OFr *recet*]

resoun, raysoun *n.* speech, statement 392; *bi r.* correctly 1344; by rights 1804; **resounz** *pl.* speech 443. [OFr *raiso(u)n, res-*]

respite *n.* respite 297. [OFr *respit*]

rest *n.* rest 1990. [OE *rǣst, rest*]

restaye *v.* to stop, turn back 1153; *to lenge hym resteyed* persuaded him to linger 1672. [OFr *rester*, 3 sg. *restait*; see OED s.v. *stay*, v.[1]]

rested *v. pa. t.* rested 2331. [OE *rǣstan, restan*]

restore *v.* to restore 2283, 2354. [OFr *restorer*]

reue *v.* to take away 2459. [OE *rēafian*]

reuel *n.* revelery 40, 313, 538. [OFr *revel*]

reuel *v.* to revel 2401. [OFr *reveler*]

reuerence *n.* honor 1243; *at þe r.* out of respect 2206. [OFr *reverence*]

reuerenced *v. pa. t.* saluted 251. [From REUERENCE n.]

rewarde *n.* reward 1804, 2059. [ONFr *reward*] See n. 1324

rewarde *v.* to reward 1610, 1918. [ONFr *rewarder*]

ryal *adj.* royal 905; **ryol** splendid 2036; **ryally** *adv.* 663. [OFr *reial*, AN *rial*]

ryalme *n.* realm 310, 691. [OFr *reialme*, AN *rialme*]

rybbe *n.* rib 1343, 1356, 1378. [OE *ribb*]

richche, rych(e) *v.* to direct, arrange, prepare 599, 1223, 2206; *hit richez* draws it to 2177; *refl.* prepare (oneself), dress 1130, 1309, 1873; *refl. and intr.* make one's way, proceed 8, 1898. [Prob. same as RUCH, but senses affected by OE *reccan*]

rich(e), rych(e) *adj.* splendid, costly, rich; of high rank; noble; flourishing 513; resounding 1916; pleasant 1744; *sb. pl.* nobles 66, 362; *adv.* richly 159, 220, 879; **rychest** *superl. sb.* those of highest rank 1130. [OE *rīce*, OFr *riche*]

rychely *adv.* richly 163; festively 931; in lordly fashion 308. [OE *rīclīce*]

richez *v.* See RICHCHE v. and RUCH(CH)E v.

ride, ryde *v.* to ride; **rod(e)** *pa. t.* [OE *rīdan*]

ryd(d)e *v.* to relieve 364; separate 2246; *r. of* clear away 1344. [OE *ryddan*]

rydyng *n.* riding 1134. [OE *rīdan* + *-yng*]

rygge *n.* back 1344 (*attrib.*), 1608. [OE *hrycg*]

ry3t *adj.* true 2443; very 1703. [OE *riht*]

ry3t, ri3t *adv.* properly 373; right, just, even; at all 1790; *r. to* as far as 1341, 2162. [OE *rihte*]

ry3t, ri3t *n.* justice 2346; claim 2342; right 274; obligation, duty 1041. [OE *riht*]

ry3t *v. pa. t.* directed; *refl.* proceeded 308. [OE *rihtan*]

rimed *v. pa. t. refl.* drew himself up 308. [OE *ry̆man*]

rymez *n.* membranes 1343. [OE *rēoma*]

ryne *v.* to touch 2290. [OE *hrīnan*]

rynk *n.* ring 1817, 1827; **ryngez** *pl.* rings of a mail-shirt 580, 857, 2018. [OE *hring*]

rynkande *v. pres. p.* ringing 2337; **ronge** *pa. t. sg.* 2204; **r(o)ungen** *pl.* 195, 1427, 1698; *trans.* rang 931. [OE *hringan*]

ryol. See RYAL

rype *adj.* ripe 522. [OE *rīpe*]

rype *v.* to ripen 528. [OE *rīpian*]

rys *n.* branch, twig; *bi rys* in the woods 1698. [OE *hrīs*]

rys(e), rise *v.* to rise, stand up, get up; **ros** *pa. t.* 1148, 1427, 1735; grew 528; **rysed** rose 1313. [OE *ārīsan*]

rytte *v. pa. t.* cut 1332. [OE **rittan*]

ryue *adv.* abundantly 2046. [LOE *rȳfe*, **rife*, adj.]

ryue *v.* to rip open 1341; **roue** *pa. t.* 2346. [ON *rífa*]

robe *n.* robe 862. [OFr *robe*]

roche *n.* rock 2199. [OFr *roche*]

roché *adj.* rocky 2294. [From OFr *roche*]

rocher *n.* rocky hillside 1427, 1432, 1698. [OFr *roch(i)er*]

rod(e). See RIDE

rode *n.* rood, cross 1949. [OE *rōd*]

roffe *n.* roof 2198; **rouez** *pl.* 799. [OE *hrōf*]

rofsore *n.* gash, wound 2346. [ON *rof* + OE *sār*]

ro3(e), rogh, ru3e, rugh *adj.* rough, rugged; shaggy 745; **roghe** *adv.* roughly 1608. [OE *rūh*, *rūg-*]

rokk(e) *n.* rock 730, 1570, 2144. [Cf. OE *stānrocc*, ONFr *roque*]

rokked *v. pp.* burnished by rolling (in a barrel of sand) 2018. [LOE *roccian*]

rol(le) *v. intr.* to roll 428; hang in loose folds 953. [OFr *rol(l)er*]

romaunce *n.* romance 2521. [OFr *roma(u)nz*]

rome *v.* to wander, make (his) way 2198. [? From OE *rāmian*]

ronez *n. pl.* brush 1466. [ON *runnr*]

ronge. See RYNKANDE

ronk *adj.* luxuriant 513. [OE *ronc*]

ronkled *v. pp.* wrinkled 953. [Cf. ON *hrukka*, *hrunka*]

ropez *n. pl.* cords 857. [OE *rāp*]

ros. See RYS(E)

rote *n.* custom; *bi rote* with ceremony 2207. [OFr *rote*]

rote *v.* to decay 528. [OE *rotian*]

rotez *n. pl.* roots 2294. [ON *rót*]

roue. See RYUE *v.*

rouez. See ROFFE

roun *v.* to whisper 362. [OE *rūnian*]

rouncé *n.* horse 303. [OFr *ro(u)nci, -in*]

rounde *adj.* round; *þe Rounde Table* [OFr *röo(u)nt*, fem. *röo(u)nde*]

roungen. See RYNKANDE

rous *n.* fame 310. [ON *hrós* or *raus*]

roust *n.* rust 2018. [OE *rūst*]

rout *n.* jerk 457. [? Rel. to OE *hrútan*]

ruch(ch)e *v. refl.* to turn (oneself) 303; proceed 367. [OE *ryccan*; cf. ON *rykkja*] See RICHCHE

rudede *v. pp.* reddened 1695. [OE *rudian*]

rudelez *n. pl.* curtains 857. [OFr *ridel*]

ruful *adj.* grievous 2076. [OE *hrēow* + *-full*]

rugh, ruȝe. See ROȜ(E)

runisch *adj.* rough, violent 457; **runischly** *adv.* fiercely 304, 432. [See expl. n.]

runnen. See RENNE

rurd(e) *n.* voice 2337; noise 1149, 1698, 1916, 2219. [OE *reord*]

rusched *v. pa. t.* made a loud rushing noise 2204; *r. on þat rurde* went on with that rushing noise 2219. [Mimetic; cf. OFr *russer*, OE *hryscan*]

ruþe *v.* to bestir 1558. [? From ON *hryðja*]

S

sabatounz *n. pl.* steel shoes 574. [See *OED sabaton*]

sadel *n.* saddle [OE *sadol*]

sadel *v.* to saddle 1128, 2012. [OE *sadelian*]

sadly *adv.* firmly 437, 1593; vigorously 1937; long enough 2409. [From OE *sæd*]

saf. See SAUE, WOWCHE

saȝe *n.* words 1202; *pl.* 341; *s. oþer seruyce* word or deed 1246. [OE *sagu*]

say *v.* to say, tell; **sayn** *pres. pl.* 1050; **sayd(e)** *pa. t.*; *herde say* heard tell, read in 690. [OE *secgan*]

saylande *v. pres. p.* sailing; flowing 865. [OE *seglian*]

sayn. See SAY, SAYNT

sayned *v. pa. t.* blessed with sign of cross 761, 763, 1202. [OE *segnian*]

saynt *adj.* Saint 1644; **sayn** 774, 1022, 1788. [OFr *saint*]

saynt *n.* girdle 2431; **sayn** 589. [OFr *ceint*]

sake *n.*; *for . . . sake* for (one's) sake 537, 997, 1862, 2518. [ON *fyrir sakir*]

sale *n.* hall. [OE *sæl*, OFr *sale*]

salue *v.* to salute; wish good morning to 1473. [OFr *saluer*]

salure *n.* salt-cellar 886. [From OFr *sal(i)ere*]

same *adj.* same 157, 1405, 1669; *pron.* in *of þe* (*þat*) *s.* with the same 170, 881, 1640. [ON *samr*]

same(n) *adv.* together 50, 940, 1318; *al(le) s.* all together 363, 673, 744, 1345. [OE *æt samme*, ON *saman*]

samen *v. trans.* to gather 1372; **samned** *pa. t. intr.* came together, joined 659. [OE *samnian*]

sanap *n.* protective cover for a tablecloth 886. [OFr **sa(u)venape*]

sate. See SITTE

saue(n) *v.* to save 1879, 2040, 2139; *subj.* 1548, 2073. [OFr *sa(u)ver*]

saue, saf *prep.* except 2171; *s. þat*, save that 394, 2229. [OFr *sa(u)f*]

sauer *adj. compar.* safer 1202. [OFr *sauf*, fem. *sauve*]

sauered *v. pp.* flavored 892. [OFr *savo(u)rer*]

sauerly *adv.* with relish 1937; to his liking 2048. [From OFr *savo(u)r*]

saule, sawle *n.* soul 1916, 1879. [OE *sāwol*]

sawes *n.* sauce 893. [OFr *sauce*]

scaþe *n.* injury 2353; *hit is s.* it is disastrous 674. [ON *skaði*]

schad(d)e. See SCHEDE

schaft(e) *n.* shaft 1458; handle 2332; spear 205. [OE *scæft*]

schafted *v. pa. t.* was low 1467. [From SCHAFT(E)]

schaȝe *n.* shaw, small wood 2161 [OE *scaga*]

schal *v. pr. t.* shall, will; shall be 1544; shall come 2400; **schyn** *pl.* (OE *scylon*) 2401; *and schale* and I will be 1240.

schulde *pa. t.* should, would, had to go 1671, 2084; was to 2244. [OE *sceal, scolde*]

schalk *n.* man. [OE *scealc*]

scham(e) *n.* shame 317, 2504; **schome** 2372; *for schame* for shame! 1530. [OE *scamu, scomu*]

schamed *v. pa. t.* was embarrassed 1189. [OE *scamian*, impers.]

schankes, schonkez *n. pl.* legs 431, 846; *vnder schankes* on his feet 160. [OE *scanca, sconca*]

schape *v.* to form; *pr. sg.* in *schapes . . . þe tale* gives an account 1626; devise 2138; *intr.* be arranged 1210; **schop** *pa. t.* arranged 2328, **schaped** 2340; **schapen** *pp.* adorned, fashioned 213, 662. [OE *sceppan*]

schaped *v. pp. adj.* trimmed 1832. [From OFr *chape*] See expl. n.

scharp *adj.* sharp; etc.; *sb.* sharp blade. [OE *scearp*]

schaterande *v. pres. p.* breaking 2083. [OE *scaterian]

schaued *v. pa. t.* scraped 1331; **schauen** *pp.* smooth 1458. [OE *scafan*]

schawe *v.* 27. See SCHEWE

schede *v.* to sever, shed; *intr.* be shed, fall 506, 956; **schadde** *pa. t.* was shed 727; **scade** *pa. t.* 425. [OE *scādan, scēadan*]

schelde *n.* shield; **(s)cheldez** tough skin and flesh at shoulders 1456; hunks of boar's flesh 1611, 1626. [OE *scéld*]

schemered *v. pa. t.* shimmered 772. [OE *scimerian*]

schende *v.* to destroy 2266. [OE *scéndan*]

schene *adj.* bright 662, 2314; *sb.* bright blade 2268. [OE *scēne*]

schere. *v.* to cut 213; **scher** *pa. t. pl.* 1337; **schorne** *pp.* cut 1378. [OE *sceran*]

schere See CHER(E)

schewe, schawe *v.* to show, lay bare, declare; look at 2036; bring out 619, 2061; offer 315, 1526; *intr.* 420, 507, 885. [OE *scēawian, sceāwian*]

schylde *v.* to defend; *God schylde* God forbid! 1776. [OE *scíldan*]

schyn. See SCHAL

schinande *v. pres. p.* shining 269; **schon** *pa. t.* 772, 956. [OE *scínan*]

schynder *v. trans. and intr.* shatter 424, 1458, 1594. [OE *syndrian,* infl. by words in *sch-* (see TG Glossary)]

schyr(e), schyree, schyire *adj.* bright, fair, white; *s. grece* white flesh 425, 1378; fat 2313; *sb.* white flesh 1331, 2256; **schyrer** *compar.* 956; **schyrly** *adv.* clean 1880. [OE *scír*]

scho *pron.* she. [OE *hēo* with shift of stress] See HO

scholes *adj.* without shoes of mail 160 [OE *sc(e)ōh* + *-lēas*; cf. ON *skólauss*]

schome, schon, schonkez, schop. See SCHAM, SCHINANDE, SCHANKES, SCHAPE

schore *n.* bank, slope 2083, 2161, 2332. [Cf. MDu, MLG *schore*]

schorne. See SCHERE

schort *adj.* short 966. [OE *scort*]

schote *v. trans.* to shoot 1454; **schot vnder** *pa. t.* jerked down 2318; *intr.* sprang 317, 2314; **schotten** *pl. trans.* 1167. [OE *scēotan,* str., *scotian,* wk.]

schowre *n.* shower 506. [OE *scūr*]

schowen, schowue. See SCHWUE

schrank(e) *v. pa. t.* shrank; flinched, winced 2267, 2372; penetrated 425, 2313. [OE *scrincan*]

schrewe *n.* villain 1896. [OE *scrēawa* shrew-mouse]

schrof *v. pa. t.* shrove, confessed 1880. [OE *scrīfan*]

schuld(en). See SCHAL

schulder *n.* shoulder. [OE *sculdor*]

schunt *n.* sudden jerk 2268. [? From OE *scunian* + *t*]

schunt *v. pa. t.* swerved 1902; flinched 2280. [? From OE *scunian*]

schwue *v.* to thrust 205; **schowue** *intr.* press 2161; **schowued** *pa. t.* 2083; **schowen** *pl.* 1454. [OE *scūfan,* str.]

scowtes *n. pl.* jutting rocks 2167. [ON *skúti*]

scrape *v.* to paw the ground 1571. [OE *scrapian,* ON *skrapa*]

se *v.* to see, look at; etc.; **sene** [OE *sēonne*] 712; *let se* let me (us) see 299, 414; **segh(e)** *pa. t.*

1632, 1705; **se3(e)**; **sy3(e)** 83
(*subj.*), 200, 1582. [OE *sēon*] See
SEN(E)

sech(e) *v. trans.* to seek, look for
266, 395, 549, 2169; *intr.* go
1052; **so3t** *pa. t.* was seeking out
1284, 1995; *out s.* tried to get
out 1438; came, went 685, 2493.
[OE *sēcan, sŏhte*]

seche. See SUCH

sedez *n. pl. s. and erbez* seeding
vegetation 517. [OE *sǣd*]

seg(g)e *n.* siege 1, 2525. [OFr
s(i)ege]

segg(e) *n.* man, knight; *gen.* 574;
in appos. to *he* 763; *voc.* 394; *vch
s.* everybody 1987; *pl.* men, peo-
ple. [OE (poetic) *secg*]

segh, se3(e). See SE, SEYE

seye *v.* to go 1879; **si3te** *pa. t.* had
gone 1440; **se3en** *pp.* come
1958. [OE *sīgan, sǣgan*]

seker. See SYKER

selden *adv.* seldom 499. [OE
seldan]

sele *n.* happiness, good fortune
1938, 2409, 2422. [OE *sǣl*]

self, seluen *adj.* same, very 751,
2147; *as sb.* self 2156, 2301; *þe
burne(s) s., Krystes s.* the knight,
Christ himself 51, 1616, 2377.
[OE *self(a)*]

selly *adj.* marvellous; wonderful
1962; strange 2170; *sb.* marvel
28, 475; *pl.* 239; **sellokest** *adj.
superl.* 1439; **selly** *adv.* exceed-
ingly 1194; **sellyly** 963, 1803.
[OE sel(d)-lic, -*lucost; sellīce*,
adv.]

selure *n.* canopy 76. [L *cēlātura*,
OFr *cel(e)ure*]

semb(e)launt *n.* appearance 148;

sign 468; manner 1273, 1658,
1843. [OFr *sembla(u)nt*]

semblé *n.* company, throng 1429.
[From OFr *assemblée*]

seme *adj.* pleasant 1085; **se-
mly(ch)** *adv.* becomingly, suita-
bly 865, 882, 888; pleasantly,
sweetly 916, 1658, 1796. [ON
sœmr]

seme *v.* to suit 1929; *impers.* 679,
848 (*subj.*); seem fitting 73,
1005; seem, appear; *semed* was
to be seen 1551. [ON *sóma* (pa.
t. subj. *sœmdi*) infl. by SEME adj.]

semez *n. pl.* ornamented seams.
610, 2028. [OE *sēam*]

semly *adj.* seemly, fitting 348,
1198; fair 685; *sb.* in *þat s.* that
fair knight 672; **semloker**
compar. as sb. one more fair 83;
semlyly *adv.* becomingly 622.
[SEME + OE -*lic, -lucor*; ON
sœmiligr]

sen(e) *adj.* plain to see 148; plain,
clear 341; *used as pp. of* SE seen
197, 239, 468, 475. [OE *gesēne*]

sendal *n.* a fine rich silk 76. [OFr
cendal]

sende *v. pa. t.* sent 2362; *subj.*
should send 1837. [OE *sendan*]

sene. See SE

sengel *adj.* single, all alone 1531.
[OFr *sengle*]

serched *v. pa. t.* examined, 1328.
[OFr *cerch(i)er*]

sere *adj.* individual 1985; various
124, 889; several 761, 822; *fele
sere* many various ones 2417;
adv. in each case 632; *sere twyes*
on two separate occasions 1522.
[ON *sér* (dat. sg.)]

serlepes *adv.* separately 501. [SERE

adj. + OE -*lēpes*, in *sundorlēpes*]

sertayn *adv.* indeed 174. [OFr *certain*, adj.]

seruaunt *n.* servant. [OFr *servant*]

serue(n) *v.*¹ to wait on 827, 851, 1986; serve God 724; *s. of (with)* serve with 482, 888, 1640; *pp.* served at table 61, 85, 114, 135, 1006, 1559; *intr.* wait at table 1651. [OFr *servir*]

serue *v.*² to deserve 1380. [From DESERUE]

seruyce, seruyse *n.* serving, service 1246, 1985; (at table) 130; (in church) 940; *s. of þat syre* celebration of Christmas 751, [OFr *servise*]

sese *v.* to seize, take. [OFr *seisir*]

sesed *v. pp.* ceased; *watz s.* had come to an end 1, 134, 2525. [OFr *cesser*]

sesoun *n.* season 501, 516, 1382; due time 1958, 2085. [OFr *saiso(u)n, ses-*]

sesounde *v. pp.* seasoned 889. [OFr *saiso(u)ner, ses-*]

sete *adj.* suitable 889. [OE *(ge)sǣte*; cf. *andsǣte*]

sete *n.* seat, place at table 72, 493. [ON *sæti*]

sete(n). See SITTE

sette *v.* to set, put; **sett(e)** *pa. t.*; *pp.* 148; to set in a seat 1083; lay table 1651; found 14; place 1593, 1937; make 1883; strike 372; do 1246; *refl.* sit down 437, 1193, 1479; *s. at ly3t* were considered lightly 1250; *s. hym on* rush at 1589; *s. on* called down on 1721; *s. solace* made merry 1318; *s. in (þe) waye* put on the right road 1077, 1971. [OE *settan*]

settel *n.* seat 882. [OE *setl*]

seuen *adj.* seven 613, 1382. [OE *seofon*]

seuer *v.* to sever 2312; *intr.* separate, 1958, (?2312); depart from 1797; part with 1987. [OFr *sevrer*]

sewe *n.* broth, stew 124, 889, 892. [OE *sēaw*]

sidbordez *n. pl.* side-tables 115. [OE *sīd-* + *bord*]

syde *adj.* dangling 2431. [OE *sīd*]

side, syde *n.* side, flank; *pl.* waist 1830; *at (bi, in)* . . . *side* at the side of, beside; *in no s.* in no direction 659, 2170. [OE *sīde*] See BISYDE

syfle *v.* to whistle, blow lightly 517. [OFr *sifler*]

sy3(e), si3ed. See SE, SEYE

sy3t *n.* sight 1721; *se wyth (in) s.* set eyes on 197, 226, 1705; *in s. holden* to see 28. [OE *gesihþ, -siht*]

syke *v.* to sigh 672, 753, 1796. [OE *sīcan*]

syker, seker *adj.* sure; assured 265; true 403; trusty 96, 111, 115, 2493; *in a s. wyse* securely 2048; *adv.* certainly 1637. [OE *sicor*]

siker *v.* to assure; *s. my (bi þi) trawþe* give my (your) word 394, 1673. [From OE *sicor*]

sykyngez, *n. pl.* sighs 1982. [From OE *sīcan*]

sylence *n.* silence 243. [OFr *silence*]

silk(e), sylk(e) *n.* silk; piece of silk 1846; *adj.* 159, 164, 589. [OE *seolc*]

sylkyn *adj.* silken 610. [OE *silcen*]

sille *n.* flooring; *on s.* in the hall 55. [OE *syll*]

syluerin *adj.* silver 886; *sb.* in *þe syluaren* 124. [OE *silfren*]

symple *adj.* plain 503; of no great value 1847. [OFr *simple*]

syn *conj.* since 919, 1892, 2440 (*with subj.*); *syn þat* 2320; *prep.* 24. [Contracted from SIÞEN]

syng(e) *v.* to sing 472, 509, 923. [OE *singan*]

syngne *n.* sign, token 625, 2164, 2433. [OFr *signe*]

synne *adv.* since then 19. [From SYN by anal. with forms like ÞENNE]

synne *n.* sin 1774. [OE *synn*]

syre *n.* lord, knight 685, 751, 1083; **sir** *title before name or polite voc.*; *beau sir* 1222; *sir swete* 2237. [OFr *sire*]

sistersunes *n. pl.* nephews 111. [ON *systrasynir.*] See HALFSUSTER

sitte, sytte *v.* to sit down; sit idle 88; sit here 290, 1531; be enthroned 256, 2442; **sate** *pa. t.* 339; **sete(n)**; *pp.* 1522; *sete on* fitted 865. [OE *sittan*]

syþe *n.* scythe 2202. [OE *sigþe*]

siþen, syþen *adv.* afterwards, next, then, since 1094; *long s.* from long ago 1440; *conj.* since 1642, 2394, 2524; (*causal*) 358, 1234; after 1; now that 2094. [OE *siþþan*] See SYNNE

syþez *n. pl.* times, occasions 632, 761, 982; *bi s.* at times 17; *þese fyue syþez* this series of five 656; **syþe** *dat. pl.* 1868. [OE *siþ*]

skayned *v. pp.* grazed 2167. [ON *skeina*]

skere *adj.* pure 1261. [ON *skærr*]

skete *adv.* quickly 19. [ON *skjótt*, *skēut-*]

skyfted *v. pp.* shifted, alternated 19. [ON *skifta*]

skyl(le) *n.* reason 1509; *bi þis s.* for this reason 1296. [ON *skil*]

skyrtes, -ez, skurtes *n. pl.* skirts of a flowing garment 865; saddleskirts 171, 601. [ON *skyrta*]

skwez *n. pl.* clouds 2167. [ON *ski*, *skiw-*]

slade *n.* valley 1159, 2147. [OE *slæd*]

slayn *pp.* slain, killed 729, 1854, 1950; **slowe** *pa. t. sg.* [OE *slōgon*] 1321. [OE *slægen*]

slaked *v. pa. t.* slackened; 244. [OE *slacian*]

sleȝe *adj.* skilfully made 797, 893; **sleȝly** *adv.* warily 1182. [ON *slœgr*]

sleȝt, slyȝt *n.* skill, 916, 1542; device 1858; *for s. vpon erþe* by any means 1854. [ON *slœgð*]

slentyng *n.* slanting flight 1160. [ON *sletta*, *slenta*]

slepe *n.* sleep 1095; *vpon slepe* asleep 244. [OE *slēp*]

slepe *v.* to sleep; **sleped, slepte** *pa. t.* 729, (*subj.*) 1190; **slepe** *pa. t. subj.* 1991. [OE *slēpan*]

sleper *n.* sleeper 1209. [OE *slēpere*]

slete *n.* sleet 729. [OE *slīet-*, *slēt*; cf. MLG *slōte*]

slyde *v. intr.* to glide, steal 1209; **slode** *pa. t. sg.* in *s. in slomeryng* was slipping into a gentle sleep 1182. [OE *slīdan*]

slyȝt. See SLEȜT

slypped *v. pp.* slipped, escaped 1858; fallen 244; **slypte** *pa. t.* were loosed 1160. [Cf. MLG, MDu *slippen*]

slyt *v. pa. t.* slit 1330. [OE *slittan*]

slokes *v. imper. pl.* stop, enough!
412. [? From ON *slokna*]

slomeryng *n.* slumber 1182.
[From OE *slŭmerian*; cf. *slūma*]

slot *n.* hollow at base of throat
1330, 1593. [OFr *esclot*]

slowe. See SLAYN

smal(e) *adj.* slender, small 144,
1207; fine in texture 76. [OE
smæl]

smartly *adv.* promptly 407. [OE
smeart + -*ly*]

smeþely *adv.* gently 1789. [OE
smēþe + -*ly*]

smyle *v.* to smile 1789. [OE
smīlan; cf. OHG *smīlan*]

smylyng *n.* smiling 1763. [OE
smīlan + -*yng*]

smyte *v.* to smite, strike 205, 2260;
smeten *pa. t. pl. intr.* in *s. into
merþe* fell into merry talk 1763;
smyten *pp.* 407. [OE *smītan*]

smolt *adj.* gentle 1763. [OE *smolt*]

smoþe *adj.* courteous 1763;
smoþely *adv.* smoothly 407.
[OE *smōþ* + -*ly*]

snayped *v. pa. t.* nipped cruelly
2003. [ON *sneypa*]

snart *adv.* bitterly 2003. [ON *snarr*
and *snart* adv.]

snaw(e) *n.* snow. [OE *snāw*]

snyrt *pa. t.* snicked 2312. [Cf. ON
snerta]

snitered *v. pa. t.* came shivering
down 2003. [Cf. Norw. dial.
snitra, shiver with cold.]

so *adv.* so, thus, in this way, this,
that, as 36; therefore 1304, 2296;
to such an extent; (in compari-
son) so too 2365; such 1761 (2),
2454; *intensive* so; *neuer so* no
matter how 2129; *half so* 2321;
so . . . to, so as to 291; *so þat so*

. . . *þat*; also without *þat*; *so
. . . as*, as (so) . . . as; as . . . as if
612, 1883; *with indef. prons.*
[OE *swā*]

soberly *adv.* gravely, with pro-
priety 940, 1278; with measured
words 2051. [OFr *sobre* + -*ly*]

soft(e) *adj.* soft, gentle 510, 516;
compar. 271; *adv.* softly 1929;
comfortably 1121, 1687; **softly**
1193, 1479; in a whisper 915.
[OE *sŏfte*]

so3t. See SECHE

soiorne *n.* sojourn 1962. [OFr
sojo(u)rn]

soio(u)rne *v.* to stay 2409; stable
2048. [OFr *sojo(u)rner*]

solace *n.* pleasure, delight 510,
1085, 1318, 1624; kindness
1985. [OFr *so(u)las*]

somer *n.* summer 510, 516. [OE
sumor]

son, sun *n.* son 113, 1064. [OE
sunu]

sone *adv.* at once, quickly, soon; *s.
as* as soon as 864. [OE *sōna*]

songez *n. pl.* songs 1654. [OE
sang, song]

sop *n.* a bite of food 1135. [OE
sopp]

soper *n.* supper 1400, 1654. [OFr
so(u)per]

sore *adj.* grievous 1793, 2116. [OE
sār]

soré *adj.* sorry 1826, 1987. [OE
sārig]

sor3e *n.* sorrow 2383, 2415; im-
precation 1721. [OE *sorg*]

sostnaunce *n.* sustenance 1095.
[OFr *so(u)stena(u)nce*]

soþ(e) *adj.* true, *and n.* truth, a
fact; *by his s.* on his word 1825,
2051; *for s.* truly 403, 2094; in-

deed; *adv.* with truth 84; surely 2110. [OE *sōþ*]

soþen *v. pp.* boiled 892. [OE *sēoþan*, pp. *soden*; ON *soðinn*]

soþly *adv.* with truth; truly 673, 976, 1095, 2362. [OE *sōþlīce*]

souerayn *n.* sovereign; liege lady 1278. [OFr *so(u)verain*]

sounde *adj.*; *sb.*, *al in s.* in safety 2489. [OE *gesund* adj.]

sounder *n.* herd of wild pigs 1440. [OE *sunor*]

soundyly *adv.* soundly 1991. [OE *gesúndlīce*]

soure *adj.* sour, sore 963. [OE *sūr*; *sūr-ēge*, bleared]

sourquydrye *n.* pride 311; **surquidré** 2457. [OFr *surcuiderie*]

sowme *n.* number 1321. [OFr *so(u)me*]

space *n.* short while; *in space* soon after 1418; at once 1199, 1503. [OFr *(e)space*]

spare *adj.* sparing; *upon s. wyse* in gentle fashion, tactfully 901. [OE *spær*]

spare *v.* to spare 1935. [OE *sparian*]

sparlyr *n.* calf of leg 158. [OE *spærlīra*]

sparred *v. pa. t.* sprang 1444. [Origin uncertain; cf. *OED, spar* v.²]

sparþe *n.* battle-axe 209. [ON *sparða*]

spech(e) *n.* speech, conversation 314, 410, 918, 1292; *pl.* words 1261, 1778. [OE *sp(r)ēc*]

specially *adv.* particularly 2093. [OFr *(e)special* + *-ly*]

specialté *n.* fondness 1778. [OFr *(e)specialté*]

spede, speed *n.* success; profit 918; *good s.* at great speed 1444. [OE *spēd*]

spede *v. trans.* to prosper, bless 762 (*subj.*), 1292, 2120; further 2216; *intr.* in *spedez better* will be better off 410; **speded** *pa. t. refl.* hastened 979. [OE *(ge)spēdan*]

spedly *adv.* fortunately 1935. [OE *spēdlīce*]

speke(n) *v.* to speak; **spek(ed)** *pa. t.* 1288, 2461; **speken** *pl.* 1117; **spoken** *pp.* agreed upon 1935. [OE *sp(r)ecan*]

spelle *n.* speech, words 1199; *expoun in s.*, describe 209; *deme hit with s.* say which 2184. [OE *spell*]

spelle *v.* to say 2140. [OE *spellian*]

spende *v.* to expend; throw away 2113; (can) utter 410. [OE *spendan*]

spenet *v. pa. t.* were fastened, clung 158; **spend** *pp.* fastened 587. [ON *spenna*]

spenne *n.* fence, hedge 1709, 1896; ground; *in spenne* (word tag) on that marked out ground = there 1074. [Cf. ON *spenni*]

spenne-fote *adv.* with feet together or kicking out 2316. [ON *spenna* + FOT(E)]

spere *n.* spear 269, 983, 2066, 2143; *attrib.* 2316. [OE *spere*]

sperre *v.* to strike 670. [OE *sperran*]

spetos *adj.* cruel 209. [From OFr *despito(u)s*] See SPYT

spyces *n. pl.* spices 892; spiced cakes 979. [OFr *(e)spice*]

spye *v.* to search out 2093; get a sight of 1896; inquire 901. [OFr *(e)spier*]

spyt *n.* doing harm 1444. [From OFr *despit*]

spoken. See SPEKE

sponez *n. pl.* spoons 886. [OE *spōn*, chip; ON *spónn*, chip, spoon]

sporez. See SPUREZ

sprenged *v. pa. t.* in *day s.* day broke 1415, 2009. [OE *sprengan*]

sprent *v. pa. t.* leapt 1896. [ON *spretta*, *sprenta]

sprit *v. pa. t.* sprang 2316. [OE *spryttan*]

sprong *v. pa. t. sg.* sprang 670; **sprange** *pl.* 1778. [OE *springan*]

spured *v. pp.* asked 901; **spuryed** 2093. [OE *spyrian*]

spurez *n. pl.* spurs 158, 670; **sporez** 587. [OE *spura, spora*]

stabeled *v. pa. t.* put in a stable 823. [OFr *(e)stabler*]

stabled *v. pp.* established 1060. [OFr *(e)stablir*]

stablye *n.* (hunting) ring of beaters 1153. [OFr *establie*]

stad *v. pp.* placed; set down in writing 33; beset 644; standing there 2137. [ON *steðja*; pp. *staddr*]

staf *n.* staff 214; **staue** *dat.* club 2137. [OE *stæf*]

stafful *adj.* crammed full 494. [Cf. Norw *stappfull*]

stayne *v.* to color 170. [ON *steina*]

stalke *v.* to step cautiously 237; stalk 2230. [OE *stalcian*]

stal(l)e *n.* standing; *in s.* standing up 104, 107. [OE *stall, in stalle*]

stalworth *adj.* stalwart 846; *sb.* 1659. [OE *stǽlwyrþe*]

stange *n.* pole 1614. [ON *stǫng*]

stapled *v. pp.* fastened with staples

606. [From ME *stapel*, staple; cf. OE *stapol* post]

starande *v. pres. p.* staring; blazing 1818. [OE *starian*]

start(e) *v.* to start, flinch 1567, 2286; leap forward 2063; *pa. t.* sprang 431; twisted 1716. [OE *stertan; cf. *styrtan*]

statut *n.* formal agreement 1060. [OFr *(e)statut*]

staue. See STAF

sted(e) *n.* steed 176, 281, 670, 823; *on s. to ryde* who ride = knights 260. [OE *stēda*]

sted(de) *n.* place; *in (þis) s.* here, there 439, 2213, 2323. [OE *stede*]

stek. See STOKEN *pp.* [2]

stel(e) *n.* [1] steel 211, 426, 575; armor 570; *adj.* 580; *attrib., s. bawe* stirrup-iron 435; *s. gere n.* armor 260. [OE *stēle*] See BAWE, GERE

stele *n.* [2] haft 214, 2230. [OE *stela*]

stele *v. intr.* to steal 1710; **stel** *pa. t. sg.* 1191; **stollen** *pp.* as *adj.* stealthy 1659. [OE *stelan*]

stem(m)ed *v. pa. t. intr.* stopped, halted 230; stood about 1117. [ON *stemma*]

steppe *v.* to step 435, 570, 2060; *wk. pa. t.* 1191. [OE *steppan*]

steropes. See STIROP

steuen *n.* [1] voice 242, 2336. [OE *stefn*, f.]

steuen *n.* [2] appointment, tryst 1060, 2194, 2213, 2238; appointed time 2008. [ON *stefna* appointment; OE *stefn*, m., time]

stif(fe), styf *adj.* stiff, unfaltering 431; unflinching, stout, strong, firm, fearless, bold; *s. and strong* brave (story) 34; *superl.* 260,

1567; *adv.* violently 671; **stifly** *adv.* strongly 606; fearlessly 287; undaunted 1716. [OE *stif*]

sti3tel, sty3tel *v.* to order, control; deal with 2137; rule, be master 2213; *s. in stalle,* stand 104; *s. þe vpon* limit yourself to 2252. [OE **stihtlian;* cf. *stihtan*]

stille *adj. and adv.* still, motionless 2252, 2293; without stirring, undisturbed 1367, 1687, 1994; uncomplaining 2385; secret(ly) 1188, 1659; privately 1085; silent 1996; *compar.* 301; **stilly** *adv.* softly, secretly 1117, 1191, 1710. [OE *stille, stillīce*] See STON(E)

stirop *n.* stirrup 2060; **steropes** *pl.* 170. [OE *stigrāp*]

styþly *adv.* stoutly, unperturbed 431. [OE *stīþlīce*]

stod(e). See STONDE

stoffed *v. pp.* stuffed 606. [OFr *(e)stoffer*]

stoken *v. pp.*² stuck; shut 782; set down, fixed in writing 33; *s. of* fully provided with 494; *s. me* imposed on me 2194; **stek** *pa. t. intr.* fitted closely 152. [OE **stecan*]

stollen. See STELE *v.*

stonde *v.* to stand; stand up 1797; stand and take (a stroke) from 294, 2286; **stod(e)** *pa. t.*; waited 2063; went and stood 322; (?)*subj.* 1768; *stondande alofte* set standing out upon it 1818. [OE *standan, stondan*]

ston(e) *n.* gem; stone 789, 2166; (stony) ground 2230, 2282 (*pl.*); pavement 2063; *stylle as þe s.* stock-still 2293; *attrib., s. fyr* sparks struck out of stone 671;

stonstil *adj.* still as stone 242. [OE *stān*]

stonyed. See STOUNED

stor(e) *adj.* mighty 1923; severe 1291. [ON *stórr*]

stori *n.* story 34. [OFr *(e)storie*]

stoundez *n. pl.* times 1517; *bi s.* at times 1567. [OE *stund*]

stouned, stowned, stonyed *v. pa. t.* astonished 301, 1291; *pp.* 242. [OFr *esto(u)ner*]

stoutly *adv.* proudly, valiantly, vigorously 1153, 1364, 1614, 1923. [OFr *(e)stout* + *-ly*]

stray. See ONSTRAY

strayne *v.* to control 176. [OFr *estreindre, estreign-*]

strayt *adj.* tight, close-fitting 152. [OFr *(e)streit*]

strakande *v. pres. p.* (hunting) sounding a call on a horn 1364, 1923. [See expl. n. 1364]

straunge *adj.* strange 709, 713; **stronge** 1028. [OFr *(e)stra(u)nge*]

stre3t *adj.* straight 152. [OE *streccan,* pp. *streht*]

strenkþe *n.* strength 1496. [OE *strengþ*]

stryde *v.* to stride 1584, 2232; *s. alofte,* mount into the saddle 435, 2060. [OE *strīdan*]

strye *v.* to destroy 2194. [From OFr *destruire*]

stryf *n.* resistance 2323. [OFr *(e)strif*]

strike, stryke *v.* to strike 287, 331, 2099, 2305; **stroke** *pa. t. intr.* was struck, sprang 671. [OE *strīcan*]

stryþ(þ)e *n.* posture 2305; *stif on þe s.* standing firm 846. [? Rel. to OE *stride* stride, pace]

strok(e) *n.* stroke, blow. [OE
strāc, rel. to STRIKE]
stroke *v.* to stroke 334, 416. [OE
stroccian]
stronge *adj.* strong 34, 1618. [OE
strang, strong]
strothe *n.* small wood; *attrib.* or
gen. 1710. [ON *storð*]
stubbe *n.* stock, stump 2293. [OE
stybb, stubb]
study *n.* study, silent thought 2369.
[OFr *(e)studie*]
studie *v.* to look and consider 230;
watch intently 237. [OFr
(e)studier]
stuffe *n.* stuff 581. [OFr *estoffe*]
sture *v.* to swing, brandish 331.
[OE *styrian*]
sturn(e) *adj.* grim, stern; firm,
tough 143, 846; serious 494; *sb.*
grim knight 214; **sturnely** *adv.*
grimly 331. [OE *styrne,* *stiorne,*
styrnelīce]
such(e), seche (1543), *adj. and
pron.* such, so great, of the same
kind; such (as), as great as if
1166, 1721; with *þat* 1011,
1426, 1658; without *þat* 46,
1321, 1393. [OE *swelc, swylc*]
sue *v.* to follow, pursue 501, 510,
1467, 1705; **swez** *3 sg.* 1562.
[OFr *sivre, siu-,* AN *suer, suir*]
suffer *v.* to suffer, permit 1967;
submit 2040. [OFr *so(u)frir,
suf-*]
sum, summe *adj. and pron.* some;
adv. in part 247. **sumquat** *n.*
something 1799; *adv.* somewhat
86. **sumquyle** *adv.* once upon a
time 625; **sumwhyle** sometimes
720, 721. **sumtyme** *adv.* for-
merly 2449. [OE *sum*] See WHAT,
WHYLE.

sumned *v. pret.* summoned 1372;
pp. 1052. [OFr *so(u)mo(u)ndre,
sum-,* infl. by OE *somnian*]
sun. See SON
sunder *adv.* in *in sunder,* asunder
1563. [OE *onsundran,* ON *í
sundr*]
sunder *v. trans.* separate 1354;
sundred *pa. t. intr.* 659. [Cf. ON
sundra, OE *syndrian*]
sunne *n.* sun. [OE *sunne*]
sure *adj.* trusty 588; **surely** *adv.*
securely 1883. [OFr *seür*]
surfet *n.* transgression 2433. [OFr
surfait, surfet]
surkot *n.* surcoat 1929. [OFr
surcote]
surquidré. See SOURQUYDRYE
sute *n.* suit; *of a sute, of folȝande
s.* of matching form or pattern
191, 859; **swete** in *of his hors s.*
to match his horse 180; *in swete*
following suit 2518. [OFr *siute*]
swange *n.* waist 138, 2034. [ON
svangi]
swap *v.* to swap 1108. [Origin
mimetic; cf. ME *swappen,* strike]
sware *adj.* squarely built 138. [OFr
(e)square, n., *(e)squarré,* adj.]
sware *v.* to answer 1108, 1756,
1793, 2011. [ON *svara*]
sweȝe *v.* to sink; **sweȝe** *pa. t. str.*
stooped 1796; **sweyed** *wk.*
swung 1429. [? From OE
swegan, parallel to *wegan;* cf.
ON *sveigja*]
swenge *v.* to rush, hasten 1439,
1615; come suddenly 1756. [OE
swengan]
swere *v.* to swear 403, 2051, 2122;
swere *pa. t.* 1825. [OE *swerian*]
swete *adj.* sweet, lovely 1204; *as
sb.* fair lady 1222; *swete, sir s.*

good sir 1108, 2237; *adv.* sweetly
1757. **swetely** *adv.* becomingly
2034. [OE *swēte, swētelīce*]
swete. See SUTE
sweþle *v.* to wind 2034. [From OE
sweþel, n.]
sweuenes *n. pl.* dreams 1756. [OE
swefn]
swez. See SUE
swyerez *n. pl.* esquires 824. [OFr
esquier]
swyft(e) *adv.* swiftly 1354, 1825.
[OE *swift,* adj.]
swyn *n.* swine, boar. [OE *swīn*]
swynge *v.* to rush 1562. [OE
swingan]
swyre *n.* neck 138, 186, 957. [OE
swira]
swyþe *adv.* greatly 1866; earnestly
1860; hard 1897; quickly 8, 815,
1424, 2034, 2259; *as s.* at once
1400; **swyþely** quickly 1479.
[OE *swīþe, swīþlīce*]
swoghe *adj.*; *s. sylence* dead si-
lence 243. [OE *geswōgen*]
sworde *n.* sword 2319. [OE
swurd]

T

ta. See TAKE
tabil, table *n.* (i) table; *hyȝe t.,*
high table on the dais 108, 2462;
(ii) cornïces (castle) 789. [OFr
table]
tacche, tach(ch)e *v.* to attach,
fasten 219, 579, 2176, 2512. [OFr
atach(i)er]
taȝtte. See TECHE
tayl *n.* tail 191, 1726; *pl.* 1377. [OE
tægl]
taysed *v. pp.* harassed; driven
1169. [Origin obscure, but rel. to
teiser, teaser, one of the first

leash of deerhounds let slip to
arouse the game]
tayt *adj.* merry 988; nimble, well-
grown 1377. [ON *teitr*]
take *v.* to take; **tas** *3 sg.* 2305; **tan**
pl. 977, 1920; **take, ta(s)** *imper.*;
tok(en) *pa. t.* 709, 1333, 2243,
etc.; **taken** *pp.* 2448; **tan(e)**;
tone 2159; to accept, receive;
capture 1210; catch 2488, 2509;
acquire 2448; choose 1966; com-
mit 2159; *t. to.* assume 1811; *t.
to yourseluen* take upon yourself
350; *t. to myself* presume 1540;
placed, situated 1811; *tan on
honde* undertaken 490. [ON
taka]
takles *n. pl.* equipment, gear 1129.
[MLG *takel*]
tale *n.* talk, speech, word(s) 638,
1236, 1301, 2133; account, re-
port 1057, 1626, 2124; story 93,
1541, 2483. [OE *talu*]
talenttyf *adj.* desirous 350. [OFr
talentif]
talk *n.* speech 1486. [From TALK v.]
talk(ke) *v.* to talk, speak (of) 108,
2133, 2372. [OE *talcian,* rel. to
TALE]
talkyng *n.* conversation 917, 977.
[From TALK + *yng*]
tame *adj.* tame 2455. [OE *tam*]
tapit *n.* tapestry; wall-hanging 858;
carpet 77, 568. [OE *teppet,*
OProv *tapit*]
tap(p)e *n.* tap, knock 406, 2357.
[Mimetic; cf. OFris *tap;* OFr
taper, v.]
tary *v.* to delay 624, 1726. [? OE
tergan, tyrgan = L *irrito, moror*]
tars *n.* costly stuffs from Tarsus or
Tharsia 77, 571, 858. [OFr *Tarse*]
tas. See TAKE

tassel *n.* tassel 219. [OFr *tassel*]

teccheles *adj.* faultless 917. [From
TECH n. + -*less*]

tech *n.* spot, stain, guilt 2436,
2488. [OFr *teche*]

teche *v.* to teach 1527, 1533; in-
form 407; direct 401, 1069,
1966, 2075; *Techez hym to* di-
rects his attention to 1377;
taȝt(te) *pa. t.* 1485, 2379. [OE
tǣcan]

tel. See TIL

telde *n.* tent; dwelling 11, 1775.
[OE *teld*]

telde *v.* to erect, set up 795, 884,
1648. [OE *teldian*, set up tent]

telle *v.* to tell, relate, speak of, say
to; recite 2188; *telles* tells of it
2494; **tolde** *pa. t.* 1951. [OE
tellan, talde]

temez *n. pl.* themes 1541. [OFr
teme]

tender *adj.* susceptible, yielding
2436. [OFr *tendre*]

tene *n.* harm, trouble 22, 547,
1008; *adj.* rough 1707; perilous
2075. [OE *tēona*]

tene *v.* to harass, torment 1169,
2002; *intr.* suffer torment 2501.
[OE *tēonian, tēnan*]

tent *n.* intention; *in t. to telle* bent
on telling 624. [OFr *atente*]

tente *v.* to attend to 1018, 1019.
[From OFr *atente*, n.]

tenþe *adj.* tenth 719. [ME *ten* +
-*þe*]

terme *n.* appointed place 1069; ap-
pointment 1671; *pl.* utterances
917. [OFr *terme*]

teuelyng *n.* labour, deeds 1514.
[? From ON *tefla*, play at tables;
but see *OED, tevel*²]

th-. See þ-

tyde *n.* time; (*at*) *þat t.* then 585,
736, 2168; at that season 2086;
hyȝe t. festive season 932. [OE
tīd]

tyde *v.* to befall; *yow tydez* is due
to you 1396. [OE *tīdan*]

tyffe *v.* to arrange, make ready
1129. [OFr *tiffer*, adorn]

tyȝt *v.* to prepare; intend 2483; *pp.*
spread 568; *t. to*, hung on 858.
[OE *tyhtan*, infl. by DYȜT]

til(le), tyl *prep.* to 673, 1979; until
734; *til þat* until 697, 991; **til,
tel** (1564) *conj.* until; *with subj.*
449, 2287. [ON *til*, OE *til*]

tyme *n.* time, period, occasion; *at
þis t.* on this occasion, now; *at
þat t.* then 1409. [OE *tīma*]

tymed *v. pp.* timed 2241. [From
TYME n.]

tyrue *v.* to strip off 1921. [? OE
*tyrfan; see *OED, tirve*, v.¹]

tit(e), tyt *adv.* quickly 299, 1596;
as tit(tyt) at once 31, 1210. [ON
titt]

tytel *n.* evidence 480; **tytle** right:
bi t. þat hit habbez justly 626.
[OFr *title*]

tytelet *v. pp.* inscribed 1515. [OFr
titler]

titleres *n. pl.* (hunting) hounds at
stations slipped as game runs by
1726. [From OFr *tiltre*]

tyxt *n.* text 1515; romance 1541.
[OFr *texte, tixte*]

to *prep.* to, towards 340, 1482;
down (up) to, as far as; until 71,
1177, 1887; for; as 1197, 1811;
with inf.; as to 291; *for to* 863,
etc.; *in split inf.* 88, 1540, 1863;
adv. to them 579; *hym to* up to
him 1454, 1903; *þat . . . to* to
which 1671, 2097. [OE *tō*]

to *adv.* too. [OE *tō*]

to-day *adv.* today 397, 470. [OE *tō dæg*]

togeder *adv.* together. [OE *tō gædere*]

to3t *adv.* hardy 1869. [OE *toht, taut, rel. to *tēon*, infl. by *tōh*]

tohewe *v.* to cut down 1853. [OE *tōhēawan*]

tok(en). See TAKE

token *n.* token, sign, indication 1527, 2398, 2509; teaching 1486; *tytelet t.* inscribed title 1515. [OE *tācn*]

tokenyng *n.* indication; *in t.* as a sign that 2488. [OE *tācnung*]

tole *n.* weapon 413, 2260. [OE *tōl*]

tolke. See TULK

tolouse *n.* fabric thought to come from Toulouse 77. See TULÉ, TULY

tomorn(e) *adv.* tomorrow morning 548, 756, 1097, 1965. [OE *tō mor(g)ne*]

tone. See TAKE

tonge *n.* tongue 32. [OE *tunge*]

toppyng *n.* forelock of horse 191. [OE *topp* (cf. *toppa*, tuft) + *-yng*]

toraced *v. pp.* pulled down 1168. [OE *tō-* + RASE, v.² or OFr *raser*, tear]

tor(e) *adj.* hard, difficult 165, 719. [ON *tor-*; cf. TORUAYLE]

torches *n. pl.* torches 1119, 1650. [OFr *torche*]

toreted *adj.* with embroidered edge 960. [OFr *to(u)ret* + suffix]

tornaye *v.* to double back 1707; **tournaye** tourney, joust 41. [OFr *to(u)rneier*]

torne *v. pp.* torn 1579. [OE *toren*, pp.]

torne, t(o)urne *v. trans.* to turn

457; *intr.* turn 1200; return 1099; go 2075; *turned towrast*, turned to disadvantage 1662; *turned tyme* time that was unstable 22. [OE *turnian*, OFr *to(u)rner*]

tortors *n. pl.* turtle-doves 612. [L *turtur*]

toruayle *n.* hard task 1540. [ON *torveldi*, infl. by OFr *travail*]

tote *v.* to peep 1476. [OE *tōtian*]

toun(e) *n.*; *in t.* (word tag) at court, among men 31, 614; *out of t.* from the court 1049. [OE *tūn*]

tourn-. See TORN-

toward(e) *prep.* towards 445, 1189; *to hir warde* 1200. [OE *tōweard, tō hire weard*]

towch *n.* burst of music 120; hint 1301; *pl.* terms of agreement 1677. [OFr *touche*]

towche *v.* to treat of 1541. [OFr *toucher*]

towen *v. pp.* journeyed 1093. [OE *tēon*, pp. *togen*] See VMBETE3E

towrast *v. pp.* twisted awry 1663. [OE *tō-* + *wrǣstan*]

towre *n.* turret 795. [OFr *tour*]

trayle *v.* to (follow a) trail 1700. [From ME *traile*, a trail]

trayst *adj.*; *þat be 3e t.* be sure of that 1211. [ON *traustr*, assim. to *traiste*, v. (ON *treysta*)]

trayteres *n.*; *a trayteres* by tricks or turns 1700. [From OFr *a tre(s)tors*] See expl. n.

traytor *n.* traitor 1775. [OFr *traïtre*, acc. sg. *traïtor*]

trammes *n. pl.* machinations 3. [OFr *traime trame*, woof]

trante *v.* to dodge 1707. [From TRAUNT]

trased *v. pp.* set as ornament 1739.
[? Same as *traced*. Cf. *OED trace*,
v.³, to plait; rel. to *trace*, sb.³, per-
haps altered from *tress*, v., from
OFr *trecier*]

trauayl *n.* laborious journey 2241.
[OFr *travail*]

trauayle *v.* to travel laboriously
1093. [OFr *travaill(i)er*]

traunt *n.* cunning devices 1700.
[Origin uncertain; cf. MDu, Swed
trant, step]

trawe, trowe *v.* to believe (in), be
sure, think; **trowoe** 813; expect
1396; *t. me þat* take my word for
it 2112; *trawe of* trust with re-
gard to 2238. [OE *trēowan*,
truwian]

trawþe, trauþe, traweþ *n.* oath,
plighted word; fidelity to oath
and compact (Trawþe), 626;
2470; compact 2348; truth 1050,
1057. [OE *trēowþ*] See VNTRAWÞE

tre *n.* tree 770. [OE *trēo*]

treleted *v. pp.* latticed 960. [OFr
tre(i)llette + adj. suff.]

tresoun *n.* treason 3. [OFr
tresoun]

tressour *n.* fancy net for hair 1739.
[OFr *tress(e)or*]

trestes, -ez *n. pl.* trestles 884,
1648. [OFr *treste*]

trewest. See TRWE

tricherie, trecherye *n.* treachery
4, 2383. [OFr *tricherie, trecherie*]

tried, tryed *v. pp.* tried 4; *adj.* of
proven quality 77, 219. [OFr
trier]

trifel, tryfle *n.* trifle 108, 1301; de-
tail 165, 960; *neuer bot t.* except
for a small point 547. [Cf. OFr
trufle]

tryst *v.* to believe 380; *þerto ȝe t.*

be sure of that 2325. [OE
* *trȳstan*, or ON * *trýsta*, rel. to
TRAYST]

trystyly *adv.* faithfully 2348. [From
ME *tristi*, rel. to TRYST v.]

trystor, tryster *n.* (hunting) sta-
tion 1146, 1170, 1712. [OFr
tristre]

trochet *v. pp.* provided with orna-
mental pinnacles (like the tines
of deer horns) 795. [OFr *troche*]

trowe(oe). See TRAWE

true *n.* truce 1210. [OE *trēow*]

trumpes *n. pl.* trumpets 116,
1016. [OFr *tro(u)mpe, trumpe*]

trusse *v.* to pack 1129. [OFr
tro(u)sser, truss-]

trwe *adj.* faithful 1845; true to
one's word, trusty, honest 638,
1514, 1637, 2354; true, accurate
392, 480; **trwee** 1274; **trewest**
superl. most certain, truest 4;
adv. honestly 2354. [OE *trēowe*]

trwly, truly, trwely *adv.* faithfully
2348; with belief 2112; truly,
rightly 380, 401, 406, 1785,
2444. [OE *trēowlīce*]

trwluf, trweluf *n.* true love 1527,
1540; **trulofez** *pl.* true-love
flowers 612. [OE *trēowlufu*]

tulé, tuly *adj.* of rich red stuff
thought to come from Toulouse
568; *sb.* 858. [Cf. TOLOUSE]

tulk, tolke *n.* man, knight. [ON
tulkr, spokesman]

turne. See TORNE

tusch *n.* tusk 1573, 1579. [OE *tŭsc*]

twayne, tweyne *adj.* two 962,
1864. [OE *twēgen*, masc.]

twelmonyth *n.* twelvemonth, year
298; *at þis tyme t.* a year hence
383; a year ago 2243. [OE *twelf
mōnaþ*]

twelue *adj.* twelve 128. [OE
    twelfe]
twenty *adj.* twenty 1739, 2112.
    [OE *twentig*] See BI, BY
twyges *n. pl.* twigs, branches 746.
    [ONth *twicg*]
twynne *adj.* double; *in t.* in two
    425, 1339. [ON *tvinnr*, OE
    getwinn]
twynne *v.* to be separated, depart
    2512. [From OE *getwinn* adj.]
twynnen *v. pp.* were twined,
    plaited 191. [ME *twīnen*, v. from
    OE *twīn*, n.]
twy(e)s *adv.* twice 1522, 1679.
    [OE *twiga* + adv. *-es*]
two *adj.* two; *in two* 1351. [OE
    twā]

Þ

þad. See ÞAT
þaȝ(e) *conj.* (*with subj.*) though,
    even if; thaȝ 493; 496, 2307. [OE
    þē(a)h, unaccented *þæh, þah*]
þay *pron. pl.* they; þayr *adj.* their
    1359, 1362; þayres *pron.* theirs;
    their affairs 1019. [ON *þeir*, gen.
    þeira]
þanne. See ÞEN
þarf *3 sg. pres.* need 2355. [OE
    þearf]
þare, þore *adv.* there. [OE *þǣr,
    þăra*]
þat *adj.* that, the *þat ilk(e)* that
    same *def. art.* (*before* ON, OÞER,
    etc.); þad 686. [OE *þæt*, neut.]
þat *conj.* that, so that; seeing that
    1209; *with subj.* that, to (*with
    inf.*); *with other conj. or inter-
    rog.*, *Þat* etc. [OE *þæt, þætte*]
þat *pron.* that, it; at that, moreover
    142, 717; of that 1211. See BI,
    WITH. [OE *þæt*]

þat *rel. pron.* that, which; who(m),
    that which, what; she whom 969;
    (that) he that 926; to whom
    1251; at what 2372; when 996,
    2085; *þat . . . hym, hys, hit*
    whom, whose, which 28, 912,
    2105, 2195. [Substitution of ÞAT
    pron. for OE *þe*]
þe *def. art.* [LOE *þe* (for *se*)]
þe *adv. with compar.* the, so much
    (the), for that. [OE *þȳ, þě*]
þe. See ÞOU
þede *n.* country 1499. [OE *þēod*]
þeder. See ÞIDER
þef *n.* thief 1725. [OE *þēof*]
þen, þen(n)e *adv.* (i) then, next,
    in that case; þanne 301 : (ii)
    than, than if 337. [OE *þanne,
    þænne, þon*]
þenk(ke) *v.* to take heed 487; re-
    member 1680; *þ. of* (*on, vpon*)
    be mindful of, remember 534,
    2052, 2397; þoȝt(en) *pa. t.*
    1023; intended 331, 1550. [OE
    þencan, þōhte] See ÞYNKEZ
þer(e) *adv. demonstr. and indef.*
    there; *þer(e) as*, where 432, 731,
    1432, 1897; *rel.* where, when;
    introducing wish 839; *þer . . .
    inne* in which 2440; *with preps.*
    it, them, etc.: þeraboute en-
    gaged on it 613; round it 2485;
    thereabouts 705; þerafter be-
    hind, after it (that) 671, 1021,
    1342, 1826; þeralofte on it 569;
    þeramongez with it 1361; þerat
    909, 1463, 2514; þerbi on them
    117; þerbyside 1925; þeras just
    as 432, 1897; þerfore, -forne
    therefore, for that reason; in ex-
    change for it 1107; þerinne in it,
    there 17, 21, 1652, 1767; þerof
    of it, to it; þeron 570; þeroute

out of it (them) 518, 1140, 2044;
out-of-doors 2000, 2481; þertylle
to it 1110, 1369; þerto to it 219,
576; at it 650; in that 2325; to
this end 757; *as . . . þerto* as . . .
(to do) 1040; þervnder under
it 185, 2079; þerwyth together
with it, thereupon 121, 980,
1610. [OE *þǣr, þēr*]

þerri3t *adv.* at once 1173. [OE
þǣrrihte]

þes(e). See ÞIS

þewez *n. pl.* manners 912, 916.
[OE *þēawas*, pl.]

þy, þyseluen, etc. See ÞOU

þider, þeder *adv.* thither. [OE
þider]

þiderwarde *adv.* in that direction
1186. [OE *þiderweard*]

þy3ez *n. pl.* thighs 579, 1349. [OE
þē(o)h]

þik(ke) *adj.* thick, stout; *adv.*
thick(ly), densely, closely; con-
tinually 1770. [OE *þicce*]

þyng, þing *n.* thing, matter 93,
1512, 1802; þynk creature 1526;
þyng(e) *pl.* 652, 1080; þinges,
þyngez 645, 1809, 1945. [OE
þing]

þynk(k)ez, þinkkez 2 sg. pres.
you seem to 2362; *impers.* it
seems good to 1502; seems to;
þink in *me þynk* I think 348,
1268, 2109, 2428; þo3t, þu3t
pa. t. impers. it seemed to; *be-
coming pers.* thought (it). [OE
þyncan, pa. t. *þŭhte*]

þis, þys *adj. and pron.* this, the;
the customary 1112, (1); *er þis*
(OE *ǣr þissum*) before now
1892, 2528; þis(e), þyse,
þes(e) *pl.* these, the; *pron.*
these (people, things) 114, 1103,

2420, 2422; *þis seuen 3ere* this
long time 1382. [OE *þis*, neut.]

þo *adj. pl.* those, the. [OE *þā*]

þof, þo3 *conj.* even though 69,
624. [ON *þó*, *þoh]

þo3t *n.* thought 645, 1751, 1867,
1993. [OE *þōht*]

þo3t(en). See ÞENK, ÞYNKEZ

þoled *v. pa. t.* suffered, tolerated
1859; endured 2419. [OE *þolian*]

þonk(e) *n.* thanks 1380; *made a
þ.* gave his thanks 1984; þonkkez
pl. thanks 1980. [OE *þonc*]

þonk(ke) *v.* to thank. [OE
þoncian]

þore. See ÞARE

þorne *n.* thorn 1419, 2529. [OE
þorn]

þose *adj. pl.* those 495; *pron.* 963.
[OE *þās*]

þou, þow *pron.* thou; þe *acc. and
dat.; refl.* 372, 396, 413, 2252,
2341; þi(n), þy(n) *adj.* thy;
þiself *nom.* thyself 395;
þyseluen *refl.* 2141; *þyn awen
seluen* 2301. [OE *þū, þē, þīn*]

þrast *n.* thrust 1443. [From OE
þrǣstan, v.]

þrawen, þrowen *v. pp.* bound
tight 194; thrown, laid 1740;
strongly muscled 579. [OE
þrāwan, twist]

þre *adj.* three. [OE *þrēo*]

þred *n.* thread; *so ne3e þe þred*
so near the limit 1771. [OE
þrǣd]

þrepe *n.* importunity 1859; contest
2397. [From OE *þrēapian* v.; cf.
ON *þrap*]

þrepe *v.* to contend 504. [OE
þrēapian]

þresch *v.* to thrash, smite 2300.
[OE *þerscan*, late *þrescan*]

þrete *n.* force, compulsion 1499. [OE *þrēat*]

þrete *v.* to threaten 2300; þrat *pa. t.* pressed 1980; attacked 1713; þreted *pp.* scolded 1725. [OE *þrēatian*]

þrich *n.* thrust, rush 1713. [From OE *þryccan*, v.] See ÞRY3T

þrid, þryd *adj.* third 1021, 1680, 2356. [OE *þridda*]

þrye *adv.* thrice 763; þryes, þryse 1412, 1936. [OE *þria* + adv. *-es*]

þry3t *v. pa. t.* thrust 1443; *pp.* pressed on 1946. [OE *þryccan*]

þrynge *v.* to press one's way 2397; þronge *pa. t.* 1021. [OE *þringan*]

þrynne *adj.* threefold, three; *on þ. syþe* thrice 1868. [ON *þrinnr*]

þryuande *adj.* abundant, hearty 1980; þryuandely *adv.* 1080, 1380. [Pres. p. of ÞRYVE]

þryue *v.* to thrive; *so mot I þ.* may I prosper as that 387. [ON *þrífask*]

þryuen *adj.* fair 1740. [ON *þrifinn*, pp. of ON *þrifask*]

þro *adj.* intense, steadfast 645; oppressive 1751; fierce 1713 (*sb. pl.*), 2300; *adv.* earnestly, heartily 1867, 1946; *as þro* equally full of pleasure 1021; þroly *adv.* heartily 939. [ON *þrár, þráliga*]

þrote *n.* throat 955, 1740. [OE *þrote*]

þrowe *n.* time; *a þrowe* for a time 2219. [OE *þrāg*]

þrowe *v.* (*subj.*) in *þrid tyme þ. best*, third time turn out best, third time pays for all 1680. [OE *þrāwan*]

þrowen. See ÞRAWEN

þu3t. See ÞYNKEZ

þulged *v. pa. t.* was patient 1859. [OE *geþyldgian*]

þur3(e) *prep.* through(out), over, because of, for, by (means of); *þ. alle oþer þynge(z)* beyond all else 645 1080; *adv.* through 1356. [OE *þurh*]

þurled *v. pa. t.* pierced 1356. [OE *þyrlian*]

þus *adv.* thus, so, in this way [OE *þus*]

þwarle *adj.* intricate 194. [(?) Rel. to OE *þweorh*; cf. mod. Lancs dial. *wharl-knot*]

þwong *n.* thong 194, 579. [OE *þwong*]

V

vayles *n. pl.* veils 958. [OFr *veile*]

vayres; *in varyes* in truth, truly 1015. [OFr *en veires*]

valay *n.* valley 2145, 2245. [OFr *valée*]

vale *n.* vale; *by hylle ne be v.* in no circumstances 2271; *in vale* by the way 2482. [OFr *val*]

vch(e) *adj.* each, every; **iche** 126, 1811; *vche a* every 742, 997, 1262, 1491. **vchon(e)** *pron.* each one, every one 657, 1028; *in apposition* 829, 1113, 1413; *v.* (*in*) *oþer* (in) each other 98, 657. [OE *ælc, ylc*]

veluet *n.* velvet 2027. [Cf. Med L *velvetum*]

venysoun *n.* venison 1375. [OFr *veneiso(u)n, veniso(u)n*]

venquyst *v. pa. t.* won victories 2482. [OFr *veintre*, pa. t. *venquis*]

ver *n.* spring-time 866. [L *ver*]

verayly *adv.* truly, assuredly. [OFr *verai* + *-ly*]

verdure *n.* verdure, green 161.
[OFr *verdure*]

vertue *n.* virtue 634, 2375. [OFr
vertu]

vertuus *adj.* of special power
2027. [OFr *vertuo(u)s*]

vesture *n.* raiment 161. [OFr
vesture]

vewters *n. pl.* (hunting)
greyhound-keepers 1146. [OFr;
see expl. n.]

vgly *adj.* gruesome 441; threaten-
ing 2079; evil-looking 2190. [ON
uggligr]

vyage *n.* journey 535. [OFr *veiage*,
AN *viage*]

vylany(e) *n.* moral delinquency, ill
breeding 634, 2375; discourtesy
345. [OFr *vilanie, vilenie*]

vilanous *adj.* ill-bred 1497. [OFr
vilano(u)s, vilen-]

visage *n.* appearance 866. [OFr
visage]

vyse *n.* vice 2375. [OFr *vice*]

vmbe *prep.* about, round 589,
1830, 2034. [OE *ymb(e)* and ON
umb]

vmbeclyppe *v.* to encompass 616.
[OE *ymb(e)clyppan*]

vmbefolde *v.* to enfold 181. [VMBE
+ FOLDE]

vmbekesten *v. pa. t.* cast about,
searched all round 1434. [VMBE +
CAST]

vmbelappe *v.* to enfold 628. [VMBE
+ LAPPE]

vmbeteȝe *v. pa. t.* surrounded
770. [VMBE + OE *tēah*, pa. t. of
tēon]

vmbetorne *adv.* all round 184.
[OFr *en tour(n)* and ME *um-
betrin*; cf. MLG *umme trint*, Dan
om trind]

vmbeweued *v. pa. t.* enveloped
581. [OE *ymbewǣfan*]

vnbarred *v. pp.* unbarred 2070.
[OE *on-* (*un-*) + OFr *barrer*]

vnbene *adj.* inhospitable, dreary
710. See BENE

vnbynde *v.* to undo, cut in two
1352. [OE *on-, unbindan*]

vnblyþe *adj.* unhappy 746. [OE
unblīþe]

vncely *adj.* unfortunate, unhappy
1562. [OE *unsēlig*]

vnclose *v.* to open 1140. See CLOSE

vncouple *v.* (hunting) to unleash
1419. See COWPLED

vncouþe *adj.* strange 93, 1808.
[OE *uncūþ*] See COUÞE

vnder *prep.* under; in 260, 1814;
see CRYST, HEUEN, SCHANKES; *adv.*
beneath 742, 868; on his heels
158. [OE *under*]

vndertake *v.* to take in 1483.
[Formed on OE *underniman*]

vndo *v.* to undo; *didden hem v.*
had them cut up 1327. [OE *on-,
undōn*]

vneþe *adv.* hardly 134. [OE
unēaþe]

vnfayre *adv.* hideously 1572. [OE
unfǣger]

vnhap *n.* mishap 438. [ON *úhapp*]

vnhap *v.* to unfasten 2511. [? Rel.
to OE *hæpsian*] See HAPPE

vnhardel *v.* to unleash hounds
1697. [From OFr *hardel* n.]

vnlace *v.* (hunting) to cut up a
boar 1606. [From OFr *lac(i)er*]

vnleuté *n.* disloyalty 2499. See
LEWTÉ

vnlyke *adj.* unlike 950. [OE
ungelīc]

vnlouked *v. pa. t.* opened 1201.
[OE *on-, unlūcan*]

vnmanerly *adv.* discourteously
2339. See MANERLY

vnmete *adj.* monstrous 208. [OE
un(ge)mǣte]

vnrydely *adv.* in rough confusion
1432. [OE *unrȳdelīce*]

vnslayn *adj.* unslain 1858. See
SLAYN

vnslyȝe *adj.* unwary 1209. See
SLEȜE

vnsoundyly *adv.* disastrously
1438. See SOUNDYLY

vnsparely *adv.* unsparingly 979.
[OE *un-* + *spærlīce*] See SPARE

vnspurd *adj.* without his being
asked 918. See SPURED

vntyȝtel *n.* unrestraint; *dalten vnt.*
revelled 1114. [ME *untühtle* lack
of discipline; *cf.* OE *tyht*]

vnto *prep.* to 249. [OE *untō*]

vntrawþe *n.* perfidy, falseness to
oath or agreement 2383, 2509.
[OE *untrēowþ*]

vnþryuande *adj.* unjust, ignoble
1499. [Un- + ÞRYUANDE]

vnworþi *adj.* of no value 1835; un-
worthy 1244. [From OE
unweorþe]

voyde *v.* to vacate, leave 345; get
rid of 1518; *v. out* clear out
1342; *voyded of* free from 634.
[OFr *void(i)er*]

vp *adv.* up; up from table 928; out
of bed 1128, 2009; open 820,
1341, 1743; away safe 1874;
vp to; *vp and doun* 229. [OE
up(p)]

vpbrayde *v. pp.* pulled up 781. [VP
+ BRAYDE]

vphalde *v.* to hold up 2442. [VP +
HALDE]

vphalt *v. pp. adj.* high 2079. [VP +
HALE]

vplyfte *v. intr.* to lift on high 505.
[VP + LYFT(E)]

vpon *prep. equiv. of* ON; upon, on
at, in; over 1831; to 2252; into
244; (*time*) at, in, on; by 47; *þat
. . . vpon* by whom 2466; *adv.* on
them 1649; on him 2021. [OE
uppon]

vpon *v.* to open 1183. [OE *openian*,
infl. by VP adv.]

vpryse *v.* to rise up 1437; **vpros**
pa. t. sg. 367; **vprysen** *pl.* 1126.
[OE *upp arīsan*]

vrysoun *n.* embroidered silk band
on helmet 608. [OFr *horso(u)n*]

vse *v.* to use; have dealings with
2426; show, practise 651, 1491,
2106. [OFr *user*]

vtter *adv.* into the open 1565. [OE
ūtor, ŭtter]

W

wade *v.* to wade 2231; **wod** *pa.
t.* stood in water 787. [OE
wadan]

wage *n.* pledge 533; *pl.* payment
396. [ONFr *wage*]

way(e) *n.* way, road; *on his w.* 670,
1028, 1132, 2074; *went his (hir)
w.* departed 688, 1557; *bi non
way(es)* by no means 1045,
2471. [OE *weg*]

way *adv.*; *do w.*, enough of 1492.
[From AWAY]

wayke *adj.* weak 282. [ON *veikr*]

wayne *v.* to bring, send 264, 2456,
2459; *pa. t.* challenged 984. [Cf.
OE *bewægnan*]

wayte *v.* to look 306, 1186, 2163,
2289. [ONFr *wait(i)er*]

wayth *n.* (hunting) kill of meat
1381. [ON *veiðr*]

wayue *v.* to wave; *w. vp*, swing

open 1743; *pa. t.* swept from side to side 306; *pp.* offered, shown 1032. [ON *veifa*, AN *waiver*]

waked *v. pp.* stayed up 1094; **woke** *pa. t.* 1025. [OE *wacian*, infl. by *wæcnan*]

wakened(e), wakned *v. pa. t. intr.* woke up 1200; would wake up 1194 (*subj.*); was aroused, arose 2000, 2490; *trans.* kindled 1650; *pa. t.* awakened 119. [OE *wæcn(i)an*]

wakkest *adj. superl.* weakest, least important 354. [OE *wāc*, superl. *wācost, -est*]

wal, walle *n.* wall 783, 787, 809. [OE *wall*]

wale, walle *adj.* choice 1403; excellent, fair 1010, 1712, 1759. See WALE V.

wale *v.* to choose 1276; pick 1238; seek 398. [ON *velja*, pa. t. *valdi*]

walke *v.* to walk 2178; be spread abroad 1521. [OE *walcan*]

wallande *v. pres. p.* welling up warm 1762. [OE *wallan*]

walour *n.* valor 1518. [OFr *valour*]

walt. See WELDE

walt *v. pa. t.* flung 1336. [OE *wieltan, wæltan*]

waltered *v. pa. t.* rolled in streams 684. [Rel. to WALT v.; cf. MLG *waltern*]

wande *n.* wand, branch; *vnder w.* in the wood 1161; **wandez** *gen.* haft's 215. [ON *vǫndr*]

wane *adj.* lacking 493. [OE *wana*]

wap *n.* blow 2249. [Mimetic]

wappe *v.* to rush 1161, 2004. [Mimetic]

war *adj.* (a)ware; *watz w. of* perceived 764, 1586, 1900; **ware** on

(my) guard 2388; **warly** *adv.* warily 1186, 1900; **warloker** *compar.* more carefully 677. [OE *wær, wærlīce, -lucor*]

war *interj.* (hunting) a warning cry 1158. [OFr *gar, war*, perh. affected by ME *waren*, OE *warian*]

warde *adv.* See TOWARDE

ware *v.* to deal 2344; employ 402, 1235. [OE *warian*²]

waryst *v. pp.* recovered 1094. [ONFr. *warir, wariss-*]

warme *adj.* warm 506, 684. [OE *wearm*]

warme *v.* to warm 1762. [OE *werman*]

warne *v.* to warn 522. [OE *warenian*]

warp *v.* to utter 2253; **warp** *pa. t.* uttered 224, 1423; put 2025. [OE *weorpan*]

warþe *n.* ford 715 n. [OE *waroþ*, shore, infl. by ON *vað*]

waschen *v. pp. intr.* washed 72; **wesche** *pa. t.* 887. [OE *wascan*]

wast *n.* waist 144. [OE *wæ(c)st*]

waste *n.* waste 2098. [ONFr *wast*, adj.]

wat. See WHAT

water *n.* water, stream; **watter** 2231; **wattrez** *pl.* 1169; *warme w.* tears 684. [OE *wæter*]

watz, was *v. pa. t. sg.* was; had been 2016, 2488; *with intr. pp.* had; **wer(en)** *pl.*; **wer(e)** *pa. t. subj.* would (should) be, was; might be 1509; *as hit were* 2171; *if hit w.* if only 1799. [OE *wæs, wæron, wære*]

waþe. See WOÞE

wax *v.* to grow 518, 522; increase 997; **wex** *pa. t.* 319. [OE *weaxan, wĕox*]

waxen *adj.* of wax 1650. [OE *weaxen*]

we *interj.* ah! alas! 2185; *we loo* ah well 2208. [OE *wǣ, wǣ lā, wel lā*]

we *pron.*; **oure** *adj.* our; **vus** *acc. and dat.*; **vs** 2246. [OE *wē, ūre, ŭs*]

wede *n.* raiment 1310; particular garment 987, 2358; *heȝ wede* armor 831; *pl.* raiment, clothes 151, 271, 508, 861; armor 2013, 2025. [OE *wǣd, gewǣde*]

weder *n.* weather 504; *pl.* storms 2000. [OE *weder; gewider*, storm]

weȝed *v. pa. t.* brought 1403. [OE *wegan*]

wel *adv.* well, without doubt, clearly, certainly; very much, fully, very; *wel connez* 1267; *wel-haled* tightly drawn 157; *wol þe wel* wish you well 2469; *w. worþ þe* good fortune befall you 2127. [OE *wel*]

wela *adv.* very 518, 2084. [OE *wellā*]

welcum, -com *adj.* welcome; *superl.* 938. [OE *wilcuma*, n., ON *velkominn*]

welcum *v.* to welcome 819, 1477, 1759. [OE *wilcumian*]

welde *n.* control; *to haue at yowre wylle and w.* to use as you please 837. [OE *gewald*, infl. by WELDE v.]

welde *v.* to wield 270; possess, use; **walt** *pa. t.* possessed 231; spent 485. [OE *weldan, wǣldan*]

wele *n.* well-being, happiness; wealth, riches 7, 1270, 1394; costliness 2037, 2432; *w. ful hoge* a great deal of money 1820; *w. oþer wo* 2134. [OE *wela*]

welhaled *adj.* pulled up tight 157. [WEL + HALE]

welkyn *n.* heavens 525, 1696. [OE *wolcen, welcn*, cloud]

welneȝ(e) *adv.* almost 7, 867. [OE *welnēh*]

wende *n.* turn 1161. [OE *wend*]

wende *v.* to turn 2152; *intr.* go; **wende** *pa. t.* in *w. in his hed* went to his head 900; **went(en)**; *pp.* in *watz w.* came 1712. [OE *wendan*]

wene *v.* to expect, think 2404; *w. wel* know well 270, 1226; **wende, went** *pa. t.* 669; *w. haf* hoped to have 1711. [OE *wēnan*]

wener *adj. compar.* lovelier 945. [ON *vænn*; cf. OE *wēnlic*]

wenge *v.* to take vengeance 1518. [OFr *veng(i)er*]

weppen *n.* weapon. [OE *wĕpn*]

wer, were(n). See WATZ, WERRE

werbelande *v. pres. p.* blowing shrill 2004. [OFr *werbler*]

werbles *n. pl.* warblings 119. [OFr *werble*]

were *v.*[1] to ward off 2015; defend 2041. [OE *werian*[1]]

were *v.*[2] to wear 2358, 2510, 2518; **were** *pa. t.* 1928; **wered** 2037. [OE *werian*[2]]

werk(e) *n.* work 494; *wylyde w.* choice craftswork 2367; **werk(k)ez** *pl.* deeds 1515; workmanship 1817, 2432; embroidery 164, 2026; designs 216. [OE *we(o)rc*]

werne *v.* to refuse 1494, 1495, 1824. [OE *wernan*]

wernyng *n.* resistance [From WERNE v. + *-ing*]

werre *n.* strife, fighting 16, 726; **were** 271, 1628. [ONFr *werre*]

werre *v.* to fight 720. [From
WERRE n.]

wesaunt *n.* esophagus 1336. [OE
wāsend, wǣsend, suff. infl. by
OFr]

wesche. See WASCHEN

west *adj.* west 7. [OE *west,* n.]

weterly *adv.* truly 1706. [ON
vitrliga, wisely]

weue *v.* to offer, show 1976; give
2359. [OE *wǣfan* as if = WAYUE]

wex. See WAX

wharre *v.* to whirr 2203. [Mimetic]

what, quat *pron. interrog.* what;
what! 309; *interj.* (screeching
noise) 1163, 2201–4; *indef.*
what(ever) 1073, 1082; *adj.*
what 460, 1047. **whatso** *pron.*
whatever 1550; **quatso** 255, 382;
what (*wat, quat*) . . . so; 384,
1406, 1407, etc.; **quatsoeuer**
1106. [OE *hwæt; swā hwæt swā*]

whederwarde *adv.* whither, where
1053; **whiderwardesoeuer**
wherever 2478. [OE *hwider, swā
hwider swā*]

when, quen *adv. interrog., indef.*
and rel. when, whenever;
whenso whenever 1682. [OE
hwanne, hwænne]

whene. See QUENE

wher(e) *adv. interrog.* where;
quere 1058; *indef.* (*with subj.*),
wherever 100; *rel.* in *where . . .
þerinne* where 16; **whereso**
wherever 395; **quereso** 1227,
1490; **whereeuer** 661; **were-
soeuer** 1459; **queresoever** 644.
[OE *hwǣr, swā hwǣr swā*]

wherfore, querfore *adv. interrog.*
wherefore 1294; *rel.* in *wh. . . .
þerfore* and so 2278. [WHER, QUER
+ OE *fore*]

whette *v.* to sharpen, whet 1573;
whette *pa. t. intr.* made a grind-
ing noise 2203. [OE *hwettan*] See
QUETTYNG

wheþen, queþen *adv. interrog.*
whence; *from queþen* 461; *in-
def.* (*with subj.*) from wherever
871. [ON *hvaðan,* ODan *hueden*]

wheþer *adv.* yet 203. [OE
hwæþere]

wheþer *adv. interrog.* whether;
introd. direct question 2186.
[OE *hwæþer*]

why, quy *adv. interrog.* why 623;
interj. why! 1528. [OE *hwī*]

whiderwarde. See WHEDERWARDE

whil(e), wyle, quyl(e) *conj.*
while, as long as; until 1180,
1435; *quyle þat* as long as 1115;
quel 822; *prep.* until. [OE *þā
hwīle þe*]

whyle, quile *n.* time 1235; *adver-
bially* 30, 1195, 2369; *a wh.* a
moment 134, 1996; *any qu.* any
length of time 257, 2058; *in a
wh.* shortly 1646; *þe qu.* at pres-
ent 1791; *þe seruise qu.* dur-
ing the service time 940; *þat
Crystenmas wh.* that Christmas
tide 985. [OE. *hwīl* (*þā*)*-hwīle*]

whyrlande *v. pres. p.* whirling
2222. [OE *hwyrftlian,* ON
hvirfla]

whyssynes *n. pl.* cushions 877.
[OFr *cuissin*]

whyte *adj.* white 1573; **quite**
2364; **quyt(e)** 799, 885, 2088;
sb. quit 1205. [OE *hwīt*]

who, quo *pron. interrog.* who 231,
682, 2213; *indef.* whoever 355.
whoso, quoso *indef.* whoever, if
(for) anyone 209, 306, 1112,
1849. [OE *hwā, swā hwā swā*]

wy *interj.* ah! 2300. [Cf. WE]

wich *adj.* what 918. [OE *hwilc*]

wyde *adv.* wide 820. [OE *wīde*]

wyf *n.* wife; woman 1001, 1495. [OE *wīf*]

wy3(e), wyghe (1487) *n.* man, knight, person, one; (of God) 2441; *voc.* sir knight; *pl.* men, people. [OE *wiga* (poetic)]

wy3t *adj.* lively 119; *superl.* most valiant 261, fiercest 1591; *adv.* ardently 1762; **wy3tly** *adv.* swiftly 688. [ON *vígr*, neut. *vígt*]

wy3t *n.* creature; *þat wy3t* she 1792. [OE *wiht*]

wykez *n. pl.* corners 1572. [ON *munn-vík*]

wil, wyl(le) *1 & 3 sg. pres.* will; **wol** 2469; **wyl(t)** *2 sg.*; **wyl** *pl.*; **wolde, woled** *pa. t.*; *pres.* wish for, desire, intend to; *becoming auxil. of future*; *I wyl to* I mean to go to 2132; *pa. t.* wished to, would (like, be willing); *wolde of his wyte* was likely to go out of his senses 1087. [OE *wil(l)e, wyl(le), wolde*]

wylde *adj.* wild; restless 89. [OE *wīlde*]

wylde *n.* wild beast 1167, 1586, 1900; *pl.* wild creatures 1150, 2003. [OE **wild, wilder*, pl. *wildru*; cf. MHG *wilt*]

wyldrenesse *n.* wilderness 701. [OE *wildeornes*]

wylé, wyly *adj.* wily 1728; *sb.* 1905. [From ME *wīle*]

wylez *n. pl.* wiles 1700, 1711, 2415, 2420. [OE *wīgel*, ONFr *wile*, OFr *guile*]

wylyde *adj.* skilful 2367. [From ME *wīle*; see WYLEZ] cf. WER(K)E

wylle *adj.* wandering, perplexing 2084. [ON *villr*]

wylle *n.* desire, pleasure, (good) will 255, 1665, 2158, 2387; *of w.* in temper, courage 57, 352; *at (his, hore, your, yowre) wylle* to (his, their, your) pleasure; *bi 3owre w.* by your leave 1065; *with (a) god w.* gladly 1387, 1861, 1969, 2430. [OE *willa*]

wylnyng *n.* desire 1546. [OE *wilnung*]

wylsum *adj.* bewildering, devious, out of the way 689. [WYLLE *adj.* + OE *-sum*; cf. ON *villusamr*]

wylt *v. pp.* strayed, escaped 1711. [ON *villask*]

wymmen *n. pl.* women 1269, 2415, 2426. [OE *wīfmen, wimmen*]

wyn(e) *n.* wine. [OE *wīn*]

wynde *n.* wind 516, 525, 784, 2004; *as wroth as w.* 319. [OE *wind*]

wynde *v.* to turn back, return 530; **wounden** *pp.* bound round 215. [OE *windan*]

wyndow *n.* window 1743. [ON *vindauga*]

wynne *adj.* delightful, lovely 518, 1032, 2430, 2456. [From OE *wynn* n.]

wynne *n.*[1] joy 15, 1765. [OE *wynn*]

wynne *n.*[2] gain 2420. [OE *gewinn*]

wynne *v.* to gain, win, get, bring; win over 1550; *refl.* in *wynne me* find my way 402; *intr.* reach 1569; come, go 1537, 2044, 2050, 2215 (*subj.*); **wan** *pa. t. sg.* 70, 2231 (came); **wonnen** *pl.* brought 831; **wan** got 1394; **won(n)en** *pp.* won, brought; *watz w.* had come 461, 1365. [OE *gewinnan*, ON *vinna*]

wynnelych *adj.* pleasant 980. [OE
  wynnlic]
wynter *n.* winter 504, 530, 726,
  1382; *gen.* 533; *pl.*, *seven w.* =
  an indefinite long period 613.
  [OE *winter*]
wynthole *n.* windpipe 1336. [OE
  wind + *hol*]
wyppe *v.*¹ to wipe, polish 2022.
  [OE *wipian*]
wypped *v.*² *pa. t.* whipped (off)
  2249. [Cf. ON *svipa*, MDu
  wippen and ME *wap, swap*]
wyrde *n.* fate 1752, 2418; *þe
  wyrde* Fate 2134; *pl.* as *sg.* 1968.
  [OE *wyrd*]
wys (*vpon*) *adj.* skilled (in) 1605.
  [OE *wīs*]
wyse *n.* manner, fashion; *on fele w.*
  in many ways 1653; *in no w.* by
  no means 1836. [OE *wīse*]
wysse *v.* to guide, direct 549; *sub.*
  739. [OE *wissian*]
wysty *adj.* desolate 2189. [OE
  wēstig]
wit, wyt *v.* to know, learn 131, 255,
  1864; *wyt at* learn from 1508;
  wot *1 sg. pres.*; **wot** *pl.* 1965;
  wyst *pa. t. sg.* 1087, 1712, 2125;
  wyst(en) *pl.*; *wyt 3e wel* be as-
  sured, 1820. [OE *witan*; *wāt*, sg.;
  wiste, pa. t.]
wyt(e), wytte *n.* intelligence, un-
  derstanding, cleverness, good
  sense, reason; *pl.* wits 2459; con-
  sciousness 1755; *fyue wyttez* five
  senses 640 2193. [OE *(ge)witt*]
wyte *v.* to look 2050. [OE *wītan*]
with, wyth *prep.* with; (i) (= OE
  mid) with, having, among, in,
  amid, by, through; *w. hymseluen*
  in his (your) own mind 1660,
  2301. (ii) (= OE. *wiþ*) with,

against, at, from; *wyth þis* (*þat*)
  thereupon 316, 1305. *adv.*
  wherewith 2223. [OE *mid,
  wiþ*]
withalle *adv.* entirely, altogether
  106, 1926. [OE *mid alle*, ON
  með ǫllu]
wythhalde *v.* to hold back 2268;
  withhelde *pa. t.* 2291; **wyth-
  hylde** 2168. [OE *wiþ* + *haldan*]
withinne, wythinne *adv.* in,
  inside, within; inwardly 2370;
  prep. 1435, 1732, 1742. [OE
  wiþinnan]
withoute(n) *prep.* without. [OE
  wiþūtan]
wyttenesse *n.* witness 2523. [OE
  gewitnes]
wlonk *adj.* noble, glorious, lovely;
  sb. 1988; *superl.* 2025. [OE
  wlonc]
wo *n.* woe 1717, 2134. [OE *wā*]
wod. See WADE
wodcraftez *n. pl.* woodcraft 1605.
  [WOD(E) + CRAFT]
wod(e) *n.* wood, forest; *in* (*bi*)
  wod in the woods 515, 1628,
  2084. [OE *wudu*]
wode *adj.* mad 2289. [OE *wōd*]
wodwos *n. pl.* satyrs, forest trolls
  721. [OE *wuduwāsa*]
wo3e, wowe *n.* wall 858, 1180; *bi
  wo3ez* on the walls 1650. [OE
  wāg]
wo3e *v.* make love 1550. [OE
  wōgian]
woke, wol(ed), wolde. See WAKED,
  WIL
wolues *n. pl.* wolves 720. [OE
  wulf]
wombe *n.* stomach 144. [OE
  wamb.]
won(e) *n.* course (of action) 1238;

multitude, host 1269. [ON *ván*,
hope, fair prospect, etc.]

wonde *v.* to shrink from fear 488,
563. [OE *wandian*]

wonder *n.* wonder, amazement
238; *have w.* (*of*) be amazed
(at) 147, 467, 496; oddity, marvel
16, 480, 2459; *of Arthurez
wonderez* from among the mar-
vellous tales about A. 29; *predic.*
wonderful 1322, 1481; *adv.* won-
derfully 2200. [OE *wundor*,
wundrum, adv.]

wondered *v. pa. t. impers.*; *hym
w.* he was surprised 1201. [OE
wundrian, pers.; ON *undra*,
pers. and impers.]

wonderly *adv.* marvellously 787,
1025. [OE *wunderlīce*]

wone, -ez *n.* dwelling, abode.
[From OE *wunian* v.; cf. ON
ván]

wone *v.* to remain, dwell, live 257,
814, 2098, **wonyes** 2 *sg.* 399;
wonde, woned *pa. t. pl.* 50,
701, 721; **wonyd, wonde, wont**
pp. 17, 1988, 2114. [OE *wunian*]

wont *n.* lack 131. [ON *vanr*, neut.
vant]

wont *v. impers.* there lacks; *er me
w.* before I have to go without
987; *neked wontez of* little time
is wanting till 1062; *yow wonted*
you lacked, 2366. [From WONT n.]

worch(e) *v.* to work, make; do
1039, 1546; *absol.* act, do 238,
2253; *w. bi*, act according to
2096; *let God worche* let G. work
as He will 2208; **wro3t** *pa. t. and
pp.* made 399; wrought, devised,
3, 22, 2344, 2361; acted 677,
1997 (*pl.*). [OE *wyrcan*, *worhte*,
wrohte]

worchip, worschyp *n.* honor,
honorable treatment. [OE *weorþ-
wurþscipe*]

worchip *v.* to honor 1227. [From
WORCHIP n.]

word(e) *n.* word 224, 314, 2373;
statement 1792; fame 1521; *pl.*
words, talk; *grete w.* boasts 312,
325. [OE *word*]

worie *v.* to worry 1905. [OE
wyrgan]

worlde *n.* world; *alle þe w.* all
men 1227. [OE *woruld*]

wormez *n. pl.* dragons 720. [OE
wyrm]

worre *adj.* worse; *þe w.* the worst
of it 1588, 1591. [ON *verri*, infl.
by WORS adj.]

wors *adj. compar.* worse 726;
worst *superl.* worst 1792, 2098.
[OE *wyrsa*, *wyrsta*]

wort *n.* plant 518. [OE *wyrt*]

worth *adj.* worth 1269, 1820. [OE
weorþ(e), *wyrþe*]

worþe, worth(e) *v.* to become, be
made done 1202; (*as future of
'be'*) will be: *me worþez þe bet-
ter* I shall be the better 1035;
worþez to shall become 1106,
1387; *me schal w.* it shall hap-
pen to me 1214; *subj.* let it be
(done) 1302 be (*with pp.*) 2374;
wel w. þe may good fortune be-
fall you 2127; *w. hit wele oþer
wo* come what may 2134;
worþed *pa. t.* came to pass 485;
subj. would fare 2096; *pp.* be-
come, been made 678. [OE
weorþan]

worþy, worthé (559) *adj.* worthy;
valuable 1848; honored, noble
559, 1537; *sb.* noble lady 1276,
1508; fitting 819; **worþyest** most

excellent 261; *adv.* courteously 1477. [OE *wyrþig* infl. by *wyrþe*]

worþily, worþyly *adv.* in honor 1988; courteously 1759; with honor 1386; suitably 72, 144. [OE *weorþlīce* infl. by WORÞY]

worþilych *adj.* honored, glorious 343. [OE *weorþlic*, infl. by WORÞY]

woþe *n.* danger 222, 488, 1576; **waþe** 2355. [ON *váði*]

wouen *v. pp.* woven 2358. [OE *wefan*]

wounded *v. pp.* wounded 1781. [OE *wundian*]

wounden. See WYNDE

wowche *v.* to vouch; *subj. I w. hit saf* I would vouchsafe it 1391. [OFr *voucher sauf*]

wowes 1180. See WOЗE *n*

wowyng *n.* lovemaking 2367; *þe w. of* the temptation by 2361. [See WOЗE *v.*]

wrake *n.* distress 16. [OE *wracu*]

wrang *adj.* wrong 1494. [ON *rangr*, older *vrangr*]

wrast *adj.* loud 1423. [OE *wrǽst*]

wrast *v. pp.* disposed to 1482. [OE *wrǣstan*, twist]

wrastel *v.* to wrestle 525. [OE *wrǎstlian, wrǣstlian*]

wrathed *v. pa. t.* troubled, grieved; afflicted 726; *impers. in you w.* you were angry 1509; *pp.* brought to ruin 2420. [From OE *wrǽþþu*; cf. *gewrǣþan*]

wreзande *v. pres. p.* denouncing 1706. [OE *wrēgan*]

wro *n.* nook 2222. [ON *(v)rá*]

wroзt(en). See WORCH(E)

wroth(e), wroþe *adj.* angry, wroth 319, 1660; unhappy 70; furious 525, 1706, 1905; **wroþely** *adv.* fierce(ly) 2289; **wroþe-loker** *compar.* more harshly 2344 [OE *wrāþ, wrāþlīce, lucor*]

wroth *v. pa. t.* stretched himself 1200. [OE *wrīþan*]

wruxled *v. pp.* wrapped 2191. [OE *wrixlan*, wind to and fro; cf. *wrigels, wrēon*]

Y

yзe *n.* eye 198; *pl.* 228; **yзen** 82, 304, 684, 962. [OE *ē(a)ge*]

yзelyddez *n. pl.* eyelids 446, 1201. [LOE *ēge(h)lid*]

ymage *n.* image 649. [OFr *image*]

your-, yow(re). See ЗE

yrn *n.* iron 215; blade 2267; *pl.* armor 729. [OE *īren*]